WHO THE HELL
ARE WE FIGHTING?

WHO THE HELL
ARE WE FIGHTING?

The Story of Sam Adams and
the Vietnam Intelligence Wars

C. MICHAEL HIAM

STEERFORTH PRESS
HANOVER, NEW HAMPSHIRE

For Grace and Sophia

Library of Congress Cataloging-in-Publication Data

Hiam, C. Michael.
Who the hell are we fighting? : The story of Sam Adams and the
Vietnam intelligence wars / C. Michael Hiam. – 1st ed.
p. cm.
Includes bibliographical references and index.
ISBN 13: 1-58642-104-5 (alk. paper)
ISBN 10: 1-58642-104-2 (alk. paper)
1. Vietnamese Conflict, 1961–1975 – Military intelligence –
United States. 2. Adams, Sam, 1933-1988. 3. Vietnam
(Democratic Republic) – Armed Forces – Organization.
4. Mat trân dân tôc giai phóng miên nam Viêt Nam –
Organization. 5. United States. Central Intelligence Agency.
I. Title

DS559.8.M44H53 2006
959.704'38-dc22

Maps by Molly O'Halloran

FIRST EDITION

Contents

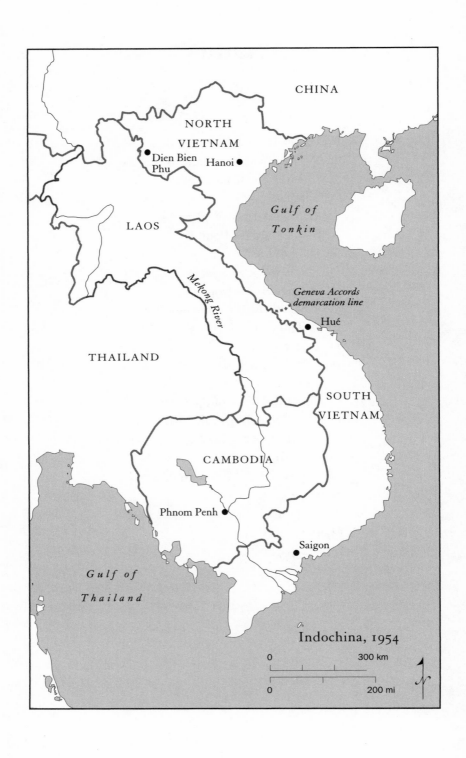

CHINA

NORTH
VIETNAM

Dien Bien
Phu

Hanoi

*Gulf of
Tonkin*

LAOS

Mekong River

*Geneva Accords
demarcation line*

Hué

THAILAND

SOUTH
VIETNAM

CAMBODIA

Phnom Penh

Saigon

*Gulf of
Thailand*

Indochina, 1954

| 0 | 300 km |
| 0 | 200 mi |

N

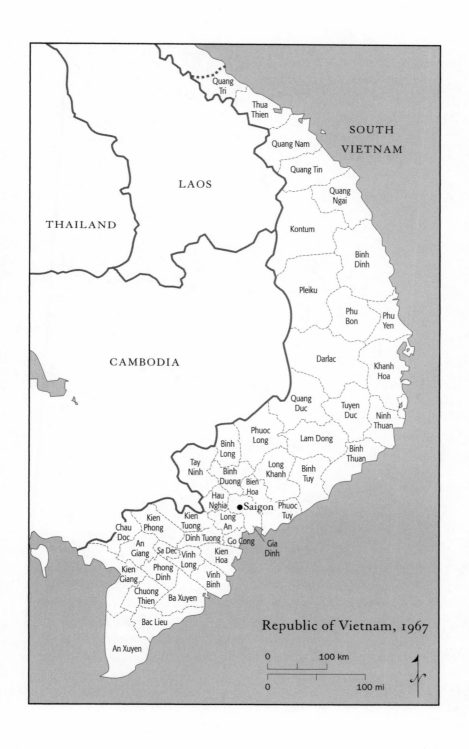

THAILAND

LAOS

SOUTH
VIETNAM

CAMBODIA

Quang
Tri

Thua
Thien

Quang Nam

Quang Tin

Quang
Ngai

Kontum

Binh
Dinh

Pleiku

Phu
Bon

Phu
Yen

Darlac

Khanh
Hoa

Quang
Duc

Tuyen
Duc

Ninh
Thuan

Phuoc
Long

Lam Dong

Binh
Long

Binh
Thuan

Tay
Ninh

Binh
Duong

Long
Khanh

Binh
Tuy

Bien
Hoa

Hau
Nghia

●Saigon

Phuoc
Tuy

Chau
Doc

Kien
Phong

Kien
Tuong

Long
An

An
Giang

Dinh Tuong

Go Cong

Gia
Dinh

Sa Dec

Vinh
Long

Kien
Hoa

Kien
Giang

Phong
Dinh

Vinh
Binh

Chuong
Thien

Ba Xuyen

Bac Lieu

An Xuyen

Republic of Vietnam, 1967

0   100 km

0   100 mi

N

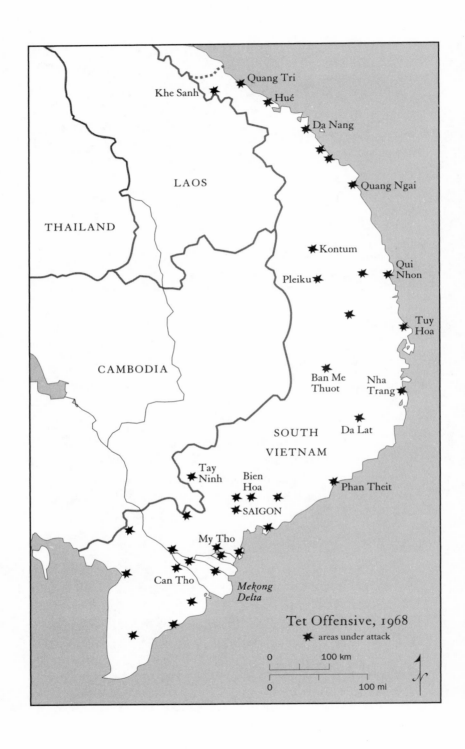

Tet Offensive, 1968

✳ areas under attack

Prologue: Tet, 1968

In defeat, Sam Adams readied his classified files for the transfer downstairs. Appearing far younger than his thirty-four years, Adams was a man of patrician good looks and an all-American affability, although that affability would have been subdued on this day. There were a lot of files to go through, indeed four safes' worth of files, and each file was in its own way a reason why he felt he had to leave: Accurate intelligence had been suppressed and, worse, deliberately compromised. This melancholy chore went efficiently enough, though, so that by five P.M. Adams was done with his files and could depart for home. The official move would come in the morning.

The next day Adams returned to the office, named for the title of its chief, the Special Assistant for Vietnamese Affairs (SAVA), early. Not that by moving two floors away in CIA headquarters Adams was going anywhere far, but still there were farewells at SAVA that needed to be made to secretaries, colleagues, and, dutifully, to the boss who had been so much a part of the deception: This was the special assistant himself, George Carver. Adams would also, of course, want time to go through the overnight cables in from Saigon, and just maybe have one last chance to update the enormous topographic layout of Khe Sanh that dominated the Vietnamese Affairs Staff Related Activities Center (VASRAC), located in a darkened and secure room in the office. Days started slowly at SAVA and so certainly, perhaps Adams reasoned to himself, the farewells could wait a bit.

It was January 31, 1968. Adams routinely punched in the code to enter the office, but when the buzzer sounded and the door opened the scene was not what he had expected. The secretaries were typing madly, and the usually quiet VASRAC was teeming with officials gesticulating to one another and frantically updating maps with red pins. Adams managed to catch someone's attention and was hurriedly told that the Viet Cong were attacking across the northern and central parts of South Vietnam. Cities with names like Nha Trang, Man Me Thuot, Kontum, Hoi An, and Da Nang had been hit, along with smaller towns, villages, and hamlets, in surprise attacks. It was an all-out invasion, but one that was coming from within South Vietnam as Viet Cong units based on the outskirts of population centers were bursting in to take over. Adams postponed his departure from SAVA that day and watched as the offensive unfolded.

The latest intelligence reports from South Vietnam became outdated almost the moment they arrived, but apparently the Viet Cong had actually seized the ancient capital of Hué and the offensive, as feared, was already in the southernmost region of the country. The real shocker, though, came when word reached Washington, DC, that Viet Cong commandos were right smack in the middle of the U.S. embassy compound in Saigon.

At SAVA, Adams learned of these events as they became known, and he helped out amid the bustle where he could, but he also resignedly took time away from the office for the mundane task of going to the CIA employee credit union to cash a check, and for having a leisurely lunch. It was not that Adams didn't care; it was just that he realized that what was happening that day in Vietnam, half a world away, had been foreseeable. As an intelligence professional, this fact sickened him.

Sam Adams had not predicted the giant Viet Cong offensive, although in the weeks prior he had seen in the intelligence to which he was privy strange and ominous stirrings: Viet Cong agents in Saigon had been falsifying identity cards that would allow them access to the city; Viet Cong defections and desertions had dried up, suggesting that the Communists were on a heightened state of alert; and intercepted Viet Cong radio messages were referring to something called "N-Day." That this newest intelligence had been ignored was bad enough, but what really upset Adams was that the U.S. military in South Vietnam, headquartered in Saigon and called the Military Assistance Command, Vietnam (MACV), was deceptively *under*counting, and in many cases outright ignoring, Viet Cong strength, and had been doing so for years.

Just days into the 1968 New Year, as but one example, U.S. military intelligence officers at MACV had quite arbitrarily cut ninety-six hundred Viet Cong guerrillas from the enemy strength estimates. These enemy strength estimates in military parlance were called the order of battle. "The decline" in the Viet Cong order of battle, an incensed Adams noted when he saw that MACV had taken an ax to the most recent Viet Cong strength figures, "was damn peculiar for an enemy that was supposed to be planning for a big attack." Then there was MACV's unwillingness to acknowledge the existence of support units for the Viet Cong Ninth Division, located outside Saigon or, around Da Nang, of the Viet Cong T-89 and T-87 Battalions. This latest intelligence discrepancy on MACV's part looked, Adams thought when he discovered it, "fishy." Yet for Adams, as he related, "Most things looked fishy to me nowadays," as they had for the past year or so. Only months earlier, during the summer of 1967, Adams had fought almost literally tooth and nail against the compromised intelligence being put out by the U.S. military in Saigon, and now in early 1968 he had not given up that fight by any means, but at SAVA he had been betrayed by George Carver, and this he could not forgive. Adams returned after lunch to packing his files. Tomorrow, Viet Cong offensive or no Viet Cong offensive, he would continue his own fight from elsewhere in the agency.[1]

*

In retrospect a brief Associated Press dispatch reporting an unusual Viet Cong assault (presumably including the nonexistent T-89 and T-87 Battalions) on the coastal city of Da Nang was a last-minute tip-off to the larger offensive. The assault on Da Nang, according to the wire service, had resulted in eight hours of house-to-house fighting, five American casualties, and more than twenty million dollars in damage done to airplanes at the nearby airbase. The date was January 30, 1968, the start of Tet Mau Than — the Vietnamese holiday in celebration of the Chinese lunar new year. It was later learned that local units of the Viet Cong had jumped the gun.

At three A.M. Saigon time (already midafternoon at SAVA) on the thirty-first, the *tong cong kich/tong khoi nghia* (general uprising/general offensive) proper got under way with a breathtaking act of audacity on the part of the Viet Cong. A sixteen-member team of commandos from the C-10 Sapper Battalion had breached the U.S. embassy walls and, once inside the compound, held out for six hours before U.S. Army MPs and American newsmen and television crews stormed the gates. When MACV commander General William C. Westmoreland arrived on the scene, the first floor of the chancery building was still smoldering and bodies of the Viet

Cong sappers lay sprawled on the embassy grounds. For the benefit of the gathered reporters and cameramen Westmoreland, who only moments before had thought it too unsafe to leave his Saigon villa, gave an impromptu press conference. Everything was fine. "The enemy's well-laid plans went afoul," Westmoreland reassured. "Some superficial damage was done to the building. All of the enemy that entered the compound so far as I can determine were killed."[2]

Westmoreland's confident tone, though, was not echoed either by what he had promised the American people only three months earlier, or by events that were fast occurring all across South Vietnam.

It was in November 1967 that Westmoreland, at President Lyndon B. Johnson's behest, flew back to Washington. In the nation's capital Westmoreland had spread the good news. To a congressional committee on Capitol Hill, to reporters at the National Press Club, and to viewers of *Meet the Press* on television, Westmoreland reiterated his *light at the end of the tunnel* theme and predicted that victory in Vietnam was less than two years away.

The trip home had been an impressive public relations coup for Westmoreland but now, as he stood at the gates of the U.S. embassy in Saigon, the gathered reporters could see that the general's earlier confidence seemed misplaced. Not only had the embassy been brazenly attacked, but throughout Saigon violence raged unchecked. Independence Palace, navy headquarters, and the Joint General Staff Compound, as well as the main radio station, were under Viet Cong attack. Crowded and polluted Saigon had never been considered a battlefront before. The urban warfare was captured on film and the film flown at once to Japan; there it was converted to images, which were sent via satellite to America. The pictures broadcast into the nation's living rooms were raw, many of them rushed onto the airwaves unedited, and the scenes of carnage were shocking to Americans.[3]

Meanwhile, outside Saigon the rest of South Vietnam seemed to be aflame: Provincial capitals and district towns were under Communist threat; the ancient city of Hué was in the firm grip of the Viet Cong; in Da Nang the fighting raged on; and across the country hundreds of thousands of Vietnamese civilians flooded into safe areas, creating a massive dislocation of the population and an instant refugee crisis. And there was more. The enormous U.S. base at Camranh Bay — the one President Johnson favored for his visits to South Vietnam — was hit hard, MACV headquarters was threatened by the enemy's Ninth Division (ironic, given that MACV had only recently discounted large elements of the Ninth), and in countless communities strewn across the South Vietnamese countryside areas once thought by the Americans to have been "pacified" fell to the Viet Cong one by one.[4]

The damage, though, wasn't confined to South Vietnam. In Washington, D.C., the pain was felt acutely in some quarters. "What happened?" one senator on the Hill asked. "I thought we were supposed to be winning this war?" "This is really disturbing," another member of Congress said. "We've been led to believe we were on top of things militarily and past the stage when we were subject to this kind of thing." The columnist James Reston noted of Washington, "Something has happened here in the last few days, some conflict between logic and events. How could the Vietcong launch such as offensive against the American Embassy and the American bases all over South Vietnam? How could the North Vietnamese, who were supposed to be getting weaker, like the Vietcong, gather a force large enough to challenge the U.S. Marines at the demilitarized zone?" The bewilderment was understandable. Journalists, politicians, and the American public had been led to believe that, in Westmoreland's words, "We have turned the corner," but now it looked as if years of unwinnable war lay ahead.[5]

In the aftermath of the Tet Offensive, 3,895 officers and men of the U.S. Army, Air Force, Navy, and Marine Corps, 4,954 officers and men of the Republic of Vietnam (South Vietnam) Armed Forces, and approximately 14,300 South Vietnamese civilian men, women, and children were dead. Also in the aftermath, the bottom had fallen out of American domestic support for Vietnam. This would be the legacy of Westmoreland's intelligence operation at MACV, a legacy of providing estimates that were born of political expediency, and a legacy that, as Sam Adams would try to tell his fellow Americans over the next two decades, fatally undercut all of the sacrifices that they had made in Vietnam.[6]

1

A DOWNWARDLY MOBILE WASP

My dear Mrs. Gordon" wrote Dorothy Adams. "Enclosed is my check for seven hundred dollars. This, I understand, is half the yearly tuition. Sammy is very enthusiastic about going to you." In the same letter Dorothy also wanted to arrange for her son's trip to his new boarding school. Dorothy's wish was to have her Sammy make the journey alone: "Mrs. Van Rensselaer told me that [her son] Philip will go by train to Garrison — I should like to make the same arrangement." Students and their trunks arriving at Garrison, New York, were driven the short distance from the station to the Malcolm Gordon School. "I hope that things work out well," Dorothy's letter concluded, "and that Sammy won't be too homesick at first. After all, he is very young." At the time the letter was written, September 10, 1940, Sam Adams was seven years old.

Sam was small compared with the other boys that first year away at school, and he was miserable. School was frightening. At night he would cry himself asleep. Terrified, the little boy felt he had nothing in the world and that nobody cared about him.

By the looks of the old photographs Sam was the youngest student. "When he came here," the school noted later, "he apparently had very little interest in anything outside of his particular toys." He was bullied. The bigger boys would smack him with broomsticks, but he never told any of this to his mother. "Sammy's letters home have been very happy, which pleases me no end," Dorothy later informed the school.

Sam Adams's parents divorced when he was an infant but his father, Pierpont "Pete" Adams, lived not far away and worked on Wall Street. Pete appears to have visited his son at school once, and this during Sam's second year and only after the headmaster, old Malcolm Gordon himself, had written Pete enticingly, "I am very anxious to see you and to have you see the school. . . . Trains between Garrison and New York run frequently." The following year, 1943, found Pete stationed at a naval air base in Kansas, and he wrote Malcolm that except for this impediment, "I can think of nothing I would rather do than spend the day with you all at Garrison." It seems likely, however, that Pete's sentiments were less than sincere.

When Sam was sent to the Malcolm Gordon School his parents had both newly remarried. Custody of Sam was supposed to be shared equally, although the chore of raising the child was eventually pushed upon Dorothy alone, with Pete seeing him on weekends and vacations. Dorothy was not maternal toward her son and, as an avowed Anglophile, she kept him in long curly hair befitting a little lord until age four. Sam was raised by the nanny; when he was barely of age his mother shipped him off to camp for the summer. He would forever harbor a fury at his mother about being treated this way, but during his first year in Garrison he pined for her. Busy with her social life in Manhattan, Dorothy rarely, if ever, visited her son at school.

Homesick, the young Sam Adams found himself at the small school along the Hudson River. He is remembered by schoolmates as a straightforward fellow who stuck to the basics; an even-headed, cheerful, easygoing, and pleasant person to be around. He was open, amenable to everybody, and not a teaser or nagger or clique former. Sam's nickname was "Sparky" but he is also recalled as being phlegmatic. School photographs reveal a handsome, nicely proportioned little boy with lots of dark hair, high cheekbones, and slightly buck teeth. In the black-and-white prints Sam looks shy.

The home of the Malcolm Gordon School was a big brick manor house designed in the gothic tradition by Richard Upjohn, architect of Trinity Church in Lower Manhattan. In the manor lived old Malcolm Gordon, the school's founder and headmaster, and his wife, the very formidable Mrs. Amy Gordon. Also in residence were two young masters just out of college to assist in the teaching and discipline. Rooms for the thirty or so students were located both in the manor and an annex. The living was not luxurious, but the showers were hot and the food plentiful. Helping out was a grounds and house staff whose ranks would be gradually depleted by the coming war.

Order was kept through the vigilance of the Gordons. "They were all over you like a tent," said a schoolmate of Adams's, Byam Stevens. There was no corporal punishment of any sort, but there was also no undue sentimentality: The occasional pair of young combatants who could not agreeably resolve their differences were told to go out behind the squash courts and settle their business there. And the Gordons hardly encouraged levity. "It wasn't a laugh in a carload; they were not a funny bunch," recalled Stevens.

Church was every Sunday, the boys walking two by two down the winding road to Saint Philip's, and the school was a very moral place. Stevens observed, "I find myself explaining so many behaviors, things that were inculcated way back then. I think one of them is being good. You weren't naughty, you were good." The boys wore a crest with the three boars' heads of the Gordon heraldry on their blue blazers, and the Gordon motto was constantly invoked: *Non Nobis, Sed Allis* (Not for Ourselves, But for Others). According to Stevens, "Sam, and I suppose myself, was imbued by it. Throughout your life you do things that are good for the community or whatever, and it came from there."

The academics provided by the Gordons and the masters were rigorous, largely rote memorization. Writing and reading were emphasized, as was public speaking. Students had to regularly present before the school on a subject of their choice. Sam held forth on various topics: "Squirrels," "Ants," and "The History of Flying." Good study habits were fairly drilled into the boys. Old Malcolm Gordon was a rough taskmaster of a teacher, and from him the boys knew all of the countries and capitals of Africa by heart. Malcolm Gordon also taught the school's only history class, which unvaryingly began with the ancient Greeks in the fall and ended with the American Civil War in the spring. "So," remembered Stevens, "after several years of this, if you hadn't gotten it you weren't listening."

Sam Adams remained homesick, according to what he later told his friend Joan Gardiner. "But he learned," explained Gardiner, "that he would be acknowledged and rewarded for doing well. He learned that the only way he would get response from people was by accomplishing academically."

For the summer recess of 1941 Dorothy had her son sent away to Camp Wallula in New Hampshire; indeed Sam was to spend most, if not all, of his summers as a child in one camp or another. Dorothy even paid extra to have her son held over at the end of camp — and after all of the other children had left — so that he could be sent directly back to boarding school.

The war in Europe undoubtedly fostered Sam's interest in things military, and he showed an early proclivity toward analysis and statistics. In a paper receiving the Gordons' highest grade, a gold star, he wrote: "If Amarca gets in war eveybody will be unhappy. All the belammt [blame] will be on Garny [Germany]. the goornt ordered 3000,000 solgers to fite if Amarca gets in the war, 50,000 war plans are ned-ed for the Goornt of the U.S.S.."

When war did arrive old Mrs. Gordon mustered the entire school in an upstairs room and announced to the boys that the Japanese had bombed Pearl Harbor. "She could not tell us what would become of us or them or anything," recalled a classmate, Roger Stone, "but it was a very chilling and an amazing moment if you're seven years old; you don't really know what a war is."

By March 1942 the report from Malcolm Gordon was that "Sammy is making real progress, and certainly he is happy. His school work is satisfactory, and his improvement in general knowledge is most satisfying to us. . . . [He has] a desire to enter into the activities of the school." And there were a great number of activities to be entered into. The boys were always busy with hiking, knot tying, horseshoe throwing, woodworking, and, constantly, the putting on of plays, some of which the boys and the Gordons wrote themselves. Spring break began with a trip to the city so that the school's annual theatrical could be performed at the Amateur Comedy Club on East 36th Street. These were elaborately staged affairs with fantastic costumes. In the 1943 play Sam was cast as a spy. Back on the campus more practical activities included cleaning up the pine woods, retarring the roof, and painting the skate house.

Sports were a major part of the curriculum and incoming students were permanently assigned one of two teams: the Hudsons (Sam's team) or the Highlanders. The competition was intense with much partisan spirit as Hudsons and Highlanders confronted each other in touch football, baseball, soccer, track, and ice hockey. (But despite this, or perhaps because of this, Adams would nurse a lifelong antipathy toward any type of organized athletics.)

The school struggled through the 1943–1944 academic year with dwindling resources. The masters had gone to the war, and the entire burden for running the school fell upon Malcolm Gordon. On May 26, 1944, he announced to the startled audience assembled for Closing Day exercises that operations would cease for the duration.

Sam can be seen in the 1944 Closing Day photograph lined up with the other boys. He has a nice smile and, at eleven years old, looks tall for his age — but too young to have already spent four years away from home.[1]

*

Like Sam Adams, Edward Ames was also a new boy at the Buckley School in the fall of 1944, the other forty or so students in sixth grade having been together since kindergarten. Ames was just after Adams in the class list, and so the two were frequently seated together. They became close friends. Ames thought that this was partly because "We were both sort of young for our age and struggling a little bit socially. Buckley was quite an extraordinary school and the people who went there were pretty well educated, pretty self-confident, pretty accomplished kids. I was no rube from the country but I was less mature, and I think Sam was the same."

As with academics, the athletics at Buckley were superb, but Sam took this fully in stride. "Sam I remember being a hacker," said another classmate, John Lorenz. "He didn't care about making any special teams. As I recall we'd be almost hiding in the locker room rather than be out there in the midst of dodgeball." And Sam made no pretenses about looking prim and proper. "The thing I remember about Sam particularly," recalled Lorenz, "he wore gray sweats, top and bottom with a drawstring, and he was one of the sloppiest-looking guys. In the phys. ed. department the instructors were all ex-military, and here he was with his sweats all falling down: But always with a smile. He had this aura of kindness and humor."

Home for Sam during the two years that he was at Buckley was 60 East End Avenue. He lived with his mother, Dorothy, and her second husband, Charles Arthur "Tubby" Clark. Also in residence were Sam's older sister, Judith Adams, and his younger half sister Alix Clark. (Sam's half brother, Nichols Clark, would be born to Dorothy and Tubby later.) By all accounts Sam got along well with Tubby, who was a jovial bon vivant, but Sam's relationship with Dorothy was always distant and strained.

By 1945 Pete Adams had returned from the military and his son Sam would again be spending time with him at his home in Connecticut, or at the summer place in the Adirondacks. Since the divorce from Dorothy, Pete had remarried twice; the children from his second marriage, Mary and Cally, became Sam's younger half sisters. Unlike Sam, who would grow to more than six feet and was of calm disposition, Pete was short in stature and had a Napoleonic temper. Sam was frequently the target of Pete's wrath. Cally remembered, "My father often blew up at Sam because Sam was a dreamer and not a click-your-heels-together-and-salute type."

It was through his father that Sam could claim close identity with the American past. A distant ancestor, Henry Adams, emigrated from England to Massachusetts in 1638 to become the progenitor of the Adams clan in America. Henry and his wife, Edith Squire, had eight sons and one daughter. It was son Joseph and his wife Abigail Baxter who would produce the presidential Adams lineage, and it was son John and his wife Ann (last name not known) who produced Sam's. After four generations in Massachusetts, John and Ann's descendants moved north to frontier territory in New Hampshire, but like their famous cousins they also heard the call of an emerging nation. Sam's great-great-great-great grandfather John Adams got word of Lexington and Concord from his farm in Mason and rushed south in time to fight the British at Bunker Hill.[2]

Pete Adams kept a room in Redding Ridge for his son that was filled with hundreds of leaden toy soldiers. Sam and his toy soldiers were legendary, vividly remembered by all who knew him as a child. Sam would arrange his soldiers in historically accurate order for the great battles of the Civil War. The vast armies under his control, the precision of the lines, the ensuing bloodbath — to what psychological purpose did this all serve the little boy? It is an open question. What is known is that he, from about age seven to twelve, spent hours upon hours in his world of toy soldiers and Civil War re-creations. Although Pete issued orders to the boy's siblings not to go into the room where Sam garrisoned his troops, infiltration was inevitable. "He had the entire Confederate and Union Armies, with horses and everything, set up for the Battle of Gettysburg," recalled Cally, "and then I would come along and change it all, having the Grays square dancing with the Blues. And Sam would show up and say, 'Oh,' and he knew it was me and then he would reset the battle. He never got mad at me. He would let me watch him play."

*

In the fall of 1946 Sam Adams would not be returning to Buckley. The young adolescent — he was now thirteen — was again headed for boarding school. This time it was the Saint Mark's School in Southborough, Massachusetts, and upon arrival Adams apparently did not feel out of place. From the beginning, recalled his Saint Mark's classmate Peter Hiam, "Sam acted like a kid who understood institutions. He didn't look like somebody who looked homesick or wistful. He really understood the boarding school life."[3]

The school was not progressive, and sports, not academics, were the big thing. Adams, though, remained disinterested in athletics, and Hiam recalled him as being "goofy, uncoordinated. Sam would walk around with his legs sort of thrashing — he was just gawky."

At Saint Mark's, Adams retained his quiet demeanor, but classmates soon noticed that he possessed a good sense of humor and an inquiring mind. "Sam had very strong particular interests," remembered Hiam. "For example, he had a very strong interest in the Civil War. At an early age he knew more about the Civil War than anybody else I knew. He read not only the standard histories, but he got into all sorts of minutiae about the Civil War. Supply lines, railroad lines, all the things that influenced the outcome of the war. Sam was somebody who was sort of compulsive about details and knowledge." Adams also began to follow events in the wider world, and in time became an avid reader of newspapers and weekly news-magazines. Politically his sympathies grew liberal and Democratic. Another classmate, Edward Ballantyne, recalled that "he was just a very interesting guy. Not exactly what Saint Mark's probably had in mind; if they wanted a model student, Sam would not have been one. But he certainly made his mark in many ways."

A mediocre student at best, only two years short of graduation Adams set his sights on the top academic prize, the Founder's Medal. His study habits, which up until then had not been exemplary, underwent a complete transformation. He now worked tremendously hard and put in extremely long hours. "He would work night and day," said Ballantyne. "He was going to show Saint Mark's that he was someone to be reckoned with." With a few other classmates who also wanted to do exceptionally well, Adams made it a point of pride to get up very early in the morning, sometimes as early as two or three, and stay up very late in the evening. Studying after the bedtime hour was prohibited, and so the ambitious scholars would secretly cloister themselves in the library basement, or upstairs in an empty classroom. Wakefulness was aided by doses of NoDoz. The night watchman was a friendly sort who exchanged banter with the boys but otherwise left them alone.

This surge in effort paid off. Adams's progress was now charted monthly by his academic adviser with palpable ardor: "A whale of a difference over last year. . . . Splendid. . . . Improving all the time. . . . We couldn't ask for a better scholastic job. . . . Delighted that Sam continues to do so well. . . . Deserves the very greatest credit. . . . Sam is entitled to hearty congratulations. . . . A magnificent job."[4]

Out of nowhere Adams had rocketed to the top of his class academically, a position he would retain off and on until graduation. He was not, however, a model student in other respects. The sixteen-year-old was feeling his oats and had begun to earn a reputation for being a renegade, albeit an enigmatic one. "People knew Sam broke the rules," recalled Hiam, "although they didn't know particularly which rules, but they knew that he was just not somebody who joined in the school spirit. He had sort of a subversive effect on the school in that way." "Sam," another classmate, Carlson Gerdau, remembered, "was a rabble-rouser, inciting younger students to get into mischief." Jack Madden, the class giver of nicknames, called Adams "the snake," or sometimes "the sneaky snake." Tuesday nights Adams and another classmate, Hunter Ingalls, would creep off campus and take a bus to nearby Marlborough to see a movie: The next day Adams would post his review of the film in the corridor.

By the time sixth form (twelfth grade) was drawing to a close, Adams would be looking forward to college. His final report ended with his adviser stating, "I shall watch his Harvard and later career with earnest interest."

On June 15, 1951, a day after Adams turned eighteen, his parents, Pete and Dorothy, and his siblings were gathered in Southborough to hear Eleanor Roosevelt deliver the commencement address. In her speech that morning Mrs. Roosevelt warned of a race to feed the hungry: "The people in the world today with enough food to eat are in the minority," she intoned. "This is a tremendous challenge and it is just a question of who is going to do it. It means disaster if Russia, which intends to enslave the world, can do it more easily." It was a real Cold War send-off for the new graduates of Saint Mark's.[5]

*

Harvard was the college of choice for the Saint Mark's class of 1951. Freshman year in Harvard Yard, Sam Adams roomed with Carl Gerdau, Peter Hiam, and Edward Ballantyne. Other Saint Markers were nearby. Adams was as happy as he could be, but Gerdau found it socially stifling: "I had gone to Harvard knowing thirteen people, and by the end of my freshman year I knew twelve" (one Saint Marker had dropped out). "It was all Saint Mark's," said Hiam, "it was really a continuation of Saint Mark's — except all the rules were off."

Adams used his newly acquired liberty at college by beginning a four-year odyssey of movie watching. That Adams loved the movies certainly did not make him unique among the undergraduates, but he displayed this passion more strongly than others. Adams saw a tremendous number of films. He liked action films best, but he would watch anything and everything: single features and double features, Hollywood films and foreign films, good movies, but usually terrible movies. He would go to all-night showings in theaters that doubled as flophouses and smelled of urine. Adams would crash invitation-only movie premieres, and he even convinced the Brattle Theater in Harvard Square to revive the Humphrey Bogart classics.

In Cambridge the taverns shut down early, and Adams had to find his noncinematic entertainment in the various after-hour establishments across the river. He and his classmates mainly frequented clubs in Scollay Square. The prices were outrageous, and the rye whiskey with ginger ale came in tiny little cups. The Old Howard and the Casino had burlesque shows. "We liked the Casino better," Hiam said, "more stripping, raunchier jokes. It was full of college boys." Adams particularly enjoyed a Mediterranean club in the South End, drinking uzo, eating roast lamb with friends, and then suddenly disappearing only to emerge moments later on stage with the belly dancers.

Adams's inhibitions would dissolve in alcohol. Hiam explained that "he would drink but he wouldn't get mean, he would get the opposite of mean; he would get more generous and friendly." Returning hungry at three or four in the morning after a night out on the town, Adams and friends once went to get something to eat at the Hays Bickford (the "Bick"), a greasy cafeteria in Harvard Square. During the day the Bick played host to Widener Library types who discussed great things about English literature, but after hours it catered to a different clientele. On this occasion a Wonder Bread van was parked out front. The keys were in the ignition and the driver was in the Bick drinking a cup of coffee. Adams saw the van and announced that he was going to distribute the bread to the poor. He jumped behind the wheel and roared off.

At Harvard, Adams continued with his casual mode of dress. He did wear the jacket and tie required for most college occasions, but "his shirt would always be out, collars would be sticking out," said Ballantyne; "he always seemed like an unmade bed." And, remembered John Lorenz, his old friend from Buckley and also a Harvard classmate, "Sam didn't bother to brush his hair that much."

In four years at Harvard, Adams underwent no epiphany of scholarship. His performance throughout was a solidly B and C affair. When given the choice he took history courses, and by graduation he had only taken a scattering of classes outside the subject. These included Industrial Psychology (B+), Music 1 (dropped), Natural Sciences (C+), and Slavic 150. The Slavic course, taught in English, was on Russian literature. Adams had a few shots of vodka before going into the final exam, held in the morning, and did not do at all badly (B+). But in general Adams's grades were, noted Ballantyne, "far below what he was capable of doing." There were obvious obstacles to better marks. "Sam never went to class," said Gerdau, "and tended to come to you if you were in the same class and look at your notes a few days before the exam."

On campus Adams eschewed the various campus clubs, such as the Phoenix SK, The Gas, and The Iroquois, that were only known about by, and only open to, those who came from eastern private high schools. "These were snooty and exclusively for preppies, and Sam was being bombarded to join, but he refused," said classmate James Witker. "He had an extraordinary sense of fairness and egalitarian values, and he thought that it was not right to be a self-styled elite."

Adams spent a great deal of time at Harvard reading and talking about the Civil War. "He was obsessed with the Civil War," said Gerdau. He would stay up at night with friends, eating smoked eel and discussing tactical and strategic aspects of the conflict. Lorenz joined him in these bull sessions and recalled, "He had maps, battle maps; he loved that. It wasn't like he was a Rebel; he definitely was for the North and against slavery." Witker was also there: "Twenty years later I read things in Shelby Foote that I first heard from Sam back then. Sam brought the Civil War alive for us."

Sam Adams was always poor. He called himself a rich kid without the money, and he was willing at times to make sacrifices for cash. Through the Harvard student agency he and Lorenz got day work helping a landscaper. "This guy," said Lorenz, "wanted us to dig and plant, for a dollar an hour, and we worked like slaves." Lorenz put in a couple of ten-hour days with Adams; on the third day, "Sam is pounding on my door at seven A.M. saying, 'Wake up,' but I said, 'I am not going to do it, I ache in every bone.' But he went and did it. To do that for ten dollars you had to be hurting, because it was backbreaking work." Adams eventually settled upon another vocation. He went to the blood bank whenever possible. "He was being paid for his blood," explained classmate Charles Kivett, "and then he would go to the movies a few times."

*

Summers when Harvard was on break Adams traveled to Southampton on Long Island. His mother and stepfather rented a house there for the season, but Adams led a separate existence from them during those warm months by the sea. He lived on their deck for one summer but seems to have found a room somewhere else for other summers. He did not have access to cooking facilities or, for that matter, food. "My memory," recalled his second wife, Anne Adams, "of what Sam said was that he survived on bologna. I am not even sure if he had money for bread: starving."

The summer between his third and fourth year at Harvard, Adams was invited by a local student, Marilyn Kendle, to be her Southampton High prom date. Beforehand, they and some other couples went to a dinner party hosted by a Mr. and Mrs. Johnson. The Johnsons' eldest daughter, Sue Johnson, was also going to the prom. "And I think that when Sam walked in that house he thought it was right out of *Father Knows Best*," said Sue. "We lived in downtown Southampton, we had a comfortable house, it was all aglow, everybody was all dressed up, my father was there, just tickled pink about this gathering, and my little sisters were there passing cheese and crackers all dressed up." Sam Adams took an immediate liking to the Johnsons' eldest, "and after that," Sue recalled, "I think he spent every single evening at our house."

Sam and Sue went out together, often with her two younger sisters, Mary and Laura, in tow. Sam liked Sue's sisters, and they in turn liked him. Once they all rented a rowboat and pretended that they were harpooning Joanna the Whale by throwing the oar at a floating life preserver. The couple often talked politics, Sue becoming swayed by Sam's left-leaning views so contrary to the Republicanism espoused by her family. "He really had it all figured out what he believed," Sue remembered, "and I was just sucked right in because I was ready to be influenced."

For Sue, Sam represented a wider perspective. She was ambitious, working as a telephone operator that summer, and planned to go to college. She was also crazy about Sam. The Harvard man was funny, kind, and intelligent, as well as tall and handsome. But still, Sue took issue with Sam's attire. "He really was eccentric in that he always wore the same clothes. He had these black trousers that had no crease, and lace-up shoes and a white shirt that was really dingy, and sometimes he would wear a tie with it, and he had an old tweedy jacket that had no shape. All of it looked like he slept in it."

The Johnsons virtually adopted Sam for the summer. He thought the world of Sue Johnson's parents, Elizabeth and Richard, especially of Richard, a navy veteran. The Johnsons had a lovely front porch. Sam and Richard would be sitting out there among the dripping wisteria talking intently about naval matters while Sue, inevitably, found herself waiting for Sam to go out on their date.

*

By spring of the following year most of the intellect and learning that represented Harvard 1955 was already spoken for; the seniors' draft boards had taken care of that. Sam Adams, following both his father's and Richard Johnson's footsteps, decided for the navy. He had until the following fall to report for duty, though, and so ahead of him lay one more summer of freedom in Southampton where he would, once again, feel welcomed as an almost constant guest of the Johnsons. Throughout the winter months, while he was still up in Cambridge and she was at home on Long Island, Sam and Sue had written each other every day. Sue, for her part, was now convinced that Sam was the one for her.

After graduation Sam was again in Long Island working on a Canada Dry truck when not with Sue and her family. That fall, November 9, 1955, he reported to the Officer Candidate School in Newport, Rhode Island: height six feet, one-quarter inch, brown hair, blue eyes, 175 pounds. Sue had never flown before but she chartered a small plane for thirty-five dollars and made the journey across Block Island Sound to visit him. The navy course lasted only about six weeks, and then the young candidates were graduated as commissioned officers. Sam was assigned to the naval air station in Glenville, Illinois, to learn radar interpretation. His girlfriend, by this time, had entered junior college.[6]

With a vacation coming up, Sue decided that she would fly out to visit her beau. The couple were very excited at the prospect. "I had," said Sue, "saved up my money and everything and this was the first commercial flight I had ever taken: New York to Chicago. This was really glamorous stuff." Sue's aunt drove her out to the airport, and Sam met her on the other end. "He had arranged for me to stay at this motel, and on the way he said, 'I told you that I had saved up money for this, for our visit and everything, but I couldn't get any days off, I am sorry.'" Still, there was good news: "Sam told me, 'I spent the money on a phonograph and a whole bunch of neat records that you are going to love.'" The records were labor organizing songs from the 1930s. "So there I was," Sue recalled, "in this grungy motel with this phonograph. There was no TV. The bed — you put a quarter in it and it jingled. It was a horrible little place and Sam was not there all day and there I was with that phonograph and those damn labor organizing songs." There was nowhere to go and nothing to do. And that wasn't all: "We had no money to eat!" Sue found a convenience store within walking distance and cashed checks for five dollars to buy peanut butter, jelly, and Tip-Top Bread.

Sam's next naval assignment was in California, where he wrote Sue wonderful letters. They arrived daily, and she would share them with her family. "Everybody," she remembered, "wanted to see them." But then one day the following spring, the correspondence stopped. "I thought I must have missed something," said Sue. "I just couldn't believe it. I thought he must be sick." Sue wrote Sam repeatedly but got no response. Several weeks passed until finally a letter arrived "and Sam said we shouldn't be going together and this was not going to work out in the long run." She was devastated. That fall she got a job with the J. Walter Thompson advertising agency and moved to the city.

Months passed without a word from Sam until one day a letter arrived reiterating his argument for ending the relationship. Sue was incensed. "I sat down and wrote him a letter and I said, 'I thought this was all settled, Good Bye!'" Sam then called her from a pay phone every night from California. "He must have had thirty dollars' worth of quarters and he was saying, 'Oh, you've got to come out and marry me, I've talked to my commanding officer and I've got this little chapel all lined up.'" She rebuffed him, and this time it was Sam who was devastated. "So finally he said, 'I've got special leave and I am coming home and we will go out to see your parents.'" Sue agreed, but the swell of happiness she anticipated did not sweep over her: "I kept thinking, *What is wrong with me? This is all I ever wanted for two years; it is my dream come true.*"

The marriage plans were settled during Sam's brief trip back east, but Sue's doubts only grew stronger. Sam, now in California, perhaps also began experiencing some misgivings. Sue sent him a picture of the pattern for the wedding silver, and he replied that "It looks like an ingrown toenail." Sue gave the whole marriage thing a lot of thought and came to a conclusion. She informed Sam. "And that was it."

Adams put on a brave face when writing to his friend John Lorenz. "Speaking on the subject of marriages," he reported, "I came within an ace of getting married myself not less than a month ago. I was even engaged; parents were informed, dates set, apartments were being hunted, etc., etc., when all of a sudden, through a kind of mutual fatigue, it fell through. It's sort of amusing. We're now completely broken up — after having gone together for 2½ years — (it was that girl Suzie Johnson whom I had up at

Harvard a few times in the senior year). We write, and are even exchanging Christmas presents, but no longer have the slightest idea of getting married. Have you ever heard of anything so *funny?*"

*

Lieutenant (junior grade) S. A. Adams's ship, the USS *George Clymer* (APA 27), left its home port of San Diego on February 19, 1957, for an extended tour of the Pacific. The *Clymer* had served with distinction in both World War II and Korea, and earned the official nickname "The Lucky George" due to suffering only one hit — a hit that fortunately only clipped the radio antenna. To the ship's crew, however, the vessel was known as "The Greasy George."[7]

The *Clymer* during Adams's tour was not a happy ship. The rumor in the fleet was that there were disciplinary problems among its sailors, and certainly the senior officers were hard on junior officers such as Adams. The only time Dale Thorn, who was a fellow officer on another navy ship, had reason to visit the *Clymer*, Adams was "in hack," being confined to the ship while at port for one infraction or another. But Adams had lived much of his life in eastern boarding schools, and adapting to military regimen was not difficult for him. A shipmate, William LaBarge, recalled that Adams took everything in stride. "He was a neat guy," LaBarge said, "very intelligent and funny, a lot of laughs. Sam was the only person I knew who read history books like they were novels. He was always running around the ship and carrying a history book in one hand with a finger in the pages marking his place."

Adams, though, took his naval duty seriously. His specialty was communications. and he was determined that his department be the best on the ship. The work could be hard. War games would last for days, and at their conclusion the young lieutenant, returning to his room, would open his safe and reach for a bottle of whiskey. Exhausted beyond measure, Adams could only fall asleep after a swig or two.

There were, though, enjoyable aspects to naval life for Adams, especially opportunities to experience the essence of the *Clymer*'s mission: attack transport. On one of these occasions about a thousand South Korean marines were aboard ready to reenact the U.S. landing at Inchon. The marines ate heartily of buttered rice with sugar, and also of kimchi — cabbage and garlic spiced with hot chili powder. The meal was concluded and almost immediately the first casualty emerged; one of the South Koreans fell ill. "Somebody must have really poured on the hot chili powder," theorized John Hardegree, a quartermaster on board at the time. The South Korean was misdiagnosed by the Americans as having appendicitis and rushed to sick bay, where he was promptly operated upon. Within a short period, however, the mistake became apparent as — in the confines of the rolling ship — the food began to seriously disagree with the rest of the South Koreans. There was mass vomiting and the smell, Adams later recalled, was unforgettable. The South Korean marines, however, recovered and on D-Day they scrambled down the sides of the *Clymer* and into the waiting landing craft. One of these was commanded by Adams. President Syngman Rhee and the rest of the South Korean leadership awaited the spectacle from bleachers erected on the sand. The landing craft pulled away from the *Clymer* and surged forward through the waves and saltwater spray to come crashing ashore. When the front ramp lowered, the combat-ready South Koreans ran onto the beach. Adams loved it.

Shipboard life could, however, be at other times quite dull. When all was quiet on the bridge Adams turned to Shakespeare, and he managed during his tour of duty to memorize all of Hamlet's lines.

*

The *Clymer* returned to the States in October 1958. Adams's obligations to the U.S. government were over a month later and, liberated, he headed to Mount Snow, Vermont, for a winter of skiing. For washing dishes in the ski lodge Adams received a free season pass and not much more. Surviving on lima beans and with his arms elbow-deep in dirty dishwater, the young navy veteran must have given a great deal of thought that winter to getting a real job. He had turned twenty-five and the few years spent in the service had postponed the moment of truth, but now it had arrived: What was he going to do with himself? Under intense pressure from his father to find a respectable profession Adams decided, after careful deliberation, to go into the law. He applied to law school for September 1959; he was accepted at Columbia and wait-listed at his preference, Harvard.

On Adams's first day of classes at Columbia he received word that, yes, Harvard would take him. He quickly left New York for Massachusetts. There had to have been a feeling of considerable nostalgia for Adams as he found himself again at Harvard and again living in Cambridge. He got a big apartment close to campus — but Harvard the second time around was not the experience he had enjoyed as an undergraduate.

Law school for Adams was, in fact, a disaster. He hated it, and his unhappiness took its toll. His old flame Sue Johnson visited once and became concerned that her former boyfriend was drinking too much. One night he passed out dead drunk on her bed, waking up late the next day. Adams was disgusted with himself and, quite out of character, harshly criticized Johnson for letting him sleep through his classes. The emotional strain likewise manifested itself physically. Sam developed shingles on his tongue. Never one to see a doctor, Adams sliced them off with a razor.

Sam Adams's performance that first year was dismal: Criminal Law (D), Civil Procedure (F), Contracts (D), Property (D), and Torts (C). By the spring Adams was 486th out of 503 students in his class. His second year of law school was even worse: Administrative Law (F), Constitutional Law (C), Corporations (F), Taxation (F), and Trusts (F).

On weekends Adams broke from what little studying he was doing to visit his sister Cally at nearby Bradford Junior College. Her friends adored him. Cally recalled that "he had a black VW Bug and he would take as many of us as he could squeeze in on field trips to local drinking establishments." Back in Cambridge, Adams enjoyed himself when not in class. "He ate a lot of lobster and got laid a lot," stated his brother Nichols.

A group of law students would regularly get together for martinis. Adams and another student, Waldron Kraemer, joined in these gatherings, along with Kraemer's fiancée, Jean Rosenberg. Rosenberg took note of Adams's northern aristocracy and thought that he should get together with her floor mate at Wellesley College, Eleanor McGowin, of Alabama, whom Rosenberg considered to be of southern aristocracy. Rosenberg remembered, "I was taken by Eleanor because she was a talented writer, very artistic. She was very charming and vivacious." Rosenberg and Kraemer gave a dinner party and saw to it that McGowin and Adams shared an artichoke. The pairing was a success. "I knew Eleanor was taken by the fact that Sam knew so much about the Civil War," Rosenberg explained. "It was a great interest of his."

Sam Adams was, of course, handsome and intellectual, but he was also standoffish and something of a loner in the tradition of Holden Caulfield.

This did not bother Eleanor McGowin. "Sam and I agreed about so many things. We loved books. I guess we both thought of ourselves as oddballs." Adams also had a grand sense of humor: "We did a lot of laughing together. I would laugh, he would *roar*."

After Adams's second year of law school, the summer of 1961, his father, Pete, got him an internship at a white-shoe law firm in Manhattan. By this time, however, the Harvard Law student realized that he was not destined for the bar. At the end of the internship Adams left a departing memo that concluded, "The road to hell is paved with lawyers." "Sam didn't like lawyers," his sister Cally explained. "He thought they were a scurrilous bunch." Adams told his father that he would not be returning to law school for his final year and Pete, enraged, took a swing at his son. Fraternal ties were temporarily severed and Adams, when not sleeping on the beach, stayed with a college friend in the city for a couple of months. At this low point Adams must have felt the epitome of what he would tell so many people throughout his life: "I am a downwardly mobile WASP." In a short while, however, father–son relations improved to the extent that Pete found his son a job in the Bank of New York.

Eleanor McGowin was completing her senior year at Wellesley during the fall of 1961 and winter of 1962 and her boyfriend, who was asking her to become his fiancée, was putting in time at the bank in Manhattan. For his banking job Adams had just one suit; when the trouser buttons fell off he did not bother with replacements. Instead, he took to fastening his waistband with a paper stapler. Saturdays were wash days. He would strip down, put on the suit, and take a shower. Eventually the suit jacket was soiled about midway down the front. The stain resisted the shower treatment, and so Adams placed his hand over the spot whenever in public. As Dale Thorn related, "His boss finally said, 'Mr. Adams, we are very pleased with your work, but our only concern is that there is a problem with your stomach because you have to hold it all the time.'"

Eleanor McGowin graduated from Wellesley with her degree in English that spring and with friends from college took off for France, Spain, and Italy. It was in Spain that she realized she was pregnant. The trip was cut short. Back in the States, Sam and Eleanor informed their families on a Wednesday that they would get married that Saturday. "My parents were furious," remembered Eleanor. Her mother, however, rallied and on two days' notice put on a fine wedding.

On the following Monday, and to the horror of his new father-in-law, Adams quit his job and with his bride moved to Washington, D.C. The young man now had his sights set firmly on working for the government in a capacity more attuned to his interests than banking, but the banking business paid the bills in the interim and so he found work at the National Savings and Trust Company. The job, fortunately, carried no responsibilities and Adams was able to spend many a working hour in the National Gallery.

The newlyweds rented an apartment on the corner of Wisconsin Avenue and P Street. It was a hippie place over a flower shop with a spacious terrace overlooking a garden and the police station. The Adamses had a huge kitchen and a tiny bedroom to themselves; the bathroom they shared with an abstract-artist tenant on the same floor. The neighborhood was politically left, literary, and intellectual, and the couple became connected with a lively group of people. Eleanor had a number of friends in the Washington area culled from her school days at Madeira as well as old family ties. One was Andrew Hamilton, a young staffer on the *Congressional Quarterly*. Hamilton said that he and Adams hit it off quickly. "He was very relaxed, a very funny and humorous guy." Hamilton also noted that his new friend was a real intellect: "Sam was always a voracious and critical reader."

Sam and Eleanor shared the good life with Nathan, an adopted stray dog. Nathan joined Sam and Eleanor, along with Hamilton and his wife and another couple, in a rented log cabin in the countryside outside the District. Back at the Wisconsin Avenue apartment Sam and Eleanor would hold dinners on the terrace. These occasions were graced with the discarded flowers from the florist downstairs. And soon there was another tenant in the apartment: newborn son Clayton Pierpont Adams.

Adams aced the Foreign Service exam but was turned down for employment based upon his interview. He had other career openings, however, and background checks from a potential employer were already being conducted. Individuals from Adams's past were interviewed. Sue Johnson — now Sue Johnson Yager — was one. Yager was running around her apartment in New York chasing her toddler who had a full diaper. Simultaneously, she was trying to answer questions about her old beau from a Central Intelligence Agency visitor.

In early 1963 Adams was offered a place in the CIA Junior Officer Training Program. That March his career in intelligence began when he signed the agency's Secrecy Agreement.[8]

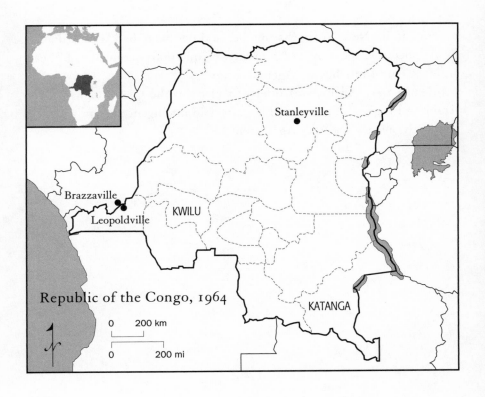

Republic of the Congo, 1964

2

CRISIS IN THE CONGO

The gleaming new CIA building in Langley, Virginia, was next to the Potomac and so close to Washington, D.C., that Sam Adams's new agency colleague Robert Sinclair made the trip to work from his home in Georgetown by canoe, paddling along with beavers and Canada geese as his fellow commuters until arriving at headquarters, ready for another day in the intelligence business. Even for those using more traditional modes of transportation, access to the CIA site was remarkably open. One could drive freely into the parking lot (as Sam Adams did in his black VW Bug) or else get on the public bus that made the CIA campus a regular stop. At the main doorway of the massive white structure, agency employees waved their badges in the general direction of a somnolent sentry; inside the building restricted areas were blocked off by guards manning turnstiles. But the security was never oppressive. At quitting time, for example, intelligence analysts had to clear their desks of sensitive material and lock their safes, yet those who wanted to bring work home with them could do so.

Adams was part of the Junior Officer Training (JOT) class that formed in the late spring of 1963. The seventy-five men and women selected for JOT were the agency's future cadre. With his old-school northeast background Adams represented the exact stereotype of the CIA organizational man: He wore a rumpled gray suit, had impeccable manners, and was the very appearance of a young Ivy League professor. But Adams's JOT classmate Kirk Balcom remembered that Adams's kind of blue-blooded background was not actually the norm for their group. According to Balcom the JOT class was "a pretty mixed bag and a really fascinating bunch of people. There were airplane pilots, there were some college kids, and also people who had been out of school for a while and had a little bit of experience."[1]

The first months of JOT training were spent at headquarters receiving a detailed orientation to the CIA and the 150,000-person-strong U.S. intelligence community. This was a huge topic that took weeks to cover. Students learned all about the different entities within the agency and how they operated. There was the Directorate of Plans, the Directorate of Intelligence, the Office of Acquisitions, the Office of Strategic Research, the Office of Geographic Intelligence, the Contacts Branch, and — for payroll and sick-leave issues — the Personnel Office. The trainees learned about what a cratologist did (guess the contents of Soviet shipping containers) and what the duties of a numbers man were (determine Soviet factory output by examining serial numbers on manufactured items). The foreign intelligence roles of the Defense Intelligence Agency (DIA), the National Security Agency (NSA), the Federal Bureau of Investigation, the Atomic Energy Commission (AEC), the State Department, and the Treasury Department were also covered in depth.

Adams and his classmates got a thorough rundown of what the international issues of the day were, especially ones dealing with the Communist threat. "We got well schooled from an insider's standpoint on the various Communist parties and philosophies, and so on, and how they operated," recalled Balcom. Adams was very engaged in this part of the learning process and he was often, according to another JOT classmate, Jerry Jacobson, very vocal in class. Jacobson recalled his classmate making "decisive comments. Usually they were right on the mark; other times not." Classroom placement was in alphabetical order, and Mr. Adams therefore got a front-row view of his new profession. He liked what he saw. "He was just very happy with his job," Eleanor Adams remembered. "He thought it was just terrific."

In addition to attending lectures the trainees were tasked to produce work samples on a given subject. Adams virtually consumed these assignments. "Sam had just an incredible mind and he had a terrific ability to grasp, and analyze, and write," recalled another JOT classmate, Ray McGovern. There were also small-group exercises as part of the course. "I remember doing one with Sam," said Balcom. "We were to build a nongovernmental agency, and Sam was clearly the brightest and most intellectually interesting star of this group. As part of the exercise we had to come up with a name for our organization." Just what that name was is no longer recalled, but it was a long one. "And we had to have an acronym for it," explained Balcom. "One guy came up with one he thought was really spectacular and then I had one that I thought was pretty good. But Sam's was just great: BEOWULF."

Toward the end of their training, the JOT class of 1963 spent six weeks at an "undisclosed location" to learn the art of spycraft. The course was a lot of fun. Trainees dressed up in fatigues every day, and the drinks at cocktail hour cost thirty-five cents (the instructors, in particular, drank a great deal). As part of their studies the students were taught how to recruit an agent and put a recorder under the bed. They took field trips into nearby Norfolk, Virginia, where they surveilled a "rabbit" through town and planted things under park benches. During the day there were lectures about CIA operations around the world; at night came practice crossings of a mock border of the type found in Eastern Europe, complete with barking dogs and barbed wire. The undisclosed location was an otherworldly place, and Adams in later years would tell those who were interested about how perfectly silent CIA planes flew low overhead while, on an adjacent lake, CIA boats sped around without making any noise at all.[2]

After six weeks those students intent on going on to become bona fide spies joined the euphemistically named Deputy Directorate for Plans (DDP) to continue with three more months of paramilitary training. Those more inclined to the analytical work of intelligence, on the other hand, returned to Langley to join the research side of the house, called the Deputy Directorate for Intelligence (DDI). Adams chose the DDI and apparently never gave much thought to becoming a foreign operative with the DDP. Eleanor explained that a couple of years later, "There was a slight chance that Sam might have had a posting abroad, but I was unenthusiastic about it because of Clayton being so small. But I don't think my coolness to the idea stopped Sam; I think he just wasn't interested."

Before leaving the undisclosed location for home, however, Adams distinguished himself by writing the parting song for his class. "Sam put it to the tune of 'Lilli Marlene,'" recalled McGovern, "a terrific song, so good that I remember it":

Good-bye to isolation
We're sad to leave The Farm
But we have to save the nation
From tragedy and harm
For we've been trained as professional spies
To tell foul lies
To Chinks and Thais
And pay Madame Nhu
And pay Madame Nhu
Please dear Mister John McCone
Won't you hear our plea?
We've worked our fingers through the bone
For very little fee
So all we ask is permission from you
To sell something to
The GRU
To help with our salary
To help with our pay
And pay Madame Nhu
And pay Madame Nhu.*

By January 1964 Adams was back at Langley and ready for real work. There were four main divisions of the enormous DDI: the Office of Economic Research, the Office of Strategic Research, the Office of Geographic Intelligence, and — the DDI's front-line operation — the Office of Current Intelligence. The OCI was essentially a top-secret news-gathering operation that produced a daily intelligence summary in three editions (one for each level of classification) as well as a constant stream of memoranda on threatening trends and developments worldwide. The OCI was where the action was, and in January 1964 Adams was not unhappy to

---

* An intelligence collage circa 1963. *The Farm* was the CIA nickname for the "undisclosed location" training site; Madame Nhu was the notorious sister-in-law of South Vietnam's President Ngo Dinh Diem and widely believed to be on the CIA payroll; John McCone was the current director of the CIA; and the GRU was Soviet military intelligence.

be sent to the sixth floor to become part of the OCI's Southeast and Southern Asia and Africa Division, Congo and Southern Africa Branch.

*

Dana Ball, branch chief of the Congo and Southern Africa, was grappling with the Congo problem, and he was delighted to be assigned the new JOT graduate. Ball got Adams a desk and showed him how to requisition office supplies, as well as how to operate the safe that would be assigned to him.

Adams, a lowly GS-9 in government rank, acclimated himself to his new surroundings in the poster- and map-bedecked walls of the Congo and Southern Africa Branch, a partitioned space within large Room 6G00. When his boss, Ball, could not be heard clicking down the hallways in his steel-tipped oxfords he was sitting at the desk directly in front of Adams's. Next to Ball's desk was that of the woman who would become Ball's wife, Janet Merkle, and next to Adams's desk was the canoeist (and analyst for South Africa) Robert Sinclair. Sinclair disapproved of the hours and hours that his co-workers spent engaged in chitchat, and some of his ire was undoubtedly directed at Adams. "Sam talked a lot," recalled Janet (Merkle) Ball; "he was a good talker." Behind Sinclair was the aesthetic Paul Stephens, frustrated that his doctorate from Yale had not opened more doors for him in life. There was also the young secretary just out of North Dakota, Colleen King, on whom Adams seemed to have developed something of a crush.

Visiting the office on occasion was the leader of Asia-Africa, Waldo Duberstein, an archaeologist by training whose shiny bald head, protruding ears, booming voice, and blustering manner left a memorable impression upon all who met him. Elwood Dreyer, the African division chief, was Duberstein's deputy and something of an old maid. Elwood once had his own deputy, chief of the North and East African Branch, Bill Newton, take Adams aside and speak to him somberly about the condition of his socks. One version of the story is that Adams's socks had holes in them; the other version holds that the socks smelled. Both versions, say those who knew Adams well, could have been true.

Prior to assuming his duties at the CIA, Adams already knew the background of a Congo situation that was, after a brief hiatus, again making front-page news. "Even before we got married," said Eleanor, "the Congo was a big thing with the deaths of Lumumba and Hammarskjöld. And Sam was really interested in that before he joined the CIA. And so it was just tremendously fascinating for his first assignment to be right in the middle of the rebellion."

The *New York Times* covered Congolese developments that January 1964 when Adams had just begun his work in Room 6G00. On the seventeenth the paper reported that, seemingly out of nowhere, a secessionist movement in Kwilu Province was threatening. The embryonic revolt in Kwilu was led by the former Lumumbist ambassador to Egypt, Pierre Mulele. That the Soviets were involved was darkly hinted at by the discovery of two Russian fur hats in a Mulele training camp, but more credible evidence, backed up by captured documents, pointed instead to Chinese Communist support. The rebels, according to the *Times*, lacked guns but were otherwise well armed with gasoline bombs and poisoned arrows and spears. They were destroying Christian mission stations in the forest and killing their inhabitants. Europeans were said to be streaming out of Kwilu, and the unrest was rumored to have spread to neighboring provinces. Tribal chiefs were being massacred, priests were being hacked to death with machetes, and Western diplomats affirmed that Mulele's revolt was a textbook case of Communist rebellion. All was in disorder. In mid-January troops from a Congolese army contingent arrested their officers, killed one, and then went on a looting spree in Baudoinville that by the end of the month still had not been brought under control.

At CIA headquarters the new analyst tried to make sense of it all. Every morning a stack of Congo material awaited Adams on his desk. There would be observations from DDP spies on the ground in Africa, State Department cables from the U.S. embassy in the Congo capital of Léopoldville, and electronic communications that had been intercepted by the National Security Agency. Because of the need to work with the NSA material Adams was given a high level of security clearance. Also on Adams's desk would be a daily raft of clippings from the CIA's Foreign Broadcast Information Service (FBIS). "And Sam went through them to see what was going on," said Dana Ball. In addition to current intelligence Adams could call upon the resources of the CIA's library, map department, and biographical section for background information (although many of the local Congolese leaders were far too obscure to have been afforded a CIA biography).

And Adams had Dana Ball as an indispensable resource. The two analysts went over the material pouring into CIA headquarters every day and had long discussions about where the situation in the faraway Congo was going. Adams would rise from his desk to converse with Ball, and during the discussion Adams would alternately prop his right foot and then his left foot up on his desk chair. At the end of the talking Adams would resume his seat. Because of this, recalled Janet Ball, "Sam always had footprints on the back of his pants."

Adams quickly became a self-taught expert on tribal Congo. He exhaustively researched the country's different tribal groups and then cross-referenced the groups in search of patterns of intertribal relationships. This complex undertaking was aided by piles of index cards, each one crammed with Adams's neat and tiny handwriting. "He had a terrific mind for detail," said Janet Ball. "He could take this mass of information and just remember all of it."

Almost immediately Adams's work got noticed. His first month on the job was not even over and his piece "Congo: Revolt in Kwilu Province Spreading" was the fourth item in the *Central Intelligence Bulletin* for January 27. The *Bulletin* was the most secret of the OCI's daily publications. The relatively few people who received it every morning were those with a need-to-know at the very highest echelons of the intelligence community, such as the president of the United States. That day in his *Bulletin* piece, parts of which remain classified, Adams painted a grim picture:

CONGO: The revolt in Kwilu Province against the central government appears to be spreading.

The "Jeunesse" bands that have been burning villages and molesting missionaries over an increasingly wide area are led by Pierre Mulele, formerly an aide in Antoine Gizenz's leftist Stanleyville regime. To date, one U.S. missionary is reported dead.

[Excised] the terrorist bands are in fact well-disciplined guerillas numbering about 2,000. There are some indications that

Mulele is receiving money and some arms from both the USSR and communist China.

Léopoldville has dispatched small units to the area, but they are reportedly not pursuing the rebels energetically. Several Léopoldville officials [excised] are said to favor employing para-commandos against the terrorists. Adoula, however, apparently fears that the paracommandos would slaughter innocent people.

Adams again made the *Bulletin* two days later. Now he warned that exile leftist elements were possibly trying to exploit the situation created by the rebellion in Kwilu Province. "The National Liberation Committee (CNL), a radical left-wing group operating out of Brazzaville," Adams wrote, "reportedly plans to foment troubles elsewhere in the Congo to draw government troops away from Léopoldville and thereby clear the way for a coup against Prime Minister Adoula."

From his desk that winter of 1964 and through the following spring Adams watched the Congo disintegrate. On February 1 his piece in the *Bulletin* noted, "The exiled former Katangan President Tshombé is reported to be planning a convention in Madrid about the middle of February to form a popular front against the regime"; on June 18 Adams noted in the *Bulletin* that Moïse Tshombé, "who is capable of posing a serious threat to the central government's authority in Katanga, is reported to have flown to Burundi to meet anti-Adoula elements."

While keeping an eye on Tshombé, Adams was also monitoring the situation in the Congolese city of Stanleyville — which, as he explained in the same *Bulletin* piece of June 18, "appears to be growing more tense. An arms-gathering raid by dissidents last week — at first reported to have picked up only a few rifles — now appears to have hauled off over 700 weapons, enough to swing the military balance in favor of the dissidents." It was in Stanleyville, deep in the African interior, that a visiting Joseph Conrad a century earlier had found his inspiration for *Heart of Darkness*, and it was just outside Stanleyville where remnants of Patrice Lumumba's followers, calling themselves the Simbas, were poised to attack.

Meanwhile, back in the capital of Léopoldville, a thousand miles southwest of Stanleyville, the political intrigue intensified. On July 1 Adams

observed in the *Bulletin* that "support for Tshombé appears to be growing.
. . . Tshombé's bargaining position is strong. Southern Katanga, richest
area of the Congo and the source of most of the government's revenue, still
supports him, and there is little doubt that he could re-establish himself
there if he chose." The next day he reported in the *Bulletin* that favorable
winds were blowing Tshombé's way. Four days later Adams wrote,
"President Kasavubu appears to be leaning toward naming Moïse Tshombé
to head the transitional government."

Adams had put himself out on a limb articulating this view, because the
U.S. State Department's steadfast opinion was that Tshombé — reviled by
other African nationalists as a pawn of the white Europeans — would
never be welcomed in Léopoldville. Notably, State took the unusual step
of going on record (termed *taking a footnote*) as officially disagreeing with
the young CIA analyst. Adams paid State no heed, though, and in the
Bulletin of July 11 he was able to write triumphantly that "Premier Moïse
Tshombé already is beset by the same security problems that confronted
his predecessor."

Stanleyville fell to antigovernment forces on August 5, and the local U.S.
consulate staff was not evacuated in time. Ray McGovern had been assigned
to the Soviet Foreign Policy Branch in Langley, although he would see his
former JOT classmate in the hallways every now and again. "And before
we knew it," he remembered, "Sam was working seventy-hour weeks. And
I said, 'What's going on, Sam?' and he said, 'Crisis in the Congo.'"

The capture of the U.S. Foreign Service people in Stanleyville had put
the American intelligence apparatus into high gear. For the CIA this was
also personal, because the American vice consul in charge of consular
affairs in the captured city was actually a DDP operative, as were three
other members of the consulate, who had been running informants and
agents in the area. The senior managers of the CIA up on the seventh floor
in Langley ordered that a Congo situation report (SITREP) be ready for
the agency's top officers first thing every day.

The early deadline meant that the SITREP had to be composed in the
dark hours of the morning in order to incorporate information gathered
from the overnight cables streaming in from the continent. "And Sam
jumped at the chance to do the SITREP," remembered Dana Ball, "and he

loved it. I said to myself, *Jeez, is he going to make it into work every time in that tiny VW of his, or am I going to get called in at three A.M. and asked to do this?*" But Ball could sleep soundly: His protégé missed not one shift throughout the long months of the crisis.

In the wee hours of the morning Adams sat alone at his desk in the Congo and Southern Africa Branch, gathering nubs of information — some of it filtering in from the Sudan where the Soviets had a staging ground for their Africa operations — and writing up that day's report. Adams created elaborate chronologies as a way to make predictions about future events in the Congo. Chronologies are basic to intelligence work, and they became Adams's favored analytical tool. The technique entails putting everything known about a person or an event into a time sequence — thus creating a chronology — and then watching for the patterns that inevitably emerge, revealing the underlying intelligence story. In terms of the Congo this meant that Adams was creating detailed chronologies of politician sightings, tribal developments, and even the comings and goings of Soviet An-12 cargo flights. With this view of what was happening where and when, Adams's political and military forecasts for the region became uncannily accurate.

The director of the CIA at the time, John McCone, had a reputation for being hands-on when it came to intelligence analysis, and soon into the Congo crisis Adams was unexpectedly called up to the seventh floor. The scene that greeted him in the director's conference room would be forever seared into his memory. "Some thirty people were there," explained Adams, "seated in leather chairs around a large mahogany table. From photographs I recognized most of the agency's higher-ups: Ray Cline, chief of the DDI, roly-poly, with crinkly red hair; Richard Helms, head of the DDP, looking, I thought, like a Mississippi riverboat gambler dressed in a business suit; and at the head of the table, John McCone, the director. He had white hair, steel rimmed glasses, and piercing eyes. Next to McCone was a big map of the Congo on an easel."[3]

The questions flew at the Congo analyst, and Adams handled them with ease. "He drove them crazy with detail, I tell you," said Dana Ball. "McCone was asking about the tribes and Adams was batting off the Bafulero, and this one and that one, and all this stuff — and Sam had his little cards." The director's meeting then shifted to other topics, and Sam sat down. When the gathering finally broke up some of the senior officers came over to the new Congo analyst and congratulated him on his performance. For Adams, the moment was one of sheer exhilaration.

*

The Simba occupation of Stanleyville continued into September, and by October the stranded American diplomats and DDPers had become hostages. A world away at CIA headquarters, Adams became a "one-man task force" to deal with the problem, and he thought of little else. Even when not at his desk he was cognitively shifting through the various pieces of the Congo puzzle. In a habit perhaps left over from his Harvard Law days, Adams always kept a long pad of yellow legal paper with him, and he could often be seen walking along the hallways of Langley then suddenly stopping to lean the yellow pad up against a wall and jot down an important thought or two that had just entered his head. Adams also did not leave the Congo when he left headquarters for the day. His old friend Edward Ballantyne came down to Virginia for a visit, and in a private moment he said to Eleanor that he assumed the Congo was off limits for Sam as a topic of conversation. "Oh no," Eleanor replied, "that's all he will talk about!"

At Langley, Adams believed that the Congo was now rightfully his. Said Dana Ball, "I can remember one time Sam wasn't around and somebody wanted a Congo expert, so I went. And Sam was mad as hell. He really was irritated. This was his damn country and, by God, he was going to be the one to talk about it."

As October was ending Moïse Tshombé in the Congo had brought international condemnation upon himself and his regime by hiring an army of white South African mercenaries to help the Congolese army retake Stanleyville. The CIA simultaneously had secretly provided Tshombé's air force with American planes and Cuban exile pilots. Adams was not initially aware of this DDP scheme, although he soon learned of it by reading a misdirected intercept. A plan was also being developed for U.S. transports to air-drop Belgian paratroopers into Stanleyville to rescue the hostages, and this Adams did know about — he had attended some of the CIA meetings where the option was being discussed. Time was of the essence, because the

Simbas were proving themselves to be exceptionally violent: "They were very savage, absolutely savage," remembered Dana Ball. "They would cut a missionary's liver out just as he was standing there."

*

At home in the United States the 1964 presidential elections were coming up in early November. The Adamses, who had moved from Washington to rural Sterling, Virginia, registered to vote. Eleanor recalled that to do this they had to go to the local Southern States agricultural store. "We went," Eleanor said, "to the back room where the manager had a billy club on the wall. He was the one who registered voters, and we had to take a literacy test." But Sam's Harvard education and Eleanor's Wellesley degree did little good: "We failed." Because Sam and Eleanor were white they were immediately due another chance. This time around the manager showed them how to correctly answer the test. It turned out that the "literacy" question was a trick one about the Constitution that relied on reverse logic. Disgusted, Sam and Eleanor were delighted when Lyndon B. Johnson, with his commitment to civil rights, prevailed on election night in a stunning landslide.

For the young and politically progressive couple the future of their country looked bright indeed. Johnson had an overwhelming mandate from the people and enjoyed sizable Democratic majorities in both chambers of Congress. He could now launch his ambitious domestic agenda of creating large-scale government programs aimed at eradicating the nation's social ills. On foreign affairs Johnson also looked promising. He was a mature leader who could, it seemed, be trusted with the nuclear button while at the same time holding the line against Communist aggression around the world, especially threats to struggling South Vietnam. The Adamses were staunchly in favor of U.S. intervention there. "We all thought this was a clear case of aggression by the North Vietnamese," Eleanor said. "They were coming down and the South Vietnamese had just wanted a chance to defend their independence."

*

American politics only briefly interrupted Sam Adams's attentions that November. Back in his republic things were heating up. With the Congolese army and the white mercenaries at the outskirts of Stanleyville, the Belgian-

American rescue attempt was finally launched on November 24. The Congo was now boiling. Dana Ball recalled being at headquarters in the Watch Office, the nerve center of the OCI, as the departures of the U.S. Air Force transports were announced one by one: "I remember as that plane goes off, that plane goes off — pretty exciting." Adams was there with Ball, and he was no stranger to the room. Those manning the Watch Office had seen a lot of Adams over the past several months. "We were a twenty-four-hour operation, so we got to know all the analysts," said Howard Beaubien, who was on the Watch Office staff. "We read all the cables and so forth and when we got hot stuff on the Congo we would call Sam. He was always very cordial, always ready to smile, and a smart guy — really knew his business." And Beaubien knew that Adams could be singularly focused. He had seen Adams, upper torso fully hidden by an outstretched copy of the *New York Times*, get off the elevator and walk down the corridor oblivious to oncoming traffic. "Now, people missed him," Beaubien explained, "because they were watching; Sam wasn't. But that's the way he was. When he got into concentrating on something that was what he did, and everything else was out there."

The Stanleyville raid in the Congo was an American success: All U.S. government employees in the city, including the DDP men, were rescued; the Simbas were driven out. In Langley, Virginia, meanwhile, Adams's reputation as a hard worker had spread among the agency's senior managers on the seventh floor. "He impressed the heck out of them," said Janet Ball. The hostage crisis was over, however, and within months the sundry rebellions in the Congo had burned themselves out. For a while things did start to look promising when Che Guevara arrived in the Congo from Cuba to see what kind of revolutionary trouble he could foment, but Guevara mishandled the opportunity and Adams was left with an increasingly peaceful country to follow. The need for the SITREP ended early into the new year. Adams soldiered on as the Congo analyst on the sixth floor of headquarters, but he was unhappy. "He wanted more excitement," recalled Dana Ball.

Still, crises or no crises, CIA analysts at Langley were expected to keep themselves busy. Dana Ball remembered the last assignment he gave his restless subordinate. "We used to have to make up these little one-page country things — where's the capital, population, what are the main products — and I asked Sam to do one for the Congo. I must have beat Sam over the head with a brick I don't know how many times to do it. He just didn't want to do it." Added Janet Ball, "I can remember Sam saying, 'Okay, Chief' — he called Dana 'Chief' — 'Okay, Chief, I'll do it, I'll get to it, I'll get to it.' He never did; he left before it got done. Somebody else did it."

The summer of 1965 had arrived and Adams began agitating for a new assignment. When he threatened to leave the OCI for the DDP, he got the attention he wanted. "As I recall," explained Ray McGovern, "the Congo sort of petered out and he was looking around for something interesting to do, and he had made quite a name for himself as an analyst, and somebody on high decided — I am sure they later regretted it — to put him on Vietnam."

3

VIETNAM

With his accomplishments on the Congo behind him and Vietnam to look forward to, Sam Adams spent a well-deserved vacation on Hoel Pond in the Adirondacks. He would have fed the chipmunks just as he had done as a child, played with his little son Clayton in the water, and enjoyed quiet afternoons reading on the cabin porch with Eleanor. At almost this exact same time, July 1965, Lyndon B. Johnson had made the decision to sharply increase the number of U.S. troops in South Vietnam. Troop levels, the president announced, were to be raised from 75,000 to 125,000. And, Johnson let it be known, whenever the U.S. commander in Vietnam, General William C. Westmoreland, wanted more soldiers they would be his for the asking. The war in Vietnam had been fully Americanized.[1]

Rested, Adams returned to Room 6G00 in early August, but now his desk, with his transfer from the Congo having taken effect, was in the Southeast Asia Branch. The setup of SEA was similar to what he had known in Congo and Southern Africa, with about five or six analysts covering different countries. In SEA these were South Vietnam, Cambodia, and Laos. And Adams would have a new boss, Edward Hauck.

Hauck, as Adams quickly learned, was a veteran Vietnam-watcher and a legend at the agency, known for his impish sparkle and wide, gap-toothed, ear-to-ear grin that made him look like an Indian lacrosse player who'd taken one too many swats on the head. Hauck's body was muscular, his head topped with a gray crew cut. But Hauck was smart and competent, and rumored to have once danced with Madame Mao Zedong.

In 1942 Hauck had been pulled from Columbia University at age eighteen because of his knowledge of Japanese. He served as a Japanese-language officer, first in India, and then with the Chinese Nationalists in southern China. Hauck learned Chinese and was subsequently assigned to the Dixie Mission, the small American team attached to the Nationalists' foe, Mao Zedong. Hauck was the only member of the mission who actually spoke Chinese. He saw Mao on a daily basis and conversed with the Communist leader frequently. For a while Hauck, with his Japanese and Chinese fluency, even led a Chinese Communist intelligence detachment behind Japanese lines. Only twenty-one years old and he was already an expert on Asian Communist guerrilla armies at war. Hauck thought highly of the military capabilities of the Chinese Communists. In particular, he admired their organization, tactics, and determination. After the Japanese surrender Hauck stayed on with Mao's forces and once found himself on the receiving end of a Nationalist attack. His final task as part of the U.S. mission was to retrieve the cadaver of an American whom the Communists had just executed — John Birch.

Once back home in the States, Hauck got a job in the Foreign Documents Division of the CIA. In 1951 he transferred departments to become an analyst on Indochina.[2]

On Adams's first day at SEA, in early August 1965, his new boss put him on the topic of Viet Cong morale. Adams was brimming with excitement about his new responsibilities, and also with optimism regarding America's prospects in South Vietnam. "Mr. Hauck," he asked, "how long do you think the war is going to last? I mean, how long before we clean it up?"

"The Vietnam war is going to last a long time," Hauck answered, his cheerful expression turning sour. "In fact, the war's going to last so long we're going to get sick of it. We're an impatient people, we Americans, and you wait and see what happens when our casualties go up, and stay up, for years and years. We'll have riots in the streets, like France had in the 1950s. No, we're not going to 'clean it up.' The Vietnamese Communists will. Eventually, when we tire of war, we'll come home. Then they'll take Saigon. I give them ten years to do it, maybe twenty."

"You're kidding," Adams gasped.

"Wish I was," Hauck said, smiling once again.

Adams returned to his new desk at the other side of the cubicle. *Good God*, he thought, *I'm only ten minutes into my first war, and already the boss says we're going to lose it.*

Adams welcomed the commotion at work later that month when it was announced that the U.S. Marines had landed on the Van Tuong Peninsula in South Vietnam in hot pursuit of a regiment of Viet Cong guerrillas. This, despite Hauck's gloomy prognosis, was evidence for Adams of real American progress in Vietnam. Adams knew a thing or two from his navy days about the power of these seaborne invasions, and he was delighted to learn that his old ship, the USS *George Clymer*, was one of the attack transports involved. Indeed, much to Adams's satisfaction, the U.S. press later deemed the American action on the Van Tuong Peninsula to be a resounding success. A large number of Viet Cong were killed with very few American casualties. Regarding Viet Cong morale, however, the recently reassigned analyst had experienced few, if any, victories of his own.[3]

Adams had hit the books in the CIA library and he read the daily Vietnam SITREP, as well as his ever-present copy of the *New York Times*, for clues as to what Viet Cong morale might be but was getting nowhere. An early attempt to apply the three-by-five index card treatment to the problem had to be aborted when Adams was told not to bother because the Viet Cong used aliases that they changed frequently. It was just not possible to compile, as it had been for the Congo, a roster of names that could be tracked over time for clues as to what was happening in the larger context. Southeast Asia was proving to be a tougher case to crack than Africa.

Realizing that he still knew precious little about his new country, Adams often turned to his office mate, Mary "Mollie" Stuart Kreimer, for the answer. Kreimer had, like Hauck, followed Vietnam for years. Her current assignment was to compile and write the daily CIA report on the South Vietnamese political situation. Kreimer was short in physical stature — a fact often exacerbated by her tendency to slink down low in her chair — but she identified with her namesake, Mary Queen of Scots (the association was with Kreimer's middle name). Kreimer possessed both a wealth of information and a sharp mind. Papers would fall from the four sides of her desk. More productive at night than during the day, Kreimer was a pleasure to work with, being perceptive and helpful, and she more than carried her fair share of the load at SEA. She was also cynical and — unlike Hauck, on whom Vietnam weighed heavily — emotionally detached from the war. But it could not be said that she served for the money, either. The CIA finance office would call her on occasion to complain that she had not cashed her most recent paychecks. Kreimer would protest, "Yes, I did," but then the finance person would reply, "Mollie, look in your purse"; there the checks would be.

In 1950, with a degree in government from Smith College, a year abroad in Switzerland, and newly graduated from the Fletcher School of Law and Diplomacy, Kreimer spent time pounding the pavement of Washington, D.C., looking for a job. She applied to the State Department and, she recalled, was asked "Do you type?" Kreimer was taken only somewhat more seriously when she inquired at the CIA. She took their test for prospective employees. "And there was a question," Kreimer remembered, "'Is the moon made of Swiss cheese?' And the choices were 'true,' 'doubtful,' and 'false.' I put down 'doubtful' because, empirically, I didn't know." The agency took her.

Kreimer was fluent in French and, she said, "I started out as a translator, which I wasn't terribly happy with. At least it was a job." Kreimer's CIA posting was not glamorous. She was part of a pool of translators who lacked security clearance to handle classified documents. Kreimer toiled away at translating French-language Vietnamese newspapers into English, relying on a French–Vietnamese dictionary because at the time there were no English–Vietnamese ones. When finally granted security clearance, "I was," she explained, "moved inside — but was doing exactly the same thing." It was two more boring years in the translation shop before she applied for a transfer and, after rejecting the possibility of joining the clandestine part of the agency ("the boss there was a terrible military person and was obnoxious"), she joined the OCI. Appropriately enough, she was assigned Vietnam.

Kreimer and one other analyst, George Sheldon, had covered Vietnam from the old CIA headquarters in Foggy Bottom next to the State Department. In his earlier career at the Office of Strategic Services (OSS) during World War II, Sheldon had worked in Indochina with the veteran revolutionary leader Nguyen Sinh Cung. Nguyen, who preferred to be called Ho Chi Minh (Bringer of Light), was an American ally at a time when the United States valued any and all assistance in its battle against the Japanese. Ho and the Americans went their different ways after the war and the OSS mission ended, but by that time Sheldon had gained insight into the Vietnamese Communists. It was Sheldon's view, which Kreimer also adopted, that the Vietnamese Communists were essentially a nationalist movement against foreign colonialism. "They wanted the French out," said Kreimer of Ho and his followers, "and Sheldon and I believed that Ho Chi Minh, if left on his own, bad as his Communist contacts were, would not become the puppet of the Chinese or the Russians or anybody."[4]

Sheldon's beliefs, however, were unacceptable to the French occupiers of Vietnam, and he was barred from traveling there. Sheldon left the CIA well before the United States was to fully inherit the French role in Vietnam. Kreimer, for her part, spent a two-year hiatus from Vietnam as an analyst for Indonesia and the Philippines before slowly transitioning back to Vietnam again in the early 1960s. By then the situation, from the American perspective, had taken an ominous turn for the worse.

*

In 1959 the Vietnamese Communists at their Fifteenth Plenum of the Central Committee decided, in secret, to renew war in Vietnam. The goal was to remove "the oppressive yoke of the imperialists and feudalists" and to "bring about independence and a national people's democracy." This renewal of hostilities would seem unnecessary because it was only a few years earlier, in 1954, that the Vietnamese Communists under Ho Chi Minh concluded their "anti-French Resistance war" with total victory in sight. The French colonialists, thoroughly defeated during that conflict, agreed to hold elections — elections that Ho and the Communists were confident of winning. Pressured by his allies in Moscow who urged caution and patience, however, Ho made a diplomatic blunder of epic proportions and agreed to postpone the plebiscite until 1956. The voting, of course, never took place (and the United States had a hand in this). Instead Vietnam broke into two separate countries: the pro-Western Republic of Vietnam in the south (capital Saigon) and the socialist Democratic Republic of Vietnam in the north (capital Hanoi). Both countries had large landmasses, and each contained a sizable population. South Vietnam had 14.5 million people and North Vietnam 16 million.

The South Vietnamese government in Saigon was under the American-backed ruler Ngo Dinh Diem. Diem was corrupt, dictatorial, and unpopular, but he was also, to the relief of the Americans, virulently anti-Communist. Luckily for Diem, the Vietnamese Communists initially abided by the peace treaty reached in 1954 and, busily engaged in their own affairs in the north, were not in a position to address their dreams of a unified Communist Vietnam until the end of the decade.[5]

Once initiated, Hanoi's secret campaign for the liberation of South Vietnam enjoyed rapid progress. Diem's cronyism and heavy-handedness had not endeared him to the peasants living in rural areas, and by 1961 his government had already lost control of much of the countryside to the Hanoi-backed revolutionaries in South Vietnam, the Viet Cong. Diem's demoralized forces, the Army of the Republic of Vietnam (ARVN), rapidly ceded ground to Viet Cong guerrillas. By late 1964 the Viet Cong were poised to split South Vietnam in two and conquer the country.

The crises kept Mollie Kreimer busy preparing a special daily CIA report on the Vietnamese situation that went to the Pentagon and State Department. Langley's efforts, though, were not popular with the military and the diplomats, because CIA prognoses for Vietnam were relentlessly gloomy; interagency relations became strained. John McCone, for example, once requested that Kreimer and her colleagues prepare a briefing for him on Vietnam in preparation for a meeting he was to have with President Lyndon B. Johnson and Secretary of Defense Robert S. McNamara. Kreimer and the other analysts were not at the high-level meeting, but when it was over the CIA director bluntly told them that he had not used their material.

"Oh?" Kreimer said to McCone.

"No," McCone answered, annoyed. "McNamara gave a very detailed briefing of his own about how well things were going, and it was just the opposite of what you were saying."

McNamara, McCone said, reported that the Saigon government had dramatically increased the number of countryside hamlets under its control in the past month, and McCone was stunned that nowhere in the CIA briefing had this been mentioned. Kreimer did not know how she and her colleagues could have been so negligent, so she went back to the data and soon discovered where McNamara's rosy statistics had come from. "We realized," she explained, "that the South Vietnamese government had recently divided its hamlets in half, so there were now twice as many hamlets under its control than there were the month before."

*

In the fall of 1965 everyone at SEA was scrambling to keep up with the daily cascade of events in South Vietnam, Cambodia, and Laos: everyone except for Adams, who was more broadly exploring his topic of Viet Cong morale. Hauck and Kreimer imparted much of their knowledge about Vietnam to Adams, but they could not help him much on the morale question. "Without guidance and not knowing what else to do," Adams said, "I began to tinker with the VC [Viet Cong] defector numbers." The numbers came from the weekly Viet Cong defector statistics compiled by the South Vietnamese government, and Adams was immediately struck by the waves of Viet Cong who were abandoning the fight. In a recent week, for example, there had been 211 defectors. Adams looked across other weeks and saw that this was by no means an anomaly: In fact, two hundred was about average for monthly Viet Cong defections. Extrapolating, Adams deduced that at this rate more than ten thousand Viet Cong were rallying to the Saigon side every year, or about 5 percent of the total number of Communist guerrillas in South Vietnam, which were then thought to total around two hundred thousand. Equally impressive to Adams, there were more Viet Cong defections presently than there had been in the past, indicating not only that there was a serious morale problem within the Viet Cong's ranks, but also that it was growing worse.

By late October, Adams was confident that he had enough of a grasp on his subject to produce a memo. In it he cautiously suggested that there was preliminary evidence of an upswing in enemy defections that was perhaps indicative of downward enemy morale. This tentative observation came after almost three months of work. It garnered no interest at Langley. For the remainder of the year Adams attempted to deepen his understanding of the Viet Cong defectors beyond aggregate numbers: "[I was] trying to figure out such things as where the defectors came from, what jobs they had, and why they wanted to quit."[6]

In South Vietnam bushels of Viet Cong documents were captured by the U.S. Army and ARVN on a regular basis, and the important ones were translated into English for intelligence analyses. Some of these translated documents were shipped to Langley, where they were ignored by all, except Adams. He took to this material greedily. Eleanor recalled weekends with her husband at the log cabin: "He would have a three-foot-high stack of documents; all of these captured documents that nobody had read!" Adams made some headway with the documents in trying to find the answers to his queries, but he longed for the chance to follow the evidentiary trail on Viet Cong morale to Vietnam itself.

When Sam Adams wanted something from the CIA he was always doggedly determined to get it, and friend and foe alike recalled with mixed emotions the incessant pestering that Adams could inflict upon others to get his way. Undoubtedly the circumstances leading up to his first trip to Vietnam were no exception. It can be imagined that only after Adams was through thoroughly hectoring various people on the sixth and seventh floors at headquarters were the funds found, the cover story created (on one trip to Southeast Asia, Adams went as a U.S. Department of Agriculture adviser), the housing in Saigon arranged, and the airline tickets purchased for his trip to Vietnam. All this accomplished, by January 1966 Adams was jetting across the Pacific toward the Orient.

*

Howard Beaubien, Adams's friend from the OCI Watch Office at headquarters, had shipped out to Vietnam for an eighteen-month stint a short while earlier. The DDI had used the huge U.S. buildup in Vietnam as an opportunity to unload employees who were not fitting in well at Langley. Agency experts on Eastern European affairs who found themselves idling away the hours in the tropical heat of Saigon knew that their CIA careers had taken a very wrong turn. Beaubien considered himself something of a maverick, and despite a degree in international relations from American University he had realized since joining the CIA in 1963 that the intelligence bureaucracy "really wasn't my game." Still, he figured, he had to give duty in Vietnam — and the differential pay that was part of the incentive — a try: "So when it came time for people to be asked to 'volunteer,'" he stated, "I was one of them."

Beaubien arrived at Saigon's Tan Son Nhut Airport on November 26, 1965. The U.S. embassy was to arrange for his transportation into the city, but the diplomats were off for the American Thanksgiving. It was a holiday in the middle of a war. "This struck me," Beaubien recalled, "as a little weird." Stranded outside Saigon, he finally got Pan Am to give him a ride into the city, where he got hold of CIA station chief Gordon Jorgensen, who found him a place to sleep for the night.

Beaubien was assigned to the CIA station's Collation Branch. "They loaded it up with a lot of us from the intelligence side — so-called analysts — there were probably thirty-five of us in that group." The Collation Branch, in the U.S. embassy annex, was where captured Viet Cong documents, as well as Viet Cong prisoner-of-war interrogation reports, were screened before being sent back to the States. The underworked Collation Branch staff also performed a minimum of analytical duties. Beaubien helped out at the branch and, for the money, pulled night shifts as the CIA duty officer at the U.S. embassy, but mainly he ran errands for his boss, George Allen, driving around Saigon in an old gray rebuilt jeep from World War II.

When Allen was out of town it was left to Beaubien to write the weekly cable back to Langley. "Ugly job," Beaubien recalled. "It was supposed to be a wrap-up of the week of finished intelligence." Often there wasn't much intelligence to summarize, however, and Beaubien would be hard-pressed to take up three pages. One time he procrastinated on doing the weekly summary, only getting around to it at the very last minute. To make it easier on himself, he rewrote some material that Langley had sent out to the Saigon station awhile ago, and then he sent the cable to CIA headquarters. Beaubien went to bed, and the next morning there was a priority message waiting for him from the agency's top Vietnam man at Langley, George Carver. The cable read: "Congratulations, great job, this is exactly what we want." Said Beaubien, "And basically what my report was, was their own words coming back to them."

For the members of the Saigon station a good deal of time was spent at the Cosmos Club, a bar that was attached to the U.S. embassy compound. The watering hole was not the private domain of the CIA, although it may as well have been. According to Beaubien, "I believe that the State Department shied away from it because of us." The Cosmos Club had survived the deadly March 1965 Viet Cong bombing of the U.S. embassy unscathed, but the interior was a wreck after the CIA patrons once went on a drunken rampage. "There were mirrors broken and stuff," said Beaubien, "and it looked like a shell had hit it."

On a typical morning the drinking at the Cosmos Club would begin at nine for a few from the agency; by midafternoon it was picked up by many more. The drinks were cheap, and salty food was served to soak up the booze. Inside bottles of "33," the local beer, one could find bugs, labels, anything. But the main action at the Cosmos Club came after work and especially on weekends, when DDPers located outside Saigon would converge on the bar on Saturday afternoon for their weekly staff meeting. Kirk Balcom, Adams's JOT classmate, was one of the visitors. "Those of us that were back from the provinces would show up there maybe on a Thursday or a Friday," he remembered, "and then it would be a party until everybody left."

The bar enjoyed many regulars, according to Beaubien, including the Saigon DDI head, his boss George Allen: "He was one of them, best patron of that place! He was a great guy, a very sharp guy. When George talked about the Viet Cong I listened to him because I believed he actually knew what the hell he was talking about." Allen's position in the "Cosmos Command" was on a corner stool where he could see his CIA lieutenants lined up at the bar on his right and left. Allen had his hands full as the top DDI officer in Vietnam, but he was always willing to mentor a newcomer.

In late 1965 during a trip back to Washington a senior officer in the OCI informed Allen — who recounted the story — "that he had a young man who'd been working on Africa, the Congo problem, who had kind of burned himself out on that and was looking for other worlds to conquer, and would I be willing to accept him and take him under my wing if he were to come out to Saigon?" Allen assented, and his new charge arrived at Tan Son Nhut on January 12, 1966. Adams wore, Allen recalled, "Khaki pants, well rumpled. You'd never have guessed he'd been in the navy, particularly as an officer. I was astonished when I learned he had been in the navy." Adams's youthful appearance also made an impression on Allen: "He seemed to me like a kid who had just been out of college, but he must have been over thirty when I first met him. Just seven years younger than I. He looked so damn boyish, and that was kind of disarming." And to Allen, Adams acted boyish. "But it was clear," Allen continued, "that Sam had a sharp mind and he was a guy who wanted to solve whatever problem he was given; he wanted to do a good job on it."

Adams, on a three-month temporary assignment from Langley, was not officially a part of the DDI outfit in Saigon and only nominally under Allen's control. "He was in Vietnam looking at Viet Cong defectors: Why did reports indicate that there were so many? Anyhow," Allen recalled, "I took him out to MACV and introduced him to some people there, and then I saw that he was looked after. He was operating mostly on his own. I'd see him from time to time and ask how he was doing, and he would tell me, 'Oh great, great, great.'"

When Adams arrived in Saigon the annual Tet holidays had closed the city down. He spent his first few days touring, among other attractions, the Saigon zoo, where he obligingly allowed himself to be used as a handsome Occidental photo prop for two Vietnamese couples. At an Indian bookstore, the Majestic, he bought a city map and a Vietnamese phrase book. The next morning he was initiated into the war when woken by a distant Viet Cong satchel charge. The following week Adams made the rounds to the Collation Branch (one employee there was busy working on a guide to Saigon's bars and whorehouses) and to the Cosmos Club, where an agency man was creating hilarity by smashing plates on the floor. Adams's lodgings were out by the airport, and every morning he walked the three or four miles to the U.S. embassy, working up — those who later in the day sat next to him noticed — a good sweat along the way. Beaubien secured some wheels for Adams. "I was on good terms with a guy in the motor pool," said Beaubien, "Mr. Phouc, a good guy. So we took Sam up there and we were able to get him a jeep. And Sam just went out on his own; I mean that guy just took off."

*

Adams's travels in Saigon brought him to the villa on 176 Pasteur being occupied by five researchers from the RAND Corporation: Leon Goure, Douglas Scott, David Elliott, Anthony Russo, and Joseph Carrier. RAND was a nonprofit research organization originally founded as a U.S. Air Force think tank, and its studies on Vietnam were for McNamara. Among the data the research group in Saigon collected were interrogations (ultimately totaling twenty-two thousand pages) of Viet Cong defectors, deserters, and POWs for RAND's Viet Cong Motivation and Morale Project. This was exactly the stuff Adams was interested in, and he dropped by the RAND villa often.

At the villa Adams was shocked to learn from the head of the team, Leon Goure, that defections — those Viet Cong who voluntarily turned themselves in to the South Vietnamese government under the Chieu Hoi (Open Arms) program — represented only a small fraction of the Viet Cong's problems. From the Viet Cong standpoint the real crisis was that many comrades were simply deserting: leaving the ranks, but not reporting themselves to the Chieu Hoi centers. Goure told Adams that for every Viet Cong defector there were perhaps seven Viet Cong deserters who had simply melted back into the civilian populace. Adams did the math, and by adding the ten thousand defectors from his earlier estimate to seventy thousand deserters he realized that the Viet Cong were losing eighty thousand men and women a year to causes other than death, injury, sickness, or capture. The situation for the Viet Cong, Adams thought, was evidently dire.

Even with the high-level security clearance that he'd earned while handling NSA intelligence during his Congo days, Adams was forbidden to travel outside Saigon. Regardless, he eagerly accepted an invitation to visit a Chieu Hoi center in Tan An, capital of the province of Long An (Prosperous and Peaceful) to the south of Saigon. At the center Adams was taken to see a dozen young men who had formerly been Viet Cong, and he was given a female Vietnamese translator, Co Yung, with whom to work. "Right away there was a problem," Adams said. "Despite her title as 'interpreter,' Co Yung knew little English. She was fluent in French, however, of which I had the high school variety, and we spoke haltingly in that language."[7]

The English-French-Vietnamese-French-English route did not allow for effective interviews of the Chieu Hoi residents, however, and so Adams decided to turn his attentions to a pile of boxes at the center. These boxes contained all of the defector reports for the province made in the past four months. Over the next week Co Yung, who was rapidly picking up passable English, and Adams went through all 146 defector dossiers on hand. The results from this census suggested to Adams that most of the Viet Cong turncoats from Long An were young and inexperienced, with around eight months' service each, and that almost all of them were from military units that were analogous to a Viet Cong home guard, not straying far from their village or hamlet base. Other defectors, such as those who had been Viet Cong administrators, were not even combatants. To Adams, this was all somewhat puzzling.

It was early February, and over the next month Adams would return to Long An twice more, expanding his harvest of Chieu Hoi records to more than five hundred. There continued to be clear indications that morale among the Viet Cong was low. According to what the defectors had told their interrogators, many of the Viet Cong greatly disliked the war. They hated the American helicopters, the U.S. bombing, the daily threat of death, and the rigors of Communist army life. Most just wanted to go home. Adams toured the province, however, and saw for himself that the security situation in the countryside was highly precarious. A South Vietnamese army officer even told him that there were an estimated 2,000 Viet Cong in Long An itself, though U.S. Army intelligence had put the number at just 160.[8]

Hearing that David Elliott of the RAND villa was working in neighboring Dinh Tuong Province, Adams traveled southwest to meet him. Elliott promised to be an important resource for Adams. This was Elliott's second tour of Vietnam, his first having occurred in uniform. About to be drafted out of graduate school in 1962, Elliott had volunteered for the army and learned Vietnamese at military language school; from 1963 to 1965 he was assigned to army intelligence in Saigon. Upon discharge, he immediately got a job with RAND and went right back to Vietnam. It was in Dinh Tuong that Elliott was engaged in a provincial case study of the revolutionary movement.

"I was doing pretty detailed stuff based on a very close reading of a lot of evidence," Elliott explained, "collecting repeated reports on places and episodes to the point where I began to get some confidence in the generalizations I was making." And Adams was using the same methodology. "Sam was going to one place, Long An, and getting a lot of information within a local context. When he went to Long An in early 1966 he systematically put together these defector records — but unlike me, Sam sort of took a wide-angle macro view and tended to extrapolate." Elliott stated that the extrapolation was "one of the potential defects of Sam's approach, which his critics, of course, jumped on. And extrapolations are risky. On the other hand, the purpose of extrapolation is to raise questions and provide insights that you otherwise would not have; then you can go in and provide the detailed documentation for it."

Elliott continued his work in Dinh Tuong into 1967, and he recalled meeting "a number of people from the agency on and off, but Sam is the only analyst that I can remember taking the trouble to come down and talk to me in detail."

*

While going about his business, Adams would occasionally check in with George Allen. "The one thing about Sam," Allen recalled, "he was always enthusiastically ready to tell what he had learned. He sort of looked to me as a guru, almost in a boyish way, and he'd come to me and say, 'Gosh, guess what I've found!' and then he would prattle on and on. He was an enthusiast with boundless energy, and boundless curiosity and dogged-ness." Beaubien saw Adams at times as well and remembered, "When he got hold of something, like a pit bull, he didn't let go." And what Adams was increasingly getting hold of was the monumental magnitude of the Viet Cong defection and desertion rate.

In Saigon, Adams had begun to review in earnest the translations of captured Viet Cong documents that came through the Collation Branch. Among the captured documents that grabbed his attention were copies of various orders from the Vietnamese Communist leadership telling their subordinates to stem the tide of desertions. Adams later summarized these Viet Cong directives: "'Christ Almighty,' they all seemed to say. 'These AWOLs are getting out of hand. Far too many of our boys are going over the hill.'"[9]

There were also a few — but tantalizing — captured reports from Viet Cong guerrilla units that actually contained defection and desertion figures. For one of the units the defection-to-desertion rate was 1 to 23; for another it was 1 to 27. Again, Adams was astounded.[10]

With knowledge of the Chieu Hoi statistics for the whole of South Vietnam, and by computing the desertion-to-defection rates that were in the captured papers from a single province, Adams did one of his extrapolations. "I set up," he explained, "an equation which went like this: If A, B, and C units (the ones for which I had documents) had so many deserters in such and such a period of time, then the number of deserters per year for the whole VC Army was X. No matter how I arranged the equation, X always turned out to be a very big number. I could never get it below 50,000. Once I even got it up to 100,000." He went on, "The significance of this finding in 1966 was immense. At that time our official estimate of the strength of the enemy was 270,000. We were killing, capturing, and wounding VC at a rate of almost 150,000 a year. If to these casualties you added 50,000 to 150,000 desertions — well, it was hard to see how a 270,000-man army could last more than a year or two longer."[11]

Adams spent the rest of his time in South Vietnam collecting further evidence of the Viet Cong's defection and desertion problem. He was convinced that he was on to something of profound significance. Statistics from the U.S. military were also indicating that for every one Viet Cong defector there were many more Viet Cong deserters. Adams returned to the RAND villa where Leon Goure — but no one else in the villa — shared his sense of optimism regarding the apparent predicament of the Viet Cong.

In March, Adams made intelligence-gathering trips north to the cities of Da Nang and Hué, and to the surrounding countryside. Once when back in Saigon, Allen told Adams over drinks lurid stories of the 1946 "Night of the Long Knives," when a band of Vietnamese Communist assassins went to work on the French population of Hanoi. Suitably frightened, Adams ran up to the Collation Branch and got himself a vintage Spanish .38 automatic and three clips of ammunition. He never had call to use the gun, however, and he returned it to its Collation Branch safe before his tour ended on April 10.[12]

Earlier, Adams had written his younger sister Alix describing his current situation and his immediate post-Vietnam plans:

17 March 66
Dear Axie,
Your first letter arrived today, about two weeks after your second. Now that everything is chronological again, I think it is safe to reply.

I am writing this in Saigon by candle-light, hungry, frightened, listening to convoys of trucks go by. The candles had to be lit when the electric power went off about an hour ago. I am hungry because the cook quit yesterday afternoon, frightened, because she might not come back, and able to hear the traffic because the air conditioner is off. Stemming the tide of Red aggression is a difficult thing to do.

Otherwise, everything is OK. Booze is cheap ($1.65 for a half-gallon of Gilbey's gin), helicopter rides to anywhere are free, and most of the natives think I'm God. Work is interesting too. My boss told me when I arrived two months ago — to sound out Vietnamese (including Viet Cong) popular opinion — that my job was to "ram a thermometer up the ass of the body politic." I haven't yet pulled it out.

Next month I meet Eleanor in Greece for a three-week vacation. Nathan will be left at a $2-a-day dog motel and Clayton in Alabama. I don't know who has the better deal. At least Nathan will be wormed.

Yr. brother,

Sam[13]

Prior to his departure for Greece, Beaubien gave Adams a small going-away party. Beaubien had a nice villa and also a great cook, and it looked to be a good time. "The last picture I have in my mind of Sam," Beaubien remembered, "was him walking in the gate with a case of beer on his shoulder."

4

GEORGE ALLEN'S WAR

When Sam Adams departed Tan Son Nhut, George Allen was just completing a two-year tour of duty in South Vietnam. Allen was permitted only the occasional trip back to the States to see his wife and four daughters, and so he made a home for himself in Saigon. Evenings he would retire to the house he shared with another member of the CIA station. The two agency men kept a small deer on the premises as well as a pet python that lived in a large cage. The python was periodically fed a duck and, as Allen recalled, "It took about a week — you could track it — for the lump to move through the python and come out the other end." Allen would play host to new DDP arrivals to Vietnam, many of them young JOT graduates, and "we'd have a little get-together and we would persuade one of them to go into the cage and then I'd say 'Oh God, there's a python!' and I'd go out and lock the door and leave the kid in there. Enough of us would be still sufficiently sober, though, to extract him if necessary."[1]

Allen's break into the world of intelligence came in 1949 when he accepted a job as a clerk-typist in the offices of the Assistant Chief of Staff for Intelligence (ACSI), the intelligence branch of the U.S. Army. As a new analyst Allen was tasked with French Indochina, a region of great concern to the United States in 1950. The Communists had just attacked on the Korean peninsula and had prevailed in China only months earlier. Now the French colonial states in Southeast Asia — Vietnam, Laos, and Cambodia — appeared to be the next dominoes to fall. Vietnam was in clearest danger due to the activities of Ho Chi Minh and his Communist organization, the Viet Minh (a contraction of Viet Nam Doc Lap Dong Minh Hoi: League for the Independence of Vietnam).[2]

Ho and the Viet Minh were products of an Indochinese socialist revolutionary movement dating back to the 1920s. During World War II, Ho and his followers had fought a two-pronged war against the Japanese occupiers of Indochina and the French colonialists who were permitted by the Japanese to administer the region. With the defeat of Japan in 1945 and the removal of the Japanese as a force in Indochina, the Viet Minh launched a purely anti-French war. By 1950 the conflict had claimed fifty thousand casualties on the French side and was becoming a political liability for Paris.[3]

During the next five years George Allen stood analytical watch over Indochina at ACSI, attempting for the benefit of American policy makers to predict twists and turns in the situation according to what was known about French and Viet Minh strengths and vulnerabilities.

To analysts in ACSI such as Allen the doctrinal and organizational aspects of the Viet Minh were complex but not mysterious. By 1950 Communist revolutionary philosophies had been propagated openly and widely. The Viet Minh represented a Vietnamese adaptation of armed socialist movements that had been seen elsewhere. These movements, known variously as "revolutionary warfare" or "people's war," were a method of struggle pioneered by Mao Zedong and the Chinese Communists in their long march to victory. People's war at the midpoint of the twentieth century was one uniquely suited for use in colonial and semicolonial societies of the type that existed throughout the developing world.

People's war was based upon two critical elements. One was the belief that the aim of the conflict was population, and not geographic, control. Gains in population control resulted in increased sources of taxation, labor, and recruitment for the revolutionary struggle. In this way people's war was an organic phenomenon, growing from within and independent of external supports. The second was the central role of the Communist political organization in the control and direction of every facet of the armed struggle. This meant that it was impossible to defeat a people's war by military means alone. As long as the political organization remained intact, then the organization could germinate future armed rebellions despite military setbacks.

At ASCI in the early 1950s, Allen was well aware of people's war theory and of the political nature of the Viet Minh, and this knowledge became integrated into his military analyses. The early Indochinese Communist

Party and its successor, the Communist Lao Dong (Workers) Party, were under Ho Chi Minh, and the party held all leadership positions within the Viet Minh. True to the ideology of people's war, the party dominated all aspects of the Viet Minh organization; an understanding of this phenomenon was important for any accurate assessment of the revolutionary Vietnamese threat. Allen explained that the party was the "heart, soul, and brains" of the Viet Minh. The Viet Minh army commanders, Allen said, "at all levels were members of their unit's party cell — frequently the leaders of that cell. Every military unit was energized by party agents. The party wrote the regulations and field manuals, controlled training, planned operations and led critiques of the results, motivated the troops, controlled personnel assignments, and rationalized strategy and tactics."

Every decision and action by the Viet Minh was placed within an ideological context, and judged accordingly. Allen related an example vignette. "After a battle," he said, "the political commissar of a unit would gather the troops together, a couple of days afterward, when he's had time to think about it." The commander, according to Allen, might then say, "All right, we've got to do some self-examination here. What are the mistakes that we committed? Did any of you see any of your comrades make an error, do something wrong?"

One of them might then say, "Well, I saw Hung over there, he ducked, and when he ducked he pointed his machine gun up in the air and he wasted some ammunition in the air and he wasn't shooting at the enemy!"

"Ah, is that *true,* Hung?"

"Well, yes, *I* did do that."

Allen explained, "There would then be criticism and self-confession, and all this would be pulled together and written up. And then they would have study sessions at each succeeding echelon to go over these things, and try to overcome them. They'd rationalize whatever was wrong as having capitalist or bourgeois tendencies of some sort. They'd say, 'We've got to overcome that tendency, get that out of our mind! And we do that with this new slogan that says, All Power to the Farmers!'"

In addition to the other attributes, it was also known in Washington intelligence circles that the Viet Minh were intensely nationalistic. The Viet Minh fight against the French, while combined with utopian aspirations, represented a continuation of centuries-old Vietnamese resentment of foreign occupation. Allen recalled an episode that occurred in 1954.

"At Dien Bien Phu," he said, "during the battle there was a breakdown in Viet Minh morale. Some Viet Minh officers complained about having to order the troops again to assault a fortified position through the minefields, over the barbed wire and everything, and take the heavy losses again that that would entail. 'We can't order our men to do that,' they said. And so they had a big self-critique, self-criticism, program by the Viet Minh units of Dien Bien Phu to get rid of these, in essence, these humanist tendencies. When [the author] Bernard Fall asked a Viet Minh colonel afterward, 'How were you able to persuade your men to do this, to assault a position that was so strongly fortified?' the colonel answered, 'We were able to convince them that the best thing they could do with their lives was to leave their bones to fertilize the soil of a free Vietnam.'"

George Allen and others in ACSI became aware of the military configuration of the anti-French resistance. The Viet Minh liberation army had four key components that French intelligence termed the *main*, *local*, *guerrilla*, and *militia* forces. These four forces were organizationally arranged in a pyramidal shape, with the top and narrowest part being represented by the Viet Minh main force units, the middle and wider part represented by the local forces, and the bottom and widest part being represented by the Viet Minh guerrilla and militia forces.

Viet Minh main force units were infantry detachments, like those that had demolished French garrisons along the China border in 1950, and capable of waging mobile warfare on a large scale. Main forces were akin to a conventional army, although lacking in aircraft and tanks and reliant on stealth tactics to overcome the technological advantages enjoyed by the French military.

At the second and middle level of the Viet Minh army were the local forces. These forces were combat strike units at the district and province level with the capacity to conduct small ambushes and other types of "low-intensity" warfare.

At the bottom level of the Viet Minh military organization were the guerrillas and the militia. The "guerrilla-militia" comprised full-time combatants in the guerrillas, and civilian part-time soldiers in the militia.

Guerrillas operated in small groups within the villages and hamlets of Vietnam, conducting classic unconventional warfare. They enforced Viet Minh authority over the populace, spied on and harassed the French, and aided the efforts of the main and local forces. The militia, in contrast, were civilian supporters of the Viet Minh who, although possessing no guns, assisted the liberation movement and the other Viet Minh forces in any way that they could. For instance, the militia used pitchforks and other agricultural implements to defend their hamlets against enemy attack.

The pyramidal structure of the Viet Minh military organization meant that the guerrilla-militia would, when dictated, move up into the local forces, and the local forces could, if called upon, move up to the main force units. Thus the Viet Minh's military assets were rooted in the villages and hamlets of the countryside and funneled upward as necessary within the force structure. As importantly, the lower parts of the pyramid, which did not depend upon the upper parts for their existence, could readily function alone. The proximity of Viet Minh main force units was not necessary for the local or guerrilla-militia forces to go about their daily tasks in support of the revolution.

The French understood the layered schemata of the Viet Minh force structure, and French military intelligence was careful to include all types of Viet Minh — the main, local, and guerrilla-militia forces — when assessing the armed revolutionary threat. In taking their fight against the Viet Minh down to the village and hamlet level, the French periodically conducted large-scale "sweep" operations to capture guerrillas. The French also constructed watchtowers in villages, established lines of small military posts in the provinces, patrolled aggressively, and committed atrocities against communities suspected of harboring the resistance. Unlike the French, however, the Americans expressed little patience for unconventional warfare at the local level, and they urged the French to focus primarily on the Viet Minh main force units.[4]

*

As the Viet Minh gained military sophistication and strength, they attempted to surround and conquer the French in remote areas far from the towns and cities of Vietnam. The Vietnamese Communists believed that if detachments of French soldiers were separated from their bases of supplies, then they could be overcome with Viet Minh main force units. But in this the Viet Minh had mixed success because of their own problems with logistics in the roadless mountains and forests of Vietnam. Initial Viet Minh efforts to surround and siege secluded French positions in 1952 and 1953 had to be abandoned due to this difficulty, although the Viet Minh met with unalloyed success in 1954 at Dien Bien Phu.

The Viet Minh attack on the French fortified complex at Dien Bien Phu, in a distant valley in northwestern Vietnam near the border with Laos, was carefully planned. To attack the French at this location the Viet Minh first performed the feat of arranging, with Chinese Communist assistance, a supply trail from the Viet Minh enclaves in northern Vietnam down to the battle zone. Using a series of relay stations at points along quickly repaired roads, bridges, and fords, the Viet Minh army moved by truck, bicycle, and foot. In areas massive artillery pieces were muscled through dense jungle. The Viet Minh eventually brought to the Dien Bien Phu theater of operations a newly formed antiaircraft regiment, three infantry divisions, one artillery division, support units, a forward command post, and the requisite amount of supplies and food for a large siege operation.[5]

The thirteen thousand French troops dug in at Dien Bien Phu found themselves surrounded by one hundred thousand combat-ready Viet Minh. The battle started on March 13, 1954, and lasted fifty-six days. Ten thousand in the French position managed to survive until surrender on May 7; Viet Minh casualties were a staggering twenty-three thousand.[6]

The French defeat at Dien Bien Phu was a defining moment in Vietnamese history. The French left the Southeast Asian scene quickly in the aftermath of their debacle, and the Vietnamese Communists had given the world an important demonstration of what they could accomplish. Allen saw their victory as "an organizational triumph, almost unimaginable." Much of the Viet Minh success, he believed, could be attributed to two factors. First, their leadership and ranks were disproportionately drawn from northern Vietnam, a region whose people were renowned for their hard work and dynamism; second, the Viet Minh believed in the correctness of Communism. "That combination of the grit and determination of the North Vietnamese," Allen said, "and their willingness to struggle and to live the Communist discipline and structure and so forth, were the two things waiting to get together. And when they did it was like the critical mass that gets atomic fission to go."

*

With the conclusion of the French catastrophe in Indochina, Allen saw that there remained a dearth of insights among U.S. military and civilian leaders regarding what had just happened in Vietnam. Despite the presence of specialists inside the U.S. government who knew a great deal about the topic, policy makers in Washington chose to remain blind to the complex Vietnam problem.

At the time the Geneva Accords were being signed in July 1954, Allen made a five-week foray into Southeast Asia. Vietnam, he found, was in a tragic state of mass migration as Catholics from the Communist-dominated north left all their belongings and fled south to live under conditions of dire poverty. Vietnam was racked with ethnic and religious conflicts, a hatred of colonialism, and mutual mistrust among those from the northern, central, and southern regions of the elongated country. Allen could readily see, however, that the non-Communist leaders in the south lacked political legitimacy in the eyes of the people, and it was obvious to him that if elections were held as planned then the Communists under nationalist hero Ho Chi Minh would win. It was also apparent to Allen that if elections were not held there would be another Viet Minh–like insurgency — and one that would be successful, even accounting for the prospect of massive U.S. counter-intervention.

Allen returned to the States and reported his sobering prognosis. It resounded loudly within the Washington intelligence community, but U.S. foreign policy, by that time geared solely toward thwarting the 1956 vote in Vietnam, remained unaltered.

George Allen soldiered on in army intelligence for the rest of the decade and, among other things, assisted in U.S. contingency planning for the event of a Communist invasion of South Vietnam from North Vietnam. One hair-raising U.S. scenario called for landing Honest John rocket battalions at Da Nang and Nha Trang to serve as a nuclear beachhead. Allen pointed out to Pentagon planners that this concept "was totally unfeasible, unworkable, and based on wholly fallacious assumptions." The idea gained credence in the American military establishment, however, and remained under consideration for a number of years.[7]

*

Following its secret decision in 1959 to no longer abide by the 1954 Geneva Accords, Hanoi launched an ambitious action program to be carried out by the Viet Cong in the south. Hanoi's hidden goals were to gain the support of the rural people in South Vietnam, to consolidate political and military power in "liberated" areas, to penetrate the South Vietnamese government and army, and to conduct across South Vietnam a campaign of guerrilla warfare, kidnappings, and — for "eliminating cruel and wicked tyrants" — assassinations and executions.[8]

Allen visited South Vietnam in May 1962, when he could tell that the new insurgency was progressing rapidly and that the pro-U.S. government in Saigon was in danger. He returned to a Washington where the intelligence community was under no less illusion regarding the Vietnamese Communist's strengths and the Diem regime's weaknesses. Allen was encouraged by the arrival of the Kennedy administration and what he hoped would be a fresh approach to the gathering crisis.[9]

The new Kennedy administration tackled the Vietnam issue head-on, and Secretary of Defense Robert S. McNamara held regular high-level conferences to vigorously address the problem. Once secret, the contents of these meetings have since been declassified.

In December 1961, the first conference met in Honolulu at the headquarters of the Commander in Chief, Pacific (CINCPAC), and McNamara made it clear to the military and civilian policy makers present that the United States would offer all assistance, and spare no expense, in saving South Vietnam from Communist aggression.

By the time of the second conference, January 15, 1962, prospects for Washington regarding South Vietnam were discouraging: U.S. Army intelligence indicated that Viet Cong operations were frequent and increasing, that the Communists were planning to surround the city of Saigon, and that 1962 was shaping up to be the year of decision for Southeast Asia. McNamara was told that Viet Cong strength amounted to as many as twenty-five thousand full-time fighters, and that this number was growing at a rate of a thousand per month. Walt Rostow of the National Security Council had recently written a paper on the theory of guerrilla warfare and concluded that to defeat a guerrilla effort up to twenty counter-insurgency soldiers were needed for every one guerrilla. The implications of a Viet Cong force numbering twenty-five thousand were therefore enormous: By Rostow's formula an anti-Communist army of many hundreds of thousands was now needed in South Vietnam. Diem's government, though, had fewer than 170,000 men under arms. Panicked, McNamara immediately authorized the rush delivery of forty thousand carbines for the South Vietnamese security forces and insisted that the Army of the Republic of Vietnam demonstrate its mettle against the Communist guerrillas by clearing and holding a large swath of the countryside.

McNamara flew out to Honolulu again for his third conference a month later. Among the attendees were Frederick Nolting, the U.S. ambassador for South Vietnam; General Paul Harkins, the senior U.S. commander in Southeast Asia; General Lyman Lemnitzer, the chairman of the Joint Chiefs of Staff; and Admiral Harry Felt of CINCPAC. Nolting and Harkins expressed optimism regarding South Vietnam, being confident that things were now turning around in Saigon's favor. McNamara asked if the twenty-five thousand Viet Cong thought to be present the previous month had now increased or decreased in number. The new head of U.S. military intelligence in South Vietnam was air force Colonel James Winterbottom, and Winterbottom answered that the number of full-time Viet Cong was believed to be in the 18,500-to-27,000 range, but that there were an additional 100,000 part-time Viet Cong operating in the countryside. Ambassador Nolting chimed in that the hundred thousand number was too low, and that millions of people lived in Communist-controlled areas of South Vietnam. McNamara had to have been stunned. Lemnitzer and Felt softened the blow by dismissing these figures as mere guesswork.

The secretary of defense, however, pressed Colonel Winterbottom for more details, and it became clear that the colonel knew nothing more on the subject other than the estimate range he had just given. McNamara was impatient, and he demanded a South Vietnam province-by-province analysis of Communist-controlled and Communist-leaning areas to serve as a benchmark for measuring progress in the war against the enemy. For similar purposes, the secretary also instructed U.S. intelligence to give him a valid estimate of Viet Cong numeric strength. The first comprehensive Viet Cong order of battle summary was about to begin.

Order of battle is a military term that would in time become part of Sam Adams's everyday lexicon. Adams would talk about the "Viet Cong order of battle" in conversations private and public, in his writings, interviews, lectures, and throughout his various testimonies under oath. It would not be a stretch of the truth to say that Adams fairly lived and breathed the subject for years on end. By way of definition, *order of battle* refers to data regarding the capabilities of an enemy: for example, its number, type, weaponry, leadership, organization, and proneness to fight or flight. The order of battle is a listing of the enemy's combatant forces by name, size, disposition, composition, equipment, location, capability, current activity, commanders, recent activity, special characteristics, and most likely course of action. In brief, to know the enemy's order of battle is to know the enemy, and order of battle work is one of the basic jobs of military intelligence.

In the aftermath of McNamara's third conference the newly created U.S. Military Assistance Command, Vietnam, started a study on the Viet Cong order of battle. MACV was a joint command, meaning that it encompassed all four branches of the U.S. armed forces. It was from MACV headquarters in Saigon that the American ground war in South Vietnam was to be orchestrated, but during its initial years of existence the MACV's mission in South Vietnam was one of assistance only. General Harkins was the first MACV commander, and Colonel Winterbottom was his J-2 (military parlance for head of intelligence at the joint-command level). The colonel's area of expertise was in making post-nuclear-bombing assessments for the Strategic Air Command; he had no specific knowledge of either Southeast Asia or of unconventional warfare.[10]

George Allen, as the newly formed Defense Intelligence Agency's senior intelligence expert on Vietnam, was asked to travel to Saigon to help set up a new entity to be called the Joint Evaluation Center. (The JEC was an early stab at interagency cooperation and was designed to provide Ambassador Nolting with unbiased intelligence, but it would be quickly swallowed up by MACV.) It was en route that Allen heard about the secretary of defense's most recent conference, and the sudden need for a Viet Cong order of battle study.[11]

At the JEC, Allen and a few other Vietnam experts who were also pulled into the effort on short notice completed the project in just six weeks. The number they arrived at for main and local force Viet Cong was somewhere over 40,000 — a massive increase from the earlier estimate of between 18,500 and 27,000 that Winterbottom had given McNamara at the secretary's last conference. By one account Winterbottom, when told of the revised figures, openly stated that they were too high and ordered a lower number, but despite this pressure the final JEC Viet Cong order of battle estimate, comprising main, local, and guerrilla-militia forces, was 120,000.

General Harkins was, like Winterbottom, upset about the Viet Cong statistics coming out of the JEC, and presumably what they might indicate to McNamara about America's lack of progress against the Viet Cong. The general fretted over the figures and finally accepted from his J-2 Winterbottom a Viet Cong main and local force strength (not including guerrilla-militia) of 16,500.

This new figure was *less than* the estimate given to McNamara earlier, and when it was presented to the secretary of defense as the conference convened it came with humble caveats that made it appear to be the result of better intelligence and not a desire to hide the truth. "While this is a reduced estimate," the official record of the conference modestly stated, "the reduction [is] more a matter of accurate reporting than of lesser numbers. . . . With regard to these facts, it is likely that we shall be getting better information in the future, inasmuch as there are now intelligence advisors down to the section level." McNamara came away from the conference encouraged, not knowing that he had witnessed the war's first arbitrary reduction of the Viet Cong order of battle estimate.[12]

*

By the end of his 1962 tour Allen had spoken frankly to General Harkins in Saigon about his misgivings regarding Colonel Winterbottom's fitness to be the MACV J-2; back in Washington, Allen was equally blunt when briefing the senior officers of the Defense Intelligence Agency in the Pentagon. Often, however, Allen's critique of the MACV intelligence effort was met with hostility by those in uniform; they thought it not proper for a civilian to judge military matters. And increasingly the DIA in Washington was being shunted aside by the MACV across the ocean in Saigon when it came to intelligence matters on Vietnam. Allen, in turn, felt less and less appreciated by his military employers. By late 1963 he had taken a pay cut to accept a position at the civilian CIA, and in January of the following year he was again in Saigon.[13]

The two or so months Allen spent during this tour were highly productive. His CIA team was given access to MACV and ARVN intelligence, made field inspections to the different U.S. military zones countrywide, pushed for coordinated intelligence efforts such as shared interrogation centers, and even briefed William Colby during the CIA director's visit to Saigon. But there were for Allen also many upsetting counter-indicators of progress, one of these being that the American military was focused on jungle fighting against the Viet Cong regulars at the expense of dealing with the enemy's irregular elements entrenched in the villages and hamlets of South Vietnam.

It was mid-1964 when Allen began his two-year tour of duty in South Vietnam. He had many different responsibilities, but one of his main areas of focus was on the "Viet Cong Infrastructure" (a term Allen coined when briefing U.S. General Richard Stilwell in 1963). The VCI was a Vietnamese Communist network existing throughout South Vietnam and one defying U.S. attempts to pacify the countryside. If Americans at home were aware of this side of the Vietnam War at all, it was in reference to press reports of the mysterious Viet Cong "shadow government" that held the villages and hamlets of South Vietnam in its grip by night, only to vanish by day. Such portrayals of the VCI as a population control organization were accurate, but not complete.

As important in terms of understanding the infrastructure from the political perspective was an understanding of it from the military one, because as with anything to do with the Viet Cong and people's war, political and military could not be differentiated. The VCI guided and controlled all aspects of the revolution. Organizationally this was achieved through the political hierarchy of the Viet Cong Infrastructure being parallel to, and branching out into, that of the armed wing of the Viet Cong. This intertwined political-military system meant that Vietnamese

Communist leaders wore two hats and ensured total political control and guidance of the armed struggle. Not just a shadow government, therefore, the VCI was part and parcel of the enemy that the Americans and their allies were fighting militarily — and this was seldom understood by the war planners in Washington.

The Viet Cong Infrastructure held little interest to the J-2 staff at MACV, who were after bigger game in the form of the Viet Cong main forces and their base camps in the jungle. The CIA's Allen was on his own in grappling with the problem, helped only by the hodgepodge of intelligence professionals Langley had sent over as part of its housecleaning efforts. Allen had economists, geographers, political analysts, and demographers working on the details of the infrastructure, along with librarian types from the agency's Central Reference Service who scanned and indexed incoming material. But none was familiar with the Far East, or was in any way a specialist on Vietnam. And of course no one spoke Vietnamese. However, by working with translated material, Allen recalled, "We would collect all of the information relating to a part of the infrastructure and put together a picture of that part, and then another part, and another part." An understanding of the overall VCI was gained, and slowly the gaps in detail were filled in. "And the idea behind it," explained Allen of this intelligence work, "is that we really couldn't undertake effective pacification in the countryside unless we knew what it was we had to eliminate; what it was we had to account for."

*

In mid-1964 when the Viet Cong appeared to be on the verge of victory in South Vietnam, President Johnson used a naval incident between U.S. destroyers and North Vietnamese torpedo boats to pass the Gulf of Tonkin Resolution, a congressional act giving him blank-check authority to expand U.S. involvement in Southeast Asia. Johnson used that authority to formalize the American air war in Vietnam by early 1965, and the American ground war soon followed. The man to lead this war would be General William Childs Westmoreland.

A year earlier, in June 1964, Westmoreland had become Commander, U.S. Military Assistance Command, Vietnam (COMUSMACV), by replacing General Harkins. For Westmoreland this was but the latest step upward in a brilliant military career that began as a horse-mounted artillery officer in the American West and was followed by leadership positions in the Ninth Infantry Division as it fought its way through North Africa and Europe. After the war Westmoreland was, successively, given command of the 504th Parachute Infantry, the 187th Air Combat Team (while it was fighting in Korea), the 101st Airborne Division, and the XVIII Airborne Corps. When not leading his troopers Westmoreland was an instructor at the Command and General Staff College, and at the Army War College. He also had spent time in an advanced management program at Harvard Business School, where friendships with America's future captains of industry were established. Just before assignment to Vietnam, Westmoreland was made superintendent of his alma mater, the U.S. Military Academy, from which he had graduated decades earlier as first captain of cadets.

Now in Southeast Asia, the new head of MACV developed a three-stage strategy to defeat the Viet Cong main forces that were situated in jungle camps miles from population centers. "So long as the Communists were free to emerge from those hideouts to terrorize the people," Westmoreland stated, and were able to "recruit or impress conscripts, glean food, levy taxes, and attack government troops . . . there was little hope of our defeating the enemy." The first stage of the Westmoreland stratagem was to establish and defend logistical points in the vicinity of the enemy's large forces. The second stage called for then invading the Viet Cong sanctuaries and routing out the fighters. With the opponent now exposed, the final stage was to engage in, as Westmoreland said, "sustained ground combat and mop up the last of the main forces and guerrillas, or at least push them across the frontiers where we would try to contain them."

Concurrent with the three-stage maneuver against the enemy's big units — which Westmoreland believed were the backbone of the Viet Cong insurgency — he gave himself two additional tasks. These were to pacify the countryside, thereby bringing the rural population under Saigon's control, and to strengthen ARVN so that the South Vietnamese could fight their own fight. But his soldier's heart was never really committed to the more messy details of unconventional warfare, and Westmoreland was happy to leave pacification and ARVN building to others. He, meanwhile, would turn his attention to whipping concentrations of enemy combatants wherever he could find them.[14]

Westmoreland, of course, had the concept of people's war completely upside down, viewing the main force elements as the roots of the struggle and the guerrilla-militia and political elements as the vines, but even if theoretically in error the U.S. power he brought to bear against the Vietnamese Communist enemy was truly awesome. George Allen witnessed the progressive Americanization of South Vietnam and the enormous amounts of war matériel pouring into the country destined for American forces. He saw a landscape changed by the U.S. military for the worse. Hilltops were flattened to accommodate artillery bases, forests were torn out to allow free fields of fire, jungles were defoliated to deny the enemy camouflage, and the ground as viewed from the air was pockmarked by bomb craters. Allen recounted that "I also observed at ground level — as I had at Tarawa during World War II — the debris of war: the death and mutilation of soldiers and civilians in the towns and cities; villages being rocketed and bombed because someone there was thought to have fired at an aircraft passing overhead, the villagers fleeing into nearby fields, wailing and flailing their arms helplessly."[15]

In June 1966, three months after Sam Adams had left Saigon, Allen finally departed Tan Son Nhut for home.

5

THE CROSSOVER POINT

Back after four months abroad, Sam Adams reported to headquarters in northern Virginia on May 2, 1966. For professional reasons Adams was happy to be back at work, and for personal reasons he was probably relieved also. The holiday in Greece had not been a success, and his marriage was in trouble. In Athens, Eleanor had suffered a miscarriage; the tragedy was complicated by the fact that Sam had not wanted the pregnancy, which was unplanned, in the first place. The marriage would last another sixteen years, but the seeds of the eventual breakup had been planted.

At Langley, the long-absent analyst spread the news that the rapid loss of men due to defections and desertions would eventually cripple the fighting abilities of the Viet Cong. Edward Hauck, Mollie Kreimer, and the rest of the Southeast Asia Branch were not so sure, but the men on the seventh floor at Langley were enthusiastic. "The findings created a big stir," Adams recounted. "Adm. William F. Raborn, Jr., then director of the CIA, called me in to brief him and his deputies about the Vietcong's AWOL problem. Right after the briefing, I was told that the agency's chief of research, R. Jack Smith, had called me '*the* outstanding analyst' in the research directorate."[1]

Adams was next called before the intelligence community's Board of National Estimates (BNE) to explain his study and its implications. This he did, and with all the commotion he had caused Adams must have welcomed Friday — it had been a busy first week back.

The following Wednesday word spread throughout Langley that Secretary of Defense Robert S. McNamara had asked the CIA to write an overall assessment of the war, to be titled "An Analysis of the Vietnamese Communists' Strengths, Capabilities, and Will to Persist." Raborn was said to be thrilled. McNamara had never sent the agency such a big assignment before, and the CIA director made it the agency's top priority. A chief question that had to be answered for "Will to Persist" was the state of Viet Cong morale, and Adams was summoned again to appear before the BNE. There he was told he was to become a member of a special "Viet Cong Morale Team" for immediate dispatch to Saigon.

The team landed at Tan Son Nhut on May 27. It consisted of Adams, veteran DDPer Emmanuelle Von der Muehll, and three agency psychiatrists. The medical men went off into the field to interview agency operatives while Adams remained in Saigon to hit the documents. At the National Interrogation Center he read all of the Viet Cong defector files, and at the RAND villa and at MACV's Combined Documents Exploitation Center (CDEC) he reviewed material that had gathered since his last visits to those places in early April. But everything he saw only underscored what he already knew: South Vietnam was awash in escaped Viet Cong recruits. Adams extrapolated out a variety of scenarios, but he could never get the number of the Viet Cong defectors and deserters below fifty thousand a year; as before, his upper estimate was one hundred thousand. Again, it seemed abundantly clear that the Viet Cong would not have the means, let alone the will, to persist much longer.

Adams's optimism, however, was tempered by the pessimism of others. Agency people whom he met on this trip informed him that his conclusions were ludicrous. The CIA people spoke of a resilient Viet Cong unbowed by disastrous defeats. The enemy, Adams was told, recuperated in the jungles, brought their units back up to full strength, and then chose where and when to fight once again. He was also informed that the Viet Cong readied their battlefields with pre-positioned caches of arms and food, and that they carefully planned their postbattle escape routes. DDPer Von der Muehll additionally impressed upon Adams the fact that the Viet Cong were defending their own villages and hamlets and, as if this wasn't enough, were urged on by the zeal of Viet Cong political cadres. Adams was beginning to get the message.[2]

The special Morale Team returned to the States on July 5 and wrote two very different summaries of the trip. The psychiatrists in their report did not believe that the enemy was suffering from low morale. "Their conclusion" — as Eleanor recalled her husband telling her of the psychiatrists' diagnosis — "was that the Viet Cong are as happy as clams." In contrast, Adams's own report restated, but this time with fresher evidence, his earlier contention that the Viet Cong faced manpower problems that were insurmountable.[3]

George A. Carver Jr. (the person delighted to have Langley's intelligence on Vietnam bounced back to him by Howard Beaubien in Saigon) was the new special assistant for Vietnamese affairs, and for Carver it was a plump assignment. The SAVA office was its own little empire separate from, and above, the other agency entities that were also working on Vietnam, and Carver answered only to the new director of the CIA himself, Raborn's replacement Richard Helms, former head of the DDP. Carver's first job as special assistant to Helms was to edit "Will to Persist," and he called the recently returned Morale Team into his office to take their reports. The psychiatrists dropped theirs off and were then dismissed while Adams was asked to remain. Carver glanced at the psychiatrists' report first and said, "Interviews, McNamara will never buy interviews." He tossed it into his out-box for disposal by his secretary. Next he looked at Adams's report. "Documents, statistics, this is more like it," Carver said and put it in his in-box. Adams left Carver's office, however, "with the uneasy feeling that he might have chosen the wrong" report.[4]

Adams returned to the nascent Indochina Division (Southeast Asia was no more; it had been disbanded in a bureaucratic reshuffling), and one can imagine him standing there, frown on his face, muttering to himself in the style characteristic of him when perplexed. He ruminated over a basic question: If the Viet Cong were defecting and deserting while also being killed, wounded, and captured at a rapid pace, how could they at the same time be keeping up such a fierce fight? "I had to ask myself," Adams would later explain of this anomaly, "who the hell are we fighting out there?" Lacking a ready answer, he saw the necessity to take on a new line of inquiry. No one in the agency was then working on the Viet Cong order of battle and, he reasoned, it was high time someone did. He informed his boss, Dean Moor, that he would be looking over the size and organization of Viet Cong forces for a while.[5]

Adams first reviewed the work that MACV had done on the problem and noted that the J-2 staff had estimated there were around 285,000 Viet Cong in South Vietnam as of mid-1966 — but Allen warned him that these MACV estimates were "illusory" and "a joke," because no accurate order of battle study had been completed since the JEC effort of 1962. Adams now realized that if he wanted valid statistics on the Viet Cong, he would have to compile them himself.[6]

In South Vietnam, MACV J-2 summarized the contents of captured Viet Cong documents and published them in the highly classified *CDEC Bulletin*. Anywhere from one to ten pages long, the *Bulletin* was put out by MACV on a frequent basis as bales of new documents were helicoptered in from the field and delivered to CDEC, where those papers that appeared to be of interest were translated. In Saigon, Adams had, of course, gone over to CDEC himself to have a look at the documents collection, but now in northern Virginia his research would have to rely in part on the *CDEC Bulletin*, of which hundreds of back issues were languishing in the CIA archives. Adams retrieved these from storage, copied them, stacked them high on his desk, and, starting with *CDEC Bulletin* 1 and ending with *CDEC Bulletin* 688, slowly went through the pile.

Adams exhausted the supply on hand and was doing other things (catching up with that day's *Washington Post*) on the morning of August 18 when the most recent number, *CDEC Bulletin* 689 — just three pages long — arrived from Vietnam via courier. The office secretary gave Adams the thin issue, and it took him but a moment to read. This event, as banal as it might seem, was in fact to be the epiphany of Adams's intelligence career — and one that would change his life forever.

Six eighty-nine was devoted to a brief Viet Cong document retrieved three months earlier in coastal Binh Dinh. A trooper from the U.S. First Air Cavalry Division had come across it on May 23, and upon translation at CDEC the document was revealed to be the "Recapitulated Report on the People's Warfare Movement from Binh Dinh Province." This account of current Viet Cong affairs in the province contained, among other things, a census of various Viet Cong guerrilla and militia categories operating in Binh Dinh:

Guerrillas

Hamlet	11,887
Village	3,194
Secret	719

Militia

Self-defense	34,441[7]

Adams glanced at these numbers. They seemed quite large. He immediately reached into his desk and pulled out the MACV order of battle statistics for Binh Dinh. "I saw the number," Adams would recall, "was 4,500 — one-twelfth or one-eleventh, whatever it is, of the number in the document. And there it had — I saw it clearly. We had been underestimating the number of enemy — probably not only in Binh Dinh, one of — one of 44 provinces, but perhaps through the whole country." Having recovered from his initial amazement, Adams became feverish with excitement. The finding went to the heart of the question of how the Viet Cong could sustain the substantial losses that they were experiencing while retaining their ability to fight. Evidently the Viet Cong could do this because their ranks were far greater in number than MACV was acknowledging. Eager to sound the alarm, "I started galloping around the CIA headquarters," Adams later said, "like Paul Revere."[8]

The eighteenth was a Thursday, and Adams wanted to formally release his intelligence find the following Monday. He worked at Langley over the weekend, reviewing all of MACV's Viet Cong order of battle estimates for irregulars in the provinces and comparing them with the *Bulletin*'s summaries of captured documents. With this fresh eye Adams soon found other provinces where MACV appeared to have missed large numbers of Viet Cong guerrillas and militia as well. Adams was now adamant that, due to systemic under-reporting, MACV's estimate of 285,000 Viet Cong should be at least doubled, if not tripled.

On Monday, Adams penned all of this onto a page or two of his yellow legal pad and handed it to the secretary to be typed up. "Recently acquired documentary evidence now being studied in detail," he stated, "suggests that our holding on the numerical strength of [Viet Cong] irregulars (now being carried at around 110,000) may require drastic upward revision." Adams's boss, Moor, assented to sending the resulting memo through the CIA chain of command. As an important communication, Adams knew, his work would be assured not only of wide distribution within the agency, but also of readership at the State Department, the Pentagon, and the White House. Adams fantasized about what the reaction might be. "I imagined all kinds of sudden and dramatic telephone calls" he would remember afterward. "'Mr. Adams, come brief the director.' 'The President's got to be told about this, and you'd better be able to defend your numbers.'" Adams wasn't actually sure what would happen, but he was sure it would be significant because he believed this was the biggest intelligence find of the war. "If the whole Vietcong Army suddenly doubled in size," he reasoned, "our whole statistical system would collapse. We'd be fighting a war twice as big as the one we thought we were fighting."[9]

The memo went out, and Tuesday became Thursday, and the expectant Adams never heard anything from anybody. On Friday the memo reappeared on his desk with an attached slip indicating that the CIA hierarchy had read it but had no comments. Despite his fantasy of the memo's having made it to the White House, the routing slip showed that it had never left the building: Adams was being ignored. Incensed, he attempted to draw attention to his assertions by initiating a memo war. From his office on the sixth floor he shot another missive up to the seventh. Now thoroughly warmed to the subject and spoiling for a fight, Adams fortified his follow-on memo with an explanation of the importance of the Viet Cong guerrilla-militia. These irregulars, Adams pointed out, played a valuable role in the overall Viet Cong strategy by, among other things, defending Viet Cong territory and serving as a recruitment pool for Viet Cong main and local forces. But again, the CIA front office expressed no interest. Adams learned that his second memo had been shunted aside and marked "Indefinite Hold."

Now doubly incensed, Adams went up to the seventh floor himself, but no one there was in the mood for combat. One senior staffer told him that he was being a "prima donna," another said that the issue of Viet Cong order of battle was Westmoreland's concern and not theirs, and yet another (this was R. Jack Smith, who had earlier spoken so highly of Adams) was too busy to see him. Adams's concern about the veracity of current order of battle numbers was mentioned deep within the final version of "Will to Persist" and twenty-five copies of his original message were distributed to other analysts in the intelligence community as an unofficial "working draft," but these actions did not represent the prominence that Adams felt his warnings deserved.[10]

It was already the first week of September; the summer of 1966 was over. For Adams the heady days of May when he had enjoyed hero status at Langley must have seemed like ages ago. It was time for a break. Mollie Kreimer, acting head of Indochina with Moor temporarily away, granted Adams a vacation.

Sam, Eleanor, and Clayton Adams stayed in an old farmhouse on Martha's Vineyard for two weeks. Sam's old school friend Peter Hiam and his wife, Helen, came over to the island for a short visit. The fall weather was beautiful and the setting — there were Canada geese gathered on the lawn — serene, but their host was not his usual lighthearted self. "We went to the beach," said Helen Hiam. "That's when I remember Sam walking up and down, pacing and talking about what was going on in Vietnam. He was just expressing a lot of emotion, a lot of tension, and a lot of feeling that there was a very significant problem that he had found. He talked about it for hours."[11]

He returned to Langley on Monday, September 26. Refreshed by ocean air, he attacked the order of battle problem with renewed vigor. It was obvious to Adams that MACV as the guardian of Viet Cong statistics had been neglectful in its responsibilities. MACV counts of Viet Cong main and local forces were apparently not being updated: In South Vietnam at any given time, according to the MACV, there were exactly 18,553 Viet Cong administrative services troops, exactly 39,175 political cadres of the VCI, and, of particular interest to Adams, exactly 103,573 Viet Cong guerrilla-militia irregulars.[11]

*

In October 1966, at the mammoth CIA complex in the woods just outside Washington, D.C., an obscure federal employee with the modest pay scale of GS-10 toiled away in Room 5G44. He was researching a major paper on the Viet Cong guerrilla-militia. Adams had assigned himself the project, and Moor had to have been inwardly wondering who was leading whom at the OCI Indochina Division.

At the same time and on the other side of the globe an extremely public figure with the government rank of cabinet secretary, Robert S. McNamara, made the pilgrimage to Saigon once again to assess the war's progress. Since his last visit there in 1965 the number of American troops in Vietnam had doubled, but for McNamara the sheen was off the American crusade in Southeast Asia. Where once he saw only what the U.S. military wanted him to see, now he saw only stalemate. The CIA paper prepared in August at his bequest, "The Vietnamese Communists' Will to Persist," would have done little to lighten his mood on the subject of Vietnam. McNamara may or may not have noted Adams's warnings about inaccurately low Viet Cong esti-mates, but he was struck by the paper's overall conclusion that U.S. efforts in South Vietnam were not likely to deter the North Vietnamese in their pursuits of a unified Communist country.[12]

As part of his briefings in Saigon, McNamara was informed that General William C. Westmoreland's war of attrition had not yet reached the "crossover point" where Viet Cong losses were to exceed Viet Cong replacements. Additionally, McNamara learned that there was no evidence the milestone would be achieved anytime soon. Westmoreland was trying to attrite the Viet Cong with all of the massive U.S. firepower at his dis-posal, but the enemy was apparently refusing to cooperate.

Based upon what he had been shown and told during his Saigon visit, McNamara wrote President Johnson that American bombing had not stopped Hanoi from supporting the revolution in South Vietnam; addi-tionally, the Saigon government and army remained weak and the Viet Cong forces remained strong. In the face of these difficulties, however, McNamara advised his president to continue his resolve in Vietnam. Then, when the time came for the inevitable negotiations that would end the war, the U.S. would be in a stronger position.[13]

McNamara's observations and recommendations to Johnson were of course state secrets, and Adams, like the rest of the world, had no knowl-edge of them at the time. Adams also did not know that his adopted issue,

the Viet Cong order of battle, was just then becoming of enormous importance politically, or that George Carver had slipped a copy of his embargoed
report on the Viet Cong order of battle numbers to the White House.

Concern within the Johnson administration over the Viet Cong numbers
can be traced back to the Honolulu conference of February 1966. The
event, which represented Johnson's first trip outside North America since
being elected two years earlier, had garnered massive media exposure.
Adams, in Vietnam at the time, would have followed in the press the
public pronouncements emanating from Honolulu with interest.[14]

Traveling with President Johnson to Honolulu were top civilian and
military officials from Washington. General Westmoreland flew in for the
meeting from Vietnam, as did the South Vietnamese prime minister,
Nguyen Cao Ky, and twenty-seven other Saigon leaders. In confidential
meetings Johnson impressed upon Nguyen and the South Vietnamese that
he expected them to enact political reforms leading toward a constitution
and free elections. In a secret side conference Johnson spoke with
Westmoreland alone. Here the president heard from the MACV commander that the Viet Cong, who had appeared on the verge of victory in
1964, were now on the defensive. Westmoreland stated, though, that he
still needed more U.S. troops in South Vietnam: He currently had 184,000
and wanted this raised to 429,000. The president, already feeling the political heat in Washington and across America for his war policies, reluctantly
agreed to this massive enlargement in forces, but he exacted a high price
from Westmoreland for doing so: The crossover point must be reached by
December 1966.

Six months later the deadline was nearing and the crossover point was
still a distance away. The Joint Chiefs of Staff (JCS) at the Pentagon had
earlier agreed with McNamara's disappointing assessment from Saigon
that victory in Vietnam was not at hand, although the JCS dismissed
McNamara's prescription that the U.S. effort be stabilized. The Pentagon
officials wanted to step up the war in Vietnam, and they asked Johnson
that this be done soon, before the U.S. ran out of options.

Driven by the differing perspectives of his military people and of his
civilian secretary of defense, Johnson gave Vietnam the greater part of his
attention. Later that same month, on October 23, he convened a meeting in

Manila of South Vietnamese leaders, U.S. regional allies, and General Westmoreland. Talking to Premier Nguyen Cao Ky and to Westmoreland in secret sessions, Johnson inquired about the military situation in South Vietnam. Nguyen stated that only Communist propaganda was preventing the South Vietnamese people from coming over to the Saigon side; if the people learned the real facts, the Viet Cong would collapse. Westmoreland, in turn, saw definite progress. "By every index," the MACV commander told Johnson, "things are improving." The general mentioned trends in casualties, defections, ARVN fighting abilities, intelligence operations, and the state of the countryside pacification program that were all going to the favor of the South Vietnamese and of the Americans.

The war, however, was far from over. In Manila, Westmoreland privately told his commander in chief that while there was "light at the end of the tunnel" the United States "had to be geared for the long pull." Separately, Johnson and his White House advisers held out hope of negotiations with Hanoi, but in the meantime they dictated that the race of attrition being run by the U.S. against the Viet Cong be won.

Later that fall the White House began to believe its own pronouncements of progress. "I suspect that we have reached," presidential assistant Robert Komer wrote McNamara, "the point where we are killing, defecting, or otherwise attriting more VC/NVA [Viet Cong/North Vietnamese Army] strength than the enemy can build up." Never mind that only a week earlier, on November 22, 1966, Komer was in receipt of George Carver's CIA note, based upon Sam Adams's September 8 working draft memo, stating that "a reappraisal of the strength of communist regular forces which is currently underway indicates that accepted (i.e., MACV) estimates of the strength of Viet Cong irregular forces may have drastically underestimated their growth, possibly by as much as 200,000 persons." If true, the critical "crossover point" had just been pushed back significantly and was perhaps no longer even within reach.[15]

*

At the OCI Indochina Division, Adams spent the remainder of 1966 preparing his paper on the guerrilla-militia. In the course of his research Adams would venture upstairs to SAVA for a visit. Don Blascak, a U.S. Special Forces army major at the time, was on assignment to SAVA. "Sort of serendipitously Sam Adams would come up every once in a while," Blascak remembered, "and ask me questions because I was advertised as a guy who'd had his feet on the ground in Vietnam." In fact, Blascak had been Colonel Winterbottom's gun carrier in Vietnam and had seen the corrupting of intelligence firsthand. "By the time I met Sam I was thirty-five years old," Blascak recalled, "and very honestly I did not have any notion that Sam was my peer. I thought he was about twenty-two because he was so boyish and young looking."

Major Blascak got to know Adams well. When the phone rang at SAVA for Blascak it would often be Adams downstairs at the OCI nonchalantly asking yet another question. "Say, Don . . . ," Adams would begin in his trademark greeting style. Explained Blascak, "Sam was casual in a sense but after fifteen minutes he was not at all casual. He would start off, 'Oh by the way, what's a caltrop?' and before you knew it you were drawn in in terms of Malay gates, and mining, and piano keying, and ambushing. He would lead you in. And what Sam was doing was educating himself in terms of what this Viet Cong thing was all about. And we talked about the main force and district guerrillas, and we talked about ten-year-old kids with AK-47s, the little old ladies with hand grenades. And that's where he began to get a feel for the depth and scope of the guerrilla influence all the way down to the village and hamlet level." Blascak noted that "Sam was hugely inquisitive; he didn't want to deal on the surface of this thing."

*

Running sixty pages long and containing more than a hundred footnotes, Adams completed his paper on the Viet Cong guerrilla-militia in December, and he now knew a great deal about the different, so-called regular and irregular, elements of the enemy order of battle. The "regular" elements were the NVA and the Viet Cong main and local forces, and as such they were not the primary focus of Adams's research, although these forces played a key role in the war.

The *NVA* were personnel drawn from the North Vietnamese Army who had been, in an arduous and dangerous trek, infiltrated down the Truong Son Strategic Supply Route (nicknamed the Ho Chi Minh Trail by the Americans). Once in South Vietnam, NVA troops fought for the Communist cause. NVA troop concentrations in South Vietnam could range from company size up to division strength, although they conducted a stealthy war largely on foot.

While the NVA originated up north, the *Viet Cong main and local forces* represented the armed wing of the National Liberation Front in the south and were indigenous South Vietnamese fighting on their own turf. Like the NVA (which often contributed soldiers and leadership to main and local force units), they had an organization, command, and staff structure similar to that of a conventional military. Main and local forces differed from each other in that main forces were more powerful and operated over a larger area, while local forces stuck closer to their district or provincial home areas.

In contrast with the NVA troops and the Viet Cong main and local forces, Adams was most interested in the under-researched elements of the enemy order of battle, the guerrilla forces and the self-defense (SD) and secret self-defense (SSD) "militia" forces. In the words of Ho Chi Minh (Radio Hanoi, 1946):

> The self-defense and militia and guerrilla forces are the forces of all our people. They are an invincible force, the iron wall of the father- land. Any enemy, no matter how cruel and ruthless he may be, who lays a hand on this force or iron wall will be smashed to bits.

Guerrilla forces were Viet Cong irregulars organized at the village and hamlet level. A South Vietnamese village consisted of half a dozen or so hamlets, and village guerrillas (*du kich xa*) were organized into companies of about fifty to one hundred people each. Village guerrillas were fairly well armed with bolt-action rifles and, occasionally, automatic weapons. Village guerrillas acted as full-time — although of course nonuniformed — soldiers. Hamlet guerrillas (*du kich ap*), in contrast, were usually part-timers, and they seldom ventured beyond their immediate locale. Armed with rifles and grenades, hamlet guerrillas were formed into squads and platoons. When situated in Saigon government-controlled territory, such as ostensibly "pacified" zones, the Viet Cong referred to guerrillas, in an oxymoron, as secret guerrillas (*du kich mat*). Secret guerrillas, if armed at all, carried only concealable weapons, like pistols or grenades. Secret guerrillas operated individually, or in cells of a few people each, and their mission was to create mischief — such as assassinating the village chief — until the time was ripe for full Viet Cong takeover.

Self-defense and *secret self-defense forces* made up the base element of the Viet Cong military structure, and the essential paramilitary link between the regular Liberation Armed Forces and the popular masses. These militia forces were peopled with men and women, and some children, with only a week or so of military training. Self-defense forces operated in zones controlled by the Viet Cong while secret self-defense forces operated in contested areas. The task of the SD (*tue ve*) and SSD (*tu ve mat*) was to defend the village, hamlet, or neighborhood if attacked, and to support guerrilla elements in offensive actions, such as establishing "kill-Americans belts" that encircled U.S. bases. The SD/SSD committed acts of sabotage and terrorism, shot at American airplanes and helicopters, operated internal security tasks, and participated in political indoctrination activities. Self-defense and secret self-defense units were sometimes used as reserve forces during large battles and represented, according to the Vietnamese Communists, "an inexhaustible source of replacements for combatants and cadres" for the main and local units. Self-defense and secret self-defense members also stood guard, dug tunnels, constructed and laid mines and booby traps, built fortifications, became members of supply transport and medical evacuation teams, and performed other unglamorous, yet essential, functions in support of the revolution. In areas where the Viet Cong was not dominant, secret self-defense members were forced to operate clandestinely in small cells. In this capacity the SSD acted as guides for NVA and Viet Cong main, local, and guerrilla forces, as couriers, and as the eyes and ears of the various Viet Cong intelligence services.

In his paper on the guerrillas and the SD/SSD militia, Adams was intent on highlighting the fact that these forces were the broad foundation of the revolutionary armed struggle, a struggle that, in the words and emphasis of North Vietnamese General Vo Nguyen Giap, victor at Dien Bien Phu, "Concretely embodied the policy of arming the whole people." The key role that the SD/SSD played in the armed struggle was highlighted when Giap said, "Indeed a strong rear is always the decisive factor for victory in a revolutionary war."

The guerrillas and the SD had historically represented the embryo of what would become the People's Army of Vietnam. Workers and peasants of the "Red self-defense" had protected the Nghe An Soviets of 1930–1931, and Viet Minh guerrillas composed the resistance army against the Japanese and the French during World War II. By 1945 Giap and the Indochinese Communist Party had realized the need for an infantry force, and the first regular units of Viet Minh were formed from consolidating guerrilla bands. However, throughout the 1946–1954 period local guerrillas and the SD, together referred to by the Viet Minh as the "popular troops," continued to be an integral part of the strategy to defeat the French. The Communists wished to make lasting French control of Vietnamese territory all but impossible. "Our strategic line," as Giap underscored, "was to extend guerrilla warfare everywhere." With the constant presence of the Viet Minh popular troops harassing them, the French by 1950 became bogged down, as would the Americans a generation later, by basic security concerns in the villages and hamlets of Vietnam. Giap explained the tactics and strategy used. "With rudimentary weapons such as swords, knives, sticks, arrows, bows, home-made rifles and bullets, mines, spike-strewn trenches, and even stones and bricks," he said, "self-defense militia and guerrilla forces succeeded in devising versatile, skillful fighting methods, and thus caused the enemy to go without sleep, lose his appetite, and be surrounded by an inescapable steel net."

Viet Cong "combat villages" represented the essence of the kind of unconventional warfare that the Americans were having such difficulty fighting. These fortified and armed communities were meant to foil the pacification program being carried out by the "U.S. puppet" government in Saigon. The guerrillas and SD of combat villages planted thorny bushes, set booby traps, and dug spike pits to make entry difficult. They had an elaborate system to warn of approaching enemy columns, and the defenders arranged for camouflaged firing sites to cover all approaches to the community. An underground tunnel network, sometimes running for miles, gave the defenders a place for concealment, a storage area for food and military supplies, a lookout station, a gun position, and, to the annoyance of the American military, a safe path of withdrawal.

Of the war gear used by the guerrillas and the SD/SSD, it was the booby traps and mines that most directly and devastatingly affected the U.S. "grunts" on the ground in South Vietnam. By the mid-1960s U.S. casualty rates from these two kinds of weapons were several times higher than what the Americans had experienced in either World War II or Korea. For example, in one major sweep, the Iron Triangle operation of October 1965, about 95 percent of American wounds and deaths were the result of mines and booby traps. It was an insidious kind of warfare that not only maimed and killed physically but also scarred psychically and — as reflected in written and filmed accounts of the war — became synonymous with the darkest side of combat in Vietnam.

The U.S. Army cataloged a list of malicious devices and tactics used by the Viet Cong. Grenades, which were light, easy to carry and hide, and readily available in South Vietnam, figured prominently in schemes to blow off legs and pierce bodies. Grenades were concealed in trees, on fences, and along trails with trip wires attached to them for detonation. Artillery and mortar shells were also rigged for explosion when the U.S. military or ARVN forces were nearby. Spiked foot and man traps were made to injure or kill. One version, for example, the "caltrop," was a metal spike based in a wooden board or concrete block. The caltrop was placed in rice paddies or underwater, and often the spike was barbed so that it could not be removed after it went through the boot and foot. To ensure additional suffering, spikes could also be covered with excrement to cause infection. Equally crude but effective devices were "Malay gates" strung along trails and paths. These released poisoned arrows, bamboo whips, and, in the words of the U.S. Army, "other swinging, barbed, or club type objects." Explosive pens and cigarette lighters were also put in obvious hiding places for the Americans to find.

When not engaged in mining and booby-trapping, Viet Cong elements at the village and hamlet level — guerrillas and self-defense — were destroying enemy lines of communications, burning American supplies of gasoline, and making motor transportation in the countryside difficult by "piano keying" — digging interlaced ditches on either side of a road to block wheeled traffic.

The last two elements of the enemy order of battle were the Viet Cong Infrastructure — also sometimes referred to as the "political cadre" or "political workers" — and the administrative services troops. In military parlance, these forces, like the guerrillas and SD/SSD, were considered "irregulars."

The *Viet Cong Infrastructure* encompassed the large and complex "hidden" Communist government that overtly or covertly controlled large swaths of the South Vietnamese countryside and significant portions of the population. The VCI encompassed functions usually associated with a government at war, such as recruitment and propaganda, along with those associated with a government during peacetime, such as dispensing justice, levying taxes, and running the hospital and prison systems. VCI "cadres" (a term the Viet Cong used to denote any type of official or specialist) could be well armed and were frequently the cause of great terror among the civilian populace.

Administrative services troops were those engaged in ordnance, courier, quartermaster, and myriad other rear command duties. The requirements of modern warfare in South Vietnam for both sides necessitated that for every fighting soldier there be at least several troops in the combat support role. Assisting the administrative services, willingly or not, was the entire population of Vietnamese Communist-controlled areas, which could at any time be called upon to house, feed, and otherwise help the amorphous Liberation Armed Forces.[16]

*

In writing his guerrilla-militia paper Adams had become convinced that U.S. war planners were discounting the significance of the Viet Cong irregulars in what was, as Adams repeatedly had to remind others, an unconventional war. "Can you believe it?" he said to a fellow analyst. "Here we are in the middle of a guerrilla war, and we haven't even bothered to count the number of guerrillas."[17]

In attempting to collect more accurate information, Adams was getting some cooperation from U.S. military analysts in Saigon working on the MACV order of battle figures. In particular, he was receiving help from the head of the MACV J-2 order of battle section himself, U.S. Army Colonel Gains B. Hawkins. In response to Adams's request, Hawkins had sent out a query to the U.S. military intelligence units in each of the forty-four provinces of South Vietnam. The response rate was spotty, but for one of the provinces, Quang Tin, the reported number of guerrilla-militia was

17,027. This was ten times the figure listed in the official MACV order of battle guide for the province. Adams loved dramatic intelligence finds like these, and they always spurred him on to more action.[18]

Adams became a memo-machine, churning out warnings on the Viet Cong numbers, MACV's erroneous statistics, and what he believed was the potential for mischief. On November 7 he noted the Quang Tin discrepancy and stated, "It would not be surprising, therefore, to see MACV revise its criteria for defining irregulars, in order to prevent a mass influx of new bodies. . . . MACV could, for example, require 'irregulars' to possess firearms; this would greatly cut down on their numbers . . . this could overlook most of the self-defense forces, many of whom are unarmed or armed only with grenades, [but] such devices account for 20% of all U.S. casualties."[19]

Adams was having a field day poking holes in the MACV order of battle. On December 2 he wrote that captured documents and POW reports indicated "that the so-called 'main force support personnel' listed in MACV's order of battle on the Viet Cong are carried at a strength far below their actual numbers . . . [they] could be as high as 100,000." On December 13 his concern that the official order of battle carried "far too few" Viet Cong administrative services troops than the evidence would support was cabled to MACV in Saigon, and MACV was also alerted by Adams that the CIA would "scrutinize the number" of armed cadre in the VCI. On December 19 Adams produced a memo concluding that while the MACV order of battle was 280,000, "A series of recent unpublished studies indicates, however, that the number of Viet Cong is closer to 600,000 and perhaps more."[20]

None of these memos, Adams said, "provoked the least response" in his superiors. The seventh floor was continuing to ignore him. "By this time," he continued, "I was so angry and discouraged with the research directorate that I began looking for another job within the CIA, preferably in a section that had some use for real numbers." For Adams, SAVA was the place to be. Allen was now there, Adams had gotten to know and like Blascak who was there also, and the special assistant for Vietnamese affairs himself, George Carver, appeared ready to champion Adams's work (and, unknown to Adams, had of course already done so). Adams's transfer request was made, and Carver agreed to take him on.[21]

Dean Moor bid his independent-minded analyst good-bye. "I know Sam was a thorn in Moor's side because he could not deter him," explained Don

Blascak, "and was kind of glad to see George take him." The OCI and Adams, it had turned out, were not a perfect match. "You weren't about to find anyone in OCI," said Blascak, "who would delve through timeless, colorless, poor translations of captured documents — my God, attention to detail. And George took him gladly because by that time Sam had amassed a wealth of knowledge."

6

TOLD TO LIE

At Camp Smith overlooking Pearl Harbor the newest MACV J-2, General Joseph A. McChristian, took his place at the center of the curved conference table. A West Point graduate, McChristian had piercing blue eyes, a beribboned uniform, and a reputation for professionalism. General Grover C. Brown, head of intelligence for CINCPAC, was also seated at the table, along with other military men such as Colonel Gains B. Hawkins of MACV and Major J. Barrie Williams of the Defense Intelligence Agency. General Earle Wheeler, chairman of the Joint Chiefs of Staff, was not in attendance, but it was he who had ordered the summit. Wheeler had recently been made aware of controversy surrounding the Viet Cong order of battle statistics, and he wanted the matter resolved forthwith.[1]

It was eight fifty-five on the morning of February 6, 1967, and the first session of the Honolulu conference convened. The conferees were to standardize and agree upon definitions, methodology, and reporting procedures relating to fifteen questions concerning the enemy's military strength — but that was it. McChristian was not going to allow the proceedings to challenge certain basic assumptions.

"Gentlemen," McChristian said, rising to his feet, "I heard some loose remarks earlier in the day that we are here assembled to arrive at a new number for the order of battle. I would like to use this opportunity to inform anyone who harbors this notion to drop it, and to drop it *at once*. The Vietcong order of battle is MACV's business, which is to say, *my* business. *Don't tread on me*."[2]

Five or six seats away from McChristian, Sam Adams of the CIA delegation sank down in his chair. Not only did Adams indeed harbor such a notion, but over the past month he had done his best to promote it. After

New Year's, when he became part of SAVA, he had taken advantage of his new position to institute a series of self-initiatives. Adams ordered the DDI to further research the Viet Cong order of battle problem, he pushed to have his guerrilla-SD/SSD paper published within the intelligence community, and he requested a hearing in front of the Office of National Estimates (ONE). As a result of listening to Adams's case, ONE agreed that the official numbers on the Viet Cong were too low, and it informed CIA Director Richard Helms in memoranda that enemy "irregular strength was about 200,000." On behalf of his newest boss, George A. Carver, Adams had also written various research papers for the staffs of the White House and the secretary of defense. These events, each very satisfying to Adams, were capped off with Carver's instructions at the beginning of February to go to Wheeler's summit in Honolulu. Unbeknownst to Adams, Carver was under intense pressure by the White House to get the order of battle discrepancies resolved, and resolved quickly.[3]

In concluding his opening remarks, General McChristian noted that "certain individuals in certain organizations" were raising questions about the categories of the Viet Cong order of battle and that Colonel Hawkins, head of the MACV J-2 order of battle section, had made a preliminary investigation into the enemy numbers. Adams slunk even lower in his chair and braced for the worst. Hawkins, a short, bald, cigar-chomping Mississippian with a crusty personality, took the floor. The colonel's remarks regarding Viet Cong strength were succinct. "You know," the colonel drawled, "there's a lot more of these little bastards out there than we thought there were." McChristian told the gathering that this meant drastic upward revisions would be needed to the various Viet Cong order of battle categories. Adams, now sitting erect, was elated.[4]

Inexplicably, Dean Moor had found his way to Honolulu as the senior CIA representative to the conference, but Adams paid his former boss little mind during the meetings and instead spent much of the five-day affair talking with Gains B. Hawkins. Adams seems to have taken an instant liking to the colonel. The first time Adams met Hawkins was in March 1966 in Vietnam, outside Hué, but a nearby Special Forces camp had just been hit by the Viet Cong and the colonel was too busy to chat. Now out of the battle zone Hawkins was free to spend time with Adams and to go over different captured documents of interest. Adams was relieved to find that he and Hawkins saw eye to eye on the order of battle issue, and that Hawkins believed current estimates for Viet Cong guerrilla-militia, officially still at 103,573, should actually be 198,000: The colonel from Mississippi was evidently a straight shooter.

From Adams's perspective the Honolulu conference was entirely a success. The meeting resulted in agreement among the military and civilian intelligence representatives present. From now on, it was understood, all studies on Viet Cong order of battle would share the same procedures, criteria, methodology, and terminology. The consensus at Honolulu was that, with these newer and more appropriate technical standards in place, the accuracy of the order of battle would improve significantly, and most believed that because of this the official estimates of Viet Cong strength were going to go up, and go up dramatically. Adams left Hawaii for home, looking forward to future collaborations with Hawkins and with MACV. "I figured," he wrote, "'the fight's over. They're reading the same documents that I am, and everybody's beginning to use real numbers.'"[5]

*

Gains B. Hawkins hailed from Flora, Mississippi, where he grew up, literally barefoot, the ninth of eleven siblings. After high school Hawkins attended tiny Delta State Teachers College until the army drafted him in his junior year and made him an intelligence officer. He subsequently served in Europe with George Patton's Third Army where, in a notable precursor to his later military career, he was briefly under the command of then-Colonel Joseph McChristian. Upon discharge, Hawkins maintained his army reserve status and returned to Delta State to complete his degree. Marriage, a master's degree in English literature, a year teaching high school, and a first child followed. Then, with the outbreak of hostilities in Korea, Hawkins was called back to active duty. Comparing his army pay stub with what he earned as a Mississippi schoolteacher, Hawkins realized that he could actually make a living in uniform, and he decided to make the army his career.

It was in the early fall of 1965 that now-Colonel Hawkins got a yearning for Vietnam. After previous postings in Japan and Hawaii he found himself deskbound and bored by a Stateside billet. General McChristian had just been named the new MACV J-2, and Hawkins wrote him asking for a job. McChristian, who had an ambitious intelligence agenda for MACV, was delighted that Hawkins wanted to join his team, and in fact the general had already envisioned the perfect job title for Hawkins: "Mister Order of Battle."

When he arrived in Saigon, Hawkins realized that heading the OB section was going to be a challenging affair, both politically and militarily. He explained, "There were almost as many vociferous estimates of the enemy force in Vietnam as there were interested parties. But Gen. McChristian wasn't interested in journalists' guesses or field commanders' 'gut feelings.' He demanded a plodding, painstaking analysis of the bits and pieces. This was to be my responsibility."[6]

Throughout the following year, 1966, U.S. forces were overrunning the enemy's different headquarters areas and in the process coming across extensive collections of enemy records. (For example, during "Operation Attleboro," September 14 to November 24, 1966, a cache of fifty-five-gallon drums was found that contained hundreds of thousands of pages of Vietnamese Communist documents.) Once bagged and tagged, the captured papers were sent to the Combined Documents Exploitation Center for processing, although frequently by the time they were captured many of the documents were already dated. This was because, Hawkins explained, "The enemy was constantly enlarging and realigning his force structure in South Vietnam during 1966 and on throughout 1967. Some of the enemy's NVA units were in the country weeks or even months before the translated documents came to the desks of the analysts. Some of the minor Viet Cong units were dissolved long before we learned about it. It was a desperate game of catch up." Hawkins, though, worked "ungodly hours" and began to gain on the enemy.[7]

Success came slowly. First, NVA units at the battalion and regimental level were identified. Next, and after months of trial and error, the five NVA divisional headquarters became known. The big break, though, came with the help of the National Security Agency back at Fort Meade, Maryland. Documents taken off a dead NVA officer were decoded, and the first NVA "B-Front" was identified. With this find Hawkins and his men could decipher the entire NVA command structure, from supreme headquarters up north in Hanoi to the smallest combat formation down south in the Mekong Delta.[8]

By the early spring of 1967 Hawkins and his team were ready to show off. A briefing was scheduled for McChristian, and a graphic representation of the enemy's force structure was created. There were solid lines for confirmed enemy units, dotted lines for suspected units, and dashed lines for units still in the making. A young army captain conducted the briefing and Hawkins, leaning up against the far wall, enjoyed the show. The seemingly confused nature of the enemy's armed organization had, thanks to the hard work of his men, given way to clarity. "I thought to myself," Hawkins said, "'Goddam, they've got that sonofabitch literally nailed to the wall.'"

Such progress pleased McChristian, although as subordinate to General William C. Westmoreland, he was devoting 95 percent of MACV's intelligence capacities to the "big unit war" that Westmoreland was intent on waging. Enemy command structures and organizational alignments were all very well, but McChristian knew that his boss really wanted J-2 to physically locate enemy base areas out in the countryside so that U.S. and allied troops could eviscerate them. This type of location work, which was complex and challenging, entailed taking photographs from the air and using computer programs to identify possible NVA troop and Viet Cong main force enclaves hidden in the mountains and jungles of South Vietnam. But as a result of this emphasis on the big units, the MACV J-2 order of battle section, as Hawkins stated, knew relatively little about the "hordes of people in variously designated guerrilla-type groups."

While busy with the big units, McChristian did not ignore the Viet Cong irregulars entirely and ordered that a methodical accounting of these forces be done at the village and hamlet situation. A localized intelligence collection program was therefore instituted by MACV. The young American military officers did their work out in the countryside and, in a slow and tedious process that took the political sensitivities of the South Vietnamese military and national police into consideration, their intelligence was compared with what the local DDPers knew. The combined data eventually reached Hawkins in Saigon. Newly informed by intelligence gathered by Americans situated in South Vietnamese rural communities, Hawkins was able to compile updated Viet Cong strength figures — and the numbers were much higher than the old MACV estimates.[9]

Under Hawkins the MACV OB section also made headway on statistics for the Viet Cong Infrastructure. A young officer in the section, Lieutenant Kelly Robinson, amassed data on the VCI cadres and saw that the Viet Cong maintained fairly consistent personnel levels from village to village, and hamlet to hamlet. Robinson determined how many Viet Cong functionaries were typically in the various branches of the infrastructure (recruiting, propaganda, tax collection, and so forth) for an average village and hamlet, and calculated accordingly. "And here again," Hawkins explained, "as in the case of the irregulars, we had confirmed our beliefs that there were a whole lot more of them than our old estimate showed."

But there were yet other, even lesser-known, parts of the huge Viet Cong apparatus, an apparatus that Hawkins had come to believe consisted of between four and five million people in South Vietnam alone, not counting supporting elements in North Vietnam, Laos, and Cambodia. These components included, for example, the Viet Cong–sponsored civilian groups that gave village and hamlet dwellers a self-interest in the revolution. A "myriad skein of organizations," Hawkins said, they were "called variously the farmers groups, the fishermens groups, the midwives groups and every sort of group by profession or occupation that could be dreamed of."

In addition to these organizations there were the Viet Cong administrative services, the ones who, as Hawkins explained, did the "fetching and toting" for the Viet Cong armed forces. And just how many Viet Cong, Hawkins wondered, were there in the administrative services? As the evidence piled up he realized to his disgust that administrative services troops could well number into the hundreds of thousands — a nightmarish proposition. "There seemed to be no end to them," he said. "They came on and on like a steady stream of tiny, brown piss ants flowing unceasingly, inexorably toward a broken piece of watermelon lying on the ground under the shade of a sweet gum tree in Mississippi."[10]

*

After the Honolulu conference Sam Adams returned to Langley and to bad news: It turned out that the only thing resolved in Hawaii was that

MACV was to be the sole custodian of the order of battle numbers. A separate agreement had apparently been reached on the matter between Dean Moor and General McChristian behind everyone else's backs. On the CIA's part this was nothing less than, as George Allen termed it to Adams, a "sellout." And indeed, the February Viet Cong order of battle statistics came in shortly thereafter. The numbers were basically the same as before. MACV subterfuge continued unabated.[11]

With the battle renewed Adams was in fine spirits, and regarding the Viet Cong he was learning more every day. "Sam cruised the halls at flank speed," his former colleague at the Congo and Southern Africa Branch Robert Sinclair remembered, "always in the same rumpled gray suit and red tie, always with an untidy sheaf of paper under his arm, always twirling the chain of his badge. He would collar me, rather like a genial version of the ancient mariner, and tell me about his latest discoveries. Nobody, it seems, had systematically exploited the mass of Vietnamese Communist documents we captured during our military operations."[12]

Adams was, like Hawkins, benefiting from the intelligence bonanza created by American military advances in South Vietnam, and if copies of the captured documents were not available at Langley, Adams would go over to the Pentagon and bring back a pile. He also got himself on the DIA distribution list so that he was privy to the same documents that MACV was reading in Saigon. And in all this material Adams was finding things the military overlooked. "As an example," Don Blascak recalled, "MACV would have six documents that talked about Phu Quak Island as a point where there's infiltration from the north, and Sam would come up with fifteen or twenty documents saying the same thing, including six or seven that MACV never had."

For the winter of 1967 Adams seems to have ceased formal efforts to contest the official order of battle; there are no loaded-and-armed Adams memos on the subject from this period. Indeed, Adams had a patron in his boss, George Carver, and Carver did nothing to dissuade Adams from his work. In a sign of approval, he even promoted Adams a grade in salary to GS-11. Operating, as he had in Saigon, only loosely under the control of George Allen, Adams continued to rake through heaps of captured enemy documents. His attentions, as always, were drawn to Viet Cong elements that posed a danger to U.S. efforts in Vietnam but were being ignored by MACV.

The "assault youth" was one such element. From what Adams could determine, assault youth were an outgrowth of the local Viet Cong SD/SSD forces that comprised fresh-faced enthusiasts for the Communist cause and for Vietnamese independence. Due to their high degree of political indoctrination, personal fanaticism, and acts of bravery on the battlefield, assault youth were permitted to wear special uniforms with distinctive scarves and badges as a sign of their honored place in the revolution. But more importantly from the standpoint of U.S. intelligence, these Viet Cong youngsters were well organized, were heavily armed, and, Adams believed, could number into the tens of thousands. He informed MACV of this but was told that the assault youth would remain off the official order of battle pending the availability of "sufficient data."[13]

And there were other Viet Cong elements that bore watching and also had not made it onto the official order of battle. Among them were Viet Cong sappers, special action troops, combat engineers, scouts, and something called the "armed public security forces." Adams became particularly concerned about the latter and what appeared to be their extensive and sophisticated espionage system. He worked on George Carver for permission to make a research trip to Vietnam to study the problem; Carver obliged. By early April 1967 Adams was again winging his way to Saigon.

Adams had done his homework on the armed public security forces before traveling to Vietnam, having compiled a fat file on them back at Langley, and information gleaned on this trip would serve him well over the next two or so years as he periodically returned to the subject. Adams again toured the provinces as part of his investigation and talked to Viet Cong defectors. He learned that the forces were controlled by the Bo Cong An (Vietnamese Communist Ministry of Public Security). "Closely modeled on the Soviet KGB," Adams explained, "the Bo Cong An has its seat in Hanoi, in the same building, ironically, as the old headquarters of the French colonial Surete. The ministry runs police operations on both sides of the 17th Parallel, and is in direct radio contact with each of the 38 VC provinces in South Vietnam. By this means, it keeps close tabs on the Viet Cong's complex police bureaucracy, which employs not only prison officials but a variety of functionaries such as typists, file clerks, researchers, investigators, radiomen, cryptographers, agent-handlers, administrators, armed policemen and large numbers of operatives who compile blacklists . . . [of] 'reactionary' politicians, South Vietnamese government officials, and others targeted for execution."[14]

In Saigon the Bo Cong An was not the only thing on Adams's mind, of course, because he was desperate to discover what was going on in the MACV OB section. To his disappointment, however, his friend Hawkins was away — and in the colonel's absence at MACV, Adams was most definitely persona non grata.

Adams and the most recent MACV order of battle estimate arrived back at Langley at about the same time. The numbers for May stood at 292,000. It had been nine months since Adams had discovered the crack in MACV's facade with *Bulletin* 689, and nothing had changed.

*

With America in early 1967 irrevocably committed to the war in Southeast Asia, and with the enormous financial costs of the conflict now threatening a healthy U.S. economy at home, for Lyndon B. Johnson and his administration there was now a race against time to demonstrate headway in South Vietnam. The situation there demanded changes, and to liberate General William C. Westmoreland from all but combat-related responsibilities a special U.S. ambassadorial position was created to head "the other war": the American-backed South Vietnamese village and hamlet pacification program. This "four-star civilian" job was given to Robert Komer, National Security Council adviser, former CIA operative, and unabashed Vietnam War booster whose hard-charging style had earned him the nickname "Blowtorch Bob." Komer would run the awkwardly titled Civil Operations and Revolutionary Development Support (CORDS) program as if it were his own private fiefdom.

Komer's enthusiasm for the war and his control of CORDS, however, did not translate into actual progress. In fact, things were worsening in South Vietnam after Komer got there, and the political implications of this at home in the U.S. were obvious to all. In the Pentagon, for example, the chairman of the Joint Chiefs of Staff, General Earle Wheeler, reacted with dismay when in March he received a report from Westmoreland that said the NVA and Viet Cong had dramatically increased attacks using their "big units." Wheeler cabled Westmoreland with instructions to "do whatever is necessary to insure these figures are not . . . released to news media or otherwise exposed to public knowledge," explaining that "if these figures should reach the public domain, they would, literally, blow the lid off Washington."[15]

Later that month, on March 20, yet another high-level U.S. conference to review the war was held. Westmoreland and Wheeler, along with Admiral Ulysses S. Grant Sharp of CINCPAC, met in Guam with President Johnson and the current leaders of South Vietnam, Nguyen Thieu and Nguyen Cao Ky. Thieu and Ky had a new South Vietnamese constitution literally in hand, and they were pleased to announce that free elections would soon take place in their country. Behind closed doors, Westmoreland adroitly handled Johnson's concerns about enemy strength.

"Are they," Johnson asked regarding the Communist Vietnamese, "bringing in as many as they're losing?"

"Up until now, no sir," Westmoreland answered. "Their gains have exceeded their losses. However, if the present trend continues I think we might arrive at the cross-over point. Perhaps this month, or next month. And by the cross-over point I mean where their losses are greater than their gains."

At the conference also was National Security Council member Walt Rostow, who like Robert Komer was a hawk on the war issue and also an eternal optimist. Rostow was present when Westmoreland reviewed for Johnson the current Viet Cong order of battle numbers (287,000) as well as the enemy infiltration rates from North Vietnam into South Vietnam. Infiltration by the NVA, Westmoreland stated, was thought to be about seven thousand per month. This number of new fighters slipping over the border to tackle U.S. and South Vietnamese forces might have seemed to some to be alarming (especially since the number did not include Viet Cong conscription and recruitment of indigenous South Vietnamese), but Rostow argued that at this point enemy manpower just had to be declining. Rostow noted to Johnson (as Adams had similarly noted a year prior to his superiors at Langley) that the Viet Cong were defecting to the Saigon side in large numbers. "I must confess," Rostow wrote, "that I am greatly impressed by the fact that the Chieu Hoi figures have remained over 1,000 per week for 5 weeks. If that can be sustained for, say 6 months, I find it hard to believe that the VC infrastructure can hold up."[16]

Out of the Guam meeting, then, came among other things the impression that the war of attrition had already turned to the favor of the U.S., and that the Viet Cong were half a year away from collapse. This aggressive hopefulness was, however, greatly tempered — if not ruined — by Westmoreland's secret request afterward for eighty to two hundred thousand more American troops. In April, Johnson summoned Westmoreland home to talk it over.

At the White House, Westmoreland informed the president, "The VC/NVA 287,000 order of battle is leveling off" and that "as of March, we reached the 'cross-over point' — we began attriting more men than Hanoi can recruit or infiltrate this month." But the general was anxious to hasten the war of attrition. "With the [U.S.] troops now in country," as Westmoreland explained it to Johnson, "we are not going to lose, but progress will be slowed down. This is not an encouraging outlook, but it is a realistic one." The alternative to gradual victory — an alternative Westmoreland greatly preferred — was to send in many more American soldiers. The president was dismayed. "Where does it all end?" Johnson asked. "When we add divisions, can't the enemy add divisions? If so, where does it all end?" It would end, Westmoreland answered, in five years with the present American troop strength in Vietnam at 470,000, in three years if that troop strength was increased to 565,000, and in only two years if it was additionally raised to 665,000.[17]

Johnson, though, was in no rush to add troops; politically he could live with the slow but steady progress that Westmoreland had ensured him was taking place. Johnson did not accede to any troop increases, and Westmoreland returned to Saigon empty-handed. On May 19 the MACV commander again secretly asked Johnson for more troops, two hundred thousand in all, with half that number immediately. Westmoreland was again denied.[18]

*

Adding to Westmoreland's sense of urgency that May was intelligence coming from his own J-2, General Joseph McChristian, that the enemy order of battle was not 297,000 as everyone had been led to believe, but instead almost double that: 500,000.

Sometime between May 10 and May 15 McChristian met with Westmoreland privately to discuss a cable meant for Washington that would detail these new, greatly increased estimates. "I took that cable in to General Westmoreland," McChristian said, "and I stood in front of his desk and handed it to him. I gave him a little bit of background on what it was." McChristian explained to his commander that the cable summarized a new intelligence study just completed by his staff showing NVA and Viet Cong strength to be half a million. "He read it," McChristian would recall later about the draft cable. "He looked at me and he said, 'If I send that cable to Washington, it will create a political bombshell.'

"'General, I don't see why it should. Send me back [to Washington] and I'll explain to anyone who wants to know what we've been doing to collect this information.'

"'No, leave it with me,'" Westmoreland, according to McChristian, replied.

The cable was never sent, and McChristian was angry. "This was the first time," he explained, "that General Westmoreland had ever held up one of my intelligence reports."[19]

Then on May 28 Westmoreland was given another jolt when briefed by Colonel Gains B. Hawkins and Lieutenant Kelly Robinson. The topic of the briefing was the results of two large-scale studies, code-named RITZ and CORRAL, which had just been completed. RITZ covered the Viet Cong SD/SSD, while CORRAL dealt with the VCI. According to these two new studies, Westmoreland was told by Hawkins, the Viet Cong order of battle should be revised to reflect a strength of *more than* five hundred thousand. Hawkins would recall the general's reaction: "He expressed surprise. He voiced concern about the major increase in the irregular forces and infra-structure that we had found. He expressed concern about possible public reaction to the new figures — that they might lead people to think we had made no progress in the war." According to Robinson, Westmoreland said when learning of the new numbers: "What am I going to tell Congress? What is the press going to do with this? What am I going to tell the President?" Hawkins also would later remember words to that effect. The "substance of General Westmoreland's statement," according to Hawkins, was: "What will I tell the President? What will I tell the Congress? What will be the reaction of the press to these higher numbers?"[20]

Like McChristian's cable, the RITZ and CORRAL studies were never let out of MACV. "The general," Hawkins explained, "did not accept the new numbers."[21]

Within three weeks of having his order of battle cable killed by Westmoreland, McChristian was packed off to Fort Bragg, Texas. He and his type of intelligence were just not fitting in well with the American leadership in Saigon. Ambassador Komer made him aware of this when McChristian learned shortly before leaving that the intelligence collection apparatus at the village and hamlet level that had been laboriously constructed would be dismantled. The departing J-2 stormed into Komer's office to complain. "Have a good trip home, Mac," the CORDS chief said. Irate, McChristian next confronted Westmoreland. "Don't worry about it," the MACV chief said. McChristian felt like he "had been kicked in the stomach."[22]

*

McChristian's replacement was his West Point classmate and longtime personal nemesis, General Phillip B. Davidson. Davidson, like McChristian, was a World War II veteran, and career military intelligence officer. It was on Davidson's watch, however, that two of the largest intelligence failures in American history had taken place. One occurred back in June 1950 when Davidson was chief of the Plans and Estimates Branch in General Douglas A. MacArthur's Far Eastern Command in Tokyo. At that time Davidson had failed to foresee the North Korean invasion of the Republic of Korea. Just five months later, Davidson also missed signs that three hundred thousand Communist Chinese were about to invade the peninsula — and when they did the American and South Korean forces were almost pushed into the sea. With those twin intelligence disasters behind him Davidson, improbably, was now in Vietnam as the newest J-2.

Under Davidson the estimates function of MACV J-2 took on a whole new look. Assisting Davidson were his two top deputies, Colonel Charles A. Morris and Colonel Daniel O. Graham. Morris was a veteran military intelligence officer but Graham, an enthusiastic and ambitious West

Pointer who had only recently become Davidson's protégé, was far newer to this type of work.

Colonel Graham was short, he had a butch haircut, and his army nickname was "Mad Dog." In one incident Graham, then in command of the 319th Military Intelligence Battalion, ended his dinner toast for his young lieutenants and their dates by throwing his glass against a stone wall. His officers immediately followed suit. "The resounding crash," Graham would remember fondly, "brought the club officer on the run. Before he could say anything, I said, 'Get the glass swept up, I and my officers are going to dance.'" But not everyone could make it to the dance floor, because several of the female guests had to be escorted to the dispensary for cuts. Graham enjoyed the notoriety, and he was pleased to have dodged the bill for damages. "Years later," he boasted, "I would hear of how my battalion had 'wrecked' the Fort Shafter Officer's Club. . . . I nor my men paid for our glass-breaking."[23]

With Davidson's blessing, Graham merged the MACV J-2 office of Current Intelligence with that of Estimates and gave himself control over the resulting entity, called the Current Intelligence, Indications, and Estimates Division (CIIED). As chief of CIIED, Graham immediately had McChristian's favorite, Colonel Hawkins, exiled to the Combined Intelligence Center, Vietnam (CICV). Given free rein to make the OB estimates as he saw fit, Graham would compile the "all source" data (signals, imagery, and human intelligence) in the privacy of the top-secret CIIED "tank" and then present them to Westmoreland, Komer, principal MACV staff officers, and the U.S. commanders of the different corps areas at his regular CIIED intelligence briefings. It was at these affairs, Graham stated proudly, that "many of the key decisions of the war were made."[24]

One of Graham's responsibilities was to prepare the essential "crossover analysis" for Westmoreland, and because of this Graham would tolerate from the J-2 staff no figure for Viet Cong strength above three hundred thousand. With their mandate clear, the analysts quickly found themselves trimming estimates from the various enemy force categories in order to keep below the ceiling: They were being told to lie. For men like Hawkins those areas where Viet Cong order of battle reductions could plausibly be defended were soon exhausted, and the job became increasingly torturous.

For Hawkins himself it became too painful. Knowing that his superiors wanted not real intelligence but instead "intelligence to please," he simply asked them what end data they wanted and then gave it to them.

Hawkins counted down the days until his tour of duty was over and he could return Stateside. In the meantime, he said of Davidson and Graham: "These people are taking over. It is their war to fight. Maybe [my] higher figures *are* wrong. Whatever the case, it is their war and the consequences are theirs. Give them what they want, bless them and get your ass out of here."[25]

7

SNIE 14.3-67

Robert S. McNamara no longer trusted his military men. In April 1967 he quietly asked the CIA for an objective assessment of the war, and the appraisal he received was not encouraging. Viet Cong strength, Langley told him, was five hundred thousand; the American pacification program had stalled; and the air campaign against North Vietnam would not achieve its desired results.

CIA Director Richard Helms disliked McNamara's furtive courtship of the agency. During World War II, Helms, a Williams College graduate with experience as a foreign reporter, had been essentially drafted into the OSS. After the war, and after realizing that he lacked the financial independence to fulfill his dream of becoming a newspaper publisher, Helms decided to make the newly formed CIA his career. Diligent, alert, and above all loyal, Helms perhaps more than anybody else understood the agency's role within the Washington, D.C., power structure — and understood that the CIA was rightly the president's. McNamara's secret request had put Helms in a tricky situation vis-à-vis the White House, and he would need to consider the political implications of this for upcoming Special National Intelligence Estimate 14.3-67.

SNIE 14.3-67 would assess, on behalf of the president and the Joint Chiefs of Staff, the Vietnamese Communists' abilities to prolong the war. *Special* indicated that the estimate request came from outside the CIA, *14.3* stood for Indochina, and 67 was the year. As intelligence products go, the SNIE 14.3-67 document would be an influential one, and Helms predicted internecine warfare within the intelligence community over its production. He well knew that Vietnam War statistics were a contentious commodity in D.C. power circles, and fearing the worst Helms resignedly warned his lieutenants at Langley that the "Vietnam numbers game" would be played "with ever increasing heat and political overtones" in the year ahead.

George Carver, however, didn't share his boss's reticence for controversy. He viewed SNIE 14.3-67 as a golden opportunity to advance SAVA's prestige and influence. Through back channels Carver had just told the White House that MACV figures for the Viet Cong "may be extremely low," to the CIA hierarchy Carver said that these statistics "should be raised, perhaps doubled," and to the State Department he confided that the true number of Viet Cong are "more than 300,000" and "as high as 500,000."

Carver on this matter had the backing of many at headquarters who believed that "the company" was on the right side of this issue. Adams, home from his third trip to Vietnam, enjoyed one of his periodic resurrections as agency hero.[1]

SNIE 14.3-67 was to be drafted by the Office of National Estimates (ONE), an entity set up in the early days of the CIA to serve as the capstone of the analytical effort. The Board of National Estimates directed ONE, and a small staff carried out its orders. The staff's work was coordinated with all interested parties, and ideally ONE's final estimates represented unanimity. If total agreement was not possible, dissenters had two options. They could accept the estimate generally but "take a footnote" with their specific objections, or else they could appeal to the U.S. Intelligence Board and argue for more substantial changes. Helms as director of the CIA was also the USIB chairman, however, and had the final say on all estimates.

A ONE staffer, Robert Layton, now back at headquarters from his stint at the Saigon Collation Branch, was tasked to draft SNIE 14.3-67. He often consulted Adams on the matter. Adams told Layton that the MACV numbers in use since "time immemorial" didn't make sense anymore, and Layton was receptive to including higher estimates for Viet Cong forces in SNIE 14.3-67, believing that Adams could always back up his view with hard evidence. But there was conflict: "Sam and I had a lot of slinging matches because he had his standards, some of which I knew damn well you couldn't sell." Adams was not always happy with Layton but, Layton said, "At least I was willing to listen to him; we could talk to some degree the same language."

In Layton's version of SNIE 14.3-67, Viet Cong strength was guessed at 460,000 to 570,000, with the higher figure being "closer to the actual total Communist strength in South Vietnam." Most of these enemy forces, as Layton detailed in his draft, were in village and hamlet guerrillas and the SD/SSD.[2]

The ONE's ruling body, the Board of National Estimates, convened on June 23 in a large conference room at Langley to finalize SNIE 14.3-67. A retired army general chaired the meeting. There were many present: representatives from the State Department's Bureau of Intelligence and Research, the Pentagon's DIA, the intelligence branches of the army, air force, marines, and navy, the NSA, and the CIA. The CIA came into the meeting with its Viet Cong figure of five hundred thousand, well above and beyond the figure DIA thought more than adequate: 296,000.

Layton made the CIA's case that first day of 14.3-67, and then Adams took over. The proceedings reached gridlock. Adams, Layton recalled, struggled to keep his composure. "Like many people who feel strongly about something, at times Sam let his enthusiasm carry him to the point — not literally but figuratively — of grabbing people by the lapels and shaking them. Sam was very fair-complexioned; he would get red, very red in the face. His voice would go up. In a charitable sense Sam did not tolerate fools very easily."

Adams could get frustrated but overall he was pleased with how things were going. "There was some minor slippage in a couple of categories," he would remember, "but otherwise the CIA held firm." Carver instructed him not to budge. By the end of June, and with the DIA refusing also to give ground, the estimative process came to a halt.[3]

Helms learned that the two sides remained far apart, and he was hardly about to send a fractious document on to the White House. He convened an interagency meeting of the BNE, CIA, and DIA in late June and said that the order of battle question was "the most important disagreement about the war," insisting that "we've got to come to an agreement." When none came by early July, however, Carver was silently dispatched to Saigon. There he met with General Davidson and explained that the impasse had to be broken. But Davidson gave him no opening. Carver sent

a cable to Helms. "The chief problem," Caver wrote of Davidson's objections, "is the political and presentational one of coming out with a brand
new set of figures showing a much larger [VC] force at a time when the
press knows MACV is seeking more [U.S.] troops."

Carver then volunteered a clever way of making SNIE 14.3-67 more
palatable for Davidson. This was to break the Viet Cong order of battle
down into two parts. There would be, Carver proposed, a "military" component of NVA, Viet Cong main and local forces, guerrillas and administrative services, and a "nonmilitary" component of Viet Cong SD/SSD and
infrastructure. The military segment would number three hundred thousand and the nonmilitary two hundred thousand. MACV could thus continue using the number 290,000 for enemy combatants in dealing with the
press, while top-secret SNIE 14.3-67 would maintain that total Viet Cong
strength in all its various guises was 500,000. Although not asked for his
opinion, Adams learned of the semantics; they were fine with him. His
only goal was to finally get real numbers across the Oval Office desk.[4]

General Davidson was agreeable to Carver's idea but Davidson's boss,
General Westmoreland, was not. Deadlocked again, SNIE 14.3-67 was put
on hold. An accord, it was hoped, would be reached when 14.3-67 recon-
vened on the seventh floor at Langley. At that time the DIA would turn its
fight over to MACV's order of battle specialist just in from Vietnam —
Colonel Gains B. Hawkins.

*

As scheduled, the estimate preparation resumed in early August (the lull in
the tribunal had allowed Adams time to complete his massive study of the
Bo Cong An). Layton had gone back to Vietnam in July, and so advocacy
for the CIA stance at SNIE 14.3-67 fell totally upon Adams. Hawkins was
there on reopening day, and Adams was happy to see him. *Here's good old
Gains B. Hawkins*, Adams thought. *Everything's going to be all right. He
agrees that the numbers are way higher.* Accompanying Hawkins — and evidently his "keeper" — was Davidson's deputy MACV J-2, General George
Godding.[5]

Right off, Hawkins presented revised MACV Viet Cong order of battle
statistics:

	Previous	Revised
NVA, VC main and local:	120,400	120,400
Administrative services:	24,800	26,000
Guerrillas:	65,000	65,000
SD/SSD:	47,800	—
VCI:	39,200	87,500
Total:	297,200	298,900[6]

Adams would recall doing "a double-take. I said, 'What's going on here?'" There was something odd, Adams noticed, to some of the figures. In the revised numbers the Viet Cong self-defense and secret self-defense forces had disappeared, while the VCI expanded in numbers in almost direct proportion to the SD/SSD loss. The guerrillas, meanwhile, had totaled sixty-five thousand in MACV's previous estimate and remained unchanged in its revised one, despite intelligence known to MACV that Viet Cong guerrillas currently numbered well over one hundred thousand. It all was, Adams found, "awfully damn peculiar."

For the next ten days Adams publicly tussled with Hawkins over how and why MACV had arrived at these revisions, especially those for Viet Cong irregulars. Hawkins obligingly provided answers and even gave Adams copies of his raw intelligence data. But the data often contradicted Hawkins's own testimony, and Adams interpreted this as the colonel's way of subtly undermining the MACV position.

Adams grilled Hawkins on the disappearance of the self-defense and secret self-defense forces, and Hawkins replied that these militia, having rudimentary training and armaments, were not combatants. But, Adams knew, here Hawkins was being illogical. The fact was that MACV didn't discriminate when it came time to tally the SD and SSD for other reasons, such as those that made the American military effort in Vietnam look good. Adams asked at one point, "Damnit, Colonel, if you count them when they defect, or when they're dead, why can't you count them when they're still alive?" Hawkins demurred in giving an answer and Adams, seeing that Godding was watching Hawkins's every utterance, well knew that his colonel friend was in an untenable position.[7]

While SNIE 14.3-67 droned on at Langley, General Davidson told his staff in Saigon that weekly Viet Cong strength figures "will hereafter be cleared personally by me." Davidson explained the mission. "What we have got to do," he instructed, "is to attrite main forces, local forces, and particularly guerrillas. We must cease immediately using the assumption that these units replace themselves. We should go on the assumption that they do not, unless we have firm evidence to the contrary. The figure of combat strength, and particularly of guerrillas, must take a steady and significant downward trend."[8]

The self-defense and secret self-defense forces in particular were a problem for Davidson because they inflated the Viet Cong strength numbers to a politically unacceptable degree, and it was time they go. Henceforth, the exclusion of the SD and SSD from the official estimates became the MACV line. On August 19 Robert Komer, having gotten wind of CIA attempts to retain the SD/SSD in SNIE 14.3-67 despite MACV's protests, cabled Carver from Saigon. The CORDS chief pleaded with Carver to support Davidson's position. "MACV is determined to stick to its guns," Komer cabled, "and you can well imagine the ruckus which will be created if it comes out — as everything tends to on Vietnam — that the agency and MACV figures are so widely different."

The next day General Westmoreland's number two at MACV, General Creighton W. Abrams, concurred. Abrams wanted it made clear that the MACV "command position" was that the self-defense and secret self-defense forces must be dropped from the order of battle. "If SD and SSD are included in the overall enemy strength, the figure will total 420,000 to 431,000," Abrams cabled from Saigon. "This is in sharp contrast to the current overall strength figure of about 299,000 given to the press here." The problem, Abrams explained from Saigon, was that "We have been projecting an image of success over the recent months" and "when we release the figure of 420,000–431,000 the newsmen will immediately seize on the point that the enemy force has increased about 120–130,000. All available caveats and explanations will not prevent the press from drawing an erroneous and gloomy conclusion as to the meaning of the increase."[9]

Finally, word arrived at Langley from Westmoreland himself. If the SD/SSD numbers remained in the estimate, and if those numbers were ever released to the public, Westmoreland said, "No possible explanations could prevent the erroneous conclusions that could result."[10]

Yet with Carver's protection, the SD/SSD survived, and the Viet Cong order of battle figures at last seemed ready for placement in SNIE 14.3-67. Where MACV and CIA still could not agree, two different figures were to be reported:

	MACV	CIA
"Military" Viet Cong		
NVA, VC main and local:	121,000	(Same)
Administrative services:	40,000	60,000
Guerrillas:	60,000	100,000
Subtotal:	221,000	281,000
"Other" Viet Cong		
SD/SSD	120,000	(Same)
VCI:	90,000	(Same)
Subtotal:	210,000	(Same)
Grand total:	**431,000**	**491,000**[11]

In addition to these entries, Adams managed to squeeze a few thousand Viet Cong assault youth into the CIA column. But this was a minor victory compared with what Adams and Carver must have imagined was a far greater one: CIA numbers for all Viet Cong categories would be protected and advanced by an unassailable Special National Intelligence Estimate. To get this far a few allowances to MACV had been made, and the total number of Viet Cong was still below where it should have been — which was, Adams thought, six hundred thousand — but at last MACV was forced to break through its artificial three-hundred-thousand barrier.

On the seventh floor at Langley, CIA director Helms took one look at the divergent MACV and CIA proposals in SNIE 14.3-67 and knew that a split decision such as this would never stand. Helms had many things to think about other than the 14.3-67 saga, and at this epoch in the drama he was ready to move on. What did he care if the military, against the CIA's better advice, wished to accept faulty intelligence? The men in fatigues were the ones fighting the war and not the analysts at Langley, and more than once Helms had barked at Carver to "Work it out!" with MACV, but to Helms's annoyance nothing had been worked out, and his patience was at an end.

General Westmoreland in Saigon was also anxious to arrive at a common set of enemy strength figures. The Joint Chiefs of Staff in the Pentagon were of the same mind, although according to notes taken at the chief's August 25 meeting it is evident that the military brass cared more about the public relations aspect of the issue than they did about the actual enemy order of battle. "The JCS fully appreciate the public release problem and view it as the major problem," the notes said, and "While concerned about the figures, [the JCS] consider them of lesser importance."[12]

For those arguing SNIE 14.3-67 on both sides the proceedings at Langley had by now run on interminably; an adjournment was mercifully declared on August 28. Adams dashed to a plane for Alabama, where Eleanor and Clayton were already vacationing. No sooner had he arrived, though, than the phone rang. It was for him, George Carver on the line. Carver told Adams to pack for Saigon. Helms and Westmoreland had arranged for a summit at MACV to resolve the numbers dispute once and for all.[13]

*

Adams arrived in Saigon on September 8. His first stop was the U.S. embassy, where he was greeted by Ellsworth Bunker, an old friend of his father's from the Wall Street firm of Butler, Herrick and Marshall. Bunker had left the brokerage business to pursue a career as a cold warrior and in this he had been successful, most recently earning himself the position of U.S. ambassador to South Vietnam. The visit at the embassy was a pleasant one; Adams had no inkling of Bunker's intense anger at the CIA. In fact, the ambassador had just cabled Walt Rostow at the White House in fear that the agency's estimate of five hundred thousand Viet Cong might be leaked. Such a disclosure would undermine pronouncements of American progress being voiced by the embassy and by MACV. "I intend to mention it to the president in my coming weekly," Bunker wrote Rostow. "The credibility gap would be enormous, and is quite inconsistent with all the hard evidence we have about growing enemy losses, declining VC recruitment and the like."[14]

The numbers negotiations between MACV and the CIA began the next morning at the new MACV headquarters building ("Pentagon East") on the Tan Son Nhut airbase. The numbers controversy was big news throughout the vast U.S. intelligence community — the talk of American clandestine types around the globe — and there was great interest in its eventual outcome. The State and Defense Departments had flown in their delegations from Washington, D.C., and from Langley, Virginia. Present were Adams, George Carver, Dean Moor (once again), and a ONE staffer, William Hyland. David Close of the CIA Saigon station was also there as the local agency representative. MACV, for its part, was more than adequately represented with General Phillip Davidson in attendance along with General George Godding, Colonel Charles Morris, Colonel Daniel Graham, Colonel Gains B. Hawkins, Colonel David Morgan, and Lieutenant Richard McArthur. The MACV public information officer, General Winant Sidle, was also there and sitting at General Davidson's right elbow.[15]

Major J. Barrie Williams was with the Defense Intelligence Agency group. He was no stranger to the order of battle issue, having been first at the Honolulu conference and then at the lengthy 14.3-67 hearings at Langley. In his Pentagon posting Williams was the Viet Cong order of battle expert for the Joint Chiefs of Staff. He had watched as evidence from the vast document finds in South Vietnam of late 1966 and early 1967 showed a far larger Viet Cong force structure than U.S. military intelligence had initially realized. Notably, the guerrillas and self-defense forces, the elements responsible for so much of the booby-trapping, pungi-sticking, and other types of low-level warfare taking place in Vietnam, had ballooned exponentially. "The documents indicated that just the guerrillas themselves," Williams explained, "may be numbering 112,000, and already this starts to knock the number that we had been carrying, 296,000 or something, to around 400,000. This is starting to worry people."

Soon the talk at DIA was that there could be as many as 450,000 to 500,000 Viet Cong in the hamlets, rice paddies, and jungles of South Vietnam. The evidence for this could not be ignored, and everyone in the Pentagon realized that it would have profound implications for the selling of General Westmoreland's entire war strategy. The DIA, however, was not at liberty to make any revisions to MACV's estimates because MACV represented the "soldiers in the field"; their "command position," which Major Williams and his Pentagon colleagues were "enjoined to defend," was that Viet Cong strength be capped at three hundred thousand. Williams thus found himself taking the MACV side on the numbers debate and supporting things that Williams knew were "total and utter horseshit, just total and utter."[16]

In addition to playing defense for bad intelligence, military intelligence professionals such as Williams were expected to finagle the figures as well. Williams remembered one scene that occurred in his Pentagon office, sometime in early August, when he was hosting military delegates to SNIE 14.3-67. The group was finalizing MACV's Viet Cong strength estimates for the proceedings at Langley and its leader was Colonel Daniel Graham, flown in from MACV to add backbone to DIA's position. As Williams and the rest watched in amazement Graham unilaterally lined out enemy force numbers and wrote in lower figures. Colonel George Hamscher of CINCPAC was at this cutting session, and he was appalled. "There was no re-analysis, no re-examination of supporting evidence, no recourse to OB files, no respect for the work of analysts," Hamscher would later complain. "It was a 'blue pencil' operation, and we haggled and bargained, even blustered. It progressed from unprofessional to wrongful; and it amounted to falsification of intelligence."[17]

"Look Danny, we can't do this, this is wrong," Hamscher protested at the time.

"If you've got a better way to do this, let's have it," Graham replied.

Hamscher did not and he watched in silence as one Viet Cong unit after another was, he said, "bloodlessly" wiped out at the Pentagon.[18]

The decimated enemy strength figures were supported by a "queasy" DIA delegation at the SNIE 14.3-67 meetings in August. Williams saw that General George Godding, Hawkins's handler from Saigon, was himself having serious difficulties swallowing the low numbers and wanted some flexibility to the MACV position. However, every time Godding telephoned MACV from Washington for permission to increase the numbers he was refused. Fearing that Godding had missed the point, General Davidson in Saigon became so concerned that in a cable to his wavering delegate he spelled out the objections to CIA's higher Viet Cong numbers, and to the agency's insistence that the SD/SSD be retained.

"Further consideration reveals the total unacceptability of including the strength of the self-defense forces and the secret self-defense forces in any strength figure to be released to the press," Davidson cabled Godding. "The figure of about 420,000, which includes all forces including SD and SSD, has already surfaced out here. This figure has stunned the embassy and this headquarters and has resulted in a stream of protests and denials." Davidson continued, "In view of this reaction and in view of General Westmoreland's conversations, all of which you have heard, I am sure that this headquarters will not accept a figure in excess of the current strength figure carried by the press. Let me make it clear," Davidson concluded, "that this is my view of General Westmoreland's sentiments. I have not discussed this directly with him but I am 100 percent sure of his reaction."[19]

Despite this blunt hint Godding had by the end of August, of course, allowed his estimates for 14.3-67 to fairly resemble the agency's numbers. General Westmoreland was "deeply concerned" about this, and Godding would pay dearly for his generosity toward the CIA. "When we went back to Saigon after that," Williams said. "General Godding was treated as though he had the plague because he could not carry the day for the MACV position."[20]

*

The MACV–CIA Saigon summit would last five days, September 9–13, with the agreement announced on the fourteenth. General Davidson chaired the summit, and on day one he saw that "Carver, a 'power player' in the agency, was to discuss the broad issues, while Adams, armed with his few treasured documents, handled the detailed argumentation." But Carver and Adams could barely get a word in edgewise, the conference initially being smothered by numerous MACV presentations, all of them orchestrated by Colonel Daniel Graham.[21]

The MACV speakers depicted a Viet Cong enemy as sick, hungry, frightened, running low on ammunition, and numerically in a state of substantial decline. Graham himself reported that Viet Cong recruitment and conscription in South Vietnam had dropped off dramatically and, concurrently, that the flow of North Vietnamese troops coming down the Ho Chi

Minh Trail to bolster their comrades in South Vietnam was drying up. Graham explained that the crossover point in the war of attrition against the Vietnamese Communists had, as a result, been reached. Adams caught a glimpse of Gains B. Hawkins and the colonel, Adams noted, looked embarrassed and uncomfortable.[22]

The CIA representatives were not impressed by the Graham show, and the summit quickly degenerated into acrimony and personal attack. Davidson recalled that he had "sat in on hundreds of conferences attended by both civilians and military, and none of them ever approached this one for animosity and boorishness." Davidson felt that "Carver and his delegation" were "arrogant and overbearing — the experts come to show these military intelligence neophytes how to 'do' Order of Battle." This agency attitude only hardened Davidson's opinion. He became proudly and increasingly inflexible, noting with pleasure that Carver "described me — not to my face, of course — as a 'hard-nosed son of a bitch.'" Toward Adams and his "voodoo intelligence" Davidson was entirely dismissive. Adams, "in his egoistic obsession," Davidson explained, naively believed that his "superficial study" on the Viet Cong was destined to change U.S. policy toward Vietnam. It was laughable. Graham had equal disdain for the "zealot" Adams and the "fuss" Adams had made at CIA about there being six hundred thousand Viet Cong. Adams, Graham thought, had simply become "psychotic on the issue."[23]

Carver, in turn, was insulted by Davidson's behavior. "I was," Carver told Helms in a cable sent back to Langley, "frequently and sometimes tendentiously interrupted by Davidson," who "angrily accused me of impugning his integrity." Carver also told Helms that Davidson informed him that the MACV order of battle estimate was the "final offer, not subject to discussion. We should take it or leave it."[24]

When that first day concluded an army officer from MACV gave Adams and Carver a lift to their quarters. The MACV man explained their predicament: "Our main problem is that we've been told to stay under 300,000."[25]

Over the next two days of negotiations Adams tried to keep up as the MACV figures for different Viet Cong order of battle categories, he related, "bobbed, weaved, slithered, and sometimes altogether vanished." During one juncture Colonel Graham revealed that analyses showed the

SD/SSD to be an ineffectual militia, and to prove his point Graham provided MACV's latest numbers for these forces, a figure well under what Adams believed was a realistic guess. As Adams rose to present an alternative estimate he was immediately challenged by Davidson.[26]

"Mr. Adams," Davidson demanded, "what is your evidentiary base for your estimate?"

"Two documents," Adams admitted and resumed his seat. Davidson could barely contain his disgust. His aide, Colonel Charles Morris, leaned over to share a thought with the CIA man. "Adams," Morris confided, "you're full of shit."

Next it was MACV Lieutenant Colonel David Morgan's turn to stand up and give his estimate. J. Barrie Williams remembered what happened: "And he gave an estimate that was just seriously in contrast as to the magnitude with the one that Sam Adams did. And he finished and General Davidson sat there and kind of smiled."

Adams raised his hand, though, and said, "Sir, I have a question, what is your evidentiary base?" There was no answer, according to Williams, and Adams again asked, "What was your documentary base for your estimate?"

General Davidson confidently turned to Morgan and said, "Colonel, he asked you a question. How many documents did you use to make this estimate?"

"Sir," the colonel said, looking ill, "one document."

"With that," Williams remembered, "General Davidson got up and stormed out of the room."[27]

This was a nice little moral victory for Adams, but the Saigon meeting would end in utter defeat for the CIA, and for Adams this disgrace would become the lowest point of his career. A premonition of the nadir came on the second day when a note, unbelievably, was circulated openly stating that MACV would add fifteen thousand Viet Cong guerrillas to the 14.3-67 order of battle estimate if CIA agreed to drop its insistence that the SD/SSD be included.

Adams was naive to the notion of bureaucratic give-and-take, just as he was naive to the concept of compromising intelligence for the sake of politics. He and Carver read the note simultaneously, and Adams recalled that "I said something to the effect that this kind of bargaining might be acceptable in a rug bazaar, but goddamnit, it wasn't intelligence." Adams suggested they quit the conference and fly back to Washington right then and there. For all he cared, MACV officialdom could take a footnote to 14.3-67 if it didn't like the agency's estimates. Adams had had his fill, but Carver came to Saigon to smooth over MACV–CIA differences and not to acerbate them.[28]

Carver had an impeccable pedigree for the CIA — raised in China by missionary parents, Yale graduate, doctorate at Oxford on Thomas Hobbes — and it took the agency two tries before it could convince him to become a spy. After ten years in the clandestine services Carver went into the research side of the house, where he had two articles published in *Foreign Affairs* to his credit as well as being Helm's handpicked man to handle Vietnam. Carver, looking forward to further advancement at Langley, was not about to fail in his assignment to Saigon; he was, in fact, coming around to Helms's view that CIA must extract itself from, in Carver's words, "this politically touchy subject" whose "major differences lie in realm of conceptual and presentational methodology rather than in genuine disagreement over sustentative facts."[29]

But even with this new thinking, Carver was having a tough go of it with General Davidson. "So far," he cabled Helms, "our mission frustratingly unproductive since MACV stonewalling, obviously under orders." All indications were "that General Westmoreland (with Komer's encouragement) had given instruction tantamount to direct order that VC strength total will not exceed 300,000 ceiling." Carver explained why: "Rationale seems to be that any higher figure would not be sufficiently optimistic and would generate unacceptable level of criticism from the press. This order obviously makes it impossible for MACV to engage in serious or meaningful discussion of evidence of our real substantive disagreements, which I strongly suspect are negligible."[30]

Four days into the so-far futile negotiations Carver dined with CORDS chief Ambassador Komer to see if a deal could be reached. First, though, Carver would have to endure a one-hour "Blowtorch Bob" monologue on the subject of the Viet Cong order of battle. The ambassador was not happy with the CIA and the way it was pushing its higher estimates. "Look

George," Komer yelled, "you guys have got to back off, you have just got to goddamn well back off! This issue is bigger than the numbers, it's bigger than the estimate!" Komer told Carver that if CIA's numbers appeared in SNIE 14.3-67, in no time "some goddamn dove from the State Department will leak it to the press. And it'll be seized on by everyone who is against the war in Vietnam. It will destroy everything we have accomplished out here in the past year and a half in the way of creating an image of progress and success on the war. You guys have got to goddamn well back off!"[31]

Later that evening Carver cabled Helms and asked for guidance. Adams and others held that Helms gave Carver specific directions at this time to cave, but if there was a cable ordering capitulation it was subsequently destroyed. Helms, who has disputed the notion that he ever cabled surrender orders, said that no instructions to Carver were required. "He already knew my basic views," Helms explained, "that because of broader considerations we had to come up with agreed figures, that we had to get this OB question off the board, and that it didn't mean a damn what particular figures were agreed to."[32]

Done with the cables, Carver went back to his room and drafted a compromise that he knew would be amenable to MACV — one that would entirely rid SNIE 14.3-67 of Viet Cong irregulars. Toward noon the next morning, September 13, Carver met alone with General Westmoreland. The CIA delegation was kept in the dark; even Westmoreland's own chief of intelligence, General Davidson, was locked out of the discussion. Davidson found this insulting, and Westmoreland was never to give him an explanation for the breach of military protocol.

At the conclusion of Carver's and Westmoreland's private meeting MACV had gotten everything it wanted — and more. The agreed-upon order of battle "spread figures" (the "spread" insisted upon by Komer to avoid providing the press specifics) were henceforth to be:

NVA, VC main and local:	119,000
Administrative services:	35,000–40,000
Guerrillas:	70,000–90,000
Total:	224,000–249,000[33]

The order of battle table was lacerated beyond recognition. While enemy regular forces (NVA troops and Viet Cong main and local forces) were cut only a couple of thousand, administrative services troops had been slashed 50 percent and the SD/SSD and the VCI had been sheared off altogether. Westmoreland and Carver agreed that the VCI numbered between seventy and ninety thousand, but because this group was not "military" it had no place in the order of battle table; it would be dealt with separately within the text of SNIE 14.3-67. As for the SD/SSD, assault youth, et cetera, Westmoreland and Carver agreed that under no circumstances was 14.3-67 to attempt any quantification of these forces.[34]

Major J. Barrie Williams had waited a long time for the numbers debate to end and he was curious as to its resolution. He immediately saw how it came about. "The categories," he said, "were jimmied for the purpose of not going above 300,000." Ambassador Bunker learned of the settlement and was "most pleased," while Carver himself thought the impossible had been achieved. From Saigon he cabled Helms the glad tidings by quoting favorite philosopher Thomas Hobbes: "Circle now squared."[35]

*

Robert Layton in Saigon did not attend the summit at MACV but he learned of what was going on through his housemate, David Close. "Some kind of resolution had been reached," Layton recalled of September 14, "and we decided to hold a get-together. Carver didn't come to it; he had bigger fish to fry. It was going to be a relaxing affair." This prediction, however, was wrong. Layton continued, "Our rickety Vietnamese furniture took a real test. It turned into a slinging match. Clearly Sam was not happy with the compromise. I am not sure anybody was happy. So Hyland, who was probably the most senior of the group, was taking the MACV position in talking with Sam." Hyland told Adams: "Sam, don't take it so hard. You know what the political climate is. If you think they'd accept the higher numbers, you're living in a dream world." The argument continued and, said Layton, "As wine and booze flowed and as the evening wore along tempers got more frayed and so forth. And so it wasn't a pleasant evening." Having drunk too much scotch, Adams awoke the next day with a hangover.[36]

Back in Langley, George Allen was shown the settlement with MACV, and he said it "damn near made me puke." Allen was enraged at the lower numbers and particularly incensed that the SD, SSD, and VCI had vanished into thin air. Westmoreland, as he had done before, was insisting that these elements were militarily no threat, but the assumption went against everything the CIA and other agencies knew to be true about the enemy. Allen had by now studied Vietnamese Communist political-military strategy and tactics for almost two decades and he thought, "Why the hell does CIA or any intelligence staff exist *but* to make judgments about things like that?"[37]

After work Allen told his wife, Dola, that he intended to quit the agency. The outcome of the MACV–CIA meeting was nothing less than the prostitution of intelligence. But in talking things over with Dola he backed down. "I had four daughters," Allen explained, "one of them sophomore in high school — and three coming up behind — and the only thing I know is intelligence. I persuaded myself, *Well, stay and try to win the next battle*. But Sam decided to do what he did."[38]

*

Adams returned to Langley from his fourth, and what would be his last, trip to Vietnam on Monday, September 18. A CIA promotion in grade to GS-12 awaited him from Carver, but the extra money (annual pay nineteen thousand dollars) did nothing to assuage Adams's outrage. At the end of the month he was given the opportunity to express himself. Special National Intelligence Estimate 14.3-67 still had to be officially concluded, and in preparation for this final effort Adams and a group of CIA officials met privately with the Board of National Estimates.

In friendly territory once again Adams described what had happened in Saigon and the bargaining that made the VCI and the SD/SSD disappear. He also said that MACV knew its Viet Cong numbers were far too low and gave an example of how MACV estimates for administrative services troops had been arbitrarily scaled down. The audience of intelligence professionals accepted the veracity of what Adams was saying and it was agreed that, based upon Adams's witness, the fight with MACV was indeed not over. MACV had apparently been, in the words of one board member, "cooking the books." There was displeasure that CIA could collude in this activity; after the meeting board chairman and legendary agency man Sherman Kent came up to Adams to pose a question. "Sam,"

Kent asked earnestly, "have we gone beyond the bounds of reasonable dishonesty?" Adams replied that, yes, the CIA had.[39]

Over the next six weeks Adams scrambled to head off Helms's signature on SNIE 14.3-67. Adams railed against the new numbers agreed upon with MACV, and he swayed some over to his side. Ronald L. Smith of the CIA's Office of Economic Research told Adams that the numbers "couldn't have honestly been an honest depiction of the situation." Assisting Adams in his cause was a proposed MACV press briefing on the new Viet Cong estimates. The briefing took liberties with what had been agreed to with the CIA in Saigon by further downgrading the Viet Cong force categories and numbers. The head of the OER, Paul Walsh, called the proposed MACV publicity piece "one of the greatest snow jobs since Potemkin constructed his village." George Carver himself termed the planned press briefing a "clumsy piece of dissimulation."[40]

Sobered by MACV's willingness to bend the facts, the agency broached the idea of again including the SD/SSD in the order of battle, but Ellsworth Bunker in Saigon would have none of it. In yet another cable to Walt Rostow of the White House, Bunker wrote that restatement of the militia would raise questions in the press about why it had been removed in the first place. "Given the overriding need to demonstrate progress in grinding down the enemy," Bunker argued, "it is essential that we do not drag too many red herrings across the trail."[41]

Time was running short, and Adams continued frantically to put forth his case before the Saigon agreement was to be set in stone by Helms. After leaving Saigon, Robert Layton said, "Sam clearly carries his *I'm not happy* message home, and in a way he gets more and more entrenched in his views." Williams remembered Adams's demeanor at this time and said, "Sam was well spoken, but his emotions were on his sleeve. When Sam is angry there is no question you are going to know he is angry. He was driven, he got all the data and he would hold on to it, and ride it, ride it, ride it, convinced of the rightness of his cause."

Adams spent a week writing a carefully crafted argument to Helms asking for a stay of execution. The Saigon agreement, he contended, was deeply flawed in many respects, among them was that it ignored "the probability that the number of Viet Cong, as currently defined, is something

over half a million. Thus it makes canons of gaps, and encourages self delu-
sion." But it was all for naught. A BNE member, Abbott Smith, regretfully
told Adams that the board had no alternative but to ratify the Saigon
agreement because Helms had all but approved it. What choice, Smith
asked rhetorically, did they have?[42]

Helms signed SNIE 14.3-67 on the morning of Monday, November 13,
1967. The document, blue-covered and emblazed with the seal of the CIA,
ran about thirty pages and was officially titled "Capabilities of the
Vietnamese Communists for Fighting in South Vietnam." In the weeks
since the Saigon agreement MACV had surreptitiously lobbied Helms to
further crop the numbers; as a result total Viet Cong "capabilities" were
put at just 188,000 to 208,000.[43]

The estimate was done with, yet for Helms the problems it created per-
sisted. Now he had to explain to President Johnson why the new order of
battle tallies looked so different from those previously produced by the
intelligence community. Helms wrote in a covering memo to Johnson that
because the newest 14.3 estimate was "sensitive," "controversial," and "at
variance with our former holdings" he had actually considered not signing
off on it at all, but — he assured the president — the numbers "can stand
on their own two feet."

Highlighting the positive, Walt Rostow wrote to Johnson in a covering
memo to Helms's covering memo that the new estimate showed "a substantial reduction in guerrillas," "a slight reduction in main force units,"
and "a fairly good chance" for a decline in the Viet Cong Infrastructure.
"Manpower," Rostow stated, "is the major problem confronting the
Communists."

Helms, however, assiduously avoided optimism in presenting the estimate before a special cabinet meeting a few days later. He cautiously
emphasized "the perplexing question of force levels" and the "statistical
uncertainties" inherent in the newest estimate. Helms additionally told the
cabinet that the numbers must be "closely held" because they could cause
problems if used as a metric proving progress in the war. "We can't let the
press in on this," he said of the strength estimates. "We must still be careful
in talking about the number of people in the game." President Johnson
agreed, apparently giving credit where credit was due. "Bunker and

Westmoreland have stayed up nights working on these figures," Johnson said, "and I would like to keep them all off the record for now."[44]

The cabinet was impressed with the document's authoritativeness. Secretary of State Dean Rusk believed the numbers were "the best available estimates as to the enemy strength available to anyone" and not "in any way incomplete or misleading." McNamara was likewise unaware of any problems with the estimate, and later said that if he had been he "would have immediately sought to raise the issue to the surface and resolve it."[45]

While kept from the public at large, SNIE 14.3-67 became part of the New Year's intelligence package Helms sent to every member of Congress.[46]

*

Disgusted by the Helms endorsement, and by George Carver's disgraceful cave-in to Westmoreland, Adams stalked the halls of Langley relaying his displeasure to any and all who would listen. Carver must have been bracing for an Adams memo — and it came. "I do not feel that SAVA has been sufficiently diligent in bringing to the attention of the intelligence community the numerical and organizational strength of our adversaries in Vietnam," Adams wrote. "I feel we (the CIA in general and SAVA in particular) have basically misinformed policy makers of the strength of the enemy. The pressures on the CIA and SAVA, I realize, have been enormous. Many of those pressures — but not all — have originated from MACV, whose Order of Battle is a monument of deceit. The agency's and the office's failing concerning Viet Cong manpower, I feel, has been its acquiescence to MACV half-truths, distortions, and sometimes outright falsehoods. We have occasionally protested, but neither long enough, nor loud enough." Adams then stated his wish to leave SAVA. Carver, ever the gentleman, graciously accepted the notice of resignation, which would come into effect February 1.[47]

For the remainder of 1967 Adams had enough work to keep himself busy. He continued to catalog and count Viet Cong units as revealed to him by the captured documents, he further researched the Bo Cong An, and he kept current with the CDEC Bulletin (now at number 9,000). There was also perplexing intelligence coming in from Vietnam that called for attention. Inexplicably, the Viet Cong were in a mad scramble to reorganize their forces, while simultaneously the once steady stream of Viet Cong defectors into the Chieu Hoi centers had mysteriously dried up. In puzzling over this Adams also became aware of General Westmoreland's public relations offensive.

The offensive officially began November 11 at MACV headquarters. General Winant Sidle, Davidson's right-hand man at the MACV–CIA summit, delivered a dazzling three-hour-and-twenty-minute briefing for the press corps. (This was the same briefing that the CIA had been given an advance copy of, and had found so repellent.) Tom Buckley was at Sidle's show in Saigon and on the twelfth reported on what he had seen and heard (*New York Times*: "U.S. Aides Say Foe's Strength And Morale Are Declining Fast"). According to Sidle, Buckley wrote, enemy losses over the past six months were not being replaced by new fighters and that, tellingly, the Viet Cong in the mountains and jungles were "often on the verge of starvation." Viet Cong morale, Buckley stated according to what Sidle had said, "was sinking fast" with "evidence that enemy troops were being forced into battle with machine guns at their backs."

Three days later, on November 15, Westmoreland landed in Washington, D.C., to lead the public relations offensive personally. There, Hedrick Smith on November 22 covered this next phase of the campaign (*New York Times*: "Westmoreland Says Ranks of Vietcong Thin Steadily"). In an address to the National Press Club, Smith reported, Westmoreland attested that Viet Cong guerrilla forces were "declining at a steady rate"; they "could no longer fill their ranks from the South" and "must depend increasingly on replacements from North Vietnam." An outright U.S. military victory in the classic sense was not likely, Westmoreland said, but the Vietnam War had finally entered a phase "when the end begins to come into view." The enemy, Westmoreland confided, was losing — "But apparently . . . hasn't realized it yet."

After this appearance Westmoreland moved his center of operations over to the Pentagon, where Neil Sheehan, also of the *Times*, followed the offensive (November 23: "Westmoreland Sure of Victory"). Westmoreland promised that recent U.S. successes in South Vietnam were "the beginning of a great defeat for the enemy." At the Pentagon, however, Westmoreland took some flak. Why, the press wanted to know, had the Pentagon been holding to the original enemy strength figure of 297,000 up until just yesterday?

"The general," as Sheehan reported Westmoreland's response, "said that figure included political cadre." But the question lingered, and Westmoreland found his encampment in Washington exposed.

Two days later support came from Sidle in Saigon. There, Tom Buckley reported Sidle's explanation for the revised figures for Viet Cong strength: "enemy documents captured in recent United States Army raids into Vietcong strongholds provided much more detailed information, which enabled a new assessment." Because of this new assessment, Buckley wrote, MACV could more accurately size up the enemy and "sort out large numbers not in a military category," which included "political cadres, local defense units and fifth column squads."

But resistance by the press to the new figures was growing, and Sidle in response readied more public relations ordnance. Military officers made available to Buckley now said that American commandos had captured a high-level North Vietnamese officer who provided the information, allowing for, Buckley wrote, the "sweeping revision of estimates." This intelligence "helped analysts arrive at a lower — and in their view more accurate — estimate" than was previously possible.

The sheer implausibility of this tall tale must have left Sam Adams seething. He saw all the headlines, such as "Westmoreland: The Enemy Is Running Out Of Men" (November 18) or "War Of Attrition Called Effective By Westmoreland" (November 20), and he read all the articles. Westmoreland, with Ambassador Bunker in tow, was on *Meet the Press*, Westmoreland was appearing before the Senate Armed Services Committee, Westmoreland was briefing President Johnson. The time, Adams thought, was ripe for counteroffensive.

The attack on the Westmoreland position began inauspiciously, November 25, with lunch at the Moon Palace, a Chinese restaurant on Connecticut Avenue. Adams dined with his reporter friend Andrew Hamilton, who had a desk in the Pentagon newsroom. It had been clear to Hamilton for some time that the Pentagon was preparing the press corps for good news. "The Pentagon public numbers game," Hamilton explained, "had consisted of floating the current estimate, totaling roughly three hundred thousand, to reporters 'on background' as a buildup to releasing the crossover numbers cited by Westy when he came to Washington in

November." When those numbers were released, however, Hamilton noticed the absence of the SD and SSD forces — forces that he had been told were responsible for many of the American casualties — and he had an inkling that Westmoreland was perhaps misleadingly comparing his new, lower, order of battle figures with the former, higher, ones. At the lunch Hamilton asked Adams about this and, Hamilton recalled, "Sam simply told me I should follow my instincts as I described them to him."

Three weeks later "Westmoreland's Progress Report" was a cover story in the December 16 issue of *The New Republic*. In the article Hamilton wrote that the previous month's press offensive by Westmoreland should be considered "as part of a political campaign, not as a candid review of the war situation." As an example of the politics, Hamilton detailed how the Viet Cong order of battle categories and numbers had been twisted and tortured, all for the appearance of success. Hamilton also hinted at the price General McChristian, formerly of MACV, paid for being "very competent and a 'realist'" regarding his intelligence on the enemy strength figures: McChristian had been sent Stateside.

After enduring all that Westmoreland, Bunker, and Sidle had been saying publicly in the past month, for Adams there was relief in finally seeing his side of the story in print. Following Hamilton's scoop, Hedrick Smith wrote the next installment.

Smith's article appeared on the front page of the *New York Times*, December 20. "Government officials," Smith led off, "say privately that they now estimate enemy military and political manpower in South Vietnam at 418,000 to 483,000, much higher than the figure of less than 300,000 reported in 1966." Smith quoted an unnamed source as saying, "In terms of destroying the enemy's structure of power, we are farther away from our goal than we thought we were last year" and "the more we find out, the worse it looks." Smith displayed a remarkable knowledge of recent developments regarding how U.S. intelligence was treating the Viet Cong order of battle, developments that were supposedly secret. Smith informed his readers that "the Government changed its method of keeping score in Vietnam this fall and the figures for 1967 cited by General Westmoreland are not strictly comparable to those used in 1966." He went on to describe how the exclusion of the infrastructure and self-defense militia had led to lower estimates, but that in reality "the enemy organization is — and has long been — numerically much more formidable than Washington previously reckoned."

General Davidson and Colonel Graham were outraged at the disclosures. Komer cabled Langley and complained about the leaks, but the Johnson administration, whose "success offensive" continued unabated, was unfazed. This massive public relations effort, planned by the White House over the summer of 1967 and culminating in Westmoreland's November visit to Washington, had made a notable and positive impact on the home front. As the year ended seven out of every ten Americans approved of Westmoreland's military leadership in Vietnam, and for the first time in months Johnson's positive poll ratings eclipsed his negatives. Americans were sold on the official version of the war.

As 1967 came to a close the order of battle controversy slipped from public view. The major news story related to the war was Robert S. McNamara's unexpected resignation. For seven years as secretary of defense, McNamara had overseen the U.S. escalation in Vietnam, but privately he had lost hope in the cause and had come to distrust the U.S. military and what they were telling him. "I didn't believe we had reached the crossover point," McNamara, many years later, said — "I didn't believe the strength would decline."[48]

8

A LUGUBRIOUS IRONY

One legacy of the September order of battle ruckus was a hardening of lines between CIA and MACV working-level types in Saigon. After the summit J-2 staffers treated their local CIA counterparts as if they were foreign agents, and agency personnel resented both this and what they felt was the military's continued foolery with the numbers.

Isolated from the order of battle issue in Saigon were Robert Layton and his CIA station colleagues James Ogle and Joe Hovey. In late 1967 the three were going over newly captured enemy documents when they noticed something out of the ordinary. "To our reading," recalled Layton, "the tone was different. It was a tone of, *We are approaching a momentous turning point in the war, we are approaching something decisive; it's going to be larger, it's going to be bigger, and it's going to involve the cities.*" Joseph Hovey also remembered, "Up until now the enemy had been doing this and saying that. Now everything is shifting gear. They're talking in a whole different vein."[1]

Interrogation reports as well as clandestine intelligence coming into the station were indicative of the same thing, and warnings duly went out from the CIA station to Washington, D.C. One of them reached the White House. There Walt Rostow took notice, and he contacted the U.S. embassy in Saigon. What were these dark forebodings, Rostow wanted to know, and what did they portend for the war? In a rushed response Layton, Ogle, and Hovey spent their Thanksgiving Day writing a short summation of the intelligence data. The following morning they submitted it to the U.S. embassy.

For the next two weeks Layton, Ogle, and Hovey continued on the case. Eventually they worked up a full-blown political and military analysis. They decided, unasked, to submit something to Washington and to ensure notice they sent it through both State Department and CIA channels. A secret cable was readied, which read in part, "Recent captured documents indicate that the enemy believes the situation is favorable to the VC/NVN," and because of this the enemy were planning a "1967/68 Winter–Spring Campaign" and were "placing heavy emphasis on its historical significance and decisive nature" that will in all "likelihood determine the future of the war."

The analytical "thinkpiece" arrived in Washington on December 8. There, Layton said, "it sort of flew in the face of the *We've turned the corner* thesis." The cable drew no reply of any kind. Undeterred, the three men continued to forward "smaller snippets of analysis" Stateside, but the Thanksgiving summary and the December 8 analytical paper were the two seminal ones cabled to Washington. Meanwhile in Saigon, Layton recalled, "MACV thought we were full of bologna. They didn't take it seriously, and they didn't think our work would have any effect — and they were right."

At Langley the second paper was read at SAVA, and Carver ordered his deputy George Allen to write a covering memo to dispute its conclusions. Allen's covering memo stated that the CIA Saigon station was well off the mark, that the analysts there couldn't see the forest for the trees, and that intelligence available to Langley and not to Saigon contradicted the paper's central premise of an imminent threat to South Vietnam's cities. "I realize now that we should have gone to Saigon and asked those guys how they came to that conclusion," Allen would later say. "We should have worked it out. The reason we didn't was that we were just frustrated with the whole thing. We had just concluded the MACV OB meeting in September and we just didn't do it." Instead of working it out, Layton explained of his paper, SAVA "pissed all over it."[2]

New Year's 1968 came and went. Rumblings that the Viet Cong were indeed up to no good, however, were by this time being heard by others in the U.S. intelligence community. Major Don Blascak was at SAVA, and he and the rest of the staff "knew that all kinds of shit was about to happen, but nobody was brave enough to say what." Then at about four o'clock in the afternoon of January 31, Carver was giving Undersecretary of State Nicholas Katzenbach and Deputy Assistant of State Philip Habib a tour of the VASRAC facility when a "flash" newswire arrived down the pneumatic tube. Carver had just finished explaining to the two State

Department officials that the ongoing Tet holidays in South Vietnam were a period of potential trouble.[3]

"This is what I mean, gentlemen," Carver said while passing the teletype to his visitors. "SAIGON (AP)" the item read. "Suicide squad of guerrilla commandos infiltrated the capital and at least three are reported to have entered the grounds of the new U.S. embassy near the heart of the city."[4]

"This cannot be!" Habib yelled.

Habib's words were echoed throughout Washington. At the NSA alarms were going off; at the State Department there was chaos. Over in the Pentagon's National Military Command Center a special gray phone was ringing off its hook as word came in that Ambassador Ellsworth Bunker was locked in the embassy code room and needed rescue.[5]

At SAVA, Carver called off the tour and rushed up to the seventh floor. An hour later he came down with CIA Director Richard Helms. Helms wanted to know how the situation at the embassy was, and Blascak replied that they had not heard.

"Get me the duty officer at the American embassy in Saigon!" Helms barked.

Blascak immediately worked the lines, reaching the White House switchboard, then the Manila switchboard, and finally the Saigon switchboard. Saigon inquired what number at the embassy was wanted and Blascak asked for any number, so he was given the line for the reception desk. It was picked up by a marine guard; with him was a CIA case officer — not the CIA duty officer, but he would do. The phone at SAVA was handed to Helms.

"Whom am I talking to, son?" Helms asked, and when he got the name of his CIA man on the scene Helms inquired, "How's it going there?"

"Well sir we can't really see much, we're under a table in the main lobby."

"Well, you're doing a great job there, keep it up."

Helms ended the call and immediately phoned the White House with the news. "I've talked to them on the ground," Helms said, "and they assured me that everything is under control."

Everything was *not* under control. Viet Cong sappers had blasted their way into the American embassy, where they would remain for more than six hours, and at Tan Son Nhut the MACV was threatened by three battalions from the Viet Cong Ninth Division. The Independence Palace and the South Vietnamese military headquarters were meanwhile under attack, and three Viet Cong main force divisions were encircling the city. Nor was the onslaught confined to Saigon. Almost every provincial and district capital in South Vietnam was enduring a fierce Viet Cong assault, and practically all parts of the country were aflame. Viet Cong mortars and rockets replaced Tet fireworks in Hué, Hoi An, Phan Thiet, Dalat, Xuan Loc, and scores of other places, and a major set-piece battle, akin to Dien Bien Phu, was in the offing around the U.S. Marines dug in at Khe Sanh near the Laotian border.

Afterward William C. Westmoreland and Phillip Davidson would insist that they had advance knowledge of the attack all along, and Daniel Graham would echo this in the years to come, but the whereabouts of all three in the wee hours of the thirty-first makes this claim suspect. Westmoreland was at his villa on Tran Quy Cap Street in the middle of Saigon, Davidson was also at his residence in the city and had to defend his house with orderlies and housemates, and Graham was fast asleep at his downtown bachelor's quarters and was, when the attack hit, forced to form a scratch platoon of field-rank officers to protect the premises.[6]

On the thirty-first SAVA was a beehive of activity as attempts were made to keep up with the massiveness of the enemy offensive. Details, even twenty-four hours after the initial assaults, were hard to come by, but it was clear that the Viet Cong were throwing everything and everybody they had into the harmonized attacks. The entire Viet Cong political-military apparatus had come out of hiding and was rising up against the Americans and the Saigon regime. Sam Adams must have believed that all those Viet Cong so recently written off the official strength figures were getting their revenge, and doing so with a fury. He watched the action at VASRAC and noted that the maps were being pricked with colored pins signifying Viet Cong units coming out of nowhere. The magnitude of the offensive, the enormity of the undertaking, the hundreds of thousands of Viet Cong combatants and supporters involved — all put the lie to MACV intelligence assertions.

Adams observed the scurrying around VASRAC and thought about these things, but then he broke off and concentrated on the work at hand.

In a bizarre juxtaposition, on this the most momentous day of the Vietnam War so far, Adams could be seen amid the bustle pushing a shopping cart filled high with his captured documents. He was quietly moving down a floor to the Office of Economic Research, his resignation from SAVA coming into effect the next day.

*

News of the Tet Offensive reverberated across the United States. It was a shocking escalation of the war and Americans, most recently the beneficiaries of the "success offensive," were little prepared for the riveting images of violence coming into their living rooms from Vietnam. The Viet Cong were supposed to be hiding out in the jungle hinterlands awaiting destruction by General Westmoreland's forces, but instead the Communists were openly invading the city of Hué, besieging parts of Saigon, and turning Khe Sanh into a mud-splattered battlefield reminiscent of 1944 Europe. The war footage on the evening news was raw and some of it, such as that showing Saigon's police chief summarily executing a Viet Cong suspect, deeply troubling.

Many Americans now questioned what their country was doing in Vietnam and, more importantly, wondered how it could get out: Opinion polls showed a sharp drop in support for the conflict. In Congress war skepticism reached new heights, and a chord of concern about U.S. intelligence was struck. Only a week into the attack, February 8, Senator Robert F. Kennedy of New York remarked, "Our enemy, savagely striking at will across all of South Vietnam, has finally shattered the mask of official illusion with which we have concealed our true circumstances even from ourselves." Kennedy noted critically that U.S. forces were "unable to secure even a single city from the attacks of an enemy whose total strength is about 250,000. Now our intelligence chief tells us that of 60,000 men thrown into the attacks on the cities, 20,000 have been killed. If only two men have been seriously wounded for every one dead — a very conservative estimate — the entire enemy force has long been put out of action. Who, then, is doing the fighting?"[7]

But most ominous for President Johnson, and for war hawks inside and outside his administration, was that the press — which had once hailed the Vietnam crusade — was now leery of the venture. The *Wall Street Journal* of February 23 editorialized that "the American people should be getting ready to accept, if they haven't already, the prospect that the whole Vietnam effort may be doomed, that it may be falling apart beneath our feet." Four days later grandfatherly Walter Cronkite warned solemnly in a television special that "It now seems more certain than ever that the bloody experience of Vietnam is to end in a stalemate."

*

The offensive gave General Davidson the opportunity to sneak in even more reductions to the enemy order of battle, and meanwhile General Westmoreland publicly proclaimed Viet Cong losses — held at the time to be twenty-four thousand — a "disaster" for the enemy.

In early February, Adams conferred with his old nemesis George Carver more than a dozen times, insisting that the CIA once and for all make a clean break from MACV's fabricated estimates. By way of argument, Adams pointed out that during Tet the urban attacks were carried out by the very same SD/SSD, assault youth, and other so-called nonmilitary forces that had been banned by the Saigon agreement. But in the wake of the Tet debacle the politically astute Carver needed no advice from Adams. He now wanted to put as much distance as possible between himself and his September agreement with Westmoreland. On February 15 Carver readied Helms for the about-face by telling the CIA director that MACV's intelligence process has "unfortunately been designed more to maximize the appearance of progress than to give a complete picture of total enemy resources" and therefore suffered from "a built-in bias for a persistent underestimate of enemy capabilities."[8]

Helms remained aloof for the time being, but Carver and the other agency lieutenants scrambled to assert their independence from U.S. military intelligence. Cables were sent from Langley to the CIA Saigon station voicing headquarters' newfound concerns that enemy troops had been dropped from the official order of battle. A DDI memorandum of February 21 concluded that, contrary to MACV assertions, Viet Cong/NVA regular forces emerged from Tet largely unscathed because the assault youth, SD/SSD, and other "irregular" forces had borne the brunt of the fighting. And at the OER Adams, back in favor yet again, was approved to do a whole slew of new CIA studies on the Viet Cong. By mid-

March, Helms himself had come around and was perfectly comfortable using the agency's resurrected numbers of five to six hundred thousand when describing enemy strength.[9]

*

On a very cold day that winter Adams and his wife and child moved into their new place a few miles outside Waterford, Virginia. Sam and Eleanor had been eyeing the land for more than a year. It was 214 acres of hilly fields bordered by a dense, vine-entangled wood of oak, ash, and hickory. From the highest point of the property Maryland could be seen to the north, with West Virginia and the Blue Ridge Mountains visible to the west.

The place cost the Adamses five hundred dollars an acre — money Eleanor had recently received from her grandmother's estate — and with the land came a stone house built in the Pennsylvania Style by its original Quaker owners. The deed was dated 1757, the most recent renovations done to the structure were completed in 1810, and currently living in the house (it had been used infrequently in latter years as a weekend retreat) were black snakes. The reptiles were evicted, and Sam and Eleanor got down to the business of making a home for themselves.

As a result of the move to Leesburg, the morning commute into Langley was now considerably longer. During the drive, however, Adams could look forward to the day's work ahead. His new boss, Ronald L. Smith, was an expert in Viet Cong manpower issues and had sat through the SNIE 14.3-67 meetings at Langley with no illusions regarding MACV's manipulations with the numbers. "The entire process," Smith stated, "was ridiculous from an intelligence standpoint." Meanwhile Adams's old boss, George Carver, was busy trying to make the White House understand the direness of the Vietnam situation. On the seventh floor Helms was by this time openly dismissive of whatever numbers were coming out of MACV.[10]

While the agency had unshackled itself from the U.S. military's Vietnam intelligence, President Johnson and his White House advisers were just then realizing the folly of having relied on that same intelligence for so long. It was clear to them that the military was providing a current picture of the NVA and Viet Cong that was both contradictory to itself and at variance with what it had been before.

A week into the attacks, February 7, General Wheeler informed Johnson and the National Security Council that enemy losses were an astounding twenty-five thousand, but the next day the Joint Chiefs of Staff told Johnson that Westmoreland needed more troops to offset an increase in enemy strength of fifteen thousand troops. On February 10 Secretary of State Dean Rusk remarked to Johnson, "I can't find out where they say those 15,000 extra enemy troops came from. They say that these battalions came in between December and January." A day later Walt Rostow, having researched the order of battle numbers for December and January, confirmed to Johnson that there had been "no significant change" to enemy strength. Yet on the heels of this confirmation came a startling request from General Wheeler that would appear to dispute an unchanging enemy order of battle. Wheeler prepared Johnson for the shock by first noting that the enemy "still has sizeable uncommitted reserves"; then, on February 27, he dropped the bombshell: Westmoreland in Vietnam was in desperate need of 206,000 more men.

This sent the White House reeling. Such a major jump in U.S. troop numbers was militarily and economically unfeasible; politically it would be an outright admission that the war was going terribly. Johnson permitted a trusted few to mull over the secret request. On March 4 the task force reported back to the president and one of its members — McNamara's replacement, Secretary of Defense Clark Clifford — turned to his old friend Lyndon B. Johnson and said, ruefully, "For a while, we thought and had the feeling that we understood the strength of the Viet Cong and the North Vietnamese. You will remember the rather optimistic reports of General Westmoreland and Ambassador Bunker last year. Frankly, it came as a shock that the Vietcong–North Vietnamese had the strength of force and skill to mount the Tet offensive — as they did."[11]

The reason for Clifford's shock was revealed two weeks later on the front page of the *New York Times* ("U.S. Undervalued Enemy's Strength Before Offensive: C.I.A. Reports Forces Were Significantly Larger Than Intelligence Estimates"). Adams had given Neil Sheehan the scoop, and Sheehan now wrote all about the military's lower numbers and the CIA's higher numbers in 1967, about the subsequent deletion of the VCI and the SD and SSD from the order of battle, and about the compromised intelligence contained in the special national intelligence estimate. Sheehan also reported, based on his "well-placed informants," that the NVA and the Viet Cong had in the wake of Tet "probably replaced the majority of their casualties with recruits."[12]

In Saigon, General William C. Westmoreland reacted with dismay to the *New York Times* story. He sent a cable to Washington expressing his deep concern that the article contradicted the 297,000 estimate his command had released to the press, and that there was a "leak" somewhere. After sending the cable, though, Westmoreland thought about how his concerns might be interpreted and sent a follow-on message saying that he wished to with-draw the cable. "Have destroyed all file copies in this headquarters," Westmoreland informed Washington, "and request that you do likewise."[13]

Whatever concerns Westmoreland had about Sheehan's article, however, were far eclipsed by another Sheehan piece. This one, co-authored with Hedrick Smith, exposed Westmoreland's request for 206,000 more troops. A source at the Pentagon told Smith and Sheehan, "We know now that we constantly underestimated the enemy's capacity and his will to fight and overestimated our progress. We know now that all we thought we had constructed was built on sand."

Revealed to the public, Westmoreland's request for more U.S. soldiers became a devastating development for the White House as the president's poll numbers dropped precipitously. Americans would not tolerate the continuing investment of lives and limbs in a war that had, apparently, no end in sight.

The Johnson presidency was now beginning to unravel.

On March 13 Johnson only narrowly won the New Hampshire primary after a challenge by peace candidate Senator Eugene McCarthy.

On March 23 Johnson announced in a press conference that Westmoreland — in a tacit admission that the general's "big unit war" was a failure — would be pulled from Vietnam to become the army chief of staff in Washington.

On March 25 George Carver, under Helms's direction, gave a grim and sobering assessment of the Vietnam situation to Johnson's informal group of war advisers, the elder statesmen known as the "wise men." The wise men were stunned at Carver's unrelentingly gloomy CIA assessment on all aspects of the war, and one of them, Arthur Goldberg, turned on the military representative present, General William E. DePuy, and demanded to know how in the aftermath of Tet he could still claim enemy strength was just 230,000: "General, I am not a great mathematician, but with 80,000 killed and with a wounded ratio of three to one, or 240,000, for a total of 320,00, who the hell are we fighting?"[14]

On March 27 Carver and Helms went over to the White House where they were met by President Johnson, Vice President Hubert Humphrey, NSC adviser Walt Rostow, Generals DePuy, Wheeler, and Abrams, and Johnson's son-in-law, Patrick Nugent (apparently present to witness a bit of history).

Carver began the CIA briefing, which would last an hour and fifteen minutes. Johnson appeared annoyed and agitated throughout and, when not getting up to take phone calls, interrupted Carver constantly. Carver was delivering two pieces of very bad news. One was that CORDS, the pacification program under Robert Komer, was a failure: In only four of South Vietnam's forty-four provinces could it be said pacification was succeeding. The other piece of very bad news was that official estimates of the enemy strength were off by a factor of more than two. There were presently, Carver told the president, six hundred thousand NVA and Viet Cong active in South Vietnam. The crossover point had never been reached.

Johnson repeatedly asked Carver "Are you finished yet?" and when Carver was finally done the president jumped up and stalked out of the room — before returning immediately. Carver said that the president then "pumped my hand, thanked me warmly for my presentation, and made some very flattering and gracious remarks about my overall work and contribution to the national effort."[15]

On March 31, four days later, Johnson told a shocked nation that he would not seek reelection. He would instead, he said, devote all his energies to finding peace in Vietnam.

*

The MACV J-2 staff survived the Tet Offensive unscathed, although the building was practically defenseless until a company from the U.S. Army Twenty-fifth Infantry Division finally showed up late in the day February 1.

Throughout the rest of South Vietnam, meanwhile, U.S. forces were beginning the difficult task of extinguishing the uprisings. The Vietnamese
Communist offensive subsided in March, flared anew for a while, and then
died out entirely by June.[16]

By the time it was all over Tet had become an unmitigated battlefield
defeat for the Vietnamese Communists. They suffered as many as forty-
five thousand killed while never seriously threatening either American
forces in South Vietnam or the authority of the Saigon government. For
the Communists, the hoped-for popular uprisings in the cities never mate-
rialized, and in the countryside the Viet Cong political-military infrastructure was decimated. The village, hamlet, and secret guerrillas, the
self-defense and secret self-defense forces, the people in the infrastructure,
the assault youth, and the other known and unknown parts of the Viet
Cong political-military system were virtually blown away.[17]

On the American side success also brought problems. Just three days into
the offensive, and with the enemy death toll already having surpassed the
ten-thousand mark, General Davidson and his intelligence officers were
faced with a serious dilemma: how to account for all the Viet Cong dead.
These casualties were fast gaining on January's order of battle numbers,
numbers that Davidson — inconveniently in retrospect — had put at their
lowest levels since 1966. And equaling vexing for Davidson, just what force
categories were the cadavers to be assigned?[18]

The lower-level enemy and "nonmilitary" elements had, of course, been
earlier banished from the order of battle, which meant that room would
have to be made for the freshly killed Viet Cong somewhere else. It was
decided to put them in with the guerrillas. Fortuitously for MACV, U.S.
military intelligence offices had earlier constructed a parabolic curve to
account for the "growth" of Viet Cong guerrilla forces in late 1967. This
statistical exercise was necessitated when MACV's optimism got ahead of
itself and the order of battle numbers for Viet Cong guerrillas dropped to
zero. The guerrillas were consequently re-formed by the U.S. military and
the guerrilla ranks reconstituted, coincidentally, in time for Tet. The tens
of thousands Viet Cong dead who really belonged to the SD, SSD, assault
youth, or political cadre could as a result be turned into, for MACV book-
keeping purposes, expired guerrillas.

Back in Washington the director of the DIA, General Joseph Carroll, had like others at the Pentagon already been feeling "some queasiness" over the MACV estimates and was now after the Tet calamity feeling decidedly ill. The general dispatched his subordinate, Major J. Barrie Williams, across the Pacific to come up with legitimate figures, once and for all, on enemy strength. "The numbers," Williams said of the pre-offensive estimates and the post-offensive facts, "were just not jiving." Williams made the trip on Carroll's behalf but reasoning with MACV, he noted, was a fruitless endeavor: "Probably the most frustrating thing you have ever been into."

At MACV headquarters Williams was introduced to the Intelligence Data Handling System and the "spring methodology." This methodology ensured that any new intelligence figures entered into IDHS on the enemy would, via an algorithm, "spring" back to the old, pre-Tet, MACV order of battle numbers. The evidentiary base was free to move in any direction, up or down, yet the official estimates would remain pat. A young officer on the J-2 staff, Bernard Gattozzi, had written the code to make this possible. Williams knew that the trick was nothing but "a little computer game," but he gave Gattozzi his due. "Bright man," said Williams of Gattozzi. "You get Bernie against the wall and he would just kind of smile at you because he knew what the hell was going on." Williams reported back to General Carroll in Washington and Carroll wanted to know if MACV would yield on its enemy strength figures. "Sir," Williams replied, "I can't get them to come off a dime."

The President's Foreign Intelligence Advisory Board ordered that a Tet postmortem group fly out to Vietnam in mid-March. The PFIAB team's task was to determine if there had been an intelligence failure before the offensive. The high-level group was handpicked by its leader, Richard Lehman of the CIA, and consisted of top intelligence and military professionals as well as some more junior officers such as Major Williams. The team interviewed all of the principal South Vietnamese and American players in Saigon, visited every corps area, and generally perused South Vietnam up and down for evidence of an intelligence failure before returning to Washington to write a twenty-two-page report for the PFIAB on how the United States had failed to predict the offensive. But the paper first went to General Duke Spivey of the Joint Chiefs of Staff, who sent it right back for major revisions. "Gentlemen," Spivey had to remind the PFIAB group, "U.S. forces are never surprised. U.S. forces are never ambushed."[19]

*

With enemy forces still entrenched in the city of Hué and the Tet Offensive having not yet run itself out, George Allen was sent by the agency on a fact-finding mission to determine the offensive's long-term political and military impact. All three major urban areas of South Vietnam — Saigon, Hué, and Da Nang — as well as thirty-six provincial capitals, sixty-four district towns, most major air- and military bases, and hundreds of villages and hamlets had all endured debilitating enemy attack, Allen knew, and he put the figure of enemy attackers at four hundred thousand.

Allen toured South Vietnam for two weeks and talked to many officials. In Saigon he met with Ambassador Bunker and with the MACV J-2 staff. Allen listened as Vice President Ky spoke of President Thieu's incompetence, and the next day Allen listened as President Thieu spoke of Vice President Ky's treachery. During his travels in the countryside Allen saw that ARVN had abandoned wide areas to the opposition and realized that the average South Vietnamese, despite the presence of more than one million allied forces in her country, felt completely defenseless. South Vietnam after Tet was a demoralized society, and Allen was convinced that, despite taking heavy losses, in the background still lurked the Vietnamese Communists, regrouping and readying themselves for further large-scale action.[20]

*

Colonel Gains B. Hawkins, his MACV tour finally ended, was again stationed at Fort Holabird, Maryland, when he paid Adams a visit at Langley in early January, only weeks before the Tet Offensive. The two analysts greeted each other warmly and talked order of battle. There was some discussion of the past, and Hawkins confessed to Adams that July, August, and September of the previous year had been "the worst three months of my life," but otherwise the colonel maintained silence on all he had been through. Bound by the Uniform Code of Military Justice and by responsibilities to a wife and four children — youngest age seven — Hawkins was not at liberty to jeopardize his career or his pension to disclose what he had seen and done at MACV. Adams understood and did not press his friend for details. In late February, Hawkins — perhaps in return for this favor — invited Adams down to Fort Holabird to lecture on the Viet Cong. Afterward the colonel gave a lunch in the CIA man's honor in which he paid Adams the highest possible compliment. "Sam Adams," Hawkins toasted, is "the best OB man in the business."[21]

Hawkins was now counting down the months until retirement, but the opportunity for a star was literally within reach. The position offered to him was an important one: chief of order of battle estimates for Vietnam. The posting would be at the Pentagon; Colonel Hawkins would become, if he accepted, General Hawkins. "This was a moment of supreme irony," he said. "How could I sit at a desk in the DIA and challenge the very figures I had helped invent at MACV? Or how could I continue to defend intelligence estimates which I did not believe?" Hawkins declined the job, and the promotion that came with it, and looked forward to returning to his native Mississippi.

During the summer of 1970 Hawkins, due to leave the army that November, was for one last time under the command of his admired general, Joseph McChristian. Hawkins was working on a project for the general, a project that necessitated access to filing cabinets in the labyrinthine basements of the Pentagon. It was there that Hawkins sat in a little straight-backed chair with sheaves of old Viet Cong documents in his hands. The documents told of a defeated enemy organization, an organization that during Tet had been shattered, its most dependable leaders killed, its guerrilla and local forces decimated, its administrative services in disarray, and its hierarchy engaged in mutual recriminations. Hawkins "read on and on with mouth agape." He realized, "Our armed forces had literally kicked the shit out of the Communists during Tet. The term is overworked, but they were in a state of emotional trauma. They were ready for mopping up."

Hawkins put the documents down and remembered how the news media in 1968 had credited the Viet Cong with having achieved a momentous psychological victory over U.S. forces. "How could this have been?" he wondered. "The answer came easily. The answer was bitter. It gave off a mournful, melancholy taste." Hawkins sighed. "MACV had shot itself in the foot with a blunderbuss. MACV couldn't take it back after Tet and say with any degree of credibility that MACV had inflicted a calamitous defeat on a large and powerful enemy."

Hawkins leaned back in his chair. "It was a case of lugubrious irony," he said.

"*Lugubrious* irony?"

The colonel answered his own question.

"Find a better word if you can."[22]

9

THE ADAMS PHENOMENON

By the spring of 1968 CIA director Richard Helms realized the numbers debate with MACV would have to be reopened. The figures he'd acceded to the previous fall had proven, of course, to be unsupportable in light of the Tet Offensive. On the sixth floor at Langley, George Carver informed Adams. "I went 'whoo-ee!' and dashed downstairs and wrote a cable to Saigon," Adams recalled. "And then all hell broke loose."[1]

The inevitable conference got under way at CIA headquarters on April 10, 1968. Adams was not invited to attend but except for his absence the scene in the conference room at Langley was similar to past order of battle affairs, with the usual CIA, DIA, CINCPAC, and MACV crowd present.

Helms appeared to make a brief opening appeal. "We've got to be honest," he said, "we've got to be above board, we've got to put our best stuff on the table, we've got to negotiate these common needs so our best people can put this in print." Helms left and the head of the MACV delegation, Colonel Daniel Graham, stood up. "I don't care what the fuck Mr. Helms says," Graham told the conferees, "the MACV position is going to prevail."[2]

The DIA representatives at the talks were attempting to be the "honest brokers" between CIA and MACV, but to no avail. Both sides were clinging to intractable positions. "It was just a terrible, terrible situation," recalled J. Barrie Williams, who was again with the DIA group. But MACV was in no mood for compromise, and in fact now sought a larger chasm between its numbers and those of the CIA. "I can remember," Williams said, "Danny Graham just unilaterally striking strengths off of units to get within a given range."

General Phillip Davidson monitored the proceedings with concern from Saigon, but in the end he had nothing to fear. His chief of estimates, Graham, never let things slip Stateside. According to Williams, "Graham was given a mission to do, and he did it very well. I can't approve of his integrity or anything like this, but he was going to keep the numbers down, and he was rewarded for it." Soon-to-be-General Graham would henceforth enjoy rapid advancement. "One star, two stars, three stars," said Williams of Graham's subsequent promotions. "Davidson took care of his boy."

*

Snubbed from the negotiations with the military, Adams learned of the outcome secondhand. "At the end of the conference," he said, "the agency's top count of VC was just below 600,000. Among other things, we'd marched the self-defense militia back into the estimate." This hardly mollified Adams; the damage, he knew, had already been done. An agency colleague explained that "I think one of the things that really drove him — in fact he said it on a number of occasions — was he felt so sorry for the young guys who were conscripted, the people who were being killed unnecessarily because some politicians and bureaucrats tried to protect themselves and wouldn't listen to the truth. That was a major, major thing for Sam; he would talk about the body counts all the time; the U.S. casualties and the tragedy of it all." There had to be, Adams believed, accountability.

Douglas Parry was a young economist and one of Adams's new colleagues at the OER. Parry shared Adams's sense of outrage. "You realize that in most other trades," he told Adams, "these people would be in deep trouble. They lied about the OB before Tet, which caught them by complete surprise as a result, and now they're trying to think up ways to get out of it. There ought to be an investigation. Somebody should be told about this."

Parry was idealistic. "I had been a Mormon missionary in Austria," he said of his youth, "but I remember years before that, in '56, it was the Hungarian Revolution and I remember going home at night and just getting in front of the radio and hearing what was going on. I was terribly emotional over that; we had promised those people, 'If you strike for freedom we'll back you' — and we just let them get slaughtered."

As a Mormon missionary Parry went to Austria at age nineteen; at the end of his assignment he and his fellow missionaries decided to tour a little. He wrote a letter, avoiding mention of any religious affiliations, to the

University of Budapest Komsomol. The Komsomol (Communist Union of Youth) extended an invitation, and "They were great, my gosh did they put on a party for us." Out of shape from two years of sedentary missionary work, Parry and his friends struggled through a game against the University of Budapest basketball team but nevertheless managed a win. Back at their Soviet-style hotel the missionaries discovered a trapdoor under the bed. Exploration revealed a series of tunnels connecting all the rooms.

Parry returned home and continued to be intrigued by foreign affairs. This interest eventually led him to the Sino-Soviet Institute at George Washington University and then, in a roundabout way, to the CIA and in early 1967 to the OER. At the OER his first task was to determine how many Viet Cong there were in each South Vietnamese province.

"So I work out this computer program," he recalled. "I had thirty-five variables, like religion, highlands; whether the province was coastal or in the delta." Plugging this all in, "I came up with these things, wild silly ass guesses, but things started computing." Parry's computer estimates began to resemble the numbers found in the captured documents. "They were matching up. So then I thought we could put something together. I talked to Ron Smith about it, and Ron says, 'You know, there is a guy up in SAVA who is doing this, his name is Sam Adams, and go talk to him.'"

SAVA was an intimidating place. "I mean it looked like a war room. People writing on the boards, some of the rooms were dark, and I met Sam; and what a shock. He looked like an Ivy League professor of olden days. I can remember the suit he wore. It had a hole in it so what he'd done, he'd gathered the surrounding material together and then sewn over it." There was in fact more than one hole. "So he had these little pimples all over his suit."

Adams was instantly receptive to Parry, and Parry became a gatherer of information for Adams, bringing him whatever news he had managed to find on the Viet Cong numbers. "We had these documents," said Parry, "and they just didn't square with MACV's order of battle. It was a joke. I would always go and talk to Sam about it and we would look at this stuff together. He was very good, he wasn't highbrow, he wasn't egotistical, he wasn't protecting his position, he really believed in finding the truth and getting it out; and he was willing to look for it anyplace."

Adams kept Parry informed of the numbers controversy with MACV as it unfolded, letting him see copies of the classified cables that exposed the politics behind the fraudulent intelligence. "The question Sam had," Parry recalled, "was if he had a duty to do something, and he finally decided that he did." The decision came the day after Johnson announced his intentions not to run for reelection. Adams said to Parry, "Whoever the next president is, he ought to be warned what's gone on down here. This is a good time to do it."

Adams went up to the seventh floor and entered the offices of the CIA inspector general. The IG himself wasn't in, but a Douglas Andrews was free to meet with Adams. "What can I do for you this morning?" the smiling Andrews said.

"I've come to file a complaint," answered Adams. "I feel the conduct of American intelligence on Vietnam has been far less than satisfactory, and that the director and the head of the DDI might well have to be replaced. I want an inquiry started to alert the incoming president."[3]

Having taken the first step, Adams composed his thoughts carefully into a memorandum, "Re. Complaints about research on the Viet Cong." The first charge that Adams leveled in this memo was "a misuse of research manpower." The CIA, he stated, had devoted next to no resources on the Vietnamese Communist enemy in South Vietnam.

The second charge was "a misdirection of research effort." Here the complaint was that before Tet, "research on the Viet Cong political apparatus was neglected, existing research was ignored, as was primary source material from RAND interviews, POW reports, and captured documents."

The third charge was "a want of courage in advancing well-documented findings concerning Viet Cong manpower." At the CIA, Adams accused, there had been a "want of mettle" and "timidity" in defending accurate order of battle estimates. "Since 30 January 1968, the day the enemy Tet offensive began, the CIA has apparently determined to confront MACV on strength estimates," he wrote. "The show of pluck, it appears to me, came too late."

The fourth and final charge concerned "lethargy in correcting past failures." This was the most far-reaching indictment. Here Adams wrote, "History will probably record that one of the principal reasons the United

States became mired in the Vietnam War was a failure in intelligence. We did not realize what we were getting into, did not know what we were looking at when we got there, and are only now discovering the consequences of our ignorance and myopia. Certain medium- and low-level intelligence officials familiar with Vietnam warned what might happen, but their warnings were too often disregarded, or drowned in the babble of the uninformed." Adams continued, "Once the U.S. was heavily involved in Vietnam" the "lack of foresight in developing a coherent body of research on the southern enemy became inexcusable. In failing to do its homework, the research community has allowed its country, with inadequate warning, to sink deeper and deeper into the Vietnamese mire, with increasingly little hope of honorable extrication. The disservice came about because of sloth, timidity, and bad scholarship."[4]

In concluding the memo Adams asked for three things. One, that the IG thoroughly investigate the charges. Two, that copies of the memorandum be sent to the White House staff and to the President's Foreign Intelligence Advisory Board. And three, that copies be sent to Richard Helms and to Helms's deputy director of intelligence, R. Jack Smith.

On May 27 the signed complaint was given over to the IG. Adams kept one copy for himself, one he gave to Douglas Parry, and one he passed on to Neil Sheehan of the *New York Times*. Adams wanted a member of the press corps to have a duplicate lest something happen to him. To preserve the evidence that buoyed his complaints, Adams began sneaking classified materials — memos, analytical reports, cables, codes, electronic intelligence, captured documents — out of the building at the end of work each day. This he usually did by folding the papers into his *Wall Street Journal*, although occasionally he more brazenly stuffed them in his briefcase.

At work Adams endured what would become a familiar waiting game and eventually was called into the IG's office for the initiation of a formal inquiry. The IG was a man named Gordon Stewart, and he was none too friendly. Before introducing Adams to the two IG inspectors who would handle the case, Stewart warned him gravely that it "would be a mistake" to take his complaints outside the CIA.

The two inspectors took the matter seriously, interviewing Adams and, among others, George Allen and George Carver of SAVA, Paul Walsh of the OER, and R. Jack Smith of the DDI. From what the inspectors could tell Adams was not your typical troublemaker and had identified some interesting problems in regard to intelligence on Vietnam. The inspectors' work was completed August 1, and the resulting report went to Stewart.

There was more waiting before Adams was again called up to the IG's office. Stewart had read the report and was solemn. The accusations leveled against the CIA were serious, he informed Adams, and merited further consideration. Adams was told that the director, Richard Helms, was aware of the charges and that Helms had personally appointed a special review board to look into them. The select panel would be made up of Admiral Rufus Taylor, Lawrence Houston, and John Bross. These were all solid agency men: Taylor was the CIA deputy director and Helms's number two man at Langley; Houston was the CIA general counsel and had been since the day the agency was founded in 1947; and Bross was an OSS veteran, senior CIA officer, and one of Helms's closest advisers. Adams was asked to cooperate with the board; he replied, "Of course I would."

The weeks passed, and there was no sign of life from the special review board. Adams and his family took their annual vacation in the Adirondacks, and upon return to work in mid-September, Adams was disheartened to learn that Bross, a canoe enthusiast, was on "holiday exploring the lakes" — and not expected back for a month and a half. If anything was going to happen with the board it obviously, Adams knew, wouldn't occur while a third of its membership was busy paddling around somewhere.[5]

Adams became agitated and pushed to have his concerns aired outside the agency. He went to the CIA general counsel's office for legal advice and spoke with a Mr. Ueberhorst. "Would I be breaking any laws," Adams asked Ueberhorst, "if I took my memo and carried it over to the White House myself?" Ueberhorst proffered no legal opinion but did obliquely warn against doing this.[6]

A specific threat came a week later when Adams was called into the office of Colonel Lawrence White, the CIA executive director and the number three man at the agency after Helms and Taylor. White warmed up while Adams, writing rapidly and nodding politely, transcribed his words verbatim onto a yellow legal pad. "I would like you to know," White began, "that if you take your complaint independently to the White House

— and even if you obtain the results you desire by doing so — your useful-
ness to the agency will thereafter be nil. Let me repeat that: Nil." Then
White got serious. Leaning over his desk he told Adams, "If you continue
on this course you will never hold another job anywhere in the world for
the rest of your life and we can — that's something we can do, the agency
can do this." Adams had all thirty-five minutes' worth of threats typed up
by the South Vietnam Branch secretary as a memo of conversation. Adams
attempted to give White a copy the following week, but the colonel,
Adams explained, "backed away from it, unfortunately tripping on the
carpet as he did so. 'I'm too busy to read that sort of thing,' he said."[7]

White, however, was not the only one who could make threats. Adams
told White it was essential that "the incoming administration receives
timely warning of the CIA's failures over the past two years." Concerning
these failures, Adams told White, "I think they are far too big to be dealt
with by the people who made them. Therefore, please tell the director that
I intend to take action no later than the end of the month."[8]

November came and Adams uncharacteristically voted Republican. He
believed that Hubert Humphrey would only continue Johnson's failed
Vietnam policies and that a fresh face in the White House was needed.
Adams was plotting ways to get a copy of his memorandum of complaints
into the hands of President-elect Richard Nixon when, figuratively
speaking, the agency blinked. It was November 8, three days after the
voting, and an audience with Helms was unexpectedly granted.

*

The morning meeting between the OER South Vietnam Branch analyst
and the CIA director got under way at ten twenty-five A.M. Richard Helms
had heard of the "Adams phenomenon" then sweeping the agency and also
of Adams's reputation as a scribe of sorts. "I'd rather you didn't take notes,"
Helms requested as Adams sat down and readied blue ballpoint pen and
yellow legal pad. "Now tell me," Helms went on when the danger of tran-
scription had passed, "what's the matter? Are your supervisors treating you
unfairly? Are they being too slow on promotions?"[9]

"No," Adams answered, his problem was that he, Helms, had "caved in
on the numbers right before Tet." Adams, as he recounted his end of the
conversation, "enlarged on this theme for about ten minutes," while Helms

"listened without expression, and when I was done he asked what I would have him do — take on the whole military?"

Adams replied that, yes, "Under the circumstances, that was the only thing he could have done; the military's numbers were faked."[10]

Helms realized that Adams was accusing him of being a traitor to his own agency. He was not amused. Adams was, Helms recalled, an "opinionated" young man "many years junior than me" who "thought he was smarter than anyone else." Helms knew full well that "every single analyst" at Langley had agreed with Adams on the Viet Cong numbers; Helms was painfully aware that the MACV compromise "wasn't a happy episode for the CIA" and that "I participated in it and I shoulder some of the responsibility." Yet Helms was also acutely aware at the time that Langley had but a finite amount of influence with President Johnson, and that this influence could easily dwindle away to nothing if not used sparingly. For this reason he was hardly going to fight for Pyrrhic victories of the type Adams demanded.[11]

"You don't know what it's like in this town. I could have told the White House there were a million more Vietcong out there, and it wouldn't have made the slightest difference in our policy," Helms said.

"We aren't the ones to decide about policy," Adams retorted. "Our job is to send up the right numbers and let them worry." He then requested that he be allowed to tell the policy makers that they had been duped by faulty intelligence.[12]

Okay, Helms said, and just whom did Adams wish to see?

Adams answered that he wanted to see the "appropriate members of the White House staff and the President's Foreign Intelligence Advisory Board" but "didn't know who the appropriate members were."

Helms asked if "General Maxwell Taylor and Walt Rostow would be all right?"

This was, replied Adams, "not only acceptable, it was generous."[13]

Helms informed Adams that he would arrange the appointments. With the interview concluded the CIA director got up from behind his desk and accompanied the analyst to the door. "At the last moment," Adams said, "I remembered a question. By extraordinary coincidence, Helms had spent the previous weekend in Alabama, visiting one of my wife's uncles, Earl

McGowin. He'd even slept at Edgefield, a large house with white pillars where Eleanor had grown up." (Helms, with his CIA bodyguards and secret radiophone, had made quite an impression on the McGowin clan.)

Adams just couldn't resist, and so he asked: "By the way, how's Uncle Earl?"

"Uncle Earl?"

"Earl McGowin, sir, he's Eleanor's uncle."

The association between Adams and McGowin was quickly established. Helms, Adams said, "chuckled" and then "started laughing so hard he had to lean against the wall for support. This lasted maybe fifteen seconds. When he recovered, he said: 'Excuse me for laughing. It struck me as funny. Uncle Earl's just fine.'"[14]

It was five minutes past eleven A.M. when Adams left, and Helms was no longer in a lighthearted mood. He was, in fact, incredulous. "That someone in Sam's junior position," Helms stated, "should expect that I should bother the White House to give him a hearing about his concerns — well, you can draw your own conclusions."[15]

*

The Helms interview spurred Adams to work the complaint full time. He did the rounds on the seventh floor, now having access to all the top command, including R. Jack Smith. Smith was named in Adams's complaint as one of those CIA administrators in need of firing. "Sam came to interview me," Smith recalled, "and he brought along a yellow pad and wrote down all my answers and so on, which was a little surprising. I was the deputy director of intelligence, he was an employee — of not a very high rank certainly — and no one else ever did that sort of thing. It was a little out of line."

Smith said that Adams "wanted to know why he wasn't getting fuller attention, why his view wasn't prevailing, and he wanted my approval to take the case outside of the agency." Smith gave a version of the Helms argument that back in '67: "Our job was to provide a number which the administration could use." Adams, though, didn't buy this. "There was no question when you talked to Sam," Smith recalled, "that here was a man who had a very rigid concept of his rightness, and very inflexible. There was no give-and-take. He had found the truth and he wanted to carry it for-

Sam Adams (*front row left*) and Roger Stone (*front row right*). Garrison, New York, 1944.

Harvard.

Harvard Studio
Boston

Shouldering Laura (*left*) and Sue (*right*): The Johnsons virtually adopted the Harvard man. South Hampton, New York, October 1955.

Lieutenant (jg) S. A. Adams.

"The Greasy George."

Eleanor and Sam (left hand hiding an ink stain). Douglaston, New York, August 15, 1962.

The self-defense and militia and guerrilla forces are the forces of all our people.
— Ho Chi Minh

Man and a boy prepare a spiked bamboo weapon. South Vietnam, 1965.

Women erect obstacles to prevent U.S. helicopters from landing. South Vietnam, 1965.

Villagers in a trench carry grenades. South Vietnam, 1966.

Fourteen-year-old girl teaches her younger brother to fire an AK-47. Thua Thien Province, South Vietnam, 1968.

A young Douglas Parry during his Mormon mission in Austria, 1962–1963. Afterward, Parry and his colleagues would be honored guests of the Komsomol (Communist Union of Youth) in Budapest, Hungary.

Mary "Mollie" Kreimer in the late 1960s. Kreimer began her intelligence career armed only with a French–Vietnamese dictionary.

Howard Beaubien and his jeep. Saigon, South Vietnam, June 1967.

A vacationing Robert Klein, circa 1970. For Klein, joining the CIA was "very much a case of running from rather than running to."

Danny Graham told Congress that Adams had "a mental problem."

MG PHILLIP B. DAVIDSON, JR.
Jun 69 · Mar 71

Davidson despised Adams and his "voodoo intelligence."

Don Blascak as S-2 for
U.S. Army Special
Forces, Detachment C-4.
South Vietnam, 1965.

J. Barrie Williams while commanding the
Fourth Battalion (Provisional) 525 Military
Intelligence Group, IV Corps. South Vietnam,
1970 or 1971. (Insert: IV Corps crest.)

Adams respected "good old Gains Hawkins" (*right*) perhaps more than anyone else in the world.

Five hundred dollars an acre: The Adams farm outside Leesburg, Virginia. The title was dated 1757, but the house was renovated in 1810.

Relaxing on his farm. At work, Adams had come into
his own as a CIA rebel, July 1969.

The Pentagon Papers: Jean Kraemer (*left*) and Eleanor Adams (*right*) see Adams off
to Los Angeles to testify for Ellsberg and Russo, March 1973.

Alex Alben (*lower left*) in the CBS newsroom. New York, 1980.

Directly following his deposition (*from left to right*) Colonel J. Barrie Williams is joined during Oktoberfest by David Boies, Ellen Brockman (a Cravath paralegal), Robert Baron, and George Crile. Munich, West Germany, 1983.

General Westmoreland
and his lawyer, Dan Burt,
arrive for the first day of
trial, October 10, 1984.

White knight serene:
General McChristian
after testifying against
Westmoreland,
February 6, 1985.

Mike Wallace, a defendant along with Sam Adams and George Crile, leaves the U.S. Courthouse, February 20, 1985.

Robert Baron on what would become the final day of testimony. (Behind Baron and only partially shown is CBS attorney Catherine Flickinger.) February 13, 1985.

It was a surprise ending. In Baron's apartment (*left to right*) Jim Noonan (a PR man for CBS), George Allen, and Mike Wallace celebrate the televised announcement.

After the trial and on the road to the cloud forest: Anne Cocroft with Clayton and Sam Adams. Costa Rica, March 1985.

(Overleaf) Foley Square, New York, New York.

ward. He felt that those of us who didn't agree with him, those of us who didn't accept his position, were guilty of standing in the way of the truth."

Smith denied Adams's request to move the inquest outside headquarters, and there the relationship ended. Afterward, though, Smith heard about Adams from time to time. "My executive assistant said to me one day," he recalled, "'you know, I just saw Sam Adams walking down the hall. You know, he walks on his socks.' I said, 'What do you mean, he walks on his socks?' He said, 'He wears long stockings and he doesn't have any kind of garter and they come down over his heels of his shoes and he walks on them.'"

Another official who endured the Adams interview was Edward Proctor, associate deputy director of intelligence. As an experienced numbers man, Proctor had already taken it upon himself to examine the Adams allegations and came away convinced that "There is no way that Sam or anybody else could have scientifically addressed the OB; the data were just not there." The work Adams had been doing was a case in point. "Sam's data were fragmentary. He had no statistical basis for making a sound estimate. Anecdotal stuff, not scientific. He had a feel but nothing else. His methodology was discontinuous; it wasn't a sample but a collection of things." A main problem for Proctor was the classification scheme Adams had used. "He only counted whole people, not considering what proportion they actually added to the Viet Cong structure. For example, should an unarmed person be weighted the same as an armed person? What if a rebel was only active one day a week: Did he count the same as someone who was active four days a week?"

Even assuming Adams was coming up with something worthwhile, Proctor faulted him for not promoting definitive findings through any one of the agency's various publications. "Sam never completed his work. He never gave me anything I could hold. He never published anything that had been peer-reviewed, a research article that would stand on its own two feet." Rather, Adams gave Proctor work "that was all discourse, 'more study needed,' never a conclusion." Proctor came to believe that "something drove him, I think it was his family history of being an Adams from the Revolution. The need to get attention; to be recognized and fight the battle; to be right at the expense of others." Proctor had ultimately no other choice but to conclude that "Sam wanted to be fired so then he could have a real cause to fight for."[16]

During their meeting Proctor told Adams, "The real problem is you. You ought to look into yourself."[17]

*

On November 11 — only three days after meeting with Adams — Helms traveled to the Hotel Pierre in New York where Nixon awaited him. The president-elect said he wanted Helms to stay on to be his director of the CIA. Helms, however, could not reveal the reappointment because Nixon, in his inimitable style, wanted this kept secret.[18]

In an unfortunate bit of timing, it was just then that Adams pushed to have the incoming administration present at his promised meetings with Rostow and Taylor. On November 18, as Adams would remember, "I wrote letters to Mr. Rostow and General Taylor telling them who I was and asking that they include a member of Nixon's staff in any talks we had about the CIA's shortcomings." Adams then "forwarded the letters, through channels, to the director's office, asking permission to send them on." Adams had already given Helms a good chuckle and a hearty laugh over the McGowin connection, and with this naive request he perhaps did so again. "Permission was denied," said Adams, "and that was the last I heard about meeting with Rostow and Taylor."

Adams had also heard the last of the "special review board," the board having never issued any kind of finding, assuming that it had ever conducted any kind of investigation. However, in the absence of a board report Adams decided to write one himself. The Adams report would cover not only the order of battle episode, but diverse other topics as well. Using his trademark composition technique of writing and cutting until a manuscript of stapled yellow snippets was created, Adams, as he recounted it, "put together a thirty-five-page paper explaining why I had brought the charges and why, among other things, the Sitrep was a less than adequate publication. My paper was ready for typing on Nixon's inauguration day, 20 January 1969." Four days later Adams asked permission to send it to the PFIAB and to Walt Rostow's replacement at the White House, Henry Kissinger. No, Adams was told by Admiral Taylor, he couldn't send anything downtown on his own. The CIA was a team, and if Adams didn't want to be a team player then he should resign. The date was January 31 — one year since the start of the Tet Offensive.[19]

With the possibility that his days at the agency were numbered, and with them the chance for him to seek redress within the system, Adams went back to his farm and buried his trove of purloined papers. Those he did not bury he gave to supporters for safekeeping. An agency colleague, Lydia Weber, put her own career at risk by agreeing to keep some for him.[20]

Despite having taken these steps to preserve the evidence, however, Adams still held out hope that his complaints might be properly dealt with here and now in 1969, rather than at some distant date and in circumstances that he could only imagine. Adams, who always had an odd collection of contacts "downtown," gave a bootleg copy of his thirty-five-page report to John Court, a member of Kissinger's National Security Council staff. Adams received word back a few weeks later from Court that his report "had gotten around all right, but the decision had been made not to do anything about it."

Adams gave up. "If the White House wasn't interested, I'd reached the end of the line. I felt I'd done as much as I possibly could, and that was that. Obviously, the time had come to take stock in my career at the CIA." Adams did so and concluded: "It was pretty much in shambles." He was now working under "special restrictions," meaning that he couldn't attend meetings where non-CIA people were present or become involved in interorganizational efforts such as the just-completed SNIE 14.3-68 or upcoming SNIE 14.3-69. And, of course, any return trips to Vietnam were completely out of the question. Discouraged, Adams turned his attentions to a problem that he had been neglecting for months now: the activities of the Viet Cong's Military Proselyting Section.[21]

On this task Adams could no longer count on the help of Douglas Parry, who had left Langley for the University of Utah Law School. Still, in Parry's place help for Adams had arrived in the form of a new OER hire, Robert Klein.

*

For Klein joining the agency was, he said, "very much a case of running from rather than running to." Looking forward to graduation from Brooklyn College in the spring of 1968, but not to being drafted for Vietnam, Klein took the advice of an economics professor who suggested he apply to the CIA. "I could work in the CIA as an economist and not have to get killed," he explained, "a heck of a deal."

Klein arrived at Langley and the OER fresh out of college. The CIA, he discovered, was a good employer and one that offered unique perks. There was a spy novel collection at headquarters that employees were encouraged to peruse for ideas, or one could help oneself to any of the excellent maps put out by the Cartography Department; for those who took vacations abroad management would generously cover the costs of holiday photos — provided a second set was left at Langley.

As a peace activist and draft avoider Klein's assignment at the OER was, as luck would have it, the South Vietnam Branch. He was shocked to see how lightly the agency took the war. "There were no resources at the CIA," it seemed to him, "devoted to Vietnam." His colleagues, only about twenty in all, didn't speak Vietnamese and had no knowledge of the culture. Plus, many appeared to be engaged in "pointless work, like estimating the South Vietnamese rice harvest." One of the analysts was not even interested in Vietnam and hankered to join the FBI but could not pass the bureau's spelling test. "And this," said Klein, "used to cause infinite derision."

Adams was Klein's first boss, and Klein quickly noticed that Adams was an unusual entity. "Sam knew more about odd things than any other human being I have ever met," Klein recalled. "He had this astounding eclectic database of stuff — history, Civil War stuff." Adams, of modest government pay, lived on a sizable farm out in the countryside, and he soon invited Klein out for a visit. "I came out that Saturday and the tie that I saw him wearing on Friday around his neck was holding up his pants." It was also obvious that Adams had a special place at the agency. "Sam had done this IG thing," Klein said, "which I think scared a lot of people. I know his boss, Ron Smith, treated him with a great deal of deference." Adams was also respected by those not threatened by his complaints. It was June 1968 when Klein started at the CIA and, he recalled, "The Tet Offensive had just ended. The bad guys had come out of the woodwork and Sam, who had been arguing on the OB issue that there were more of them out there than anybody realized, was suddenly a hero. Sam was very much recognized inside the agency as a great, top analyst, and even more so among the analysts themselves. To put it mildly, the analysts loved him; he had tremendous credibility with them."

Klein also realized of his new boss, "Here was a guy who was awesomely intelligent." Adams was prone to use words like *peccadillo* that Klein had never actually heard uttered in speech, and "was incredibly eclectic and staggeringly well read; he just read and read and read." And with the eclecticism came some oddities. Adams arrived at the office one fall day, for instance, wearing a heavy leather bomber coat. He hung the garment next to the desk of an OER colleague, Joseph Stumpf, and Stumpf, who himself was a fastidious dresser, wrinkled his nose. "Oh," Adams said by way of apology for the odor, "the dog's been sleeping on that coat all summer." At other times Adams refused to remove his sports jacket at the office, his dress shirt underneath being too old and torn up to reveal.

Klein had no sooner gotten to know Adams a little than the inspectors descended. This was at the height of the IG inquiry and, Klein recalled, "they interrogated me, which was a little intimidating at the time, because what did I know?" In fact, Klein said, "I really didn't know shit. So the IG guys kind of realized that I wasn't a great source of information about the whole story." Instead, one inspector started grilling Klein about his knowledge of Adams personally. "I remember him asking me, 'Is it true that he's rich?' And I said, 'Yeah, he's got a big farm out in Virginia and, yeah, he's pretty rich.'" The inspector commented on this. "And," Klein recalled, "there was a note in the guy's voice, like, *Holy cow, why would he be working here? Why would he be doing this if he is rich?*"[22]

Adams gave Klein a big assignment, although Adams was himself too busy with the IG affair to be of much help. Adams in his past readings of the Viet Cong documents, according to Klein, "had noticed that the 'bad guys' said they were fighting the war on three fronts. The military front — that was the whole OB discussion, guys with guns — the political front — which was the National Liberation Front and the Communist Party — and the 'military proselyting war.' Nobody knew what military proselyting was; they didn't know what it meant." It was time for original research.

"Find out what military proselyting is," Adams said.

"How the hell do I do that?"

"Go down and put in an information request into the computer," Adams answered.

Klein did as instructed and "began getting reams of documents, I mean stacks and stacks of shit. POW reports, very little in the way of communications intelligence, and mostly documentary evidence referring to 'Military Proselyting Subsection G, Achievement Mission Q in Quadrant R' — that kind of thing."

Klein was initially very excited, although the thrill didn't last. "First job and I started wading into this stuff and it was unbelievably awful, because I didn't know anything. I was really a crappy researcher." Klein continued unhappily with his haphazard research for seven or eight months before finding his Rosetta stone. This was a Viet Cong training document, replete with some low-level codes, that finally explained the nature of military proselyting.

The Vietnamese Communist's Military Proselyting Directorate, it turned out, had three functions. The first was to run the Viet Cong POW camps in South Vietnam. Here there was the opportunity for the directorate to transform captives into Viet Cong agents before setting them free. The second function was to conduct psychological warfare activities against the Saigon regime and its allies. The third function was to place *noi tuyen* — "fifth columnists" or "penetration agents" — in the Army of the Republic of Vietnam.

"I showed the document to Sam," Klein recalled, "and Sam immediately went to the subversive penetration agents and said, 'How many are there? Get the documents, let's start tallying them up.' Now Sam and I started working together. Until then I had been on my own, but now Sam was interested."

Adams introduced Klein to his method of extrapolation, a method that required the construction of what Adams called an "organigram." Adams would sketch an organigram, which was basically an organizational chart, on a napkin before drawing a more elaborate rendition on a piece of yellow legal paper. The basis behind the organigram was that the Viet Cong used the same organizational structure in every locality of South Vietnam. Atop the Viet Cong organization, as Adams sketched it, was the Province Party

Committee; just below it was the Current Affairs Committee. From there Adams showed how the organization branched out into a dozen sections before filtering down into myriad subsections and smaller parts — more than one hundred functional units in all.[23]

The work, however, was not over with the completion of the organigram. Now it was time to fill in the numbers. Klein explained, "What Sam said was that 'If I have information on one or two of these units I don't need confirmation that these other units exist because they always exist in the organizational structure.' So he would extrapolate the number of enemy, bad guys out there, based upon his organizational chart instead of hard facts."

Klein went through back copies of the *CDEC Bulletin* (now at number 22,000) with an eye toward mention of *noi tuyen*. He started compiling figures and with Adams created an organigram based upon the documentary evidence. Klein recalled, "We ended up extrapolating from the documents and projecting that there was something in the order of fifty thousand Viet Cong agents in the South Vietnamese army." Adams was ecstatic. "Sam took great glee in this; the kick of finding this." It was a momentous discovery because fifty thousand agents represented about 5 percent of the Saigon regime's entire military. "I remember Sam saying, 'My God, the place is riddled with quislings.'" Klein didn't know what *quislings* meant: "I had to look it up."

The quislings were not only in ARVN but also in South Vietnam's national police, where seventy Viet Cong agents had been recently arrested (including the police chief's dentist), in South Vietnam's Parliament, and in South Vietnam's Joint Chiefs of Staff. One Viet Cong agent was even responsible for delivering sensitive documents of strategic value to MACV. All in all, Adams stated, the activities of the *noi tuyen* represented "by far the biggest agent network in the history of espionage."[24]

The existence of so many Viet Cong agents in South Vietnam's military and security apparatus, Adams and Klein thought, would be a severe blow to Nixon's "Vietnamization" strategy. This strategy, announced in May 1969, involved turning responsibility for the war over to the Saigon regime; yet if that regime was Communist-infested, the prognosis for Vietnamization looked questionable indeed. Also at risk, Adams and Klein believed, was the CIA's Phoenix Program. This new program represented U.S. recognition — tardy though it was — of the importance of the Viet Cong Infrastructure because it was designed to identify and assassinate Viet Cong operatives at the village and hamlet level. The effectiveness of Phoenix, however, was in jeopardy because Viet Cong agents were in some cases the South Vietnamese army liaisons to the program.[25]

Klein wrote a fifty-page paper on the Viet Cong proselyting problem that was finished in December. The paper, however, was not allowed out of the OER. Klein was outraged and so was Adams, who needed no prompting to come to Klein's aid. "Sam often cast himself in the position of having to fight the agency and the hierarchy and the establishment because of the morality of it, and the need for it," Klein said. "And that was all true. But there was also in Sam a gleefulness, a joy, a pleasure, even a seeking-out of opportunities to do that. He enjoyed tilting against the establishment windmill. I remember Sam saying things like, 'I've got money, so they fire me so what.'" Adams knew exactly what to do with Klein's suppressed paper. "Sam gave a copy to a guy called John Court on Kissinger's staff. Court gave a copy to Kissinger, Kissinger discussed it with Nixon, Nixon discussed it with Helms who didn't know shit about it, and the roof came in on me and Sam." Adams, corruptor of youth, could no longer be trusted with Klein: "At this point I was taken away from Sam."

*

Adams had by now long been a pariah in some quarters. The head of the OER Logistics Branch, Paul Walsh, stormed into Lawrence Houston's office during the IG inquiry requesting permission to terminate him ("Can't we fire the sonofabitch?"), and word from R. Jack Smith was that DDI staff should avoid the disgruntled analyst. "It was generally known," said Adams's JOT classmate Ray McGovern, "that Sam was rabidly pursuing some vendetta or crusade, and it was just better not to talk to him."[26]

Undeterred, Adams continued with work he deemed valuable, such as his lectures on the Viet Cong at "Blue U," the teaching facility of the CIA Office of Training. His students there were clandestine operatives, and for Adams dealing with them was refreshing. "In contrast to many higher-ups at headquarters," he recounted, "most Vietnam-bound DDP-ers couldn't give less of a damn about office politics. The majority were headed for the provinces, so that their main interest was what they were up against."

Adams also kept current with the Cong Bo An — and he didn't forget about enemy military proselyting, either. His attempts to interest the DDP's Vietnam desk into addressing these two problems failed, though, the desk chief demurring, "For God's sake don't open that Pandora's box. We have enough trouble as it is." Still, by sheer dint of will Adams got a seventh-floor conference to address the subject. Present were Adams; the SNIE 14.3-69 chairman, James Graham; Adams's boss Ronald L. Smith of the OER and (undoubtedly seething) Paul Walsh, also of the OER; some DDP officials; and Robert Klein and Douglas Parry. Parry, having completed his first year at law school, was back at Langley for the summer researching, under Adams's tutelage, Viet Cong stealing and faking of South Vietnamese ID cards. Adams said of the conference, "I shot off both barrels — that is, Robert's list and Doug's cards." Still, "The briefing fell flat. Always polite, Mr. Graham said: 'Thank you Sam, that was very interesting.'"[27]

*

Robert Klein soldiered on at headquarters after being removed from Adams's seditious influence. Klein was told to forget about Viet Cong military proselyting and concentrate instead on American casualties. Klein's job was to determine U.S. killed in action (KIA) and U.S. force level ratios and how they would effect the preservation of the Saigon regime. "We were going to scale back the number of troops in the war," Klein explained, "and we were losing, say, a hundred a week at that point, but if we cut the number of troops in half would that mean that we would lose fifty a week? And would that force level be enough to keep the South Vietnamese government in operation? It was essentially a political study."

Under the supervision of Joseph Stumpf, Klein used a "nifty desktop device" to run regression equations in an attempt to forecast American KIAs under varying troop strength conditions. But "It came to pass after a while," said Klein, "that this was an idiotic exercise because the number of U.S. killed was not a function of how many of us were there, but of how many of us they decided to shoot." American combat deaths were the result of enemy activity, Klein reasoned, and had little to do with the number of

Americans in South Vietnam. "To say that there was a statistical relationship between casualties and troop levels was a phony issue." Klein's paper pointed this out, but Stumpf disagreed: "He told me that I massively misunderstood statistics." Klein was given a warning: His career was on the line, and his paper would have to be rewritten.

"I at this point became incendiary," he said. *"My God,* I thought, *tens of thousands of American boys are dying on the battlefields of Vietnam and we are fighting with the numbers."* Klein decided he had no future with the CIA and wrote a blistering letter of resignation. "Sam was a partial author of that letter; we drafted it pretty much together."

Klein departed for graduate school, and leaving Langley "was one of the most liberating moments I have ever had — I was so happy to get out." Klein felt that he had no future with the agency: "Because, as Sam said, 'If you tell them the truth, you are going to end up running the doughnut machine.'"

10

A THOREAU TYPE

Adams was sorry to see Klein go. It was late 1970 and, Adams said, "By now my fortunes had sunk to a low ebb. For the first time in seven years, I was given an unfavorable fitness report." The report was shown to Adams by the same person who wrote it, his boss, Ronald L. Smith. According to Smith, "Mr. Adams does not take direction well and has had a marked tendency to work [only] on what he deems important or interesting at any given time." Smith noted that "his highly independent attitude has disrupted the performance and progression of junior personnel. I believe that the discontent leading to the recent resignation of a junior officer was in large measure the result of his close association with Mr. Adams who was his first supervisor. These deficiencies," concluded Smith, "combined with his strong personal views concerning the conduct of intelligence on the Vietnam War, cost him balance and objectivity to the point he became a net liability to the Branch and his employment in the OER became undesirable. Therefore, Mr. Adams has been reassigned to a position where he will be less directly involved in the war. RATING: Marginal."[1]

"This meant," Adams recounted, "I had to leave the Vietcong branch and join a small historical staff, where I was to take up the relatively innocuous job of writing a history of the Cambodian rebels." He considered resigning from the agency, "but the job still had me hooked."[2]

The banishment from the OER was undoubtedly also the result of Adams's special efforts earlier that fall to get Klein's military proselyting paper accepted by the seventh floor. Klein's study had, Adams complained to his superiors, been labeled "gloomy" and unfairly reviled as "inflammatory, contentious, and argumentative." But Adams's final appeal in this matter failed, and the paper's chances for distribution were dead — that is, until a summary version appeared on page one of the *New York Times*.[3]

"The Central Intelligence Agency," the October 19 story read, "has told President Nixon that the Vietnamese Communists have infiltrated 30,000 agents into the South Vietnamese Government in an apparatus that has been virtually impossible to destroy." These thirty thousand agents, the *Times* account continued, were supported by "tens of thousands of part-time agents and Vietcong sympathizers." The article asserted that South Vietnam was rotten with enemy subversives who had bored their way into government, military, and police posts at all levels, and also into South Vietnam's political and religious organizations. The newspaper story gave as an example a case: "All members of a village council in an ostensibly pacified district recently were discovered to be Vietcong agents."

The following day Klein, who was now at the MBA program at Columbia University, got a call from his former employer. "Saw your paper in the *Times*," the voice on the phone said. Klein denied involvement: "I told them I knew nothing about it, I even volunteered to go through a lie-detector test." But Langley didn't follow up, and "I later learned — Sam told me — that he had released my paper to Neil Sheehan."[4]

*

Exiled to the DDI Special Research Staff, Adams started work early in 1971 on the Cambodian rebels, a group the French-speaking leader of Cambodia, Prince Norodom Sihanouk, had christened *les Khmer Rouges* (the Red Cambodians). Knowing little about the Khmer Rouge, but eager to find out, Adams descended to the CIA archives, where he was to spend the next several weeks educating himself.[5]

Adams's initial research was completed in mid-May, nearly a year to the day since the start of the "incursion" by U.S. and South Vietnamese forces into Cambodia. Prior to that event Secretary of State William Rogers had reiterated America's respect for Cambodian "neutrality, sovereignty and independence," but at the opportune moment Richard Nixon ordered an invasion. His opening occurred in late April 1970 when Prince Sihanouk's reign dissolved into anarchy and chaos. Nixon, in response to this crisis, gave MACV permission to do what it had long wanted: launch U.S. forces across the South Vietnamese border and attack NVA and Viet Cong sanctuaries in Cambodia.[6]

Now twelve months later Nixon's plans were for U.S. forces to depart from the country and to leave the fighting there to the armies of South Vietnam and Cambodia. Indeed, the situation for the United States almost looked promising. Phnom Penh was in friendly hands and in the countryside hostile Khmers were said to number only five or ten thousand.

Working on his own — although no less than three DDI offices at Langley were supposedly responsible for Cambodia — Adams discovered in the winter and spring of 1971 something that others had not. This was, Adams said, "the extraordinary story of what the communists had been up to in Cambodia." The captured documents told of a large and complex Viet Cong advisory system for the Khmer rebels; of sophisticated Khmer chains of command, radio nets, hospitals, and training schools; of Khmer artillery companies, commando battalions, infantry regiments, and "even," Adams marveled, "a division."

Fearing that U.S. order of battle statistics for the Khmer Rouge were questionable, Adams inquired around as to their origin. No one at Langley knew, so Adams called over to the DIA. From somewhere within the vast Pentagon building he reached a noncommissioned officer, a Sergeant Reisman, who said the Khmer numbers were from a study done a year before by the Cambodian government. But hadn't, Adams wondered, the statistics ever been updated? No, Reisman answered, everyone at the DIA was busy with other things. "They hit us with too much shit," the sergeant griped.

It was Friday afternoon and Adams was hardly about to leave this important, but obviously neglected, piece of intelligence work for Monday. On Saturday he waded into a mass of captured documents, POW interrogations, and CIA field reports. It took him a week to compile an updated Khmer Rouge order of battle; by Friday, June 5, his work was done. The Khmer rebel numbers, Adams determined, greatly exceeded those postulated by the old Cambodian government study and now totaled between 100,000 and 150,000. To his disgust, Adams noted that an entire enemy army had been raised in Cambodia "while we weren't looking."[7]

Adams readied a memo on the Khmer Rouge order of battle, and he informed his newest boss, Deputy Chief of the Special Research Staff Walter P. "Bud" Southard, of its existence — but didn't actually give him a copy. "Experience told me," Adams said, "that the Cambodian draft might run into heavy weather." Southard, a Far Eastern scholar of careful work habits and quiet temperament, did not detect trouble. Upon hearing word of the memo, "He looked up distractedly from his typewriter and nodded."

This was yet another Friday, and Adams once again spent his weekend at headquarters. On Sunday he completed his study and called his contact at the NSC, John Court. "That evening," Adams "stopped by the Executive Office Building (next to the White House) and handed him a Xerox copy in a manila envelope." On Monday morning Adams submitted the study to Southard's boss, Harold P. Ford. Ford read the memo and, Adams related, "said that under no circumstances was it to leave staff channels."

Southard toned down the paper and forwarded it to the Manpower Branch, the OER keeper of the Khmer Rouge numbers, for action. There a manpower analyst, Herman Dowdy, was given the assignment. Dowdy read the work Adams had done and was not impressed, calling the analysis "structurally unsound" and predicting that it "would never see the light of day." Adams was informed by the OER that troop estimates for the Khmer Rouge were to run no less than ten thousand and no more than thirty thousand, and that the Khmer Rouge guerrillas, self-defense, and service troops didn't belong in the order of battle.

Adams made the trek to the seventh floor to complain to George Carver. As Adams related the sequence, Carver became annoyed and the next day told Ford that he "didn't know how to control his underlings." Ford, to show who was boss, warned Adams that he'd "sent people packing before" and wasn't afraid to fire him. Adams was ordered to get back to work on the history of the Khmer Rouge and leave the numbers strictly alone.

Ten days after receiving the Khmer Rouge numbers study from Adams, John Court replied that the paper had merit and suggested that Adams provide another bootleg copy to the Pentagon. In the cafeteria of the Defense Department building Adams slipped one to a DIA analyst and a friend, David Siegel, and Siegel gave a copy to Sergeant Reisman, who kept it out in plain view. "In August," Adams said, "Bud summoned me to his cubicle to tell of an irate phone call." The call had been from Paul Walsh, one of whose OER employees had just been over at the Pentagon and saw Adams's paper on Reisman's desk. "Bud looked me in the eye," said Adams, "and asked if I was responsible. I replied uneasily that I was not."

After hearing from others that Adams was in fact carrying on at the Pentagon, Southard and Ford sat Adams down and had him compose a memo for the file stating what his responsibilities were and were not to be. Southard and Ford patiently tried to get Adams to see things the DDI way. "Sam," Ford said, "you are hurting yourself with this style, going behind the back of your bosses. You were brought in here to work on the Khmer Rouge and this work is very important." Ford hoped that the message had gotten through to the rebel analyst. "Sam was," Ford remembered, "a brilliant fellow but as a boss he was a pain. You never knew where he was or what he was doing. He was so much trouble to handle that it brought into question whether it was worth having him around."[8]

Adams had taken a fall for leaking his Khmer numbers paper to the NSC and DIA, and his sacrifice had gone unrewarded. Neither of these two bureaucracies cared to support him in his cause, and so his was the lone voice of dissent as the CIA rolled out its Khmer numbers that November. Langley's estimate, which was later given to the White House, put Khmer strength at fifteen to thirty thousand. Dejected, Adams poured his energies into his history of the Khmer insurgents. The finished paper, Adams recounted, would become "the last words I wrote that were published by the agency."[9]

With the conclusion in February of his Khmer history, which was one year in the making, Adams endured another periodic evaluation, this time from his newest boss, Bud Southard. "As other supervisors have noted," Southard wrote, "Mr. Adams is a highly intelligent, resourceful, and hard-driving researcher, who can discuss things of importance and can write clearly and forcefully about them. As other supervisors have also noted, Mr. Adams is also independent, headstrong, overly certain of his own judgments, and prone to get emotionally involved with his subject. A tendency to free-wheeling can engage Mr. Adams on various fronts more heavily than he should be, and at times without the knowledge or consent of his supervisor. One particular asset, assiduous researching, is often a fault in that an Adams paper is likely to be late" and only "brought forth in pain and turmoil."

Having stirred up all too much controversy over Indochina, Adams was taken off Cambodia. As Southard stated at the end of the review, he was now to research "Chinese Communist strategic thinking."[10]

For Adams, however, this new subject would have to wait because the Manpower Branch had once more bungled the Cambodian intelligence. On March 13, Adams said, "a fresh CIA memorandum arrived on my desk again fixing the Khmer numbers at 15,000 to 30,000." The Manpower Branch had done no further work, Adams learned, on the numbers since its faulty study of the previous November. Reflexively Adams grabbed a stack of three-by-five index cards and, he recounted, "Reported to Bud's cubicle to ask if I could work upstairs for a while on 'filing.'" Luckily for Adams, Southard was "Busy as usual at his typewriter" and "replied absently that it was OK with him."

Over the next month Adams carved time out from his regular duties for Southard to complete a detailed accounting, index card by index card, of all Khmer Rouge military units known to exist. Partisans upstairs at the OCI provided an unused desk from which Adams could work; Southard wasn't apprised of these extracurricular activities until April 11, when Adams presented him with a draft memorandum titled "The Communists' 'Combat Strength' in Cambodia." The memo, Adams hoped, would make the seventh floor finally take the Khmer order of battle problem seriously.[11]

In the memo Adams reiterated his earlier contention that a realistic number for Communist strength in Cambodia was not the low figure accepted by the Manpower Branch but instead a figure that "exceeds 100,000." Southard took the memo into his hands and, Adams related, said in reference to himself, Adams, and Ford, "What are you trying to do — get all three of us fired?" Loyal to his subordinate, however, Southard sent the piece at once to the DDI front office. There it was killed.[12]

Upon learning of his memo's fate Adams became glum. He realized that the Khmer Rouge numbers fight was a hopeless cause. "The agency was busy with other matters, and I became increasingly discouraged. The Cambodian affair seemed to me to be a repeat of the Vietnam one; the same people made the same mistakes, in precisely the same ways, and everybody was allowed to conceal his duplicity."[13]

*

The Easter Offensive launched by a recuperated Viet Cong organization in April 1972 looked to Saigon and Washington like the beginning of the end. Although the demise of South Vietnam was stayed awhile longer, and the Viet Cong beaten back, this newest offensive became, Adams exclaimed, "the last straw for me. As usual, it was a complete surprise, and I decided that something, goodness knows what, had to be done about American intelligence." Adams vowed to get hold of a man who might have some answers: Gains B. Hawkins.[14]

Hawkins had, as Adams learned, retired from the U.S. Army and moved to the small farming community of West Point, Mississippi. Adams phoned Hawkins requesting a visit and the retired colonel, now supervisor of transportation, buildings, and grounds for the West Point schools, told Adams to come down to West Point as his guest. Adams jumped at the opportunity and quickly asked permission from Southard to take a few days' vacation time.

The visit, however, was tedious for Hawkins as Adams, in the sweltering heat of June, peppered him with hundreds of questions regarding events of five or six years ago in Saigon. "I found it difficult to remember the details," Hawkins said. "I guess I didn't want to remember. The thing had become a blur." But this hardly deterred Adams from a relentless inquiry into what transpired behind closed doors at MACV. "Sam's persistence aroused some antagonisms. He seemed to be challenging all of our order of battle techniques. Worse still, he seemed to suspect Gen. McChristian. This, to me, was only slightly less than sacrilegious. I became annoyed, and Sam's visit ended on a sour note."[15]

Returning home to Virginia, however, Adams was thrilled. Hawkins, reluctant though he may have been, did relay to Adams all he knew about MACV chicanery, telling him, for example, that when Westmoreland was apprised of the real numbers in May 1967 the general "almost fell off his chair," and that afterward a lid was placed on the order of battle. Energized by all this new information Adams threw caution to the wind and over the next six months launched a personal crusade for intelligence reform. He gave John Stennis, head of the Senate Armed Services Committee, a thirteen-page paper detailing the order of battle scandal's chronology and players; for good measure he passed another copy on to the House of Representatives. And at Langley he revived and revised his previous complaint to the CIA inspector general.

But the results for Adams, as before, were disappointing. An official at the IG's office informed him that the agency "ought not to be seized with the problem since it seemed primarily a military matter," and someone from Senator Stennis's staff informed him that his paper "was an interesting document" but doubted that the Intelligence Subcommittee would take the paper up "because it hadn't met in over a year and a half." Meanwhile the House, Adams reported, "was likewise unresponsive." Congressman Lucien Nedzi, for example, told Adams that he was too busy for such things because the "forthcoming elections obliged him to concern himself primarily with the question of busing."[16]

Taking his cue from the IG, however, that the agency should not concern itself with military affairs, Adams then asked that his concerns be made known to the U.S. Army. On December 8 Adams gave a memo to the IG explaining that the army should be notified that Westmoreland "may have originated orders imposing a ceiling on the official MACV order of battle in 1967," and if true, "such orders violate Section 207, Article 107 ('false official statements') and Section 881, Article 81 ('conspiracy') of the Uniform Code of Military Justice." According to Adams, "a full investigation" — including, if necessary, criminal prosecution — was warranted.[17]

On the seventh floor the IG — undoubtedly horrified at having to be party to this affair — informed the Pentagon that a CIA staffer had an unusual request: that a court-martial be held for retired U.S. Army Chief of Staff General William C. Westmoreland. At the DDI top people such as Paul Walsh soon learned of this latest Adams gambit. They were furious.

Adams somehow escaped being fired, and in late January of the new year a letter arrived for him from the Department of the Army, inspector general of investigations and complaints. No action could be taken on his request for an investigation, the army missive to Adams read, because his employers at the agency had failed to properly forward information regarding the complaint. With undisguised annoyance, the army letter also reminded Adams that he'd "already been told" by his CIA superiors to keep his grievance confined to Langley.[18]

*

The day of this latest put-down, January 23, 1973, Adams caught up with his unread copies of the *New York Times*. A front-page headline that had appeared three days before caught his attention: "Pentagon Paper 'Secrets' Cited in Public Documents." The article was generally related to the ongoing legal problems his old acquaintance from the RAND villa in Saigon, Anthony Russo, was having with the U.S. government and was specifically related to the phony numbers contained in SNIE 14.3-67.

In terms of Russo's legal problems, he along with fellow RAND alumnus Daniel Ellsberg had made public the secret history of the Vietnam War titled "United States–Vietnam Relations, 1945–1967" that McNamara had commissioned in the summer of 1967. McNamara's secret history took eighteen months to complete and involved the participation of thirty-six scholars drawn from the Defense Department, RAND, and several universities. In all, the history would consist of three thousand pages of text and another four thousand pages of supporting documents such as memos, intelligence estimates, and cables. Highly classified, the forty-seven-volume "United States–Vietnam Relations, 1945–1967" was never intended for public consumption.

Ellsberg, a converted war opponent who in his earlier capacity as a RAND employee had worked on the history, grew impatient that no one was leaking it and in frustration gave a purloined copy of the massive chronicle to Neil Sheehan in 1971. The story broke in the *New York Times*; once it was made known, McNamara's secret history of the war became known as the Pentagon Papers. Russo had helped Ellsberg acquire and copy the Pentagon Papers for Sheehan; for his efforts Russo was facing 35 years in prison while Ellsberg was looking at 115. The resulting trial was now under way in Los Angeles. On the stand on February 19 — as Adams was reading with extreme interest four days later — had been General William G. DePuy.

DePuy's appearance at the criminal proceedings, according to the *Times*, was as an expert witness for the prosecution, testifying about the massive classified study that General Earle G. Wheeler wrote in 1968 just weeks after Tet. (Although not one of the original documents assembled for the McNamara project, eight pages of the "Wheeler Report" were given to

Sheehan along with the rest of the papers, and the government, in its case against the defendants, considered this act to be among the most damaging.) DePuy had explained to the jury in testimony on the eighteenth that the Wheeler Report was vital to national security because it detailed U.S. intelligence estimates of enemy capabilities during the Tet Offensive.[19]

Adams must have put his copy of the *Times* down in amazement. He knew, of course, all about the intelligence contained in the Wheeler Report to which General DePuy was referring: This was none other than MACV's made-up numbers for enemy gains and losses of early 1968 that were entirely based on the by-now thoroughly discredited SNIE 14.3-67 order of battle numbers. How could, Adams asked himself, men such as Ellsberg and Russo go to jail for this? It would be an utter travesty of justice, and so Adams dropped whatever else he was doing and got to work composing a memo for CIA General Counsel Lawrence Houston — the man who had been one-third of the "special review board" back in 1969.

The memo was completed the next day, and Adams delivered it to Houston, who probably thought that he had heard the last of Adams. The memo informed Houston that the Wheeler Report being used as evidence against Ellsberg and Russo was based upon "numbers which had been deliberately fabricated in late 1967" by MACV officials and that its release, consequently, in no way threatened national security. Accompanying this memo were three others Adams had prepared explaining the intelligence cover-up at MACV as told to him by Hawkins the previous spring. Adams asked Houston to kindly forward these documents to the Department of Justice without delay.[20]

Not Houston himself but a lawyer from his office got back to Adams on the morning of the twenty-ninth. The lawyer patiently explained the intricacies of criminal law to Adams and then assured him that his four memos would be "invalid as evidence." Adams quickly penned a reply to Houston: "Although the various reasons he advanced may indeed be cogent, it seems to me that any decision regarding the documents' validity belongs to the Justice Department, and not to the Central Intelligence Agency." Adams then lectured Houston on the 1963 *Brady v. Maryland* decision "in which the Supreme Court decided to overturn a conviction because the prosecution failed to give the defense material which tended to exculpate the accused. Surely," Adams reasoned, "the CIA ought not to become a party to this kind of failure — even to the extent of preventing the Justice Department from exercising its own judgment." Knowing by now Houston's propensity for the bureaucratic runaround, Adams gave him until noon, February 1, to forward the memos to Justice or else, Adams promised, he would do so himself.[21]

It was a week later and the day before February 1 when Adams was informed he would be let go. In his following "Memorandum for the Record" he described what happened. "Walter P. Southard," Adams wrote, "deputy chief of the special research staff of the DDI, told me that in my upcoming fitness report, due out shortly, he would recommend my 'divorce' (as he put it) from the agency. In the subsequent half-hour-long discussion, which occurred as we nervously paced the corridor, Mr. Southard indicated that he thought my work was satisfactory, that I was not insubordinate, and that I got on well with my fellow workers. The main problem, he indicated, was the long-standing friction that existed between me and the DDI hierarchy, the latest example of this, he indicated, was my overt act in going to the CIA Inspector General (IG) last December. It was this overt act, he indicated, that was behind the decision to fire me. I would like to make clear that I harbor no animosity towards Mr. Southard. Personally, I like him a great deal, and think him a man of considerable integrity." Adams concluded, however, that "I would also like to make clear that I believe that there is a close connection between the memorandum of 8 December 1972 and the threat of Dismissal of 31 January 1973."[22]

Adams had apparently made himself clear, and later that same day Houston thought it prudent to send Adams's memos to the Justice Department at once.

Bud Southard, after reading what Adams wrote about the conversation in the corridor, and perhaps also after being queried by Houston about it, wanted to explain his side of the story. According to notes he took, Southard admitted that while "speaking unofficially" with Adams on the thirty-first he did mention that Adams and the agency should get a "divorce on grounds of incompatibility" and that the December 8 complaint to the IG was but a case in point and not the only reason — this being, Southard said, Adams's "campaign against the officers of the Directorate of Intelligence." But "I went on to say," Southard explained, "that Mr. Adams struck me as a free spirit, a man who marches to his own drummer (a Thoreau type) whereas the agency like any organization involves a hierarchy, a chain-of-command, the imposition of external authority; and that my observation of Mr. Adams led me to believe — rightly or wrongly — that he would always tend to be resistant to external authority."

How the subject introduced itself during the nervous conversation in the corridor is not known, but apparently Adams told Southard that while he did not currently have any money, his wife, Eleanor, would "inherit a bundle when her father dies." Upon this news Southard encouraged Adams to take up writing. "As the possessor of private means to keep himself afloat while getting established," Southard predicted, Adams "could possibly make a success of it." Adams politely rejected the career advice and informed his boss that his intentions were not to leave Langley at all but to be employed instead in "a reformed agency."[23]

The general counsel's decision to release the Adams memos to the Justice Department instigated a series of confidential exchanges between the two offices, and it was reluctantly agreed between CIA and Justice that the trial judge in Los Angeles would have to be alerted. Shortly thereafter Adams was requested by a CIA attorney, IG deputy John K. Greaney, to consolidate his four memos into just one document. Adams did as asked, and on February 7 Greaney told him that his document had been sent to the West Coast. Satisfied, Adams promised Greaney that he "would accept whatever the Judge decided" regarding the document's admissibility in court and "had no intention of contacting the defense independently."

That same day in Los Angeles the harried defense lawyers for Daniel Ellsberg and Anthony Russo received an official "Notice of Information Which the Court May Consider 'Brady Material.'" This notice was submitted by the prosecution and dealt mainly with recent testimony given by a key government witness, General Paul F. Gorman. "In accordance with the Court's statement that the views of anyone favorable to the defense on any issues involved in this case are 'evidence of innocence,'" the notice read, "defendants are advised of the following:

1. A Mr. Samuel A. Adams, Route 4, Box 240, Leesburg, Virginia, has expressed the view that he has information which would rebut statements of Government witness William DePuy as reported in a newspaper.

2. A Mr. Chester Cooper, 7514 Vale Street, Chevy Chase, Maryland, has expressed the view that testimony of Government witness Paul Gorman as reported in a newspaper was untrue.

3. David A. Munro, 802 Bluebird Canyon Drive, Laguna Beach, California, has expressed the view that the Government's prosecution . . . case is a criminal conspiracy, meeting secretly and acting illegally.

4. A person whose name and address are unknown has expressed the view that Government witness Paul Gorman is responsible for the cruelty and poverty in the world and that he persecutes any person that tries to improve the world.

The chief lawyer for the defense, Charles R. Nesson, was not amused. He dismissed the facetious list as a "funny attempt by the government on a matter which to us is extremely serious." The judge in the case, William Mathew Byrne Jr., declared that the notice wasn't what "I consider to be *Brady* material" and agreed with the defense that such notices should not be a "matter for humor."

The ploy to disguise Adams's identity and the import of his information had worked, and news of this reached the general counsel's office at Langley. There a smug Greaney showed the unsuspecting Adams a copy of the CIA's Memorandum for the Record explaining the disposition of his document. "Judge Byrne," according to the agency's interpretation, "did not consider this to be exculpatory material and, therefore, would not require Samuel Adams's name to be given to the defense."

Adams and his *Brady* memo, which of course had never been given to Byrne, may well have escaped the attention of the Ellsberg and Russo defense team if not for the government's attempt to kill two birds with one stone. Adams, it transpired, was not the only legitimate person on the government's list of people who claimed knowledge of exculpatory material. Taking another look at the notice, the defense came to realize that person number two, Chester Cooper, was no kook but was in fact a retired CIA analyst and former White House staffer for McGeorge Bundy. This piqued Nesson's interest, and he asked Byrne to review *in camera* (privately) that which Cooper wanted to tell the court, and to rule whether it must be made known to the defense.[24]

That same evening at a Los Angeles cocktail party Nesson was chatting with a *New York Times* reporter about the government's unusual *Brady* notice when he mentioned the name "Sam Adams" in passing. It was only then that Nesson learned Adams was with the CIA. The reporter informed him of this fact, and also that Adams was an "extremely capable intelligence analyst" and had waged a "one-man campaign" against "senior military officers who, he believed, had consistently falsified figures on enemy troop strength." Within minutes Nesson placed a call to the defense team's chief consultant, Morton H. Halperin, and immediately after talking to Nesson, Halperin placed a call to a farmhouse outside Leesburg, Virginia.

Now it was Adams's turn to be surprised. Over the phone he asked Halperin why the defense was calling him now when the judge in the case had already read, two weeks ago, his exculpatory material *in camera* and deemed it irrelevant. Halperin assured Adams that Byrne had never so much as laid eyes on the material. Adams, realizing all at once that everything he had been told by the IG's office was a feint to keep him from testifying, told Halperin that "I have been had."[25]

A Saturday meeting in Houston's office at Langley was hastily arranged among the IG lawyers, Adams, and a legal consultant for the Ellsberg-Russo defense team. Adams, pledged to secrecy as an agency employee, refused to answer the questions posed to him by the defendants' consultant and, predictably, was delivered a subpoena on the spot.[26]

With Adams's name, occupation, and employer now in the public domain, Seymour M. Hersh of the *New York Times* took the opportunity to introduce Adams to his readers. Exaggerating the family lineage slightly, Hersh called him a "direct descendant of his colonial namesake, a Harvard man and an official of the Central Intelligence Agency." Hersh continued that "Mr. Adams has been waging a one-man campaign against top Army officers who he believes deliberately falsified critical intelligence information a month before the Vietcong began their devastating Tet offensive at

the end of January, 1968." Hersh then detailed Adams's efforts to force a
CIA investigation into the matter, Adams's request to have Westmoreland
court-martialed ("Army officials said last week" — Hersh noted — "that,
'based on the information presently available' they do not 'intend to investigate the Adams allegations'"), and Adams's wish to remain part of the
Viet Cong order of battle estimate process. While Adams had failed in all
three, Hersh explained, his CIA colleagues still "professed admiration for
his integrity." The *Times* reporter quoted a former CIA insider as saying,
"The trouble with Sam is that he has always been right. He always told the
truth and never cared whose toes he stepped on."[27]

*

Wally and Jean Kraemer happened to be visiting the farm on the weekend
before Adams was to leave for Los Angeles to testify for the defense, and
Jean remembered the decrepit state of his wardrobe. "Sam really didn't
have appropriate shirts and there wasn't time to buy him any; but we got
him barely presentable anyway." Wally said that his friend wasn't hesitant
to take the stand. "Sam was ebullient, enthusiastic! He was looking forward to it. Most people when they are subpoenaed have the same enthusiasm as if they had been summoned to their proctologist."

*

In West Point, Mississippi, two smiling army counter-intelligence agents
showed up on Gains B. Hawkins's front porch only moments after the subpoena was delivered. The subpoena, Hawkins explained, "came as a bombshell" and he was angry with Adams — it had to have been Adams — for
getting him embroiled in the Ellsberg-Russo defense. "I despised Ellsberg
and his partner," Hawkins said, "and considered the publication of the
Pentagon Papers an enormous psychological benefit to the Vietnamese
communists." The army agents wanted to know if there was any veracity to
what the Ellsberg-Russo defense team intended to say about military intelligence during the war: that the enemy strength estimates had been fooled
with. "No," Hawkins was quick to answer, "there was no hanky panky at
all. None at all." Their mini-interrogation done with, the two agents bid
Hawkins good day, but the retired colonel was still stuck with the subpoena.

Obeying the order to testify, Hawkins reluctantly made two trips out
to Los Angeles to be questioned under oath by the defense team but his

depositions were suspect and, at the last minute, Nesson did not trust the retired colonel enough to place him on the stand. "I was committing — or at the very least flirting with — perjury," confirmed Hawkins of what he told, or did not tell, Nesson. "Never mind how questionable my judgment was at the time. It just didn't seem fair that one seamy episode in an otherwise solidly successful intelligence effort should be cited in defense of an act which had caused irreparable harm to our own side. God, how I wanted us to 'win' that war."[28]

Freed suddenly from having to appear in court for the defense himself, Hawkins watched as Adams was about to take the stand and to testify against the officers and men of the U.S. Army.

"Sam," Hawkins said sadly, "this is the end of our friendship." For Adams the moment would be "The closest I ever came to abandoning the course I had set for myself." In a few seconds Adams would have to make a decision: "I was forced to compare what I knew about Hawkins — his honesty, his humor, his love for his family, his loyalty towards the Army — with what I saw roundabout. This included the wiles of both the prosecution and the defense, the posturing of Ellsberg, and the hokery of the media, as its representatives scrabbled about, looking for 'angles' in the story." Adams pleaded with his friend not to abandon their friendship. "Please, Colonel, not that," Adams said.

"Well, I suppose you know what you're doing," Hawkins growled. "Go on up there and give 'em hell."[29]

*

Adams finally had his day in court. When he testified on Monday, March 6, he was on top of his game. "Incidentally, I'm a researcher and not a spy," he quickly told the jury upon taking the oath. "That's why I can get up here and talk to everybody. Were I a spy, I would not." Under friendly questioning by Nesson, Adams testified, among other things, to being a U.S. Navy veteran who served for "three years, four months, eleven days." He additionally testified to having studied the Viet Cong since 1965 and "trying to dope out what made those guys tick, keep going in the face of what we could throw at them." Adams then began talking about "the order of battle," but Nesson asked him to first define the term.

"Our estimate," Adams answered, "of how many baddies there are out there fighting against us."

The trial up to this point had been dominated by colorless Defense Department types, and the jury of Los Angelenos appeared to wake up. Sanford J. Ungar of the *Washington Post* noted of Adams, "As he testified, he became increasingly animated, and moved around so much on the witness stand that his shirttail was hanging out in back by the time each recess came around."

During Adams's testimony Nesson had a paragraph of the Wheeler Report projected onto a courtroom screen. Among other things, this stated that the enemy "had peaked his force total to about 240,000 just before Tet." Asked to comment on the paragraph, Adams replied that everything in it was either "extremely inaccurate" or "extremely suspect." Adams then got off the stand and, taking a green marker and standing at an easel in the middle of the courtroom, listed the categories of "self-defense militia," "secret self-defense," "infrastructure," and "assault youth" missing from the Wheeler Report. He demonstrated that by including these forces the actual order of battle on the eve of Tet was at least 440,000.

Under cross-examination by the lead prosecutor, U.S. Attorney David R. Nissen, later that afternoon, Adams was challenged to defend the publicizing of the Wheeler Report: Even if he disagreed with its contents, Nissen wondered, might not the report still have been of interest to the enemy? Adams was quick to note that the report was just "another example of how bad U.S. intelligence was at that time," and that the only information it might reveal was "that Gen. Wheeler didn't know what was in his own order of battle."

His testimony was supposed to last only a day, but Adams continued on March 7 with Nissen casting aspersions on Adams's own estimates. Nissen said mockingly that, according to Adams, "the entire population" of South Vietnam belonged in the order of battle and, anyway, wasn't the order of battle the army's business and not the CIA's? Adams gave ground by admitting that the CIA's responsibility for making enemy strength estimates was "cloudy" while the military had a "clear mandate" to do so, but in turn he ridiculed the military's "peculiar" intelligence methodology when it came to the Vietnamese Communists, stating that it was overly conservative and prone to producing misleading numbers. Adams, by way of example, explained that an enemy unit only made it into the MACV statistics if American or South Vietnamese forces "took a prisoner or captured a document" from that unit. Under this standard, Adams testified, Viet Cong antiaircraft units were often not included in the order of battle. "The pilots got the flak in the air, but this didn't fit the criteria," Adams deadpanned. "It was my feeling that if you see someone shooting at you, you put it in the Order of Battle."

On the morning of the eighth Adams was again on the stand. Nissen, taking up where he had left off the day before, described Adams as a person who, when not studying the Code of Military Justice in an effort to have General Westmoreland indicted, was a chronic complainer within the CIA, someone given to conspiracy theories, and a junior analyst whose intelligence findings were at odds with those of his superiors. This strategy, however, became waylaid when Adams explained how CIA lawyers had "lied" in an attempt to "prevent me from testifying in this court."

"You were advised," Judge Byrne asked of the witness, "that the documents were given to this court and later found out they were not presented?"

"That's right," Adams answered. "I was convinced that the materials had been shown to you."

"And later learned they had not been?"

"Yes."

Adams was finally excused to make time for the next defense witness, McGeorge Bundy, national security adviser to Presidents Kennedy and Johnson. The next day Adams could bask in his good press. Martin Arnold of the *New York Times* reported that Adams's testimony had been punctuated with humor that "brought loud laughter from the courtroom." His article continued, "A woman spectator, wearing a dark brown corduroy jacket and buff colored trousers said: 'He's restored my faith in the C.I.A. He's the best public relations the C.I.A. had had in years.' Similar comments," Arnold wrote, "were heard from other spectators."[30]

*

Adams returned to an unwelcoming Langley. His testimony and the publicity it generated had not been appreciated on the seventh floor. To make matters worse, *Los Angeles Times* columnist Joseph Alsop, a dedicated war hawk, had as much as demanded that Adams be fired. Calling Adams's testimony "garbage," Alsop said that the agency needed a "forceful cleanout in some areas." Then, as if on cue a week later, March 19, Maurice

Ernst, chief of the OER, told Adams — just as the two were entering the cafeteria — that he "had been declared excess to the needs" of the CIA because his "skills" were "no longer applicable." This incident became notorious around the building, although as time passed Adams received no further word regarding his supposed termination. Officially there was only silence, and so with no other duties to perform Adams spent his days calling different agency offices trying to get a straight answer from somebody. None came, however, and Adams was convinced that his superiors lacked the "machismo" to fire him outright.[31]

Raring for battle, Adams next wrote to the head of the DDI insisting that he be formally told of his employment status within the next twenty-four hours. "If I have not heard from you by then," Adams stated on April 4, "I will respectfully assume that the decision to declare me in excess is final, and that I need wait no longer." With still no word by April 15, Adams called the reporter Seymour Hersh and arranged for lunch. Three days later Hersh wrote in the *Times* that "Samuel A. Adams, the Central Intelligence Agency analyst who testified about military deceit at the Pentagon papers trial, said in an interview today that he has apparently been discharged."[32]

Hersh also wrote in the article that Adams acknowledged being "personally reprimanded or threatened with dismissal at least 12 times in his 10 year career" and that "Mr. Adams's friends in the agency have repeatedly professed admiration for his integrity and his willingness to contradict official policy to express his point of view. They also note, however, that Mr. Adams has not received a promotion in at least seven years." Regarding the alleged threat of dismissal Hersh was informed by a "spokesman for the agency" that "of course" Adams "had not been sacked."[33]

But Adams's employment status remained in doubt because the statement Ernst made outside the cafeteria had never been rescinded. In addition to living in this state of limbo, Adams also suffered the indignity of being treated at headquarters like an enemy spy. His office safe had been opened and searched without his permission, the career-minded at Langley kept their distance from him, and on the seventh floor a psychiatric report was ordered up (Adams, the CIA doctors ruled, "had become unbalanced").[34]

Perhaps in an attempt to ease the tension, Adams wrote a couple of memos. One was for the assistant to the director, Angus Thuermer, and read:

1. This is to inform you that I have begun inquiries about publishing a magazine article. Its tentative title is "How to Get
   Fired from the CIA."
2. Please inform the proper authorities. Thank you in advance.[35]

The other was for Edward Proctor. In it Adams demanded that "I either
be promoted to GS-19 or be fired" — and if Proctor were to promote him,
Adams promised, then he would fire Proctor.[36]

But the seventh floor didn't share Adams's sense of levity, and the
ostracism at work began to affect him. A colleague recalled that Adams
didn't appear to be his usual happy self. "Sam was very discouraged.
Morose. He was wandering the halls with nothing to do."

At his farm Adams became convinced that his phone was being tapped and
that his house had been bugged. "It was a very scary time," Eleanor remembered, and the thought that family conversation was no longer private only
added to the sense of paranoia. "We went outside to talk about anything that
might have to do with his job." Adams was spooked by the airplanes that flew
low over the house, and indeed his car was followed once while he reconnoi-
tered around Union Station to pick up a mysterious woman (it was Dorothy
Clark — his mother). On another occasion Adams had been shadowed on
foot, and the next day he saw his tracker in the hallways of Langley. Adams
gave him a cheerful wave and grin and said, "Oh, hi!"

At other moments, however, Adams felt far less cocky, and at his nadir
he thought he might be arrested, tried for treason, and executed. Eleanor
also feared for her husband's safety: "I was always afraid something terrible
might happen to Sam; that it would be some unexplained car accident."

Adams's deteriorating situation at the agency prevented all chances that
his latest project on Chinese Communist strategic thinking, assigned one
year previous, would receive any recognition, let alone that which it
deserved. What Adams found in his research — which naturally for him
had veered off into order of battle issues — was that the CIA's numbers,
vintage 1958, for the Chinese People's Liberation Army (PLA) were no
longer accurate. Instead of having two and a half million troops as thought,
the PLA order of battle was now in the range of six to seven million.[37]

Adams did not push the PLA issue with any great passion, but when it
came to Cambodia he was determined to make a noisy last stand, and he

had of late achieved a victory of sorts. Due to his pestering, the agency's order of battle estimates for the Khmer rebels were allowed to "creep up to 40 to 50 thousand." This was done by the Manpower Branch, Adams explained sardonically, not only in response to his entreaties but also "to cover ourselves" at the agency just in case things in Cambodia went bad. But while the Khmer numbers were now somewhat more realistic, U.S. intelligence was still oblivious to a central fact of the Cambodian conflict.

This fact, which Adams learned from reading the captured documents, was that the Khmer insurgency was no longer a proxy for the Vietnamese Communists but was instead a bona fide Cambodian affair with Cambodians fighting Cambodians. "Far from being a foreign aggression" perpetrated by Hanoi, Adams held, "the Cambodian struggle is now a straightforward civil war." This war pitted the Khmer Rouge against the American-backed government in Phnom Penh, with the Khmers, Adams stated, having "out-recruited, out-organized and outfought the govern-ment." Overly focused on the dwindling role that the Vietnamese Communists were playing in Cambodia, the United States had paid no attention to the indigenous rebellion. As a result of this "intelligence neg-lect," Adams steamed, "we are left to watch in confusion as Cambodia falls to Cambodian Communists."[38]

Adams was determined to get the Cambodian intelligence story out. He informed CIA management "that a Mr. Lowenstein of the Senate Foreign Relations Committee has expressed an interest in talking to me about Cambodia," and also that he intended to submit an article, to be titled "A Cambodian Post Mortem," to the *New York Times*. Regarding the proposed article Adams demanded to know if he was still an agency employee, and as such still subject to having to clear it first with the CIA censors. This got the attention of the general counsel's office. On May 3 Adams was informed that he had never "been declared in excess" at all, and would indeed have to submit his article for classification review.[39]

With this news Adams became outraged about his March "dismissal" all over again, but this time for a different reason. The mock-firing, he rea-soned, was intimidation and intended to keep him from further assisting Ellsberg and Russo: It had been a crude attempt at witness tampering.

Adams immediately wrote a memo to James R. Schlesinger, Helms's replacement as director of the CIA. "Put bluntly," Adams explained to

Schlesinger of the cafeteria episode, "the timing of the incident made it appear that the CIA was threatening a Defense witness. As you know, the appearance in such matters is as important as the reality."[40]

Getting no response, Adams wrote Schlesinger again and demanded a personal meeting "before close of Business today concerning the possibility of your involvement, or that of the White House, in the incident of 19 March 1973." Adams was particularly insistent that Schlesinger answer "the key question 'Was the White House involved?'" Adams told Schlesinger that if no response was forthcoming then "I will relay" to the Ellsberg-Russo lawyers out in Los Angeles "what has transpired in the last few days. The Defense can make what they will of your failure to answer my question."[41]

Three days passed without an answer from Schlesinger. Finally, John Greaney contacted Adams. "I can state flatly," Greaney wrote, "that there is no basis in fact for any inference that the White House has shown any interest in your case." Before Adams could take the next step, however, the Ellsberg-Russo trial had come to an unanticipated end. This occurred on May 10 when Judge Byrne was informed by the prosecution "that an FBI employee recalls that in late 1969 and early 1970 Mr. Ellsberg had been overheard talking from an electronic surveillance of Dr. Morton Halperin's residence." Late 1969 and early 1970 was when the Justice Department was beginning to investigate Ellsberg and his activities, and the contents of any conversations that the future defendant had with the person who would become his chief consultant at trial was certainly *Brady* material. Byrne demanded that all FBI records pertaining to the surveillance (a phone tap) of Halperin's residence be turned over to the court. The FBI claimed no records could be found, and Byrne threw the entire case out the next day.[42]

*

Upon hearing the news Adams was disheartened — even embittered. He had hoped to have gotten a jury verdict of innocence for Ellsberg and Russo based upon his testimony. It might have been the breakthrough Adams was looking for, the chance to finally expose the Vietnam War deception fostered upon the American public by a colluding intelligence community, a deception that, he believed, was "bigger than Watergate." But now, with the bizarre ending to the trial, that opportunity was lost.

Tucked away at CIA headquarters with literally nothing to do (they had even taken away his phone), Adams made the best of it and informed

Southard that, should something come up, he would be at his desk writing his memoirs. But after a few days of this, Adams knew it was time to go.

In his last memo for the seventh floor, written May 17, 1973, Adams explained why he was resigning. "My main reason," he said, "is the belief that U.S. intelligence has been neither honest enough nor thorough enough in conducting research on the war in Indo-China. The failures in research have led to repeated misjudgments of the nature and strength of our adversaries there. The latest misjudgments concern the rebels in Cambodia. U.S. intelligence grossly underestimates their numbers. And it does not admit that the Khmer insurgents, who are virtually independent of Hanoi, are engaged in a civil war." Adams then added the words that he would repeat so many times to so many people throughout the rest of his life: "I hope one day to rejoin the Central Intelligence Agency, and resume my job as an analyst."[43]

The general counsel's office asked that Adams sign the "termination secrecy agreement" as was required by all employees, but Adams, after consulting with the ACLU, felt that the agreement was "overly broad and unenforceable" and refused. After a decade at Langley, Adams left headquarters for one last time a few days later. It was a month before his fortieth birthday.[44]

11

INVESTIGATIONS

Newly freed from the CIA and eager to publicize U.S. intelligence failures in Southeast Asia, Adams almost immediately published op-ed pieces in the *New York Times* ("Truth in the Balance") and the *Wall Street Journal* ("The Foe We Face in Cambodia"). From W. W. Norton he received a twenty-thousand-dollar advance for a book to be titled, in honor of the SNIE fight of '67, *Fourteen Three*. He also made the rounds on Capitol Hill, poking his head into dozens of Senate and congressional offices. Members of the Asian and Pacific Affairs Subcommittee took an interest in his allegations, and on June 6 he was invited to testify before them.[1]

By summer's end, though, the excitement had dissipated and Adams prepared to write his book. Going out to a wooded area he literally dug up his sources — the documents he had buried five or six years previously. He explained that "some water had gotten into the box as well as some worms" but otherwise most of the papers inside were in readable condition.[2]

Adams also began turning his attentions to farming at this time, the summer and fall of 1973, which was something that he had just started with a small herd of Black Angus cattle; it would grow into an operation smaller than a full-time farm but larger than a hobby. The farming for Adams was a joy, but writing was difficult going at first. Not getting much of it done around the farm, he accepted an invitation from the local librarian, Jean Curuthers, to use the attic of the Purcellville Library. "He would put on a coat and tie," remembered Eleanor of this arrangement, "and go and write his book without any distractions."

Adams soon established a routine for himself: farming, writing, and having lunch with a fellow writer and friend, John Gardiner, at the White Palace diner in Purcellville. Adams also maintained a busy social and cultural life with Eleanor, although at home the couple hadn't spent so much time together since Adams joined the agency in 1963, and fault lines in the marriage had become apparent. "Right at the time when he left the CIA," Adams's son Clayton said, "there were a lot of arguments, a lot of strain. The dominant feature — my memory of the household — was it was very, very strained between the two. There was more conflict than not."

Writing toward his patriotic deadline of July 4, 1976, Adams was in the attic of the library one day in early 1975 when a visitor, George Crile, appeared. Crile, a young and ambitious editor at *Harper's* and friend of Andrew Hamilton, had heard of Adams's project and wanted to turn it into an article. Crile's brand of journalism was investigative, and he and Adams quickly realized that they could work together. At Crile's direction Adams wrote something and, even though he had earlier refused to sign the termination agreement, submitted it to the CIA's Publication Review Board for classification review. The PRB returned the draft, stipulating where many deletions would have to be made and, in an editorial comment, noting that the punches aimed at former CIA director Richard Helms "were below the belt."[3]

*

By March, as the final draft for *Harper's* was being readied, South Vietnam and Cambodia were in danger of falling to the Communists. Adams shared his sense of doom with the readers of the *Wall Street Journal* by describing an incident in the Mekong Delta. "It was a routine execution," Adams wrote. "A notice had arrived from Viet Cong provincial headquarters the day before, sentencing the prisoner to death. That morning he was taken from his cell (really a bamboo cage), led about 200 yards down a narrow, winding dirt path to a clump of bushes and told to kneel. He did so and a VC guard shot him through the right temple. They buried the corpse in a shallow grave behind the bushes and later in the day crossed his name from the jailer's list and added it to a list of the dead." Adams went on, "Although this incident happened in 1967, it is apt [to be repeated] today because the Communists seem not only about to capture the capital of Cambodia, Phnom Penh, but they are setting themselves up to move eventually on Saigon. And when these cities are taken, the number of 'enemies of the revolution' who will fall into Communist hands will number in the hundreds of thousands. The question becomes: How many will they kill? On the prognosis of past performance, my outlook is on the gloomy side — probably many thousands."

Adams predicted that one hundred thousand South Vietnamese might be on the Viet Cong's postvictory death list, and although "no similar guess has been made for Cambodia," Adams wrote that "there is a good deal of evidence that the Cambodian rebels have executed fairly large numbers of people."[4]

Saigon fell to the Vietnamese Communists in late April. The *Harper's* cover story for May was titled "Vietnam Cover-Up: Playing War with Numbers," and subtitled "A CIA Conspiracy Against Its Own Intelligence." At Langley an agency man who had sympathetically observed Adams's battle with MACV and the seventh floor back in 1967, Richard Kovar, remembered the sensation this story made at the agency. "The article hit the DDI's office," he said, "like a bombshell — or a stink bomb." A memo was circulated within the research directorate that called Adams "a frustrated and embittered ex-employee" and explained that according to the PRB much of the *Harper's* story, "over fifty percent," contained "material not included in the submitted draft."[5]

In coordination with the timing of the May issue of *Harper's* Adams pressed the President's Foreign Intelligence Advisory Board for a full investigation of his charges that pre-Tet intelligence had been manipulated. The PFIAB declined to do so, although not before it asked the new DIA director — none other than General Daniel O. Graham — to respond. Graham dismissed the ruckus raised back in 1967 among intelligence professionals over the Viet Cong estimates as having been nothing more than "honest differences of opinion" and opined that no wrongdoing on his, or on the military's, part had ever occurred.[6]

The times, however, had changed since the days when an ambitious Colonel Graham was lopping Viet Cong units off the order of battle with his blue pencil, and the altered political climate in post-Watergate Washington was such that Adams's allegations about U.S. intelligence would no longer be ignored.

*

On Capitol Hill the Democratic congressman from Baltimore County, Maryland, Clarence Long, read the *Harper's* article. He was troubled by the allegations that the article raised about Vietnam War intelligence and asked one of his young staffers, Gregory Rushford, to read it also. Rushford, an air force veteran and expert on national security matters, was in no hurry to do so. "I thought," Rushford recalled of the magazine and of the magazine article's author, Sam Adams, "what would *Harper's* know about the CIA, and who is this guy?" However, Rushford did read the article, and like his boss he was alarmed at its accusations.

Rushford recognized that the Vietnam War intelligence cover-up was something to be looked into; more importantly, "Long recognized this also." Rushford had the congressman write a letter to the current CIA director, William Colby, asking if what Adams was saying was true. "No, no, nothing to it," Rushford recalled Colby writing back in so many words. Adams, Colby stated, "was a fine young man," but his *Harper's* article had "overblown" the importance of the Viet Cong numbers dispute, a dispute that was really, Colby assured, a very minor matter.

Dissatisfied by the CIA brush-off Rushford went out to Leesburg to meet with Adams in person, and Adams related what had happened to the pre-Tet intelligence and how America had been unprepared for the offensive. In the weeks ahead Rushford, now working for the newly formed Pike Committee, took the time to meet regularly with Adams to learn all that he knew. Besides names and dates, Rushford also received from Adams descriptions of the secret documents that would tell the tale of American intelligence corruption in Southeast Asia. Based upon these descriptions requests were made to the CIA. Rushford said, "We got the documents declassified and turned over to the committee; the whole record, four or five feet of documents. These were copies of the ones Sam had buried in his backyard, the ones with the wormholes."

Two congressional groups, the Pike Committee (House of Representatives) and the Church Committee (Senate), were for the first time in U.S. history launching a serious inquiry into America's foreign intelligence activities. The Church Committee met with Adams, heard what he had to say, and in its final report disagreed with him. With Rushford working for the Pike Committee, however, Adams could look forward to a lengthy airing of his concerns.

His date for testimony was Thursday, September 18, 1975. Rushford recalled, "Sam came up to the committee with ruddy cheeks from being outdoors all the time, and with straw stuck to his shoes, and he wore an old tweed sports coat and khakis."

*

In Room 2128 of the Rayburn Office Building the Honorable Otis O. Pike called the committee to order at five minutes past ten A.M. Adams was sworn in and promptly got down to business. "I would like now to begin quoting telegrams and memoranda, many of them within the CIA, some in the White House, some in Saigon, most of which never appeared before in public, which illustrate my assertions." He then launched into a full-bore revelation of how U.S. intelligence on the Viet Cong in the period before the Tet Offensive had been corrupted. Committee members, zealous though they may have been, were unprepared for the outpouring of classified data, and they cut their witness off. The congressmen went into a huddle to discuss the revelations and voted, six for and three against, to allow Adams the opportunity to continue. Pike warned Adams that he had to understand, however, that from now on he, Adams, and not the committee was assuming all responsibility for any spilling of state secrets.

His momentum unbowed, Adams then told Pike and his colleagues about clandestine operation Lamson 719 and how it had been fatally compromised by Viet Cong penetration agents. Lamson 719, Adams explained, was a plan devised in late 1970 and intended as a large-scale incursion by South Vietnamese troops into neutral Laos. The objective was to cut off the Ho Chi Minh Trail, but by the time the operation was launched in February 1971 even the most junior of Viet Cong soldiers knew all about it. This was because the enemy had gotten hold of the operational plans as early as November 1970 and had, Adams said, "been reading the thing backwards and forwards for months." It was all a classic example, Adams lectured, of how American failure to account for the vast Viet Cong security apparatus in South Vietnam consistently undermined U.S. initiatives during the war.

While the members of the Pike Committee digested this lesson, one of the congressmen was still transfixed on Lamson 719. "What was the result of the offensive?" the congressman asked. "What happened?"

Adams answered: "The South Vietnamese were really clobbered." This raised the question of how many agents the Viet Cong had at the time.

About thirty thousand, Adams thought. The next question dealt with how well the Americans themselves had fared at the spying game:

MURPHY: How many agents would you say we had operating within the VC?

ADAMS: At the start of the Tet Offensive we had one in Viet Cong ranks that I know about.

MURPHY: What effect, if any, did he have?

ADAMS: Well, there is actually an interesting story that goes along with this agent.

PIKE: Let me interrupt, now, just to ask a question: We are not in any manner going to endanger this man if he is active, are we?

ADAMS: No sir, he is dead.

PIKE: Thank you.

ADAMS: That is part of the story.

MURPHY: Since he is dead, would you tell us the details and what, if any, effectiveness he had?

ADAMS: This agent was run through a number of cutouts by a delightful American case officer up in Da Nang whose name I wouldn't mention even though he is retired. This guy looked, talked and acted like W. C. Fields. He always wore a white suit so the Vietcong would know who to go to if they wanted to become a spy.

At any rate, this agent handed in, in essence, the plans for the Tet attack on Danang. This fellow handed in those reports to the Marines in Danang, and he also sent a copy to the CIA station in Saigon. The station in Saigon — and I hope I have my story right; I have heard it a number of times — the station in Saigon didn't pay any attention to it and didn't forward it to Washington.

The Marines, however, did pay attention to it, and they deployed the Marine force in Danang in such a way that in fact Danang was one of the cities that the Tet attack was virtually beaten off. They just poured lead and gunfire on the approaching VC, and unfortunately also killed the agent in the process. So we were back down to zero after Tet. So the score became 30,000 to nothing.

Adams then returned to the subject of the Viet Cong numbers and of how General Westmoreland reacted when he learned from his J-2 staff that enemy strength was far larger than anyone had realized. Westmoreland, Adams explained, sat in his chair during that May 1967 briefing "practically with his jaw slack, with almost sort of a catatonic look, looking into the far distance." The general, Adams told the committee, "finally got back to his usual straight position, square jaw and so forth, but was still very much shaken . . . saying 'What am I going to tell the press, what am I going to tell Congress, what am I going to tell the President?' And then he squared himself even further up in his chair and said, 'Gentlemen, I want you to take another look at those numbers.'"

The witness was asked by the committee if he thought Westmoreland's request was tantamount to ordering an alteration of intelligence. Adams avoided a direct answer, saying only that it "indicates to me at least" that Westmoreland "was beginning to think about fudging the numbers."

The committee was coming around to the conclusion that Tet need not have caused so many U.S. casualties. One of the congressmen put the question to the witness.

> DELLUMS: Would you say that that 7,000 or 8,000 American soldiers were killed as a result of the ineptness, falsifications, and lies on the part of our intelligence community — namely the DIA and the CIA, who falsified data with respect to the strength of the North Vietnamese forces?
>
> ADAMS: I think that may be putting it a little strong because, after all, it wasn't the intelligence estimators who were shooting these guys — it was the Vietcong.
>
> DELLUMS: Let me put that question another way. . . .

Lastly, Adams told the Pike Committee that those military and CIA officials responsible for the numbers fakery during the war — people such as DIA Director Graham and former agency man William Hyland, who had since been made head of the State Department's intelligence unit — each seemed to enjoy career advancement. "These guys all made their positions by screwing up intelligence on Vietnam," Adams complained. Meanwhile,

Adams said, the working-level analysts who questioned the politicized intelligence all tended to have been subsequently fired, transferred, or held back, even though truthfulness was at the core of their job. "When I was a junior officer trainee," Adams explained to the congressmen, "we were constantly being drummed with the fact that we were supposed to be honest, objective, non-emotional, nonpolitical analysts. That was part of the indoctrination we were given." But this professional mantra had been drowned out by cries for intelligence about Vietnam that was only optimistic. The consequences, Adams contended, had been disastrous. "Although our aim was to fool the American press, the public and the Congress," he told the committee, "we in intelligence succeeded best in fooling ourselves."[7]

*

Reaction to Adams's testimony was swift. That evening the old Vietnam War hawk Walt Rostow released a statement asserting that the "capabilities of the Vietcong militia, and whether it should be included in the total strength estimate, had no bearing whatsoever on the assessment of insurgent capabilities before the 1968 offensive." Another prominent figure from the Vietnam War era, Bob Komer, called Adams's allegations "outrageous" and described the pre-Tet Viet Cong numbers debate as an "arcane" and "piddling" side issue that amounted to little more than a "tempest in an intelligence teapot." A voice dissenting from Rostow and Komer, however, was that of columnist Anthony Lewis. Lewis bemoaned the fact that, according to what Adams was saying, intelligence during the period before the Tet Offensive had been misused, and reminded his readers — for those who had forgotten their history — that the implications of this had not been insignificant at the time. At home in the United States the Tet surprise, Lewis wrote, "made the fiction of Communist weakness in Vietnam inoperative."[8]

*

The Pike Committee continued in its work for the remainder of the year. On December 3 Daniel Graham told the congressmen with a straight face, "We were not surprised by the fact of the Tet Offensive. We were not surprised by the massiveness of the numbers of troops committed. What surprised us was the rashness of the Tet attacks." When reminded that Adams had testified that in fact MACV had been unwilling to acknowledge the pre-Tet enemy strength figures, Graham responded by saying that Adams had a "mental problem."[9]

When subpoenaed to appear before the committee, George Allen was given a draft statement by George Carver — lest there be doubt, Allen said, about what the CIA "line was to be." Allen was also warned by the current CIA Director William Colby "to be very careful in answering questions." With these threats and admonishments fresh in his memory, Allen's ensuing testimony was less than candid. "I played my role on that occasion," he explained, "I regret to say, of not breaking ranks and conforming to what I now see clearly in my view was a whitewash."[10]

As the committee was completing its work the adversarial relationship between itself and the Ford administration that had existed from the beginning of the hearings grew progressively worse. The committee's confrontational style, combined with the publicizing of secret data and the making of unsubstantiated allegations by some of its members, lent the hearings an air of disrepute, causing potential allies such as Colonel Gains B. Hawkins to shy away from involvement. The nadir came when the committee's final report was leaked before it could be "sanitized." In response, the Ford administration immediately had the entire document locked up as a danger to national security, and so what was always intended to have been an open accounting of America's foreign intelligence failures was now a state secret, and Congress was furious. "The atmosphere," Gregory Rushford recalled, "was really poisoned, and then Dan Schorr of CBS published the report in the *Village Voice*. Well, that was just like being published in the *National Enquirer*, and nobody read it."

The ignored report had been written by Rushford and was everything Adams could have wanted. But sullied by its association with the *Village Voice* and that newspaper's racy personal ads, and eclipsed by the way it was leaked by Schorr, nothing came of it. Adams had been cheated once more, just as he had been shortchanged by the collapse of the Ellsberg-Russo trial, and while performing his role for the Pike Committee with distinction, the larger drama had again ended in farce.

*

The American Bicentennial came and went without the editors at W. W. Norton receiving a thing from their prospective author; nor was the publishing house about to get a manuscript anytime soon. Adams was in no hurry to complete what he now knew was to be his life's work: the telling to the world that the American intelligence debacles in Vietnam and Cambodia had been deliberate and preventable disasters. With the magazine cover stories and the congressional investigations having come and gone, Adams figured that it remained up to him alone to make the historical case, and the pressures he silently placed upon himself to do this both successfully and convincingly were enormous. More evidence — meaning more research — was needed.

Perhaps energized by examples such as the dogged Pike staffer Rushford, and by the committee's ability to call witnesses by the dozen, Adams emerged from years in the wilderness to contact his old colleagues and to plumb their memories about days gone by. He called around and found out where people were these days. He tracked down his former secretary from the Congo era, Colleen King, who was now living under her married name in Minnesota, and gave her a phone call. Adams also spoke with Dana and Janet Ball, George Allen, another former secretary, Beverly Adams, as well as Mary Gravalos, Bob Klein, Bobby Layton, Lydia Weber, Gordon Jorgensen, Mollie Kreimer, Paul Williams, Patrick McGarvey, Joseph Hovey, and a score of others.

Some were still at the CIA but many, like Adams, had left the company. Howard Beaubien for one was now running an Exxon gas station in Arlington, Virginia. Beaubien had enjoyed duty in Saigon enough but hated having to return to Langley afterward. "I felt like I was in jail," he told Adams. "That's exactly how that building felt like. They were probably as happy to see me go as I was to go." Douglas Parry was now practicing law in Chicago; Adams flew out to see him. Parry explained that he had applied to the CIA inspector general's office in the hope of becoming an agency lawyer, but they told him to finish law school first — at that point two years away — and then apply for a position. They could promise him nothing: "If we like you," they said coldly, "we'll take you." Parry thought *Screw that noise* and left Langley, never to look back.

Adams also flew to Los Angeles, where Joseph Hovey was now living. Having intended to make Langley his career since joining the agency in 1962, Hovey lasted only until December 1969. "I suddenly started to get the impression," he told Adams, "that no matter what we were doing in the intelligence community it didn't really matter. Either nobody was listening or decisions were being made not based on anything that we were producing. We had had the illusion in South Vietnam that what we were doing was important, significant, and it turned out that it really wasn't."

Adams got hold of Edward Hauck, the OSS veteran and old Asia hand, and asked him if in the early days of the war anyone had ever sought his advice about whether America should become involved. "Sure, they asked me," Hauck replied, "but they didn't listen. It's discouraging. You work your whole life on a single subject, and when it finally comes up, nobody pays attention. They're tuned into some dumb son-of-a-bitch on the evening news."[11]

The interviews of old CIA comrades were informative, but for the second part of his book — which Adams decided was to be a nonmemoir section to be called "Investigations" — he would need to talk to those on the other side. These were the former and present military men who had been part of the MACV intelligence fraud.

First, though, Adams had to have names. The principal characters he knew, people such as Westmoreland, Graham, and Davidson, but they obviously were not going to talk to him. In their stead Adams set out to learn the identities of the legions of officers who, during their tours in Vietnam (usually just twelve months), had been assigned to the lower ranks of the massive J-2 operation. These were men such as Gains B. Hawkins, men who knew where the bones were buried, and men who resented having been the ones forced to do the burying.

Based on what information about MACV he already had, Adams created an organigram of the J-2 command structure during the key period at MACV between late 1967 and early 1968. "You see who reports to whom," he recounted of his strategy. "What you do is find out who worked where, everywhere. And then the next most important thing is what days they were in Vietnam — when they showed up and when they left — because that indicates what they know."[12]

The fruits of Adams's labor began to fall slowly, one by one, into his basket. He met with Richard McArthur in Virginia in late 1975, and in 1976 he went to see J. Barrie Williams, Marshall Lynn, and Joseph Gorman. In

1977 Adams met with Thomas Black, John McIntosh, and James Meacham. In 1978 Adams talked to Joseph Price, John Lanterman, Harry White, Jerome Rinkus, Joseph McNeil, James Mauze, William Oxnard, Everette Parkins, John Rains, and George Hamscher. In October of that year Adams flew down to Florida to meet with Joseph McChristian. The harvest of 1979 was particularly bountiful: Among the many former MACV J-2 staffers Adams interviewed were Daniel Armet, Nelson Hallmark, Kelly Robinson, David Hope, Larry Pennsinger, Jonathan Saphire, Bernard Gattozzi, and, for perhaps the tenth time, Richard McArthur.[13]

There was no shortage of people willing to tell tales of underhandedness at MACV J-2. Marshall Lynn, who had been a young lieutenant and OB analyst in the section, for instance, told Adams that enemy service troop units had been arbitrarily slashed from the official estimate. Richard McArthur had also witnessed blatant cheating at MACV.

McArthur told Adams that in early 1968 he had kept, on a huge acetate wall chart, a running tally of all Viet Cong units in South Vietnam. Granted a brief leave for rest and relaxation, McArthur told Adams, he vacationed in Bangkok. Upon returning to work on the morning of February 13, 1968, he immediately noticed that someone had crudely tampered with his order of battle statistics: On his chart each of his Viet Cong unit strengths, written in grease pencil, had been erased and replaced with a number that was exactly half the original. McArthur was irate. He told Adams that he immediately confronted his commanding officer, marine Colonel Paul Weiler, about this.

Weiler apologized: "Sorry Mac, we had to do it."

"That's no answer, sir. Why?"

The colonel did his best to make McArthur see things the J-2 way, but the young lieutenant adamantly refused to part with his estimates.

Incensed, Weiler finally gave McArthur a bit of advice: "Lie a little, Mac. Lie a little."[14]

McArthur was not about to do so and within forty-eight hours, he told Adams, he found himself transferred, courtesy of Colonel Weiler, to a line unit. There the duty was far more hazardous than a desk job at MACV. At one point McArthur only narrowly escaped being hit in the head by a Viet Cong rocket.

Joseph Gorman, another former MACV J-2 staffer and young intelligence officer at the time, had been chief analyst for Viet Cong main unit forces in the American IV Corps area. Gorman talked to Adams and told him how MACV had become increasingly reluctant to accept new enemy formations. "One VC battalion," Adams explained according to what Gorman said, "was turned down by J-2 because Gorman's request form had a typographical error; another because the form's cover sheet was not centered; a third because the sheet lacked the proper red-pencil markings." Gorman said that the J-2's acceptance criteria at MACV became so rigid that "you could march a VC regiment down the hall, and they wouldn't put it in the OB."[15]

In addition to testimonials from the lower ranks, Adams got some from the upper echelons to talk as well. George Hamscher, the former colonel and CINCPAC representative to SNIE 14.3-67, described the Pentagon meeting in August 1967 in which Daniel Graham had blue-penciled enemy units. Hamscher told Adams that Graham had justified his actions by saying things like, "See, the Eighty-third Rear Service Unit, there must be a lot of civilians in there. Let's knock it down. It's not 3,100, it's 1,900. The 516th Local Force Battalion. We all know it just got clobbered the other day. Let's lower it. . . ." Another former colonel, David Morgan, backed up Hamscher's assertions. "We cut lots of units," Morgan said, "it was terribly wrong. We had no criteria for dropping people. It was guesswork. There was nothing to back it up. Why did we do it? To make ourselves look good, to make Danny Graham look correct, so we could prove we were winning the war."[16]

Former Colonel Charles Morris, Davidson's deputy J-2, had been "resentful" of his immediate subordinate in Vietnam, Daniel Graham. According to Morris, Graham had at every opportunity left the war zone for Washington, D.C., to brief the civilian leadership and promote his own career.[17]

Morris, though, had his own detractors. One of his subordinates at MACV, West Point graduate and then-Colonel Everette Parkins, told Adams that in the fall of 1967 Morris had rejected his November estimate of NVA filtration into South Vietnam as being too high.

"Ev," Morris had said, "you're not attritin' the enemy away, you're not attritin' the enemy away. Ev, you've got to attrite the enemy away."

"How the hell," Parkins countered, "can we attrite the enemy away when they are sending more and more people down here? We're not killing as many as they are sending in. No, these are the numbers, this is the methodology. I'm sticking to it."[18]

The argument continued, and Parkins lost his temper and shouted at Morris. Consequently, Morris later handed Parkins a bad fitness report — meaning that Parkins was fired from MACV and would be destined to join McArthur out in the field somewhere.[19]

Not all of the interviews were, from Adams's perspective, worthwhile. For example, he managed to schedule time with Maxwell Taylor, the former general, ambassador to South Vietnam, chief of staff of the U.S. Army, and chairman of the JCS. Certainly, Adams hoped, Taylor would shed some light on the political pressures put on the military to keep the enemy numbers low. Yet the get-together was a bust. "I prepared for my interview for upwards of a month," Adams recounted, "and in our hour-and-a-half talk got nothing save one usable quote."[20]

Some MACV sources were difficult for Adams to find. One such was James Meacham, a navy commander who was made chief of OB studies after Morris fired Parkins. Meacham appeared to have dropped off the face of the earth, and in a Hail Mary pass attempt to locate him Adams wrote him a letter and sent it to BUPERS, the Bureau of Personnel of the Navy. A short while later Meacham, who was now a military correspondent for the *Economist*, replied from England: He would be happy to meet with Adams.[21]

Without delay Adams took an airplane across the ocean and over the course of, as he noted, "19.5 hours," he and Meacham talked about intelligence during the war. Meacham, who before assignment to MACV had commanded a fleet of minesweepers, broadly hinted at improprieties with the Viet Cong estimates though, when pressed, declined specifics, only telling Adams repeatedly, "You know, you really should read the letters I sent home to my wife." Somewhat discouraged, Adams returned to the States and on November 30 wrote Dorothy Meacham, who had since the war become divorced from her husband, a gracious note asking if he could see the letters. A package soon arrived for Adams at his farm. He sat down and began to read.

*

Commander James Meacham had spent eleven months and one week in Vietnam, during which time he wrote his wife 322 letters. On July 24, 1967, Meacham had just arrived in-country and wrote Dorothy that he was staying "in the old French Foreign Legion headquarters with tall windows, high ceilings, louvers, Sidney Greenstreet fans, and a quadrangle with a swimming pool." On September 25 Dorothy heard from her husband that "I am gradually getting into the bean-counting business. It is really quite complicated and, of course, there is nothing except U.S. casualties which is more explosive politically." Four days later, on September 29, Meacham informed his wife, "I have a major crisis brewing relative to infiltration and strength figures. . . . [There is a] spiral of pressure to cook the books."

Meacham, as he explained it to Dorothy, found himself in charge of the J-2 computer operations that stored the OB data. On January 16, 1968, he wrote: "I am trying like mad to get the monthly retroactive strength calculations into the computer . . . it's like balancing about 36 bank books all at once when you haven't added up any checks for over a month."

In the letter of March 2 he reported: "Tomorrow will be a sort of day of truth. We shall see then if I can make the computer sort out the losses, since the Tet offensive began, in such a manner as to prove we are winning the war. If I can't, we shall of course jack the figures around until we do show progress."

March 19: "Lot's going on here. There are some high-level feet in the fire, and the heat is on us to quantify recruitment and infiltration since the Tet offensive. It does not matter that this kind of intelligence is basically not available, in other words, we will lie. We know the answer already — we are *winning* the goddamn war. Now it's up to us to prove it."

Undated: "The types from DIA were here and badgered me endlessly trying to pry the truth from my sealed lips. They smell a rat but don't really know where to look for it. They know we are falsifying the figures, but can't figure out which ones and how."

April 2: "West[moreland] is going to Honolulu tomorrow and has to have a bunch of poop to take with him, which means we have to tell the appropriate lies, justify and prove them, and put them in a simplified format so that his majesty can comprehend them."

May 11: "No solution of course, we just found a way to postpone the inevitable day of reckoning. I hope it comes after I am gone, because the roof may fall in. I can't say more. I'll explain when the war is over."

June 17: "The whole truth about this mess will likely never be known. For two cents, I would rat on the whole miserable mess; if I thought it would do any good, I would do it."

Finally, July 1: "I had a talk with CICV director today and let him know the truth about the doctoring of the strength figures. Now my conscience is clear. He knows the score — whether or not he acts to straighten things out is his concern. It's out of my hands."[22]

Adams put the last letter away. Rarely, since the day he discovered *Bulletin* 689, had he felt so elated.

In England, Meacham had suggested that Adams talk to Russell Cooley, the major who had helped him with the MACV computer program. Adams telephoned Cooley, who confirmed that the computerized manipulations had indeed occurred. Cooley explained it as a case of "reverse engineering" and one embarked upon at the behest of Graham. It was all an early-1968 attempt to massage, Cooley told Adams, the OB data so that "the transition into this post-Tet period look a little more smoother and rational." And there was another officer besides himself and Meacham, Cooley said, who had been in on this — an army lieutenant and a recent Boston College ROTC graduate at the time by the name of Bernard Gattozzi.[23]

Adams prowled around for this third man and found him right next door.

*

"It must have been the late '70s," Gattozzi remembered. "I got a call from Sam — I was working at the Department of Justice — out of the blue, and I didn't know Sam from a hole in the wall. He mentioned a few names of people who I knew well, people that I had worked with in Vietnam and whatnot. He was talking about Colonel Weiler, my boss's boss, General Davidson, and a few others. He knew enough people that I knew he wasn't a kook." Adams, Gattozzi said, then "asked if he could come and visit me in my office to talk about some Vietnam things that had happened about the time that I was in Vietnam, and I said 'Sure.'

"Well, Sam came in," Gattozzi continued, "he sat down — he used to write on these long yellow legal pads — and he pulled this sheath of papers out of his briefcase and he is just going, 'Okay, have you ever heard of so-and-so and have you ever heard of so-and-so?' and I was answering as fast as I could, 'Yeah, yeah, no, no, yeah, yeah, no, no.' 'Okay,' Sam says, 'this is what I have got so far,' and then he launches into a description of the deception, the deliberate miscounting of the Viet Cong main forces and local forces in Vietnam. He must have gone on half an hour nonstop, telling me about what this guy said, what that guy said. He was just animated."

Gattozzi remembered sitting through the performance "enthralled, I listened to it all, and everything he had to say kind of colluded with my recollections of the Viet Cong order of battle business." Finally, though, Gattozzi felt compelled to get a word in edgewise. He made a T with his hands.

"Sam, time out! Everything you have said is wonderful and it is true, but you are missing half the picture."

The Adams monologue stopped midsentence.

Gattozzi spoke. "What was going on and what you are finding out about counting for the Viet Cong was also going on with the North Vietnamese Army."

Adams's jaw dropped.

"I am surprised," Gattozzi recalled saying, "that you haven't mentioned not one thing about the North Vietnamese Army and the counting of it."

"'I — I — just never thought about it," Adams stammered, "I have just been concentrating on the Viet Cong."

"Well, all right, let's concentrate on the North Vietnamese Army. Same thing was going on, same intelligence deception."

Now it was Gattozzi's turn to lecture. He explained to Adams how MACV's original system — "a good system" — had estimated NVA infiltration. Listening intently, Adams got out an apple and ate it core and all ("I had never seen anyone do that before," recalled Gattozzi). The MACV accounting of NVA was an all-source methodology, Gattozzi remembered telling Adams, that took into consideration captured documents, enemy interrogations, defector interrogations, and communications intercepts. One source indicating NVA troop movements down the Ho Chi Minh Trail into South Vietnam would be a "possible," two sources indicating the same thing would be a "probable," and three sources would be a "confirmed."

"After the first month of data collection passed," Gattozzi said, "you had a feel for what was coming down the trail, after the second month passed you had a better feel, and after the third month you had a real good feeling. And after the third month of collection you had a firmed-up figure for the first month that didn't change a whole lot and was about eighty, ninety percent accurate."

The first firmed-up figure was the September 1967 one, Gattozzi explained, and it was alarming. It indicated, he recalled, "At least twelve thousand to fifteen thousand North Vietnamese Army infiltrators came down the Ho Chi Minh Trail that month." The analysts at MACV, stunned, had to break the bad news. "We would go to our superiors and our superiors would say, 'No, no, no, no, no. General Westmoreland says the infiltration is four to six thousand NVA a month. Period. That's it. That's all you can use, that number, four to six thousand.' So," Gattozzi told Adams, "I say, 'What do I do with the twelve to fifteen thousand that we are picking up each month?' 'I don't care what you do with it' was the answer, 'you just can't put it in the order of battle.'"

The analysts were in a predicament, Gattozzi told Adams: "We thought, *Holy mackerel, what do we do now?*" There appeared to be only one solution. "What we ended up doing, literally, we were keeping two sets of books," he explained to Adams. "Two of these long ledger sheets with the columns."

As the all-source intelligence data came in for October and November, the estimates of NVA infiltration grew. December, as Gattozzi recalled telling Adams, "was huge, and there were some months that, maybe, reached thirty thousand. And so we knew something was up, we just couldn't report it. And what was up was the Tet Offensive. End of January '68 they hit us with everything they had, and it was a lot more than what we thought they had."

It was during Tet, Gattozzi informed Adams, that the J-2 section was forced to reconcile its earlier assertions about the weakened strength of the enemy with obvious evidence to the contrary. He told Adams that this readjusting backward and forward had been a frustrating and difficult task, but one MACV had no choice but to accomplish: After the first days of Tet the enemy casualty figures "started coming in and we subtracted them out of the sanctioned, blessed figures — and flat ran out of enemy." Soon, according to Gattozzi, the conclusion "We won the war, might as well go home" was the sarcastic one reached by the J-2 analysts. "There was no one out there to fight anymore, we literally ran out of people. And I remember being told to go back and get this system on computer and start plugging in the numbers, back, chronologically a year and a half before that will make it come out now that there is a fighting force to still fight."

Gattozzi soon had the NVA back up to combat strength although, he recalled, "Even then it was a deflated figure. It was not based on any intelligence; it was a wild-ass guess."

Adams was dumbstruck by what Gattozzi was telling him. He went back to Gattozzi time and again — perhaps fifteen times in all — to learn more. Gattozzi, for his part, was happy to play host to the former CIA man. "Every time we met it was a thoroughly enjoyable time," he recalled. "Sam was like a breath of fresh air. We would talk and talk and talk, not just about Vietnam and the things he was interested in but about life in general and things like that. He was a great, great conversationalist, we would spend hours together — it was great."

*

The back of the Ford F-150 was loaded first with Clayton's belongings — clothes, sneakers, posters, skis, records, stereo equipment, electric guitar, and amplifier — and then with Clayton himself. In the small cab up front Sam Adams climbed into the driver's seat while Eleanor took the passenger's. It was a five-hundred-mile drive north from Leesburg, Virginia, to Concord, Massachusetts, and truck and family arrived at Concord Academy on a late-August day in 1977. Mother and father helped their son unpack and get settled in his new surroundings, but the time eventually came for the parents to return to Virginia and the new freshman to stay in

Massachusetts. Good-byes were said, and eyes blurred with tears. For the three it was a hard parting, made all the more difficult because each knew that with Clayton now away there was suddenly much less reason for Sam and Eleanor to stay together.

The marriage did not end with Clayton moving north to prep school, however, but went on essentially as it had, with the daily emotional tensions palpable. Adams, meanwhile, continued his regular commute to the little Purcellville Public Library, where the daffodils he'd planted out front when he'd started his book were now coming up faithfully spring after spring. The fact that her husband was not moving on in life must have been straining for Eleanor, but it was for his own sake that she became increasingly concerned. "It was in the late '70s or so," she remembered, "and the book became an obsession. There was no detail too small that Sam wouldn't put into it. I mean he would ask somebody who had something to do with the numbers where they were on a certain day, what the weather was like, what they had for lunch. He got into obsessive detail which — to me looking in from the outside — was totally irrelevant; he wasn't adding any new evidence to the argument. He just couldn't stop gathering material. I can't explain it other than he just didn't want to finish the book."

In time Adams dispensed with writing narrative and instead devoted his energies to expanding his voluminous collection of yellow legal pad notes. What Adams called his "master chronology," which covered the outline of the numbers episode, ran 144 pages. He then had separate chronologies for each individual involved. George Allen had a 45-page chronology, George Carver 8 pages, Bernard Gattozzi 19, Daniel Graham 66, George Hamscher 13, Richard Helms 35, Joseph Hovey 234, Robert Komer 25, Nguyen Cao Ky 44, Marshall Lynn 60, James Mauze 15, Richard McArthur 163, Buford McCharen 6, Joseph McChristian 72, Scott McClelland 27, Robert S. McNamara 10, James Meacham 238 . . . Walt Rostow 126, William C. Westmoreland (beginning with Westmoreland's birth on March 26, 1914) 135.

Referencing the spate of memoirs that came out after the war had ended, Adams also attempted to correlate where high-level officials were situated on certain days in Washington to see if he could pinpoint exactly when and where the order to corrupt the intelligence was given. He had his hunches and, by talking to contacts at the Pentagon, developed a theory that McNamara had been behind the conspiracy. But this supposition was not irrefutable. "It seemed to me that every time we had lunch," a CIA colleague recalled, "Sam had a new story, a new thesis, and he was going off in a lot of different directions. There was always some new person at that point. That was why he couldn't finish his book; he was never able to stop and put pen to paper. I can't remember him ever saying he had enough evidence to say who had actually ordered the intelligence cover-up, although he blamed LBJ for wanting to be the recipient of good news."

Surrounded by his chronologies Adams spent hours working this all out for himself, and Eleanor could sometimes hear him in the upstairs study. "He would get hugely excited," she recalled, "you could hear him just pacing around and talking to himself and laughing as if he were right onto this hot thing. But you didn't know what it was or where it was going to go. It was strange."

12

CBS REPORTS

The Adams daily routine appeared certain to continue on indefinitely. He had switched the title of his book from *Fourteen Three* to *Who the Hell Are We Fighting Out There?* but there was no finished manuscript as yet, and Adams had already outlived his editor at W. W. Norton. The routine changed, however, when George Crile showed up again in his life one cold weekend in November 1980. During a visit to the farm Crile was shown the piles of chronologies that Adams had created since their time together on the *Harper's* article. Crile was thrilled with all this new information. He was now with CBS News, and sensed that here was a story made for television.[1]

Crile returned to New York and put together a sixteen-page "blue sheet" proposal for a documentary based upon what Adams's chronologies contained. Meanwhile, he gave *60 Minutes* correspondent Mike Wallace a copy of the old *Harper's* article to read. By the end of November the blue sheet was in the hands of Howard Stringer, head of the network's documentary unit, and Wallace had agreed to be the lead correspondent should the project get the go-ahead.

The Wallace endorsement was a critical one and helped Stringer with the decision to approve the film on the condition that Crile could actually get the key players involved to talk on film. It all happened very fast, and Adams got the good news at his home in Virginia. Assuming that the documentary received final approval, Crile said, Adams would become project consultant. By early January, Adams was — incredibly almost — off the farm and at CBS on West 57th Street advising Crile on whom the best candidates were for the initial interviews. Typically thorough, Adams had listed eighty people as possibilities.

On January 18 Adams phoned former Colonel David Morgan — who had been Gains B. Hawkins's deputy at MACV — and two days later Adams and Crile were in Chula Vista, California, for the first interview. It was not an auspicious start: Morgan was unwilling to go on record. Adams explained, "He said it was one thing to tell a guy like me, it's another to spill his guts in front of God knows how many million people." Former Colonel Everette Parkins was next on the list, though he, too, refused. Marshall Lynn agreed to go on camera but Mike Wallace was unprepared for the interview and bungled it, Lynn coming across as defensive and contradictory. An interview with former South Vietnamese Prime Minister Ky Cao was friendly enough, Ky having always believed that the Americans hid accurate intelligence from him during the war. Ky, though, had no specific knowledge of any wrongdoing, and his interview would also be left on the cutting-room floor. An interview with Joseph Hovey was successful and a "take," but Hovey was former CIA and Crile and Adams really needed to crack the MACV wall of silence. This they did soon enough, first with George Hamscher's interview and then three weeks later with Richard McArthur's.[2]

February ended; Adams was paid four thousand dollars by CBS for his time that month, plus expenses. Adams was compensated a similar amount for March when he and Crile flew over to London to interview James Meacham and then flew back again to the States to film Gains B. Hawkins in Mississippi. Next on the itinerary was a flight to Florida to interview Joseph McChristian ("General McChristian," as Hawkins had written Crile earlier, "is your white knight serene, impeccable and untouchable").[3]

Toward the end of March, Crile assembled rough cuts of the Hovey, Hamscher, McArthur, Meacham, Hawkins, and McChristian interviews and showed them to Stringer and CBS News Vice President Roger Colloff. It was powerful material. Crile was given permission to go ahead with the documentary.

*

The documentary team took shape. Wallace would be "lead correspondent" while Crile would act as both reporter and producer. The other producers were to be Andrew Lack (senior), Stringer (executive), and Joseph Zigman (associate). Adams was the consultant, Ira Klein and Phyllis

Hurwitz the film editors, Carolyne McDaniel the secretary, and Alex Alben the researcher.

Alben was a recent Stanford University graduate who had worked in the CBS Special Events Unit during the 1980 elections. There one of his duties was to compile a huge fact book for Walter Cronkite. With the 1980 voting completed, however, Alben transferred to the network's documentary division, which had in the past produced such legendary works as "Harvest of Shame," the *CBS Reports* special by Edward R. Murrow about migrant labor. At the documentary division Alben's new boss was Crile, who told him to begin reading about the Vietnam War. Shortly thereafter Alben met Adams. "Sam came up to New York," Alben recalled, and "had his chronologies on long yellow legal pads." Adams's handwriting was not decipherable, however, and Alben found himself typing away while Adams read aloud. "We would spend scores of hours doing this," Alben explained. "I really was seized by the subject matter; this was something that was very exciting." Alben also liked Adams. "He had an air of mystery to me because he had the label 'CIA.' I was learning a lot about the agency and how it operated, and I was impressed by how earnest he was about this subject matter. Sam was very principled, and he was putting his life story and reputation on the line."[4]

The network gave Crile a decent-sized budget ($250,000), and the documentary team was not left wanting. Alben was busy scheduling interviews, contacting the LBJ Library for documents, and, always it seemed, going over the chronologies with Adams and Crile. The film editors were meanwhile processing the interview footage and picking through miles of old newsreel for compelling images of the Vietnam War.

Crile, with Adams and a film crew in tow, had interviewed Russell Cooley and George Allen. (Allen had agreed to this only after Crile promised him that the documentary was in no way critical of the CIA; he was nervous in front of the camera and had to be filmed for a second time, which would later become a very major issue for CBS.) Meanwhile, Wallace had interviewed Daniel Graham (pugnacious as usual and unsparing in his criticism of Adams, Graham told Wallace, "He tried to get me court-martialed . . . I think he's got a hang-up that verges on a mental problem over people refusing to accept his number at the time of the Tet

Offensive; I think it's a mental problem") and also Walt Rostow (whose interview lasted three hours and failed to offer anything of substance).[5]

Although Wallace was the documentary's on-camera star, he was having difficulty grasping the overall story. "I just remember we were going to interview somebody," said Alben, "and Mike Wallace did not remember my name. And actually he just kicked me, pushed me with his foot, and said 'What is this? What is the story? Is it a conspiracy?' And I realized that he was like any busy correspondent doing ten things at once, including doing *60 Minutes* every second or third week, but he was having problems processing all the facts of the story." Alben believed that Wallace, a veteran newsman, needed a "headline," and Alben thought he would give him one. By way of an answer to Wallace's question, therefore, Alben said that the story was about a "conspiracy to deceive the president." This seemed to satisfy Wallace. After that, according to Alben, "I think Wallace became engaged in the story very deeply."

*

The majority on the Adams list of eighty, of course, would not make it in front of the CBS cameras. There were many reasons for this besides the fact that the list was too long. Former General Phillip Davidson, for example, was suffering from cancer and reported to be on his deathbed. In another instance Adams believed that an interview with the aged Ellsworth Bunker might well backfire, telling Crile that the former ambassador to South Vietnam had certainly been "in on" the intelligence deception but that Bunker was "awfully old now, and CBS might look like it's hounding an old man to his grave." And then there were outright refusals — Helms, Colby, and McNamara being prominent ones — and also men sympathetic to Adams, such as Bernard Gattozzi, who feared for their government careers and who apologetically had to decline.[6]

During their long hours of working and traveling together Crile and Adams had their differences, but overall they were a good fit. Both were passionate about the subject, Crile being driven to make a great documentary and Adams propelled to set the historical record straight. "Sam was primarily like the kid in the candy store," said Alben. "Here were all of the people who he had been chatting with, visiting, all of a sudden you got them on tape before CBS and confirming what they had been telling him, and so it was a huge affirmation of his whole thesis." At times, though, Adams's presence was not welcomed. Crile recounted, "Sam likes to know where somebody sat in the room, what kind of haircut they had, who got travel orders at the same time." During the Cooley interview, for example, Crile remembered that "Cooley announced something innocuous and I heard a loud thump. It was Sam as he reached for his chest, pulled out his pen, and started to ask questions, quite out of control, rapid-fire." Only when Adams turned in for the night was Crile able to win Cooley's confidence and convince him to participate in the documentary.[7]

The most important week of interviewing turned out to be the second one of May. On Tuesday it was Adams's time to go before the camera. Crile, Wallace, Zigman, Alben, and the film crew flew down to Washington and drove out to the farm outside Leesburg. Crile wanted everything just right. He rearranged the furniture in the Adamses' living room and was making even more drastic changes until Eleanor had to tell him to leave the door on its hinges. The interview went well; Wallace, like everyone else, was pleased. The questions for Adams were hardly difficult for him to answer, although Wallace did throw a curveball at him toward the end of the interview:

> WALLACE: Why is this such a preoccupation of yours, almost a mania to get to the bottom of it?
>
> ADAMS: I suppose because it was, you know, I figured I had this big thing going. I felt very strong about it, and —
>
> WALLACE: It's an obsession with you.
>
> ADAMS: An obsession with me? That's a strong word, but I suppose you could say that's a case, but it's a hell of an interesting subject. I mean, if you got to be obsessed, it's not a small obsession.[8]

The interchange would not appear in the documentary.

*

The documentary team departed for New York. Westmoreland had agreed to be interviewed and, in lieu of the cash honorarium the retired general wanted, CBS was putting him and his wife up for the weekend at the Plaza Hotel. Westmoreland, who until then had only been in telephone contact with Crile, never saw anything in writing regarding the specific nature of the CBS questioning, only that it would involve a dozen or so topics relating to the Vietnam War. Recalled Alben, "I had some differences of opinion with George," and he complained to Crile, "You've got to be much more upfront about what we are driving toward." Crile told Alben, "Well, we will get Westmoreland into the room and then go into that." Alben's objections were heard, however, and the night before the interview Crile read a detailed letter over the phone to Westmoreland, who was already at the Plaza. In the letter the potential topics were pared down to five, and the penultimate one was "The controversy between the CIA and the military over enemy-strength estimates." "But," explained Alben, "we did not mention Sam Adams."

On Saturday morning, May 16, Wallace, Crile, Zigman, Crile's CBS colleague Diekhaus, and two camera crews were taken up to the Westmorelands' room. Adams was at another location and ready to give advice over the phone, if needed, to Wallace during breaks in the filming. The interview, recalled Alben, "was the turning point of the documentary story."

From the CBS perspective the Westmoreland interview went off entirely as planned, in fact even better than planned. Under questioning by Wallace the retired general appeared to be the proverbial deer in the headlights. Wallace, Crile, Zigman, and Diekhaus bid Westmoreland — still dazed from the Wallace treatment — good-bye, and the camera crews packed up their equipment. The documentary team departed the hotel where Adams and Alben were waiting impatiently outside. "We ran into this restaurant," Alben remembered, "and George was just spilling out everything about the interview. George was so wound up — he realized he had enough good stuff in there to make the documentary work."

By August the documentary process had moved into the editing room. Alben in the meantime decided to return to Stanford and to begin law school. Crile was occupied with another CBS News project about the Miami drug trade, and in his absence the film editors were overwhelmed. Joseph Fackovec was added to the crew to help out, and he, Klein, and Hurwitz toiled around the clock to get the documentary ready for its scheduled release date. Then, at the last minute, the ever-detailed Adams noticed two flaws: one, the narration contained an inaccurate description of former General Davidson, and two, Wallace had misquoted a Meacham letter during his interview of Westmoreland. Panic threatened. The Davidson error, it was decided, could simply be spliced out and hence rendered harmless, but the Meacham misquote was a trickier problem because it came in the middle of the documentary's most important interview. There was much anguish and debate within and between the documentary team and CBS News management about what to do. Finally it was resolved to have Wallace read into the soundtrack the accurate Meacham quote, while leaving the visuals unchanged. With a sigh of relief — and after ten months of hard work — the documentary was now ready for airing.

*

On Friday, January 22, 1982, newspapers in New York, Chicago, and Los Angeles carried a full-page advertisement that depicted eight uniformed military officers seated around a small table reviewing charts, graphs, and maps. Something was going on. "Conspiracy," as the bold type proclaimed and the accompanying copy suggested, was what was happening around that table. At the bottom of the advertisement viewers were informed that the *CBS Reports* special "The Uncounted Enemy: A Vietnam Deception," by Mike Wallace and George Crile, could be seen on their local CBS affiliate, Saturday at nine thirty P.M. Eastern Standard Time.

Although the film was seventy-eight minutes long, it was placed within a ninety-minute slot: Time would be needed for the Tums antacid and other commercials. The broadcast aired was a masterpiece of journalistic efficiency that used just eleven interviews to tell a very complex story. The camera work was spare, the indoor settings for the interviews somber, and the color war footage of dead bodies and captured enemy disturbing. There was throughout the seventy-eight minutes an oppressive and almost funereal feel to the documentary, a texture that matched its dark tale of intelligence deception and deceit.

*

Documentaries always fared poorly in the television ratings game, and the *CBS Reports* special, which faced insurmountable competition with both *Love Boat* and *Fantasy Island* airing on ABC during the same time slot, did not surprise. With 9.6 million viewers tuning in to "The Uncounted

Enemy" it was the least watched show that Saturday night — as it was the least watched show of all prime-time programs broadcast that week. But CBS was delighted with its product, and the network's pride showed. In addition to Friday's full-page newspaper advertisements, advance copies of the transcript had been delivered to the press, and two days before the broadcast teaser clips of the Westmoreland interview appeared, along with guests Wallace and Crile, on CBS's *Morning with Charles Kuralt and Diane Sawyer*. There was even loose talk at CBS headquarters about a made-for-television movie being already in the works.[9]

Press reaction to the program was immediate. On the morning after the broadcast the Sunday *New York Times* editorialized that the CBS program had "showed that Lyndon B. Johnson himself was victimized by mendacious intelligence," and warned that something similar might be occurring presently in regard to President Reagan and Central America. Later that week Robert Healy in the *Boston Globe* wrote that because of Westmoreland's reluctance to tell bad news to Johnson, "Washington, Congress and the American people were misled."

And then there were the accolades. An article in the *Washington Post* praised the documentary, *Newsweek* admired CBS for "trying to set the record straight," and columnist and conservative icon William F. Buckley heralded the show and wrote that "General Westmoreland for political reasons withheld from the President, probably from the Joint Chiefs, from Congress and from the American people information about the enemy." On the pages of the *Wall Street Journal* Hodding Carter III stated that CBS had "rendered an important public service" by detailing "the appalling lies which were fed to the upper reaches of government and to the American people about enemy strength in Vietnam in the late 1960's."

On Tuesday, though, a furious Westmoreland announced that he would hold a press conference at the Army-Navy Club in Washington, D.C. The conference was held as threatened. Appearing with Westmoreland were Ellsworth Bunker (who was indeed "awfully old now" and would die shortly), former General Phillip Davidson (evidently risen from his deathbed), former SAVA chief and onetime Adams patron George Carver, and — apparently returning to the MACV fold — former Colonel Charles Morris.

Westmoreland angrily informed the assembled representatives of the fourth estate that he had been the innocent victim of "notorious reporter Mike Wallace" and that Wallace had tried to "prosecute me in a star-chamber procedure with distorted, false and specious information, plain lies, derived by sinister deception, an attempt to execute me on the guillotine of public opinion." Westmoreland continued that "Mike Wallace, primarily on the basis of material provided by a former intelligence analyst for the CIA, Sam Adams, accused me of withholding and falsifying important intelligence information to the extent that generated a sinister conspiracy against the national interest. This is a preposterous hoax and will not go unanswered."

Carver then took the lectern and made less heated and more nuanced criticisms of the show's central thesis. Graham was eager to join the fray in its entirety, having even arranged taped excerpts from the documentary in order to dissect them for inaccuracies. When the tapes rolled, however, a *Washington Post* reporter pointed out that Graham had taken a Hawkins quote out of context.[10]

At the Army-Navy Club Westmoreland demanded that CBS provide him enough airtime to rebut the documentary. By way of answer, Dan Rather on the *CBS Evening News* that night promised the network would "give further study to the specific allegations made at the news conference." The "further study" turned out to be nothing more than a brief internal report written by Crile defending the program — and at CBS the Westmoreland tirade was forgotten about.[11]

Adams and his duffel bag filled with the yellow chronologies were now no longer a familiar sight at CBS since he had returned full time to his neglected farm and to his long-delayed book. Adams had hoped for a windfall of extended publicity — maybe even a conspirator or two who wanted to come in from the cold — but except for the first few days of friendly press coverage, and some letters of praise for Adams from viewers that were forwarded to him by CBS, "The Uncounted Enemy" in this regard disappointed. In February, Adams went up to Concord, Massachusetts, and to his son's school, where on the strength of the documentary he had been named Father of the Year. After having this small honor bestowed upon him, Adams went back to raising cattle and writing a book that might someday be completed, and he and his cause appeared destined to again fade into obscurity.

*

Four months after it aired the CBS documentary was the subject of the cover story for the May 29 issue of *TV Guide*. The article, titled "Anatomy of a Smear: How CBS News Broke the Rules and 'Got' Gen. Westmoreland," ran an entire eleven and a half pages and was the longest story *TV Guide* had ever published. Although nowhere did authors Don Kowet and Sally Bedell actually assert that Westmoreland was the victim of a "smear," their intent was clearly to take venerable CBS down a notch or two. In the making of "The Uncounted Enemy " CBS had, they wrote:

- Begun the project already convinced that a conspiracy had been perpetrated
- Turned a deaf ear toward evidence that suggested otherwise
- Paid $25,000 to a consultant on the program without adequately investigating his fourteen-year quest to prove the conspiracy theory
- Violated its own guidelines by rehearsing its consultant
- Allowed a sympathetic witness to view interviews of others in order to get him to re-do his interview
- Gave sympathetic witnesses soft questions while unfriendly witnesses were grilled
- Ignored witnesses who might have given a different account of the story
- Pulled quotes out of context
- Not admitted that its own paid consultant, Sam Adams, now doubts the documentary's premise

According to Kowet and Bedell, Adams had believed all along that "the conspiracy originated in the White House, not with Westmoreland. Adams has since repeated this concern to *TV Guide*. He says that in helping to prepare the CBS show, he felt more acutely than George Crile that the conspiracy originated in the White House, not with Westmoreland. 'The problem was once you get above Westmoreland, my evidence at that time was marginally circumstantial — of the rumor variety.' Now, however, Adams is convinced that Westmoreland was 'acting as a go-between rather than an instigator. In other words, he was a deputy sinner, rather than the chief sinner.' Consequently, says Adams, 'What I am doing, in my book, is I'm trying to get the smoking guns into the White House.'"

Mike Wallace would remember of the article that it "could not have come out at a worse time. It hit the newsstands while CBS's annual affiliates meeting was taking place in San Francisco and within that group the article struck a responsive chord. In years past, many conservative owners and managers of stations in the CBS family had not been happy with the network's coverage of the war in Vietnam, and the portrayal of General Westmoreland in the *CBS Reports* documentary had revived some of those resentments. And now the piece in *TV Guide* seemed to confirm their worst suspicions about the broadcast." The article caused a noticeable "tremor" at the affiliates meeting. Acting quickly, CBS News President Van Gordon Sauter announced that veteran CBS News producer Burton "Bud" Benjamin would launch a full-scale in-house investigation.[12]

Benjamin planned to interview a total of thirty-two people, a small sample by Adams's standards but apparently enough for Benjamin to complete the investigation. Benjamin's first interview was with Ira Klein, the person everyone knew was the "unnamed source" at CBS whom Kowet and Sedell had mentioned in their article. Klein had during the making of the documentary developed a deep hatred toward Crile, blaming Crile for, among other transgressions, belittling his competency during the editing process. Klein's opening to get back at Crile came soon after Westmoreland's Army-Navy Club press conference. By happenstance, Adams was visiting the CBS building on 57th Street to pick up a sixteen-millimeter copy of the documentary to show at Concord Academy as part of his Father of the Year address. Adams, Klein, and Phyllis Hurwitz got to talking in the cutting room about what Westmoreland had said at his press conference when, according to Klein, Adams made a startling admission: "We have to come clean, we have to make a statement that the premise of the show is inaccurate. LBJ had to know."

Over the next few days Klein voiced his concerns to Crile and Wallace about Adams's confession, and Andy Lack called Adams to see if what

Klein was saying was true. Adams rejected Klein's version of the cutting-room conversation. "What I imagine I was saying," Adams told Lack, "was what I was saying all the time, that it seemed to me there might have been higher-ups involved." Satisfied with this answer Lack, to Klein's great annoyance, dropped the issue. Shortly thereafter CBS became aware that *TV Guide* was looking into certain problems with how "The Uncounted Enemy" had been made.[13]

Kowet and Bedell were both experienced reporters and could not be dismissed as hacks (indeed, Bedell would soon leave *TV Guide* to join the *New York Times*), but suspicions at CBS were that *TV Guide* was out to "get" CBS. The network had long irked conservatives such as Walter Annenberg — a multimillionaire Republican with close ties with the Reagan White House where CBS was reviled as the "most liberal" of the big three networks. Annenberg was also the owner of *TV Guide*. Kowet and Bedell steadfastly denied being pressured to pursue their story, but many inside and outside CBS held that the "smear" article was unquestionably payback for the network's past reportage.

After seeing Klein, Benjamin then interviewed, one by one, all the other principals of the documentary. Adams's time came on June 21. Benjamin remembered well his first impressions of the man whom he called "the godfather" of the documentary: "Adams, one week to the day past his forty-ninth birthday, blue-eyed, his brown hair showing the first flecks of gray, was described by a woman friend as looking like 'a rustic Paul Newman.'" Benjamin welcomed Adams into his office and then immediately brought up the question foremost on his mind: Are you obsessed? Adams replied, "What is obsessed? I'm very interested in the subject. I explain how we lost the war. If this is obsessed, so be it." Benjamin carefully observed Adams during the course of the interview and came to believe that, if perhaps not obsessed, Adams could "be stubborn and inflexible."

Leaving the subject of Adams's personality to one side, Benjamin brought up the specific complaints that had been leveled against the documentary. One was that the interviews shown on the program were stacked against Westmoreland. Where in the documentary, Benjamin asked Adams, were "the Carvers, Komers, and Rostows"? Adams countered that many who agreed with the premise of the documentary had also not been given the opportunity to tell their story. "In the selection of people we asked," said Adams, "we had so many to support me that we had to slice the list of supporters. For the infiltration story, we used Cooley, but we could have had several other sources." But certainly, Benjamin asked, former General Davidson should have been allowed to come to Westmoreland's defense? "No," Adams answered. "We had so damn many people, he was just another." Benjamin asked Adams when it was discovered that Davidson was not, as he was reported to be, on his deathbed.

"Well before the broadcast, around December," answered Adams.

"You told Crile?"

"I told George, 'Holy Cow!' [but] I don't know if he tried to get hold [of] Davidson."

Benjamin then noted that Adams had initially recommended Komer as an interview prospect, and so why wasn't Komer interviewed? Adams did not disagree with the thrust of Benjamin's argument on this point. "He would have been," Adams told Benjamin, "a damned interesting interview. This is what Komer would have said: 'Of course, we did that stuff. The goddamn lying press. Of course, we did that. We had to.'"

"Might that have fortified your case?" Benjamin asked Adams.

"Yes."

And what about, Benjamin wanted to know, not using any of Rostow's three-hour interview? "I had the least to do with this one," Adams said. "I wasn't persuaded there was anything in the Rostow transcript but it wasn't my decision."

Next, Benjamin mentioned the Wallace interview on the farm in Virginia and wanted to know if Adams had been rehearsed the day before in New York. Adams said that, yes, there had been preparations for the interview but "there was no session with George when he ran the questions by me."

Benjamin then brought up the "coddling" accusation. "Did you consider your interview with Mike Wallace to be a probing interview? The kind of interview Mike Wallace is famous for?"

"I'm so familiar with it," Adams said of the interview subject matter, "it's hard to probe. I didn't feel he was an adversary. He asked a couple of embarrassing questions like 'Why are you so obsessed?' I had to come up with some lame answer." Adams did acknowledge that at times during the interview Wallace acted like a "cheerleader," and even gave Adams assistance, such as "When I ran off on a subject he waved his hand to stop me."

Benjamin lastly turned to the charge that Adams had backed off the central premise of the documentary and had told Klein in the cutting room that "We have to come clean."

Adams answered that at the time "Ira was in a state of agitation. God knows over what. He was sort of leading me into it. I said this a million times, we should have shifted the emphasis higher. I don't recall this as a big event in my life. This was something I felt from the beginning. Crile was never adverse to it. We never had the goods on who gave the orders to Westmoreland."[14]

*

Right on schedule, Burton Benjamin's report was finished July 8, not two months after the *TV Guide* article had first appeared. In his report, meant for CBS eyes only, Benjamin heaped criticism on the documentary. Among the problems he found were that "sympathetic witnesses" had been "coddled"; Adams was never identified as a *paid* consultant; Davidson should have been located and interviewed; and the editing allowed quotes to be shown out of context. Despite the journalistic transgressions, however, Benjamin's ultimate judgment was that the story itself was sound and that "If all the standards of fairness had been followed, it would not have changed the outcome of the broadcast."

Inside the offices of CBS, Wallace, Stringer, and Colloff decried the Benjamin Report, to no avail. Crile was officially reprimanded by the network on July 15, the same day that Sauter released his statement to the public. CBS's internal investigation, Sauter said, had been completed and as a result "CBS News stands by this broadcast."

Westmoreland was outraged. On August 10 the retired general again demanded airtime to tell his side of the story. Sauter instead offered Westmoreland an opportunity to appear on a televised panel along with Hawkins, Adams, Carver, Graham, and Davidson, to be moderated by Diane Sawyer. Westmoreland refused the invitation, and his intransigence was met with an unprecedented display of CBS's willingness to bend: The executive producer of the proposed show, Joan Richman, wrote

Westmoreland that she would guarantee him a full fifteen minutes on air beforehand "to say what you wish to say in the manner you wish to say it." But Westmoreland failed to see the benefit in this — especially if afterward he was expected to participate in a roundtable discussion about whether he had committed treason — and was already, as had CBS feared, talking to his lawyers.[15]

13

CRAVATH

Robert H. Baron took the first flight of the day, at six A.M., down to Washington, D.C. It was September 13, 1982, and he arrived at the Army-Navy Club early. Baron kept a low profile, and when the press conference got under way he listened intently as William C. Westmoreland announced that he was filing a $120 million libel suit against CBS Incorporated, Van Gordon Sauter, Mike Wallace, George Crile, and Sam Adams. Westmoreland told the gathering, "There is no way left for me to clear my name, my honor, and the honor of the military. Let me emphasize the issue here is not money, not vengeance. If I am successful in this case, as I believe I will be, I will not retain any monetary award for my personal use but will instead donate it to charity."[1]

Copies of Westmoreland's pleading were handed out, and Baron helped himself to one before heading back to New York and to the offices of Cravath Swaine and Moor. There his boss, David Boies, looked over the document and told him to drop everything to devote himself solely to the CBS client and upcoming Westmoreland lawsuit.

"CBS was called 'The Tiffany Network,'" Baron said, "and for the high-end media, being put on trial like this was unusual. Mike Wallace was a very high-visibility figure, and the president of the CBS News division was also." Baron realized that working on the lawsuit "was going to be not only an intense but an extraordinary experience. Boies gave me some cautionary but encouraging words. That was my introduction to the case."

The network and the four individual defendants would owe twenty-four million dollars each should Westmoreland prevail, money Adams confided to his friend Peter Hiam that he did not have. Hiam remembered Adams saying, "This will wipe me out." Hiam replied, "Sam, Westmoreland's not after you, he is after CBS. They're not going to let you sink over this." But,

Hiam said, "Sam did worry." The network, in fact, did not let Adams or Sauter, Wallace, or Crile sink: The four were represented *gratis* by Cravath as part of the CBS defense.[2]

Within two weeks Baron had met all of the defendants, and he remembered that "Sam was like no other. He was not what you expected to run into as a Cravath Swaine and Moor client. There was nothing Wall Street about Sam. He had a lot of physical presence; very informal and disarming manner. I only remember Sam wearing one outfit ever, whether he was working on the farm or in our offices at Cravath, which was sort of a brownish gray tweed coat, and his khakis that looked as if they hadn't been pressed in about a hundred years, and some kind of utilitarian-looking brown shoes and always with a bag of documents of some kind, his notes."

The notes promised to be helpful. "It was all facts," remembered Baron. "Sam had an appetite for detail the likes of which I don't think I have encountered since then." In 1964 the Supreme Court had ruled in *New York Times v. Sullivan* that the burden of proof for journalistic negligence ("reckless disregard") or libel ("actual malice") fell entirely upon the plaintiff, and because Adams had researched the story that the CBS documentary was based on so thoroughly it would be impossible, Boies and Baron thought, for Westmoreland to prevail under the rigid *Sullivan* standard.

Nevertheless Westmoreland charged ahead. His lawyer, the only one he could find who would take on his quixotic case, was Dan M. Burt. The fiercely independent-minded Burt, age forty, was head of a tiny nonprofit public interest law firm in Washington called Capital Legal Foundation. Capital Legal had a host of backers, most of them either corporations or foundations connected to wealthy individuals, and the firm, at Burt's discretion, usually took on libertarian causes in which the little guy was threatened by big government. In this respect Burt was intrigued by the David-versus-Goliath aspect of the retired soldier's fight against mighty CBS, although Burt had never tried a libel case or even argued in front of a jury before.

Burt and his new client lost the first legal skirmish. They had wanted the case tried in Westmoreland's home state of South Carolina before a friendly jury, but Boies lobbied the court to move the venue to a location more convenient for the defendants. On November 18, 1982, the case was assigned to New York's Southern District Federal Court, located in Lower Manhattan.

While losing this round, Dan Burt soon was to enjoy a major victory at CBS's expense. In early November he demanded to see a copy of the Benjamin Report; CBS refused, claiming that the document was "privileged" and not "discoverable." Boies fought off the demand until April of the following year when the court finally sided with Burt, the judge ruling that because CBS had widely publicized the Benjamin Report's existence, and had even released its basic conclusions, it was not confidential material. Benjamin's findings — all of course highly unflattering to CBS — were soon splashed across the front pages of America's newspapers. Burt declared, "We are about to see the dismantling of a major news network."[3]

From the beginning of the Westmoreland affair, the CBS goal was first and foremost to protect the integrity of Mike Wallace. The forced release of the Benjamin Report had been bad enough, and the network now wanted to avoid trial and any more damaging disclosures. To head off such an eventuality Boies was planning to file a Motion to Dismiss and For Summary Judgment. This would ask the judge to toss out Westmoreland's lawsuit and, while he was at it, find in CBS's favor. Boies knew this was asking a lot, and that he would need all the help he could get in preparing the motion.

Boies at age forty-one was a rising legal star. He had graduated second in his class at Yale Law School and made full partner at Cravath by age thirty-one. Intensely bright and extremely hardworking, with an appetite for exciting litigation, Boies surrounded himself with intelligent, dedicated, and ambitious young associates. Robert Baron had just graduated from Harvard Law School, and three other associates Boies brought in to help with the Westmoreland case were also newly minted attorneys with equally impressive credentials: Randy M. Mastro (University of Pennsylvania Law School), William F. Duker (Yale Law School), and Michael R. Doyen (Harvard Law School). To assist the team, Boies also had Cravath immediately hire defendant Sam Adams (some Harvard Law School) to be the research consultant.

*

Although not welcomed by Adams, the lawsuit was at least a diversion from having to finish his book, and also from having to make a decision regarding his marriage to Eleanor. That decision could not be delayed indefinitely with Clayton now midway through college and Eleanor arguing that the time had come for a formal split.

News of the libel suit and its potential "chilling effect" on First Amendment rights had hit the national press corps hard, and reverberations reached far and wide. Anne Cocroft, young and attractive and herself having experienced a bad marriage, was a journalist for the *Leesburg-Loudon Times-Mirror*. Upon hearing about the Westmoreland case, she recognized that there was a story here with a decidedly local angle; in fact she had earlier written a story about Sam Adams and the CBS documentary. Cocroft interviewed Adams again, this time regarding the Westmoreland allegations. The article was published, and a short while later Adams invited Cocroft out to lunch. "Call it naive," she said, "but I thought, *Why would he ask me to lunch? He must want me to write something for him.* I knew that he liked the story I had written." But Adams had no hidden agenda. "He didn't want me to write anything, he just enjoyed my company." The relationship between the two evolved, and soon they were in love.

*

Almost from the moment the lawsuit was filed, the Cravath team began deposing friend and foe alike. At the swank Cravath offices at 1 Chase Manhattan Plaza, out came Adams's list of eighty, and subpoenas were prepared. Adams also knew where to look for the documentary evidence, and subpoenas for these materials were readied as well. "He was," recalled Baron, "like a kid in a candy store with the availability of the discovery process to find facts." Adams was thrilled, Baron explained, "at the resources that were now available to him to ferret out under power of subpoena — to force the government to declassify hundreds of thousands of pages of documents ... which Sam had never seen." Capital Legal demanded a copy of everything Cravath had declassified, and Cravath demanded a copy of everything Capital Legal had declassified; by the time the trial was over an estimated half a million pages of once secret government papers would be put out into the public domain.

The depositions got underway. Among the first was that of former Secretary of Defense Robert S. McNamara, who had famously maintained complete silence of the topic of the Vietnam War since leaving his government post in early 1968. McNamara was irate at the process. His deposition by Boies — which lasted two days, March 26 and 27 — was frequently testy:

> BOIES: You are under an obligation to answer the questions, a legal obligation to answer the questions that I ask you.
>
> MCNAMARA: To the best of my memory.
>
> BOIES: (Affirmative nod.) To the best of your memory. That you are here because we have served you with a subpoena —
>
> MCNAMARA: Not only that but I am here — that's certainly the only reason why I am here. But as far as answering the questions, I would quite frankly refuse to answer them if I thought that I had a legal right to refuse them. I do not wish to engage in a discussion of my views or anybody else's views of the Vietnam War.

McNamara, though reluctant to discuss the matter, then told Boies that he was "unaware of any faking of data of any kind whatsoever relating to any aspect of the war":

> BOIES: Were you aware in 1967 that the decision as to where to draw the line as to who would be included in estimates of enemy strength was the subject of a dispute between representatives of the Defense Intelligence Agency and the MACV as well as the CIA.
>
> MCNAMARA: I have no recollection of who was on whose — what side of the dispute. I, frankly, believe the whole damn thing is immaterial. I don't want to get into judgment of your program, the CBS program, unless you wish me to and if you do I'll give you my opinion of it.

BOIES: Have you seen the program?

MCNAMARA: No. I have not, but I have read —

BOIES: I would just as soon you waited to give me an opinion of the program until you have seen it.

During the deposition Boies handed McNamara the enemy order of battle figures in the months leading up to the Tet Offensive:

BOIES: There was some change, was there not, sir?

MCNAMARA: Well, essentially none for the period — it starts here [indicating], essentially none from August '67 until November '67, the figure shown is 297,000.

BOIES: Funny you should mention that, sir. Do you have any explanation for why that was so?

MCNAMARA: It either didn't change or it didn't change enough to warrant reporting separately. These are — it goes back to the point I am trying to make, and that is that the whole damn thing is much ado about nothing because nobody in their right mind would think there were 297 zero, zero, zero, enemy in South Vietnam and particularly not when you've got the same damn figure for four months. You have to understand what these figures are. Don't get me started to — you won't want to hear me. The whole damn thing is wrong, it is a disgrace what you are doing. It is an absolute disgrace.

BOIES: Move to strike the answer as a non-response.[4]

After the McNamara–Boies duel Boies deposed William C. Westmoreland on April 4. Emotions during this deposition were also raw, and Westmoreland complained to Boies that CBS had impugned his "integrity and honor" — "the one thing I have prided myself in throughout my entire career and, as a matter of fact, throughout my entire life." Westmoreland also discounted the whole notion of the order of battle: "Nobody knew what the enemy strength was in Vietnam. It was a matter of estimates and guesstimates. What the actual strength was — I mean nobody knew, nobody knew. Nobody knows precisely to this day."[5]

*

In all there were to be sixty-six depositions taken, thirty-four requested by the defense and thirty-two by the plaintiff. The depositions were a way to both discover facts before the trial and to preserve testimony for the trial in the event that a deposed later refused, or was unable, to travel to Manhattan and appear in court him- or herself. The deposition process involved a host of characters: There were the lawyers from Cravath and from Capital Legal; there were the observers — sometimes George Crile and almost always Sam Adams; there were the court reporters; there were the paralegals; and there were the two CIA men — pleasant people — present to make sure no state secrets were spilled. The deposition process was something of a traveling circus that left New York and Washington, D.C., to make the circuit around the country and several times overseas, and as the trial neared the pace of the tour picked up. Randy Mastro recalled, "I think we had a period where I traveled every week in the year preceding the trial, most of them with Sam."[6]

Adams was an active listener during the depositions. Bill Duker remembered him taking down "what everybody was saying. The tiny handwriting that Sam was constantly updating, and he knew where in those notes on every page where every piece of information was. Sam didn't need a computer to find his way through hundreds and hundreds of pages of his meticulous handwritten notes." Duker also said, "Sam was a Boy Scout in some ways. I don't want to say he was naive because he wasn't intellectually, but he was naive about certain aspects of life. He led a fairly sheltered life in many respects, he was a CIA analyst, he was more academic in nature than most people in the world. Sam couldn't understand how people could spin the truth or distort it in some way. For Sam, the truth was sacrosanct and he didn't know that there was a whole subgroup in the world who were bad guys who didn't tell the truth. Sam could never figure out why someone would even spin the truth or distort it in some way. For him, it was like, 'Why would you *do* that?'"

The depositions were voluminous and could last days: George Carver provided 1,164 pages of testimony (7 days); William C. Westmoreland 2,003 pages (14 days); George Allen 1,030 pages (7 days); Alex Alben 432 pages (5 days); George Crile, 1,899 (15 days); Gains B. Hawkins 478 pages

(7 days); Russell Cooley 501 pages (5 days); Dean Rusk 385 pages (2 days), Howard Stringer, 821 pages (6 days); Robert S. McNamara 444 pages (2 days); Walt Rostow — only 79 pages (2 days).

In addition to the depositions a flood of affidavits came pouring into the Cravath and Capital Legal offices, each confirming or refuting the two sides to the intelligence story.

Robert Appel said in his affidavit that everyone in the OER South Vietnam Branch back in 1967 had agreed that MACV was "badly understating enemy troop strength in Vietnam." Senator Birch Bayh in his affidavit recalled that he had been "surprised by the swiftness of the enemy's attack" during Tet "and the magnitude of the offensive." John Bross said that while recognizing Adams's "obvious sincerity in advocating his views," upon investigation "I found no merit to his claims." Ellsworth Bunker dismissed the CBS documentary as "false and inaccurate in a number of important respects," and Lawrence Houston dismissed Adams as a *"fanatique."* A certain Colonel Ralph Hunt said that he recalled "no manipulation of intelligence" at MACV and someone else, Eric Kronen, swore that "I saw no evidence of deception or any conspiracy to alter or suppress military intelligence during my tour of duty." Paul Walsh called the numbers dispute "an honest disagreement," but someone named Peter Sandmann, at one time the chief of MACV's VCI order of battle section, stated that the MACV numbers had been "patently much too low" and "essentially meaningless." A Colonel Elmer Martin explained that "I came to believe that General Westmoreland had authorized his MACV intelligence staff to intentionally falsify intelligence information about enemy strength," while another colonel, Robert G. M. Storey, said that while he had no personal knowledge of a "cover-up" at MACV he had always suspected one because "intelligence officers were often fired or reassigned on short notice and without apparent reason." Robert Komer, though, said that CBS had "rehashed the same old issue with some new trimmings," and someone named John Roche stated that Westmoreland had been "mugged" by the documentary. On the other hand, former Michigan Governor George Romney, who had toured South Vietnam as part of his 1968 presidential campaign, said in his affidavit, "In retrospect, it is clear to me that the military was issuing misleading and inaccurate information about enemy capabilities and strength."

Amid the pileup of depositions and affidavits there were exhibits to prepare (they would total better than six hundred for both sides) and also the
hundreds of interrogatories that Capital Legal and Cravath were snowing
onto each other to deal with. Interrogatories are requests both for facts
known to the opposing side and for the opposing side's positions regarding
those facts. During one particularly intense blizzard of interrogatories that
lasted a fortnight Adams essentially moved into a little conference room on
the fifty-eighth floor of 1 Chase Manhattan Plaza. The conference room
was next to the corner office of Cravath attorney Tom Barr, one of the
firm's lead litigators, and the space ostensibly belonged to him. Barr had
been a drill sergeant in the Marine Corps and was known for his scowl and
dour mien, and there Adams was shuffling around his conference room in
wrinkled khakis with papers spread out everywhere. Adams did not like
the look of Barr, either, and when Barr was out of earshot he asked, "Who
is that guy? You know the guy who sits in the office next door?" It was, he
was quickly told, Tom Barr who had just won the famous IBM case. This
failed to impress Adams: "That guy looks like *a real shit bag*. I am only here
to do all this work and help out and every time I come in here he looks at
me like I came to steal his furniture or something."

*

Many who had refuted MACV in private conversations to Adams were
now ambivalent about publicly coming to CBS's defense, including even
some who had agreed to be on the program. James Meacham distanced
himself from the CBS documentary almost immediately upon learning of
the lawsuit. "I told Sam Adams and George Crile before the CBS broadcast," Meacham said in his affidavit, "that there was no conspiracy to alter
and suppress intelligence, and that no one I was associated with falsified
any intelligence." But what about those 322 damning letters sent home to
Dorothy? They, Meacham explained, "expressed my frustration at having
to do work (such as some of our studies) that I thought was silly, or a waste
of time; they expressed my pessimism about the war; they expressed my
personal dislike for some of my superiors" — but nothing more.

Former Colonel George Hamscher, who had like Meacham appeared on
the CBS program, was deposed by Robert Baron for three days of difficult
testimony in Washington, D.C. "This man," Baron recalled, "was like

many of the other officers: internally very tortured, conflicted about what had happened back then, very uneasy about putting labels on things, convinced that something bad had gone down and that he had been part of it, but very uneasy about throwing stones or casting blame." Painful though it may have been, Hamscher's deposition was an important one for the defense. "It was," Baron continued, "a very big watershed. I prepared for it with Sam and Sam was my principal assistant; he was like the researcher par excellence of all time." Baron was thankful for all of Adams's help but did not realize that the sentiment was mutual. "We get out of the Hamscher deposition," Baron said. "I am getting into a taxi and, on the sidewalk, Sam turns to me and said, 'By the way, I don't get around to saying this very often but I really appreciate what you do for me.'" Baron remembered the incident well: "I never before or since had a client thank me quite so directly or movingly."

George Allen's earlier nervousness with the whole CBS enterprise, which had of course resulted in his special treatment by Crile, now extended to the prospect of having to be a key witness for the defense. Allen had spent almost his entire adult life in the close-knit U.S. intelligence community, and although he was retired he still taught at the agency and valued personal relationships with men like Helms and Houston. Allen could never abide by Adams's contention that Helms had been a traitor, and Allen was appalled when he learned that Adams had secreted material out of Langley like, in Allen's words, "some sort of spy." "George Allen," said Baron, "was crossing a lot of Rubicons by coming and testifying."

Gains B. Hawkins would also be testifying, and he was asked by columnist Mary McGrory if he had any concerns about being on the opposing side of his former commander, General Westmoreland. "Yes there is some anxiety," Hawkins responded, "a concern that I will appear to be a fink or a rascal, or a sensation monger or worse; and some private annoyance that life in relatively quiet retirement in this little community of West Point on the black prairie of northeast Mississippi will never be the same again. But, no, too, Miss Mary, there is a compulsion here, a tardy realization that the tale must come out no matter what the personal pain or annoyance. In truth, the retelling is somewhat like the war itself. It hurts, and it is larger than all of us."[7]

Bernard Gattozzi was another former military man willing to come in from the cold, but because of his job with the Justice Department he would not discuss the case off the record. When served with a subpoena, though, he supported without qualification everything that he had been telling Adams over the years. "I am a hard-line right-wing conservative," Gattozzi explained, "and to be found on the CBS side rather than the army side was phenomenal to me. But I was not going to sacrifice my principles — I've got to sleep at night, I've got to tell the truth." What he saw at MACV "happened; that's the way it is."

*

By all accounts Dan Burt was winning the public relations war by leaking out bits and drabs of information embarrassing to CBS as they became known to him through the discovery process, and the network did not initiate an adequate offense of its own until hiring PR man John Scanlon in October 1983. During the many months remaining to the litigation Scanlon would acquit himself well, often assisted by George Crile, who eventually worked his way back into the good graces of CBS. The two organized letter-writing campaigns on behalf of CBS, attacked reporting critical of CBS, and held dueling press conferences with Dan Burt who for a full year had enjoyed the PR stage almost all to himself. While Scanlon, Crile, and Burt were focusing on the publicity, however, Boies and his small team at Cravath were readying the "truth defense."

The candid nature of the Benjamin Report, now released to the world, prevented CBS from defending its broadcast on purely journalistic grounds; the editing decisions made during the production of the documentary had just been too problematic for this. Boies therefore decided to skirt the First Amendment angle to the case — an angle that many legal observers assumed would have been the linchpin of the CBS defense — and go right where Adams had been for the past decade and a half: 1967 and the making of faked Vietnam War intelligence. Westmoreland had no cause to feel wrongly accused, Boies planned to argue, because everything alleged by the documentary was absolutely true.

Adams could not agree more. "With Sam it was never about defending himself," recalled Robert Baron. "For CBS, for George and for Mike, it was like they were on trial. Sam was just as much legally on trial as they were, but for Sam this was ultimately getting to the truth; he was never particularly interested in the actual malice defense."

In preparing the Motion to Dismiss and For Summary Judgment, Boies insisted upon a meticulous degree of documentation. "David's view, I think correctly," said Baron, "was Here's this journalistic institution, CBS, being charged with libel when it clearly did a ton of work, and what CBS was being accused of is having manipulated the material it got, manipulated film footage, left things on the cutting-room floor, and we can't do that. We can never look as if we took any liberties."

Adams was naturally not for taking any liberties, either, but he chafed at the strictures imposed by the discovery process. Baron remembered coming out of depositions and hearing Adams protest loudly, "He's just not remembering; that's *not* the way it happened, he's *lying*." Baron did not necessarily disagree, but he explained that the testimony was admissible all the same.

Adams was horrified. "It only counts if somebody had said it at a deposition? If they don't remember it's like they *never* said it? But they said it to me!" he exclaimed.

"At trial you can testify to what they told you," Baron remembered answering, "but we can't just have you on the stand for three weeks reading your notes, and we don't want to rest solely on you." Adams was hardly mollified, Baron said, and saw the legalities as "truncating history."

Truncated or not, the history had to be put into the Motion to Dismiss, and Adams and the four associates had their work cut out for them. The working hours were long. "Oh, God," William Duker remembered, "they were murderous. I would get a car in the morning at five thirty — I lived in Park Slope — and I would be there until the wee hours of the next morning, sometime two sometimes three, sometimes it was an all-nighter. We probably did one or two all-nighters a week. Back in those days at Cravath if you worked an all-nighter a messenger would go out and buy you a T-shirt and underwear. We did so many all-nighters we had a collection of shirts that were all the same and we called them the 'team shirt.'"

Baron recalled, "It was a weird dynamic; we were practically family for a time. We lived — I spent my holidays, my dinners, weekends with these people and with Sam. I would live in conference rooms with Sam for days at a time. I talked to him every day. I spent inconceivable amounts of time with him."

For Adams this was a whole new world. "He would walk around this group of lawyers," Duker said, "this category of people he had never known before, who had deep pockets and lived life in a very different way and didn't care about how much they spent on dinner or a bottle of wine. Sam was awed by it all; awed by the extraordinary wealth of Cravath."

Thrown suddenly into this milieu, Adams stuck out. "He would show up every day," Duker remembered, "in his khaki pants and blue oxford shirt with holes in his sleeves and stains on his ties and stains from his pocket pens, and his down winter jacket and blue duffel filled with papers and staplers; like he was carrying his office around with him." Although not covetous by nature, Adams with his blue duffel saw what others had at Cravath and wanted one of his own. Baron recalled, "Sam's discovery that we have these things that lawyers carry called a litigation bag and Sam realized that this was the solution, a gap that had been missing. He ulti- mately said, 'Can you guys get me one of those?' So we got him one."

David Boies was also known for eschewing fashionable clothes, his uni- form being a blue Sears suit, button-down blue shirt, and blue knit tie, and Baron noted that "there was something about Sam that David really liked, powerfully, because Sam was authentic, there was something very authentic about him, Sam was very passionate about this subject and he was a very informal guy, and David is the most informal guy around." Duker, however, recalled that "Boies himself puzzled Sam; Sam could never figure out Boies. He was really something to Sam, this guy who moved in the circles that David moved in and worked in the way that he worked, and was all over the place and could retain so much information in his head, and could kill his associates with overwork. Sam saw what was happening to us as cruel and inhumane almost, and he didn't understand that this was just the life associates at a big law firm lived."

Dinners, when there was time to eat, were at the best restaurants both in New York and on the road. Boies in particular liked red meat. Alex Alben met up with the legal team on one of their visits to Los Angeles. "Boies would only eat meat," Alben recalled, "and Sam called him 'the carnivore' or 'the shark' or something. I went to eat with them at Chasen's and Boies just ate the red meat, and the potato he just threw it off his plate; Boies wanted just pure blood. And Sam would look at Boies like, *Oh God, I'm in the hands of this madman.*"

Bedtime for Adams — when it came — was at the Plaza Hotel, and he was sick of the sumptuousness, and tired of New York. A change of scenery and some fresh air would be good for him and the young associates. "We went down," Baron remembered, "we hung out on the farm." Randy Mastro recalled, "Sam bragged about how smart his pigs were! He said he was going to be a pig farmer but didn't have the heart to slaughter them." Baron explained that "Sam was a very warm person, he took a great deal of personal interest in us, in our lives, he cared about us as people; I never doubted that, we were not instrumental to him. It wasn't, *I want you to be healthy because you are important to my defense* — it was nothing to do with that."

The pace of work quickened to a near frenzy for the four young attorneys as the finishing touches were put on the Motion to Dismiss. In the final days Baron, like an expectant father, sat up nights at the printers while the document was being born. It was a monumental legal brief three months in gestation: 379 pages in argument for dismissal, 612 pages of affidavits, 117 pages of facts, and 379 pages of exhibits. The motion was submitted to the court on May 23, 1984, and afterward Boies took his four exhausted associates to the Post House for some good steaks. "We had a really nice lunch," Duker recalled, "and probably a little too much wine and David had a limo and he told us to take the car back to the office. We drank scotch with the limo rooftop open and listened to the radio blasting Junior Walker and the All-Stars."

The Motion to Dismiss and For Summary Judgment was in fact an exemplary piece of scholarship. Detailed, precise, and lavishly supported by excerpts from sworn testimony and declassified documents, the motion told the entire sad history of the intelligence episode. The bulky motion was in every regard Adams's story, and for him the legal brief was pure history well told: It was The Truth.

If Adams was comfortable with the Motion to Dismiss and For Summary Judgment, he was not with other aspects of the case. "The whole advocacy thing was so foreign to Sam," explained Baron. "He never saw himself as an advocate, even in the role he played in the broadcast. He didn't write the script of the documentary — this is a very important fact. Sam said as much in letters to Gains and to other people around him at the time the documentary came out. He was saying, 'I would not have written the script this way. I think in substance the documentary is right but ultimately it is not my take on these events, ultimately it is George Crile's.'"[8]

The Westmoreland case had been assigned to Judge Pierre N. Leval, a highly respected juror. Leval took the Motion to Dismiss into his chambers and, when he had the time, began going through it. Two months later Capital Legal replied to the Cravath motion with a massively referenced 887-page brief of its own. With his summer reading list taken care of thanks to these two tomes, Leval was not to rule on the merits of the competing arguments until September 24.

When that time came the judge had some bad news for Cravath: "The principal bulk of defendant's voluminous briefs is dedicated to the point that summary judgment should be granted because what was stated in the documentary was true." Leval noted that while he had no opinion regarding the truthfulness of the program, the plaintiff did. "Summary judgment," the judge therefore ruled, "must be denied if there is conflicting evidence on any substantial issue."

Leval, though, had some discouraging words for Capital Legal in his ruling as well. Westmoreland's assertion that CBS had been merely prejudicial and unfair hardly, the judge ruled, constituted malice.

In the final part of his ruling, however, Leval gave renewed hope to Burt and presented more problems for Boies. Leval agreed with the plaintiff that there were numerous indications "of dishonesty and willful falsity in the editing and presentation of the evidence" by CBS, which may well have constituted "reckless falsity" and "malice" on the defendants' part. Therefore, Leval said, the plaintiff was entitled to his day in court.[9]

*

It had been almost a year earlier, on a gray November morning in 1983, that Adams made his final pass through the ancient stone farmhouse, grabbing the last of his naval prints hanging on the upstairs wall. When he went downstairs there was a painful scene with Eleanor — an argument over who owned the living room sofa. Adams prevailed and the sofa was loaded in the back of the F-150 along with the rest of his things. With a toss of a stray Civil War book into the cab, Adams got in and drove down the straight gravel driveway and past the fifty sugar maple trees on either side that he had planted years before.

Home was now a small two-story house off a nondescript stretch of Route 7 outside Purcellville. The modest dwelling with its bare, white-washed interior was soon well stocked with Plaza Hotel toiletries. There were a few neighbors close by, but the setting was rural enough to keep Adams content.

Anne Cocroft had broken off with Adams about six months into their relationship, saying to herself, *I can't do this anymore, being involved with someone who is married, it's just not much fun.* Some months afterward she met Adams again at a party, and he informed her of his plans for divorce and for renting a house in Purcellville. When he moved, she recalled, "We got back together again."

*

With the trial looming, the workload on the Cravath team increased. "We were exhausted," Robert Baron recalled. "Oh boy, I was running on fumes the last week or two. It was just crazy. Eighty hours a week was the norm." Adding to the stress was the inevitable strain among the defendants, and after a while the lawyers thought it best to handle Adams and Crile separately. Baron explained that the two were "both enormously strong personalities and very unusual personalities" that were being propelled by differing motivations. Adams was pursuing the historical truth wherever it may lead, while Crile was struggling to salvage his reputation as a journalist. Baron said that for Crile the case "was career threatening, and he was not only defending himself against the lawsuit by General Westmoreland but also attacks from within CBS."[10]

Adams's relationship with David Boies was also strained; indeed, it had never been easy to begin with. To his friends Adams was now constantly complaining about his lead legal counsel: Boies would take calls from his stockbroker in the middle of meetings with Adams; Boies went to hockey games at night instead of poring over the historical material; Boies was constantly talking about his romantic interests; Boies would not read the Hawkins deposition and was not convinced that Hawkins would make a good impression in court; and Boies was wont to quip, "The ideal witness is someone who is attractive, articulate, and willing to lie." Peter Hiam recalled that Adams "really had a lot of harsh criticisms of Boies." John Gardiner stated of Adams, "He despised Boies."

Robert Baron agreed that Boies had problems with Adams. "I am sure David had difficulty trying to get Sam to some degree focused on how we had to do things, the necessity of not publishing all of human knowledge from A to Z. And David had all us kids. There were things that we were good at but there were things we had no idea about because we had never done [them] before. And he had Sam, George Crile to manage, and he had this whole big institution, CBS, that was in a frenzy because it was under assault, and then it had done this internal investigation, there was this whole Benjamin Report angle on things — and David had to manage all of these people."

Complicating matters, Adams became incensed when Boies chose to view the intelligence controversy subjectively, from the viewpoint of the CBS documentary, instead of sticking with history in its purest form. "David is an advocate," Baron told Adams repeatedly. "He is supposed to be presenting the best case he can. He is not allowed to lie, but nobody expects David to present the most compelling version of the case for the other side's position along with his own." Still, it remained a source of potential conflict. "There were times," Baron said, "when it drove Sam crazy. He would refer to David as 'Your Danny' — it was the worst thing you could say about anybody! When he was in praise of David it was always 'David' or 'Boies' or 'Dave' or whatever, but if he was angry at David for any reason he was always 'Danny' because Danny Graham was the Antichrist."

When Capital Legal filed its brief to Judge Leval in response to the Motion to Dismiss and For Summary Judgment, Cravath offered a reply brief of its own. Baron and Michael Doyen worked on it for four days straight and then circulated the draft around the office and CBS for comments and suggestions; then they worked on it some more. The document grew to three hundred pages. Adams got a copy and called Baron to say, "This brief is so great." Baron then showed it to Boies and, Baron recalled, "David just hit the roof. 'Bob, we can't file a three-hundred-page reply brief, I mean this is the reply brief, we have already given the judge the phone book. Absolutely not.'" Baron and Doyen toiled to trim it down to two hundred pages and, Baron said, "Sam is still elated because we had really cut the fat away. And David looks at it and says, 'You guys just don't get this — just give it to me.'" Boies, Baron recalled, was ruthless. "He edited it with a meat cleaver. He was certainly right in hindsight, but I was more than reasonably demoralized by this; I was very demoralized by this and so was Doyen. Sam calls up and says, 'Well I just got the brief as edited by Your Danny and it has gone from an A-plus to a D-minus. I just hope you guys are happy.' I said, 'Thanks, Sam, just what I needed.'"

*

The trial was just days away. Robert Baron had known Adams for two years by now, and he recalled what George Crile had told him earlier. "You will be reliving Sam's research and these people in his life," Crile had said, "and you will bond with the witnesses." Crile was clearly speaking from his own experiences in making the documentary, and true enough, over the past two years Baron had indeed relived Adams's investigation and had indeed become close to the defense witnesses. They were, Baron found, a singularly impressive group of people, retired as well as active-duty CIA and military men willing to endure "the public glare" by coming out in defense of CBS, and most had been driven to make the sacrifice solely because of Adams. "Not that they owed it to him because they had a sense of debt to him or obligation to him, but they owed it to what he represented. Sam was in the end what intelligence officers were pledged to be." Back in 1967, Baron said, "they were complicit by letting themselves go along with the flow when it became clear that the numbers were going to be packaged in a way that was palatable. Everybody but Sam came to realize this. For Sam it was intolerable, and these men had reverence and respect to him for his dedication to the truth. It was just palpable in the way that they spoke about him."

14

THE LIBEL TRIAL OF THE CENTURY

The trial got under way on October 10, 1984, in overheated Room 318 of the U.S. Courthouse in Lower Manhattan. Judge Pierre N. Leval delivered a one-hour-and-fifteen-minute lecture to the members of the jury, discussing libel law and the historic nature of the case that they were about to hear. Leval told the jurors that they would not be sequestered, but he cautioned them against speaking or reading about the trial outside court during what, he said, would likely be very lengthy proceedings. To ensure that the trial would not go on forever, though, Leval also explained that he was limiting the two sides to 150 hours each for examination of witnesses.

The twelve jurors and four alternates, nine men and nine women, had been selected from a pool of hundreds. Those who made it onto the *Westmoreland v. CBS et al.* panel pleaded innocent of knowing anything about the Vietnam War or, for that matter, anything about past events, current affairs, or public officials. Names such as Colby, Helms, McNamara, Bunker, and Rostow meant little or nothing to the jurors and alternates, all drawn from New York City and suburban areas. Among those picked to decide the case were a thirty-two-year-old insurance underwriter, a twenty-six-year-old dental assistant, a thirty-three-year-old accountant, a fifty-five-year-old customer service representative, and a twenty-six-year-old laboratory research assistant. About a third of the eighteen men and women had a college education. Two of the jurors spoke only broken English.

Also listening intently to Leval's every word on opening day was the plaintiff at his desk, white-haired William C. Westmoreland sitting ramrod-straight and, at their desk, the defendants: bespectacled Mike Wallace with his slicked-back black hair that was so familiar to millions, George Crile looking every inch the handsome broadcast journalist, and

Sam Adams, who was furiously scribbling down everything being said onto a yellow legal pad. The plaintiff never so much as glanced at the three men who were the subject of his wrath, and they in turn averted their eyes from him. Watching Westmoreland at all times, though — while also doing her needlepoint, as she would throughout the trial — was his wife, Katherine "Kitsy" Westmoreland, seated in the audience.[1]

Missing in the courtroom was Van Gordon Sauter, whom Dan Burt had just dropped as a defendant. Also missing was a major part of Westmoreland's case. Burt had suddenly decided to leave unchallenged the network's assertion that Westmoreland had deceived the press, the public, and the Congress. Burt would now only contest CBS's accusation that Westmoreland had misled his military superiors and President Johnson.

The next day judge, jurors, lawyers, plaintiff, defendants, court officers, artists, reporters, and the CIA and NSA "mystery" men, there to monitor the testimony, all took their designated places. Burt introduced himself to the jury and then launched into his newly refined argument. For dramatic effect he pointed to a CBS publicity poster depicting General Westmoreland saluting President Johnson with the American flag flying in the background. His voice heavy with sarcasm, Burt said, "Here's the culprit, General Westmoreland, lying to President Johnson against the American flag." Burt told the jury that CBS had tried to "ambush" his client, had tried to "shame and humiliate" his client, had "utterly" stained the honor of his client, had accused his client of "criminal" charges, and had "rattlesnaked" his client. Burt said that the documentary was nothing more than "a work of fiction" that created "an illusion of wrong where none existed." Then Burt ran the tapes.

Although Leval had ruled earlier that no television cameras would be allowed inside the courtroom, this was still very much a TV trial; throughout the proceedings the lawyers would struggle with a mass of video monitors, cables, and tape machines as they made their respective cases. Burt got the first opportunity, assisted by two technicians, to fumble with the assembled equipment. He showed parts of Mike Wallace's unused interview of Walt Rostow. In one segment that Burt ran, Rostow was seen advising Wallace not to pursue the story. "You're gonna do great damage to the country," Rostow warned, "and you're gonna get it wrong." During the presentation Burt also got in several digs at George Crile, whom he described as needing "a story, a big story, a sensational story" in order "to prove himself."

The trial was off to a roaring start, much to the pleasure of an overflow crowd that included about seventy-five members of the press corps. When Burt sat down David Boies stood up. He'd gotten partway into the opening argument for the defense, stating that the CBS program was "true, accurate and well supported," before Judge Leval adjourned the session for the day. In the hallways reporters from many papers, including the *New York Times*, *Washington Post*, *Boston Globe*, *Philadelphia Inquirer*, *Los Angeles Times*, and *Wall Street Journal* — which would all cover the trial gavel to gavel — mobbed the lawyers, plaintiff, and defendants. This was, after all, "the libel trial of the century." Meanwhile, camera crews from the three networks, all the local New York TV stations, CNN, plus a few foreign broadcasters, waited outside on the courthouse steps leading down to Foley Square.[2]

Boies continued the next morning, presenting in court poster-sized copies of the secret cables between Saigon and Washington urging that Viet Cong irregular forces be kept off the official order of battle. "George Crile did not invent those," Boies said repeatedly. "What you have seen was not fabricated by George Crile sitting down at a typewriter." Nothing in the documentary, Boies stated again and again, had been invented by CBS: It was all historical fact.

Walt Rostow was the plaintiff's first witness when the trial resumed on Monday. At age sixty-eight the former NSC adviser was thrilled to be on the stand and talking about his favorite subject, the Vietnam War. Under questioning by Burt, Rostow discussed in the minutest of detail the intricacies of NVA/Viet Cong strength estimates and the intelligence dispute that had surrounded those estimates. Rostow exuded comfort with all aspects of the debate: He knew the players, particularly Westmoreland and Johnson, personally; he knew the numbers; he knew that others knew the Tet Offensive was coming; he knew that it was "impossible" for twenty-five thousand North Vietnamese to have entered South Vietnam undetected by Westmoreland's intelligence officers; he knew that President Johnson was so well versed on enemy troop strengths that Johnson could never have been deceived by anyone; he knew that Johnson had, in fact, personally monitored the progress of NVA troops moving south down the Ho Chi Minh Trail; and he knew that the numbers dispute between CIA and MACV was "a good faith debate" that had generated "considerable emotion on both sides."

Rostow's testimony continued the next day, but now he was in the hands of David Boies and the going was not so easy. With the jury watching, Boies led Rostow through the entire numbers episode and stopped Rostow at every weakness, at every contradiction, at every failure in his recollection of that event. This lasted a tedious two hours, during which time Boies drew some blood. He got Rostow to admit that Johnson, far from being omnipotent, was not informed that SNIE 14.3-67 had omitted the Viet Cong irregulars while past estimates had included these forces, and Boies got Rostow to counter his earlier testimony that Westmoreland had never told Johnson in April 1967 that the "crossover" point had been reached.

Former CORDS chief Robert W. Komer followed Rostow to the witness stand. The subject was the Viet Cong village and hamlet guerrillas, the self-defense and secret self-defense forces, the infrastructure, and all the rest of the "other war" in Vietnam. Under friendly questioning by Burt, Komer testified that Westmoreland had, in contradiction to the CBS documentary's premise, accepted the higher estimates for these types of forces and that no effort to hide the numbers from officials in Washington was ever made. Komer also used his time on the stand to get in some biting criticisms of Westmoreland's J-2 at the time, General Joseph McChristian, whose estimates, Komer said, were prone to gross error.

David Boies cross-examined Komer the next day, and the former ambassador lived up to his old nickname, "Blowtorch Bob." Under assault by Boies, who accused Komer of having strong opinions but of being no expert in the gathering and interpretation of intelligence, the witness turned crimson; to David Zucchino of the *Philadelphia Inquirer*, he appeared "about to burst from his three piece suit." Komer's mood was not improved any when Boies showed him copies of the incriminating cables to and from the embassy, CINCPAC, MACV, and Washington. Komer was outraged and stated that there had never been "any orders with respect to any ceiling or preconceived conclusions with respect to enemy strength in South Vietnam."[3]

With Komer's testimony Boies had once again introduced the secret cables warning of adverse press reaction to the numbers, and now on October 18 Dan Burt attempted to place these damning communications into a plausible context. In Hawaii the CINCPAC intelligence chief at the time had been General Chesley G. Peterson, and on the stand as Burt's next witness Peterson testified that these cables were not an attempt to hide the truth but rather an attempt to prevent the publicizing of incorrect intelligence. Peterson testified that he told his chief, Admiral U. S. Grant Sharp, that intelligence figures for Viet Cong self-defense forces were inflated due to "outdated estimates" and therefore did not belong in the official order of battle.

After Peterson's testimony a retired air force colonel, Edward H. Catona, took the stand to testify that in May 1967 Westmoreland had not expressed concern over the higher enemy strength figures. For the first time in the trial Burt turned an examination of a witness over to David Dorsen. Dorsen, a Harvard Law School graduate and a veteran trial attorney from the Washington, D.C., firm of Sachs Greenebaun and Taylor, was recruited by the Capital Legal team to be the courtroom litigator, but Burt had his misgivings about Dorsen; at the end of the Catona examination he banished Dorsen from the courtroom.[4]

*

During week two of the trial a speech by Robert F. Kennedy and the findings of the Pike Committee were presented to the jury. Judge Leval worried that the trial was wandering astray, and he called one of his numerous sidebar conferences to give the lawyers a little lecture. "It's not a trial about whether we won or lost in Vietnam," he scolded out of earshot of the jury. "It's not a trial about whether we were prepared or unprepared for the Tet Offensive. I'm not going to allow this trial to be broadened into some kind of historical inquiry of how we fared in Vietnam." Otherwise, Leval concluded, "we would be here until the end of time."

*

Taking the stand next was former Colonel Charles A. Morris, and when questioned by Burt he stated that no order to place a three-hundred-thousand-man ceiling on the official order of battle had ever been given, or that MACV intelligence was ever made aware of monthly NVA infiltration rates as high as twenty-five thousand. Morris (perhaps recalling the time he'd told Adams that "you're full of shit") described the MACV–CIA summit in Saigon as "a free and full exchange of ideas," adding that MACV had not rigged the affair by adhering to a preconceived intelligence estimate.

Burt next showed outtakes from the CBS film in an effort to prove that Gains B. Hawkins and James Meacham did not mean what they appeared to have meant in the documentary. Boies objected to the use of the outtakes, arguing that it was the documentary that was on trial and not the miles of footage never used, but Judge Leval let Burt use the outtakes because the plaintiff, Leval said, was attempting to prove the network's "state of mind" while preparing the broadcast. Burt ran the tapes, which were indeed embarrassing to CBS. In many instances Crile didn't so much ask questions of his interviewees as he haggled and pleaded with them to rephrase or sharpen what they had just said. An especially egregious example, as Burt was happy to point out, occurred during the Allen interview:

> CRILE: Come to the defense of your old protégé, Sam Adams.
> ALLEN: No, I don't remember. Refresh me.
> CRILE: I'll refresh you. . . .
> ALLEN: Is it really kosher to go over this?
> CRILE: Oh, this is what we do.[5]

Former MACV J-2 General Phillip B. Davidson was the next witness to be presented by Burt. Although claiming to be in good health, the retired general, who had suffered from cancer a decade before, told Leval after answering a few questions from Burt that he was too tired to continue, and the trial was ended for the day.

Davidson, having recuperated somewhat overnight, proved to be damaging to Westmoreland's side even though Burt had called him as a friendly witness. Under relentless cross-examination by Boies the old general, not looking well and having to pause for breath, repeatedly answered "I don't recall" but did remember enough to deal a serious blow to Westmoreland's case when he said that the MACV commander had to personally approve all enemy strength intelligence estimates and that the "command position" was that total enemy strength never exceed 298,000.

*

For those sitting in the jurors' box the trial was arcane and confusing, and a tendency to let one's mind wander was ever present. Juror Number Two, Patricia Roth, was an art teacher in real life, and she kept herself alert by studying the plaintiff and the defendants. "I tried to put myself in their shoes — General Westmoreland, Sam Adams, Mike Wallace, George Crile," she said. "How would I feel if I were they in the position they were in the courtroom?" Mentally, Roth drew sketches of the plaintiff and defendants.

"The general," as she referred to Westmoreland, "always sits erect. He sits alone. He sits like the commander he was. His appearance is impressive — white hair, square jaw, intense, deep eyes."

Mike Wallace, she noted, "has not been here every day, I assumed he still has to work on the programs. When he is here, he often sits low in his chair, head tucked into his shirt collar. He cranes his chin a lot and looks up at the ceiling to think. He likes to move his mouth and often wipes expressions on and off with his hand."

Sam Adams, Roth saw, "sits like a bull, his head down and his eyes staring straight out ahead. He looks like he's going to charge any minute — the whites of his eyes shining under smoldering pupils. He looks pretty serious. But when something amuses him, his whole face softens into a jolly countenance."

Roth fleshed out George Crile as "sitting between Adams and Wallace. Crile looks proper — every hair in place, a thin, alert face, thin lips, small eyes that dart everywhere. His eyes are the only part of him that give away his feelings."

Completing her sketch, Roth noted, "None of them — Adams, Wallace, Crile, or Westmoreland — appears to wear criticism exceedingly well. They all appear to be people with strong convictions — people who believe they are right."[6]

General George A. Godding, the man caught in the tug-of-war between the CIA and MACV at Langley, was forced to relive that unpleasant experience when Burt called him to the stand after Davidson. Godding testified that while MACV's numbers were presented at the Langley conference with Westmoreland's approval, there was never an attempt to put a ceiling on the numbers, or to manipulate them in any way. Boies then cross-examined Godding, and the two got into a shouting match. The elderly general and the young lawyer, both implying sincere disrespect, addressed each other as "sir" while never hesitating to interrupt the other. Boies, though, got the retired general to admit that during the August 1967 conference at Langley he had to defend order of battle "parameters" that were lower than enemy strength figures presented to Westmoreland in May.

Anthony Murry, another member of the Capital Legal team, was allowed by Burt to examine the next two witnesses, former Colonel Everette Parkins and Daniel O. Graham.[7]

Graham was now retired but could look back on a stellar career — one that had landed him jobs of great responsibility within the intelligence community. Having fought the good fight for MACV against the CIA, and winning it handily, Graham was deemed ready for the prestigious Office of National Intelligence, and by late 1968 now–Brigadier General Graham was in Langley and pursuing the cause that would consume him for many years to come: fighting the CIA on estimates of Soviet military expenditures. In this battle Graham, in a switch, argued that the CIA's estimates were far too low. Here again, Graham's willingness to take on the civilians was quickly rewarded: A stint as the deputy director for the intelligence community was soon followed by the powerful post of director of the Defense Intelligence Agency. At the DIA, General Graham pushed through his Soviet estimates and even had time to deal deftly with the Church and Pike Committees. Just before Graham hung up his uniform for good in 1976 he was awarded the CIA Distinguished Intelligence Medal.

Through with government work (although in 1980 he was mentioned as a candidate for director of the CIA), Graham next advised candidate Ronald Reagan on military affairs before becoming involved in an early concept for the Strategic Defense Initiative. Instrumental in selling the concept to Reagan in 1980, Graham went on to head High Frontier Inc., a group instrumental in promoting the "Star Wars" missile defense system.[8]

Graham took the stand, and Murry showed the jury a segment of Graham's unused CBS interview by Wallace where Graham got off a crack by saying that he had been a six-star general, "three on each shoulder." In the outtake footage, Graham told Wallace that while at MACV, he may have been guilty of "overestimating" enemy troop strengths but of nothing else. Now when questioned by Murry, Graham forcefully said that he "did not" falsify intelligence and that it was Sam Adams and Sam Adams alone who had problems with the enemy troop strength estimates. The following day Graham again took the stand and got into a drawn-out argument with Boies regarding Adams. Graham insisted, despite Boies's probing, that Adams was "the source of all this uproar" and that Adams had "a hangup that borders on a mental problem."

Graham's third day of testimony degenerated into a shouting match between himself and Boies. Graham offered a red-meat conservative defense of Westmoreland, stating that America had won the Vietnam War militarily but lost it politically. Graham accused CBS of impugning the honor of the officer corps and stated that CBS had attempted to delay the trial until Westmoreland, now age seventy, had died. Regarding the last accusation, Graham said that even in Westmoreland's absence he would have gladly continued with the lawsuit himself (Judge Leval instructed the jury to ignore this, noting that CBS had never made any effort to delay the trial). After venting, Graham testified that NVA/Viet Cong troop strength had reached a high of 550,000 in mid-1966 and then had declined at a rate of about 5,000 a month. Boies did the math, while Graham objected from the stand, and calculated that with enemy losses of 5,000 a month the total enemy strength by the end of 1967 would still be in the 450,000-to-475,000 range.

"Well," Graham said, "that's nifty arithmetic."

"It's nifty arithmetic," Boies answered, "but it also happens to work."

*

During the trial Graham ran into George Allen, there for the defense. The two got into talking about old times. "Of course," Graham blithely told Allen, enemy strength was more than three hundred thousand, but at MACV defending this estimate had been "the command position."[9]

*

The fifth week of the trial began with the deposition of a former army intelligence officer, Michael B. Hankins, being read aloud to the jury. Then came Colonel John Stewart, a former MACV official and most recently the chief intelligence officer for the Grenada invasion. Stewart defended the MACV intelligence operation and was followed on the stand by George A. Carver, the thirteenth witness for Westmoreland.

At SAVA, as Carver testified bitterly, Sam Adams "was very intolerant of people who did not share the conclusions to which he jumped" and considered them to be "either fools or knaves." Carver also said that "Mr. Adams was often in error but seldom in doubt." Carver's testimony would last three days, and at times it was unclear if he was appearing for the plaintiff or the defendants because his testimony was all over the map. What was clear, however, was that Carver was antagonistic toward David Boies. Boies was pleased to fuel that antagonism by accusing Carver of having caved in to Westmoreland and by noting that the CIA only regained "the courage of its convictions" after Carver's Saigon agreement had been scrapped.

On Friday, after the court had listened to Carver all week, the plaintiff himself stiffly took the stand. General Westmoreland, dressed in a gray business suit and wearing a regimental tie, spoke calmly as Burt asked him extensive questions about his personal and military background. When the topic finally got to Vietnam and the order of battle, Westmoreland said that he had been "surprised" by General McChristian's May 1967 draft cable that detailed dramatically increased estimates for the enemy's irregular forces, and Westmoreland was concerned "that such a cable, if dispatched," would be "terribly misleading." Westmoreland said that in particular he had objected to McChristian's inclusion of the Viet Cong irregulars in any enemy estimate. "Joe," Westmoreland would recall saying in May 1967, "we're not fighting those people. They're basically civilians." Under questioning by Burt, Westmoreland denied ever having given Johnson a rosy view of the war during their April 1967 meeting at the White House. Instead, Westmoreland testified, during that meeting he had actually asked the president for more troops.

Westmoreland was shaping up to be his own best witness. Earlier Burt had shown extensive CBS outtakes of the Wallace interview in which Westmoreland, sweating and licking his lips nervously, appeared flustered and angry, but on the stand the jury saw a different man. This version was a stately old soldier whose feelings of betrayal by CBS were, despite his reserved demeanor, painfully evident. From his martial shell, in fact, Westmoreland's humanness on the stand came out frequently. At one point in the questioning Burt wanted to know why Westmoreland had traveled to the Philippines in April 1967. Westmoreland seemed stumped by the question and after some awkward moments of silence his wife, Kitsy, piped up from the audience, "You better recall." The retired four-star general suddenly remembered and the courtroom broke out in laughter: "Yes, I know why I was there. I was there to see my wife."

Taking the stand for the second day, Westmoreland lit into the media for harming troop morale during the war and said of his soldiers that "a commander could have expected nothing more of them." Westmoreland stood by General Abrams's insistence that estimates of Viet Cong irregulars not be given out to the press because, in Abrams's words, "All available caveats and explanations will not prevent the press from drawing an erroneous and gloomy conclusion." Westmoreland testified that if these estimates had been publicized, his troops would have complained, *What the hell are we doing? We were doing a great job. Now we find out the enemy has increased when it hasn't increased at all.* He told the jury, "Yes, we were sensitive to press reaction" and would have been "dumb-oxes" not to be: "I totally agreed with General Abrams's language. I agreed with it then. I agree with it now. If I had to do it over again, I would."

Burt then asked if Westmoreland had ever ordered reductions in enemy strength estimates.

"I did not," answered Westmoreland.

"Are you sure?"

"Positive."

Dan Burt left history to one side and for the next two days led Westmoreland through his experiences with Mike Wallace and George Crile. This process was briefly delayed, though, by the cameo appearance of William Bundy, President Johnson's assistant secretary of state for Far Eastern affairs. Bundy was a busy man, and this was the only time that he could squeeze in for testimony. For those interested in glimpsing yet another figure from the Vietnam War era this was a treat, but otherwise Bundy offered little to work with for either side. After Bundy was on his way to his next appointment Burt returned to his examination of Westmoreland. The retired general said that during the Wallace interview, "I realized I was not participating in a rational interview. It was an inquisition."

The topic shifted back to history when Boies began his cross-examination and got Westmoreland to acknowledge that on April 27, 1967, he had indeed told President Johnson that the "crossover point" had been reached. Boies also got the retired general to say that his own intelligence staff had concluded that enemy irregulars belonged in the official order of battle. The exchanges between the old warrior and the aggressive young lawyer grew sharper. "You insisted," Boies accused, referring to the SNIE 14.3-67 debate, "that the enemy SD and SSD not be enumerated on a current basis." Westmoreland replied caustically that "I didn't want to be bothered" with the issue. Boies countered that earlier he had been bothered enough to intervene in McChristian's attempt to include the SD and SSD in the draft cable for Washington. "You've got this completely distorted," Westmoreland replied in a thinly veiled reference to McChristian. "Intelligence sources tend to be myopic. They get brownie points for finding more enemy. They hedge their bets. It's the old syndrome of cover your backside." In contrast, Westmoreland said, "A commander has to exercise some judgment."

In another day of testimony Boies, with Westmoreland protesting the whole way, attempted to drag the retired general into admitting that there had been immense pressure from the Johnson White House to demonstrate progress in the war, and that this was the motive at MACV to keep the enemy order of battle numbers low. "That's ludicrous," Westmoreland snapped. "Certainly not." Boies wondered why, then, were the enemy strength figures routinely reported as being 285,000 month after month. "That was strictly coincidental," Westmoreland explained.

The next morning Westmoreland, suffering back pain as a result of the 121 jumps he had made as a paratrooper, could not appear in court, and the trial was suspended for two days. When the general showed up again he probably wished he had remained away. Boies's objective that day was to demean the plaintiff's integrity and credibility, and Boies got right to work. He read from a 1971 *Time* magazine article that argued, "Westmoreland could be found guilty of Vietnam war crimes if he were to be tried by the same standard under which the U.S. hanged Japanese General Tomayuki Tamashita." Boies also quoted at length from Pike Committee findings stating MACV had given a "false perception" of enemy strength to U.S.

policy makers. He pushed at Westmoreland a pile of documents, including portions of the Pentagon Papers, in an effort to show discrepancies between the general's testimony and what he had said while commanding MACV. Boies also read from former South Vietnamese Premier Nguyen Cao Ky's memoirs. "Westmoreland," Ky wrote, "must have known all about the strength" of the Tet attack, but "I am convinced that the White House did not. American leaders in Saigon deliberately issued a string of lies to the White House, in an effort to maintain the impression that the Americans were getting on top of the Vietcong."

Westmoreland, listening to these and other words, turned red, jabbed his spectacles in the air, and gave lengthy explanations in an attempt to deflect Boies. But the lawyer relentlessly returned to his central premise — usually buttressed by Westmoreland's own autobiography, *A Soldier Reports*, and by Westmoreland's command diaries — that MACV had been under intense pressures from the Johnson administration to show progress in the war.

Agitated by Boies, Westmoreland on the stand began referring the enemy troop strength estimates as "the so-called order of battle." This drew the ire of Boies, who reminded Westmoreland that *order of battle* was in fact the official term in use by MACV during his command. Boies then followed up with a question. "You were the commander, correct, sir?"

"Mr. Boies, you know that."

"Yes, I do know that. What I was wondering is whether you forgot it, sir."

It was already the first week of December, and Westmoreland had given nine days of testimony. December 3 was a particularly trying one for the plaintiff as Boies, in a further effort to show that Westmoreland's integrity and honor were sullied well before the CBS broadcast, read a host of unflattering accounts of Westmoreland's conduct in Vietnam. Westmoreland, according to what Boies read aloud as the retired general was forced to sit quietly without opportunity for rejoinder, had engaged in producing "a string of lies," a "squalid deception," "a numbers game," and "a degraded image of the enemy." But did he ever, Boies asked of Westmoreland, attempt to take action against any of this "allegedly defamatory material"? Answering softly, Westmoreland said, "I did not."

The next day was Westmoreland's last day on the stand, and he testified briefly. When he stepped down Burt called Paul H. Nitze, the former deputy secretary of defense, as a witness. Nitze defended MACV's decision not to include enemy irregular forces in the same count as enemy regular forces. "When you aggregate elephants and flies," Nitze said memorably, "you get nonsense."

Nitze stepped down and the trial was thrown into a tizzy when Dan Burt, over the objections of David Boies, dramatically produced a memo, just found in the military archives, containing the minutes of a May 19, 1967, MACV intelligence briefing at which Westmoreland was present. The memo, however, raised more questions than it answered, and Burt's ploy to exonerate Westmoreland of intelligence suppression turned out to be a dud.

The next day, December 5, Burt embarked upon his epic although misguided examination of George Crile. Burt was looking forward to skewering his "hostile witness" with the *TV Guide* allegations, but Crile, age thirty-nine, highly intelligent, very articulate, and immaculately dressed in a gray suit, proved an elusive foe. With what seemed to be an endless supply of stamina Crile would wear Burt down in the hours, days, and weeks ahead with lengthy essay answers to his every question, and all the while taking up Burt's limited number of hours for direct examination. Crile was at times angry and exasperated, but more often than not he was a confident, even patronizing, figure on the stand, creating a glib quagmire from which Burt appeared to have no exit strategy. Burt, for instance, once asked Crile what he meant when he wrote that MACV had deceived Johnson:

CRILE: I meant what I said, given what I meant, Mr. Burt.

Another time Burt had gone on at length about the two Allen interviews when finally he paused for Crile's admission of guilt:

CRILE: Mr. Burt, much is being made about nothing.

Burt insisted that Crile had done something wrong:

BURT: You deliberately tried to mislead the viewer? Correct sir?
CRILE: Well, I can repeat my answer as many times as you like, Mr. Burt.

For those watching the Burt-versus-Crile spectacle it could be deadly dull, but for the moment all were spared from having to sit through more than one day of this: On December 6 Robert S. McNamara made his star appearance.

McNamara's day in court, representing the end of his sixteen years of public silence on the topic of the war, created international headlines. Sure enough, there were revelations. The packed courtroom heard McNamara testify about a hitherto unknown attempt to negotiate with Ho Chi Minh in 1967, and Boies — because of a tactical error made by Burt — was able to introduce a declassified memo in which McNamara told Johnson that the war could not be won and that sending more American troops would "lead to a major national disaster . . . bogging us down further."

In terms of the CBS documentary, though, there were few surprises, with McNamara repeating his deposition testimony that no intelligence deception had occurred and that the numbers debate was irrelevant. McNamara was excused, and the next four days of testimony were taken up by Burt's continued attack on Crile's professionalism and character. Thanks to Burt, it all came out, including Crile's failure to interview people who might contradict the premise of the documentary, the coddling of friendly witnesses, the grilling of unfriendly witnesses, the two interviews of George Allen, et cetera. Burt also read a note that Crile had written to Wallace in which Crile said that Westmoreland "seems not to be all that bright," adding, "All you have to do is break General Westmoreland and we have the whole thing aced."

Burt, however, found it hard to make the mud stick. He also found that simply getting Crile to answer a simple yes or no was impossible. The author Renata Adler (providing commentary in the brackets) gives an example:

> BURT: And did you believe, Mr. Crile, prior to the broadcast, that Tet was a terrific military victory for the United States?
> CRILE: [Four paragraphs containing neither yes nor no.]
> BURT: Mr. Crile, did you tell any executive at CBS, after the broadcast, that in a war of attrition Tet was a terrific victory for our side?
> CRILE: [Three paragraphs, containing neither yes nor no.]

At one point — as another Adler example of Burt's futility — Crile was asked to confirm a quote that was taken from an internal CBS memo. In the memo Crile was identified by the initial *G*:

> BURT: Did you *say those words*, Mr. Crile?
> CRILE: [Two full pages, which contain neither yes nor no but include a strange insistence that the transcript "has three dots."]
> BURT: "G," that is George Crile, isn't it?
> CRILE: I presume so.
> BURT: [Quoting "G" in the notes] "If you're talking about a war of attrition, *Tet was a terrific victory for our side*"?
> CRILE: There were three dots there, Mr. Burt.
> BURT: Three dots? Thank you, Mr. Crile.[10]

Burt seemed to be proceeding aimlessly with Crile, and Leval called a sidebar conference to ask Burt what he was doing. "I have found this examination very confusing," the judge said. "I am really quite at a loss as what the facts are that you are seeking to bring out."

A two-week recess for the holidays was announced on December 19, and Adams was given a respite from the trial routine: being picked up every morning by the limousine service for the commute down to Lower Manhattan, huddling with the lawyers, long days of listening to testimony punctuated by a brief lunch and a few breaks, and then working with the legal team late into the night to prepare questions for the next day's hostile witnesses.

When the trial started Adams was made a permanent resident of the Plaza Hotel until he finally rebelled and Cravath Swaine and Moor found him a furnished apartment in Midtown. Anne Cocroft came up from Virginia to join him. Adams, while showing the strain, was all the while in good spirits. "I would say at that time I think he was excited," Anne recalled, "really engaged and not thinking what may or may not be the outcome. Sam was just never happier than when he was engaged in something like that."

15

THE COLONELS' REVOLT

Boies continued with his velvet-gloved "cross" of Crile at the reopening of the trial, January 3, 1985, and Crile's ninth and last day on the stand as Dan Burt's hostile witness ended quickly the following morning. Jurors could now make plans for the weekend. On Monday, Burt, fast using up what remained of his 150 hours and unwilling to spend it on Mike Wallace and Sam Adams as he had planned, instead called his nineteenth and final witness, Ira Klein — the person most responsible for triggering the events that had led to the trial.

Klein, as could be expected, was no longer with CBS, and he appeared nervous when Burt led him through his testimony. The film editor, age thirty-three and, according to reporter David Zucchino, "boyish-faced" with "wavy hair," testified that Adams had told him in the cutting room, "We have to come clean. We have to make a statement that the premise of the broadcast was wrong." Klein also testified that Crile's editing decisions were "unethical" and that "Mr. Crile would not permit me to give General Westmoreland an opportunity to present his point of view." Klein used his time on the stand to throw some dirt Crile's way (such as relating the occasion, as Klein did during his deposition, when Crile in reviewing a video of Westmoreland had shouted at the retired general's image on the screen "I got you! I got you!"), and it was indeed these kinds of disclosures that had been behind CBS's wish to avoid a trial.[1]

When court adjourned after lunch, though, Boies made quick work of the film editor. Boies questioned things that he'd told Don Kowet of *TV Guide*:

> BOIES: Did you tell this reporter that you believed that George Crile was a social pervert?

KLEIN: I believe so, yes.

BOIES: Did you tell this reporter that you were just too good and that bothered Mr. Crile?

KLEIN: As I can recall, yes.

BOIES: Did you tell this reporter that Mr. Crile was devious and slimy?

KLEIN: Yes, I believe that is so.

BOIES: Did you have similar personal problems with other members of the production team, sir?

KLEIN: No.

BOIES: Let's take Mr. Alben, who you have identified as the researcher. Did you tell the reporter that we are talking about here that Mr. Alben was a homosexual?

Before Klein could answer, a panicked Burt called for a sidebar conference and asked Leval to stop the line of questioning. Boies argued, however, that he should be allowed to continue because the questioning "shows the deep seated and vicious personal bias of this witness not only toward Mr. Crile but towards CBS and the people associated with this program." Leval allowed the interrogation to continue but warned Boies not to get into the specifics regarding Klein's remarks. (At a subsequent break in the trial, Boies told reporters that he never had any intention of doing so, saying that they were "just too disgusting and too unfair to innocent people" to be read aloud in court.)

Boies pursued Klein's personal feelings toward Crile for a bit longer, then finished Klein off by exposing his complete lack of knowledge regarding, among other things, journalism, the order of battle dispute, and the Vietnam War. By the time Boies was done with him a diminished Klein left the stand, now no more than a footnote to the trial.

*

The next day the defense began its case. Boies stated, as he had countless times already, that there could be no doubt as to the veracity of the broadcast. To further buttress this claim, the Cravath team showed excerpts of the CBS interviews and read from affidavits and depositions, and throughout all of this Boies told the jurors over and over again that there was no mistaking the fact that Westmoreland had ordered the suppression of accurate intelligence. During Boies's argument, though, no live witnesses were called to the stand, and for those confined to the jury box it was a boring day. "I can vividly remember," said Patricia Roth, "studying the spot on the floor in front of me and visualizing how easily I could really lie down there."

More affidavits and depositions were read the next morning, January 10, and the day appeared to be shaping up much like the one before. Then a video of Wallace's interview with Adams was shown for the first time in court. Roth was intrigued to see the man she had been observing "buried in note taking" these last three months now actually telling his own story in his own words.

"This man on the video monitor was someone else," Roth said. "When he talked and moved and thought in front of you, he turned in to another entity.

"Then the tape went off, and he was called to the stand in the flesh.

"As I've said, I've watched him for three months. For three months I've heard all kinds of characterizations — from a mental case to a genius. I've seen the serious frown daily, and the occasional smile break out. By far, of any of the people who have taken the stand thus far, Sam Adams is the most real.

"As he approached the stand and took the oath, it was evident that he was nervous. Even in the opening statements it was evident. But it was real, and when he relaxed, he was real. It was hard to believe that this guy was capable of any kind of untruth — even trying to disguise his shyness at being a witness."[2]

David Zucchino reported how on Adams's initial day of testimony, the witness had settled "his broad frame into the witness stand" and "meticulously outlined his accusations against Westmoreland and his command" and although "sometimes digressing into trivial details" he showed "a strong command of dates and statistics." Adams also treated the court to charm and candor. Zucchino noted that "Even when his testimony turned to the substance of his allegations against Westmoreland, Adams was still folksy and compelling. He used such colloquialisms as 'something funny was going on' and 'it seemed awfully odd' in describing his realization that enemy troop strength numbers were being doctored.

"Asked in a videotaped interview shown to the jury why he went to

Vietnam in 1967 to pursue his analysis of the enemy, he replied, 'You know, there were no Viet Cong around Washington.'"

On the stand that first day Adams also described how *CDEC Bulletin* 689 had been delivered to his desk on August 19, 1966. "This thing came in at 10:30 A.M.," he testified; "By 10:32, I realized I was in deep." Zucchino reported, "The wry smile spread across his face again and again Thursday as Adams, sometimes beguiling, sometimes grave, laid out for the jury what has come to be called the 'Adams theory.' He considers his chance to testify a 'bonanza' and seemed ebullient as he addressed his captive audience."

Adams's second day of testimony was taken up by Boies as, for the first time in fourteen weeks of trial, the CBS documentary was shown in its entirety (Kitsy Westmoreland, seated in the audience, averted her eyes throughout). As the tape ran Adams dissected, point by point, every charge against Westmoreland made in the film. It was tedious going at times, but when it was over Adams provided some much-needed drama. "Finally," Zucchino reported, "just as Westmoreland had concluded his own testimony with an impassioned soliloquy defending his conduct, Adams ended with an emotional defense of the broadcast and his own long campaign to prove a 'monument of deceit' by MACV.

"Leaning forward and speaking loudly but slowly, Adams then described a visit he made last year to the Vietnam memorial in Washington, D.C. He said he had asked himself how many of the 45,000 U.S. soldiers who died in Vietnam combat — out of what he said were 52,022 total deaths — whose names were engraved on the granite memorial had been killed by enemy irregulars who Westmoreland has said posed no military threat."[3]

Boies concluded his direct examination of Adams by asking if he now had any regrets about participating in the CBS documentary: "None whatsoever, I am proud to have been part of the broadcast." Would, Boies wondered aloud to Adams, he still have joined the CIA if he had to do everything all over again?

"Yep."

*

David Dorsen began the cross-examination of Adams on January 16, and the lawyer was just barely prepared. Shortly before the holiday break Burt realized that he was in over his head and that Dorsen would have to deal with Adams when the defense put on its case. Because Burt had earlier barred Dorsen from the courtroom, Dorsen was unaware of what the defendant had earlier testified to. "I was very, very lucky," Dorsen remembered, "because we had that long break — ten days or eight days or whatever it was — over Christmas, which permitted me to read some of the trial transcript — not all of it, which to this day I have not read."

Dorsen's strategy was to drive a wedge between Adams and CBS. "I saw that Sam had a thesis," Dorsen explained, "but it was a different thesis than CBS put on the air. Sam's thesis was that Westmoreland was part of a conspiracy that lied to the press and the public. This was an important allegation and it was the thesis of the *Harper's* article. What George Crile did was make it into a conspiracy where Westmoreland lied to his superiors. This changed things tremendously because it put Sam in kind of a peculiar position. He wanted an outlet for his thesis but it became a different thesis. And in fact right after the broadcast came out he said to somebody, 'The show is great but it put too much responsibility on Westmoreland.' So Sam never really adopted it, that thesis, and he constantly was in a peculiar position of working with CBS to promote a broadcast which was not really his."

In planning for the cross-examination, though, Dorsen was not content to drive a wedge between Adams and the documentary; he also wanted to demolish Adams as a witness. "My theory," Dorsen explained, "was that he would not wear well with the jury. He was very passionate, he was very single-minded, and . . . given enough time he would look like a kook. Whether he was one or not that wasn't my problem, that wasn't my job — although I happened to feel that he was."[4]

*

Adams went into the trial just as he had waged his lonely crusade at Langley, just as he had flown out to Los Angeles to appear on behalf of Ellsberg and Russo, just as he had at various times approached Congress, just as he had worked with George Crile on the *Harper's* article, just as he had helped with the CBS program: that is, with no constituency behind him save the few who cared about integrity in the intelligence process. He never had a political base. Adams had never been a Vietnam War opponent, and this confused liberals. Adams was a critic of the U.S. military, and this annoyed conservatives. The "numbers episode" fit nowhere in the accepted historiography of the war, and academicians didn't know what to make of him. Adams argued that it was a failure in military intelligence that led to America's defeat, and this did not convince Vietnam War revisionists who believed blame belonged anywhere and everywhere except with those in uniform.

Lacking, therefore, an easy stereotype in which to guide it, the press during the trial was hard-put to comprehend Adams, and by some of the things that Adams told reporters Dorsen could well have felt that he had a chance to portray the defendant as being a "kook." For example, the *Washington Post* reported that "After one of four visits to the Cloisters Museum and viewing the unicorn tapestries there, Adams told reporters outside the courtroom, 'I'm afraid I belong in the 12th Century.'" To Bob Brewin of the *Village Voice*, Adams admitted that some thought he was "whacko" to have pursued the order of battle controversy for seventeen years, but Adams pointed out that Galileo, while also pursing the truth, had been excommunicated for believing that the earth revolved around the sun. "When was Galileo exonerated?" Adams asked Brewin. "Was it last year? Why the hell do they bother? They look silly. That means until 1983 the guy was really full of it."[5]

The press did, however, attempt to understand Adams, and it even came partway toward empathizing with him. The word *obsession* played prominently in news stories about Adams, along with descriptions of his self-deprecating humor and his distant relationship to the Presidents Adams. The defendant's rumpled tweeds, chronologies, penchant for note taking, brilliance, eccentricities, outlandish request to have Westmoreland court-martialed, and good looks also made their way into published accounts of the trial.

Although a puzzling subject, Adams's penchant for plain talk stood him in good stead with the press. He told Brewin, for example, that he had never aspired to be a "whistle-blower" because "I did not want to bother with all this goddamn crap of trying to turn people in. It's a pain in the ass." Zucchino, as others did, noticed a gentleness to Adams, and a lack of anger for a man so driven. Zucchino reported that Adams "speaks of Westmoreland charitably, calling him a 'decent' and 'likeable man.' Beyond that, he does not dare characterize in an interview the general's motives during the war. 'The last time I got into that,' he said, 'I got hit with a $120,000,000 libel suit.'"[6]

*

Dorsen hammered away at Adams during the first day of cross-examination, January 16. Dorsen accused Adams of basing his nineteen-year campaign against Westmoreland on "an old piece of paper" that was not, as Adams, thought "gospel." The defendant admitted to Dorsen that the documents like the one contained in Bulletin 689 were "varied and ambiguous" translations of the original Viet Cong ones, but nevertheless were "what the United States at that time primarily relied upon to find out about the VC." Dorsen was not convinced, though, and wondered if Adams was not the only one to be fooled by the documents:

> DORSEN: Mr. Adams, wasn't it your experience too in Vietnam that people would sometimes inflate numbers in order to get payroll increases that they could keep for themselves?
>
> ADAMS: Oh yes it was.
>
> DORSEN: And this might have been true in North Vietnam or the Vietcong and it might have been true among the South Vietnamese?
>
> ADAMS: Vietcong guerrillas do not get paid.
>
> DORSEN: They got rice?
>
> ADAMS: Yes, they got rice anyway.
>
> DORSEN: I know, but if somebody put in a document, Mr. Adams, that there were 200 rather than 100 guerrillas wouldn't that person get twice as much rice?
>
> ADAMS: No sir. They ate locally. [Laughter in the courtroom.]

Dorsen attempted to have Adams demonstrate that MACV's numbers in the fall of 1967 were really no different from those proposed by the CIA, but Adams refused to budge, explaining that the two estimates were in no way similar. Dorsen next read a CIA memo from the same period stating that while intelligence estimates "reflect an actual growth of communist forces during the past year" in fact these forces "may have actually declined." Did the memo, Dorsen wanted to know, read that the enemy strength was decreasing and not increasing? "I think," conceded Adams, "you can get that impression." Another 1967 memo was then brought out by Dorsen, this one prepared by Adams himself: The enemy "militia" — Adams had written — were "largely noncombatant." Dorsen asked Adams to explain. "I was talking about the fact that militia largely did not mix in the firefights," Adams said, but instead "laid mines and booby traps" and "doing actions which harmed American troops."

Judge Leval called it a day and the witness was excused until tomorrow. Dorsen had succeeded in getting Adams's goat. "When Sam got off the stand," Dorsen recalled, "he walked by me and looked down and said, 'You bastard.'"

The next day Dorsen sarcastically asked Adams why — if all this conspiring on the part of Westmoreland had occurred in 1967 — CBS had waited until 1983 to "notify the world." Adams answered loudly and heatedly, "It turned out that George Crile and I had to do something that somebody else should have done a long time ago." Dorsen then asked the defendant where the hard evidence was showing that Westmoreland had blocked NVA infiltration figures from leaving MACV headquarters. Adams could only answer weakly that this evidence had been either destroyed or was still being hidden by the U.S. government. But would not it have been "incredible," Dorsen pressed, for Westmoreland to have kept vital intelligence from his own troops? "Sir," Adams answered, "I find a lot of things in this whole episode incredible."

After two days of cross-examination Adams had held his own, but the cocky confidence on display earlier was often absent, and at his worst Adams appeared flustered and prone to blunder, such as when he told Dorsen that one of his estimates had been a "only a guess":

DORSEN: Is "only a guess" something less than a guess?
ADAMS: "Only a guess" is only a guess.

This was not a discourse that Adams wished to get into, and Dorsen also nicked him by comparing his current testimony with his testimony at the Ellsberg-Russo trial. In Los Angeles, for example, Adams had asserted that

General Earle G. Wheeler was present at a key intelligence briefing, but now Adams told Dorsen that he was not so sure. "I can't see why I included Wheeler in there," Adams said haltingly. "I certainly had no evidence that I can think of now."

Adams was on the stand again Monday, and Dorsen brought up a letter Adams had written to Gains B. Hawkins explaining that the "major problem" with the CBS documentary was that the "rap" on Westmoreland "probably belongs higher than that." Adams admitted to Dorsen that, as his letter suggested, the blame likely rested with President Johnson — "but that was," Adams said, "a separate story." For the rest of the day Dorsen continued to attack discrepancies and contradictions within and between the "Adams theory" and the CBS documentary — and then Dorsen brought up the money:

> DORSEN: Mr. Adams, you mentioned on Thursday afternoon that you were proud of this documentary, didn't you?
> ADAMS: Yes, I did.
> DORSEN: And hasn't this whole matter of order of battle been rather profitable for you?
> ADAMS: Profitable?
> DORSEN: Profitable.
> ADAMS: No, it has not.

Dorsen pressed ahead and discovered that Adams had been paid twenty thousand dollars by W. W. Norton and twenty-five thousand by CBS: a pittance for ten years devoted to the "whole matter" of order of battle. But surely, Dorsen must have thought, Cravath with its deep pockets was paying Adams handsomely, and he queried Adams on the stand about his dual defendant-consultant role. The line of questioning again fell flat: Adams had only requested twelve thousand dollars from Cravath since September 1982 — the princely sum of six thousand dollars a year for his time and expenses.

The following morning Adams was questioned briefly by David Boies on redirect and was then excused. After watching Adams on the stand for the past six days, reporter Bob Brewin said, "The few points Dorsen scored were eclipsed by Adams' persuasive testimony. The numbers breathed when Adams spoke. He painted word pictures that transported the courtroom audience back to the dusty Vietnamese market town where his pursuit had begun. He took them through steaming prisoner-detention centers and urged them to share his outrage over an apparent distortion that would skew the odds of survival for thousands of American soldiers. He managed to re-create the political climate of the 1960s."[7]

But when Adams got off the stand for the last time he was spitting mad. Today had gone fine but yesterday Boies had been unhappy with his testimony and, in a private moment, had given him pointers on what to say when court resumed in the morning. Adams refused to be coached, Boies became furious, Adams suggested that Boies was asking him to lie, Boies suggested that Adams was being absurdly dogmatic, and Adams became even more unmovable. The argument grew hotter and Boies jabbed Adams with the eraser end of a pencil. It was all the defendant could do not to punch his lawyer in the jaw.

For Adams the conclusion of his testimony was a turning point in the trial. With his time on the stand done with, and with the defendants' case now moving along smartly without him, Adams could feel his influence with the Cravath team attriting away.

Adams was also having second thoughts about Westmoreland's culpability. "He became very disillusioned," recalled Adams's friend from his OER days, Robert Klein. Klein was in town to see some of the trial and talked at length with Adams. "Sam initially believed that Westmoreland had deliberately, maliciously, and with intent lied to the president and cooked the books and done all that. But he wasn't so sure anymore. He was beginning to be more of the opinion that it was a phenomenon where you just don't give the president bad news, you don't give the CEO bad news, you don't give the general bad news, and that the culture that Westmoreland had inculcated in the army was such that he was being misled and lied to by people — it was just the way it was. Sam was thinking that Westmoreland might very well be an honorable man after all, and he was feeling considerable regret that he had maligned him. But Sam wasn't certain, he was kind of swinging on it, he wasn't sure."

Adams was, however, quite certain of one thing. "He had become very cynical about the American justice system," Klein said. "He basically made some comments to me along the vein that trials and the whole justice system were not what he had learned in Harvard Law — not quite as honest or straight shooting as he imagined it to be. He was not happy with that business."

*

George Allen took Adams's place at the stand, and gone was Allen's reticence to speak out about corrupted intelligence. Allen's testimony lasted three days. It was devastating. Allen began by noting that the CIA motto was John 8:32, "For ye shall know the truth, and the truth shall set you free," and went on to state that Adams had "pursued the truth with that spirit." Allen explained the history of the intelligence dispute and how at Langley, "We came to believe there was a lack of good faith in the way MACV participated in the controversy."

The next day on the stand Allen grew heated, shouting out in court that the CIA and the U.S. military had "prostituted" themselves and that the Special National Intelligence Estimate had been a "lie" and the "mistake of the century." Allen said that much of the blame belonged to Walt Rostow, who had been part of the Johnson administration's own "self deception" and effort "to influence, exaggerate and misrepresent" to the American public the situation in Vietnam. Allen also charged the agency with "selling out" to MACV and of having, under Richard Helms, "sacrificed its integrity on the alter of public relations and political expediency." Allen said that MACV was given to "falsehoods"; that by placing a ceiling on the numbers and dropping whole categories of the enemy MACV had "totally misrepresented the nature and scope" of the threat; and that this was not something "any competent, honest intelligence officer would have accepted." He told Boies, "I thought MACV's position had been unprincipled"; lest there be any doubt, Allen explained that "General Westmoreland himself was the one who had directed and had controlled the manipulation of the data."[8]

Boies asked of his witness, Why then "did you hold back on camera? Why did you tell Mr. Crile some things off camera that you were not prepared to tell him on camera?" Allen explained that the agency's testimony in front of the Pike Committee in 1975 had been a "whitewash" and "I had some feelings of guilt about my involvement in it" and was "reluctant" to "publicly acknowledge that guilt."

On cross-examination Dorsen pressed Allen to explain the "manipulations" of intelligence by MACV, but when Allen did Dorsen was disbelieving. Allen replied that, believe it or not, "This was the game they were playing, Mr. Dorsen!" The lawyer then accused Allen of testifying only to "help your protégé, Sam Adams." Allen replied in a raised voice that he was testifying only to ensure that "honest estimates are presented to the policymakers and that the intelligence process is performed with full integrity."

Later that afternoon Douglas Parry took the stand and told the jury that MACV "had no interest in knowing what the truth was but that they were using their policy objectives to define the truth."

Parry completed his testimony on Monday, and then John Dickerson, a former CIA analyst, was examined by Randy Mastro. Dickerson explained that agency people in Saigon were not allowed to attend MACV intelligence briefings, and that it was evident a ceiling had been placed on the numbers. "I told Sam that it was in General Westmoreland's command," Dickerson said, "and it was my opinion that he must have known about it. He was the commander. It happened on his watch."

Westmoreland was undoubtedly glad to see Dickerson leave the stand. The retired general was poorly prepared for the reality of court, having originally believed that the proceedings would be more akin to an open debate and that he would periodically have the opportunity to talk to the judge and jury. Such was not the case, of course, and Westmoreland, his time for testimony long since gone, had been forced these last weeks to watch in stony silence as men came forward to swear on the Bible and to testify against him.[9]

Such a man was former U.S. Marine and Congressman Paul N. McCloskey, a California Republican and one of those on Capitol Hill who had been willing to listen to Adams back in 1973. McCloskey, appearing after Dickerson left the stand, said under questioning by Michael Doyen that MACV had engaged in a "conspiracy" to issue "dishonest" intelligence and that this had been "criminal."

The next day Ronald L. Smith took the stand and praised the former subordinate who had given him so much trouble. "Sam was one of the finest analysts that I ever worked with," Smith said. "He was always full of vigor, always upbeat about getting the work done, intelligent and co-operative with the other analysts and last but not least, he was a very good writer." In contrast to Adams's efforts, Smith explained, was Westmoreland, who had hindered good intelligence by "not letting the intelligence professionals do their work unencumbered." Smith testified of Westmoreland and the official order of battle, "It was wrong for him to use the political power he had at the time to force this thing down our throats."

Richard Kovar, whose involvement with the numbers battle had been peripheral, testified on January 30. "A lot of people at CIA had papered over their conscience," Kovar said. "I myself didn't feel very good about it." But now Kovar made up for lost opportunities to speak out. "Sam Adams," Kovar had stated earlier in his affidavit, "was a godsend to the CIA's intelligence effort on the situation in Vietnam. I believed at the time, and continue to believe, that Adams was one of the best intelligence analysts I have ever encountered and, more importantly, one of the most devoted to the objectivity that the CIA purported to stand for."

In court Robert Baron, leading Kovar through his testimony, asked if Adams was a "mental case, as some have professed."

"In answer to your question, No," Kovar answered emphatically. "What Sam did wrong was that he didn't salute and shut up. He didn't close ranks. Not only didn't he shut up, he pushed his arguments and he pushed his outrage at the agency's acquiescence. And that frightened a lot of people at the agency, and it made them mad. He went after the Director of Intelligence himself."

Judge Leval was surprised that plaintiff's attorneys did not object to Kovar's speechifying, but all the energy seemed to have left the Capital Legal team. While Burt and his lawyers wilted, Adams listened to Kovar from the defendants' table. Adams's face turned red — one juror thought he could see tears in his eyes.[10]

*

Daniel Friedman, a Vietnam veteran and now a veterans' counselor, pulled out a grenade and reached for the pin that kept the device from detonating. "All you would do," Friedman said, "is loosen the pin over here, straighten the pin out so it could easily be pulled. There is some pressure on this pin, but not very much. And you would tie a trip wire, a piece of fishing line, a very thin piece of metal wire, almost anything that would be hard to see on the trail — a fishing line was used commonly — you would secure the grenade to the area that you want the kill zone to be in, and you would lace the trip wire further ahead, where your point man might set it off.

"Usually on patrol you would have a point man walking several meters in front of the body of the patrol and he would trip it off — it's usually a three to five second delay on the explosion — and the grenade would cause maximum damage."

Robert Baron — after assuring the court that the grenade was unarmed — asked the next witness, David Embree, who might do such a thing. Embree, now a college professor who'd been a private in the war, answered that old men, women, or children could have rigged this type of booby trap; in fact, anyone in the Viet Cong self-defense forces was capable of doing such a thing. Westmoreland, sitting a few feet away, smiled thinly.[11]

*

When detailed to SAVA, Don Blascak had been a major, but in late 1982 now-Colonel Blascak was at Fort Huachuca, Arizona, enjoying his own command as head of the School Brigade at the U.S. Army Intelligence Center and School. The phone rang one day, recalled Blascak, "and the secretary puts the phone call through and it's Sam — typical Sam, we hadn't spoken to each other in fourteen years — and he says, 'Hi Don, how are ya? This is Sam Adams here. I've got this little problem. It seems that Westmoreland has taken exception to some of the things we said on a documentary and I was wondering if you would consult with our legal team." And I said, 'Whatever, Sam.'"

Blascak's willingness to assist, however, was sincere. "Because I was on board with those guys when they were fighting the good fight," Blascak agreed to help, and when the trial finally got under way a couple of years later he was G-2 of army V Corps. Four days before he was due to testify, Blascak had completed the annual REFORGER (Return of Forces to Germany) exercise in Europe. "I cleaned myself up," he said, "got on a plane, a red-eye special from Frankfurt to New York, hardly got off the plane when they wanted to depose me at two o'clock in the morning." The Capital Legal lawyers thought they could break the colonel down with the early-morning deposition. "Nastiness," exclaimed Blasack. "They did it two mornings in a row, tried to catch me off guard."

Robert Baron as Blascak's "case officer" was to lead the direct examination, and Baron was highly impressed with his witness. "If ever there was a man who was the portrait of a fighting man it was Don Blascak," Baron recalled. "He was fifty-two I think at the time, but he was still buzz-cut and ramrod-straight, six foot two, and looked like he could dispatch two people at once with his bare hands if they blindsided him."

Taking the stand right after Boies's dramatic coup with the hand grenade, Blascak and his testimony were indeed lethal to Westmoreland. John Stewart — who had appeared in court for Westmoreland months before — was still in the military, but Colonel Blascak was the first man currently in uniform to come out against the former MACV commander. And Blascak came out hard. Tall, gangling, and dressed in a dark business suit, he said that Westmoreland's orders had helped produce "a lie" and "corrupt" intelligence; he said that SNIE 14.3-67 was "a carefully well packaged lie"; he said that the estimate was "just paper" and had served "a terribly disuseful function"; and, his voice rising, he said that the Viet Cong irregulars "killed people. They wounded people. They maimed people." The Capital Legal team seemed stunned by the severity of the assault, and stunned that an active-duty "full bird colonel" would dare come to CBS's defense. It was left to an exacerbated Leval to complain to Boies that the witness was making blanket accusations and ascribing motives to other people. "He has done it in spite of my instruction," Leval said excitedly at a sidebar conference. "He had done it about six times." Dorsen, though, was perhaps in no mood to confront the witness and may have even wanted to hasten the colonel's return to active duty. Blascak's testimony lasted only half a day.[12]

The remainder of the afternoon in court was devoted to the testimony of Russell Cooley. Cooley explained that at MACV if you disagreed with the intelligence manipulations, you were out of a job.

The next day, February 6, Joseph A. McChristian, Westmoreland's own former chief of intelligence, took the stand. Speaking into the microphone "as though," Patricia Roth explained, "he were addressing a battalion," McChristian related a thirty-eight-year military career that included fighting throughout Europe under Patton, the Korean and Vietnam Wars, and all the positions he had held and citations received. "The awards and medals he won are too numerous to mention here," Roth said. "But 'ooohs' of admiration could be heard from the spectators."

Then McChristian's testimony proper began. This was a moment of high drama with one retired general and West Point graduate testifying against another retired general and West Point graduate. Under questioning by Boies, McChristian said that Westmoreland's comments back in May 1967 that the draft cable for Washington would cause a "political bombshell" had been "burned" into his memory.

Like George Allen's, McChristian's testimony was far more impassioned than was his appearance on the CBS documentary, and despite David Dorsen's often successful attempts to poke holes in his memory, in court McChristian was all but indicting his former commander of conspiracy to keep the truth from Washington by removing the Viet Cong irregulars from the official order of battle. It was in Boies's redirect of McChristian, however, that Westmoreland was presented in a particularly sinister light:

> BOIES: Did there come a time . . . when General Westmoreland called you on the telephone and told you in words or substance that he thought that the conversation that he had with you in May of 1967 was a private conversation between West Pointers?
> MCCHRISTIAN: Yes, sir.

And when, Boies wanted to know, had this telephone call occurred? January 21, 1982, two days before the CBS broadcast, McChristian answered. "He thought," McChristian testified while reading from notes he had taken during the phone call, "our conversation [in May 1967] was private and official between West Pointers." Westmoreland, McChristian said while still consulting his notes, was upset that he had disclosed the contents of that conversation to CBS. "He said that he has stood up for and took the brunt of Vietnam for all of us. He as much as accused me of being the one mainly responsible for his integrity being impugned." Finally Boies brought up another telephone call "in or about June 1984" in which Westmoreland had told McChristian — in a threat that he, too, could become a party to the lawsuit — that no one was "expendable."

Thursday and Friday — the jury's usual day off — were taken up by

George Crile's reappearance on the stand. Crile once more gave a capsulation of the defense's entire argument while Boies led him through both the intelligence controversy and the making of the documentary. It was testimony terribly difficult for the jury to endure as Crile reiterated what other CBS witnesses had said on camera, had said in affidavits, had said in depositions — had said in courtroom testimony that the jurors had already heard for themselves! The entire documentary was shown all over again, including much footage that had been edited out, and just when everyone was desperately looking forward to the weekend Boies popped a surprise. He turned to a startled Dan Burt and invited him, on the defense's own time, to come up and tell Crile what "exactly" in the CBS documentary "that the plaintiff believes is false." Burt shirked the challenge and, as Randy Mastro recalled, "It was just total emasculation."

On Monday a retired major, Michael F. Dilley, testified that the Viet Cong Infrastructure was a vital part of the enemy's war effort; Dilley added that his estimates while at MACV for the size of the infrastructure was 139,000. However, Dilley said, he had cut this figure by a third. And why, David Boies asked, did he do this? "Colonel Hawkins told us to," replied the witness, explaining that "the Hawk's only stated reason for lowering the numbers is that they were too high." Dilley then told Boies that "this was entirely improper and unethical."

Tuesday "the Hawk" himself was sworn in as the defense's fifteenth witness and the second member of what George Crile termed the "colonels' revolt." Gains B. Hawkins had been visited in West Point, Mississippi, no less than ten times by Adams and the Cravath lawyers, and he was well prepared for his debut in court. The old colonel with his southern drawl and folksy ways became an instant sensation. "Are you retired, Colonel Hawkins?" Boies asked. "Yes, sir — retired, sir — 30 November 1970, sir." How many years in the service? "I had twenty-five years of duty and I got paid for twenty-nine years, thank God." There was more background questioning and more answers from Hawkins that produced laughter in the courtroom.

When the examination turned to the order of battle, Hawkins was asked if he knew Sam Adams. Yes, "he was one of the most honest men I ever met. He makes me ashamed of myself." What was the nature of the MACV estimates? They had been, Hawkins said, "skewed and screwed" until they "represented crap." Why had this happened? Because General Westmoreland had stated that higher enemy strength figures were "politically unacceptable"; Westmoreland had "established a ceiling and no competent intelligence analyst can operate under a ceiling."

That afternoon Hawkins detailed the intelligence fraud, confirming from letters he had sent home to his wife that the briefing where Westmoreland had told him, "What will I tell the President? What will I tell Congress? What if the press finds out?" occurred on May 28, 1967:

> BOIES: Colonel Hawkins, you have made some serious charges today about yourself and about others.
>
> HAWKINS: Yes, sir.
>
> BOIES: I want to ask you whether you are absolutely certain that those charges are true? — do you have any animus or ill will toward General Westmoreland?
>
> HAWKINS: No, sir, none whatsoever.
>
> BOIES: Do you have animus or ill will to the United States Army?
>
> HAWKINS: No, sir. I carried out these orders as a loyal officer in the United States Army, sir.

Dorsen objected to the last answer as being "unresponsive," and Leval sustained the objection. Still, Boies had gotten his point across to the jury, and Hawkins's testimony about being a loyal army officer was duly reported in Wednesday's *New York Times*.

David Dorsen began his cross-examination of Hawkins the next day. Hawkins played up the folksiness, saying "I'm just a country boy," and to Dorsen's irritation Hawkins's testimony was often rambling, inconclusive, and devoid of details regarding key events. Dorsen, for example, asked Hawkins about a particular intelligence briefing, but Hawkins replied that he had "absolutely no recollection" of the event; when pressed by Dorsen to try to remember Hawkins replied unconvincingly that the whole intelligence episode had been "sort of a traumatic experience" that he had put out of his mind.

Hawkins, to the delight of the courtroom audience, however, put on a show that blunted whatever headway Dorsen was making:

> DORSEN: In preparation for your testimony today, were you shown
> any documents or written material?
> HAWKINS: I have been shown various documents. I read affidavits,
> I read cables, I read some memoranda that had been prepared.
> [Pause.] Is that evil, sir? [Laughter from the courtroom.]

Eleanor Randolph of the *Washington Post* noted that Hawkins was a
"charming" although "tough witness" for Dorsen. Beneath the good-old-
boy geniality, it was obvious, existed a sharp mind, and it was apparent
that Hawkins on the stand knew what he was doing. For example, the
witness could see where Dorsen was heading but was not about to let him
get there first:

> DORSEN: Colonel Hawkins, isn't it your belief that the Communists
> . . . were great liars and that they liked to brag?
> HAWKINS: I think that the Communists were just like Democrats
> and Republicans in that way, that they all do some lying now
> and then and you find some once in a while that will tell you the
> truth. I am chairman of the executive committee —
> LEVAL: [Interrupting] I think you're going —
> HAWKINS: Excuse me, sir. [Resuming testimony] I think that in
> some instances they are great liars and that they like to brag, just
> like other people. But I will caveat that, sir. . . . I'd say most of
> the documents that we saw seemed to me to be authentic.

At another point Dorsen asked Hawkins if "you would describe General
McChristian as relentlessly ambitious." Hawkins, realizing full well what
Dorsen was referring to, answered naively, "I'm not sure that I have ever
described him as that." Dorsen, predictably, handed Hawkins a copy of an
uncompleted memoir Hawkins had written years earlier and asked the
retired colonel if he had ever seen it. Yes, Hawkins replied, he had. Dorsen
asked Hawkins to read from one of the pages (after, though, Leval had
assured the anxious CIA and NSA trial observers, who had jumped up in
alarm, that it contained no national security secrets). The passage Dorsen
had Hawkins read concerned meeting McChristian for the first time in
Europe during World War II.

"I knew," Hawkins read, "little about him then (lieutenants on division staffs don't fraternize much with colonels who were staff chiefs), but I vaguely disliked him out of what paucity of knowledge I had concerning him. He was a cold man. (And these are my impressions and presumptions.) He was a relentlessly ambitious man. He had a passion to excel. He drove his staff subordinates unmercifully. He drove himself with no more mercy. He was not a likable man."

Hawkins then put the manuscript down and — before Dorsen could make whatever point it was he had intended to make — remarked: "I think General McChristian might be proud of this statement." The courtroom burst out in laughter. "God, this is getting better all the time," Hawkins said as the laughter increased. "I'm not a bad writer, even on the first draft."

Under the rules agreed to by both sides of the case, witnesses over age sixty-five were to be excused for the day after four and a half hours on the stand. Hawkins had done his time; his testimony would continue the following Tuesday, February 19.

Retired Colonel Norman House appeared after Hawkins, and when testimony was over for the day Leval had the jury stay in the courtroom. Expect, the judge said to the members of the panel, for all testimony to conclude by next Friday, February 22, and plan for being sequestered in a hotel and out of contact with friends and family for deliberations. In the meantime, Leval admonished, there was to be no talking about the trial outside court, or reading, hearing, or seeing news accounts of the trial.

Afterward in the jury room, jurors and alternates gathered up their things for the commute home. There was a feeling of dread at the prospect of being sequestered, but also a sense of excited anticipation that the end was near. But first, thankfully, there were five full days of freedom ahead: It was only Wednesday, and Dorsen's cross of Hawkins was not scheduled to resume until the following Tuesday.[13]

*

J. Barrie Williams was, like Blascak, full colonel U.S. Army, and only the third active-duty officer scheduled to testify in the entire trial. Williams had graduated from West Point in 1958 and, along with 50 percent of his academy class, had headed straight for the billowing silk. The "airborne mafia" controlled the army in those days, and the airborne corps was the place to be for ambitious young officers. Williams was assigned to the

Eighty-second Airborne Division but suddenly found himself detailed to a three-year assignment in counter-intelligence. He trained at Fort Holabird, discarded his uniform, and spent three years in Seattle, Washington, as part of the 115th Intelligence Corps. Military intelligence had just become a regular branch of the army, and Williams "decided that I rather liked intelligence work. So I opted to transfer permanently." He learned about the Viet Cong threat firsthand during a year of advisory duty in the Mekong Delta before being sent back to Holabird for more training. After Holabird, Williams was assigned to the Vietnam desk at the DIA in early 1966. It was there in the Pentagon that now-Major Williams had a front-row seat to the "giant rat fight" between MACV and the CIA. He stayed at the DIA long enough to see the numbers episode through to its end.

"I can't prove it to you," said Williams, "but I think there was direction out of Washington that said the strength will not go above three hundred thousand, I think that came directly from the White House. And the consequence, everything that we did, every methodology MACV had, always stayed under three hundred thousand." Williams went on, "These were the kinds of things that drove Sam and the rest of us crazy. You go through all the hard work going through the documents and everything, but when the whole thing comes down to it the powers that be will tell you what the numbers are."

Williams had agreed to be deposed, and in October 1983 the lawyers flew out to Germany where he was stationed. They asked him if the DIA had been under pressure to maintain a certain order of battle number (answer: "We were not to go above 300,000"), if the estimate was kept below a certain ceiling ("You better believe it was"), and if he agreed that Viet Cong irregulars constituted a military threat ("If you have ever seen anybody with a leg blown off after tripping over a 105 shell that has been put in by some villager who is self-defense or secret self-defense, you are goddamned right they are a military threat").

At the deposition it was evident to the Cravath team that Williams had not only the military credentials but also the colorful speaking style and engaging personality that would make for a powerful witness. It was also evident how much the colonel hated Graham, and how in Germany the Capital Legal lawyers had been unable to undercut any part of Williams's deposition testimony.

Juggling his lineup for the bottom of the final inning, Boies decided to put Mike Wallace up when Burt was done with Hawkins on Tuesday and then, after Wallace, have Williams take the stand as the cleanup hitter. Boies informed Burt of his plans regarding Williams — and Burt dropped the lawsuit.

While Judge Leval and the press were informed of this over the weekend, the official Joint Statement would not be released until the next scheduled day of trial.

Crafted by Boies, the carefully worded seven-paragraph Joint Statement was read out in court on Tuesday, February 19. The agreement to end the lawsuit spoke of no monetary settlement (Westmoreland and Capital Legal received not one penny from CBS, Wallace, Crile, or Adams), and the closest it came to an apology — which was not very close — was the sentence: "CBS respects General Westmoreland's long and faithful service to his country and never intended to assert, and does not believe, that General Westmoreland was unpatriotic or disloyal in performing his duties as he saw them."

*

Denied the chance to testify, Colonel Williams was left with the larger issues.

"The question I have a hard time personally answering," he asked himself, "is, at what level in a hierarchy are you authorized to take good intelligence, or dictate the intelligence, for the results of propaganda or political impact?"[14]

Williams did not have a ready response. He tried again, simplifying the question this time: "At what point do you take good intelligence and vulgarize it into propaganda?"[15]

Williams still had no answer.

16

RECKLESS DISREGARD

Westy Raises White Flag," the *New York Daily News* screamed. A cartoon in the *San Francisco Chronicle* depicted a mad scramble for the last helicopter lifting off the U.S. Courthouse roof: "Westmoreland Declares Victory and Pulls Out," the caption read.

At Regine's nightclub, 59th and Park, a huge celebration was held on short notice. CBS rented the place for the occasion, and over the din of disco music lawyers and network executives mingled with trial witnesses and invited guests who had been flown in from all over. There were trays of food to eat and drinks in abundance. The club was crowded with people strolling around and glad-handing one another. Bernard Gattozzi went up to Mike Wallace.

"Hi, I'm Bernie Gattozzi."

"Bernie Gattozzi! Bernie Gattozzi!" Wallace exclaimed. "I don't know how many nights I went to bed with your deposition under my pillow. I couldn't believe what you were saying but, you know, it all turned out to be true."

"You went to bed with my deposition under your pillow?" Gattozzi asked. "Are you some kind of weirdo?"

"No," Wallace answered, "I just kept reading and re-reading it and thinking about it."

"Well, thank you," Gattozzi said, taken aback, "It's kind of a compliment."

David Halberstam, author of *The Best and the Brightest*, was also among the partygoers. Halberstam was, like Adams, Harvard '55, yet the two had not known each other at college; it was only years later when Halberstam learned of his classmate's odyssey at the CIA and beyond. "We ended up late in life at exactly the same place but got there by different paths; funny, because I never knew Sam at all," Halberstam said. When Halberstam finally learned of Adams's story, though, "I felt that Sam was burning with the truth." Halberstam had followed the trial with interest and, while he was approached by Westmoreland, his sentiments were biased toward the defense and in favor of agency people such as his friend George Allen. Halberstam looked around Regine's, however, and he saw the witnesses talking with the lawyers and realized that this had been, after all, just another lawsuit. "It was weird," he recalled. "There were these CIA men who did this for the passion, and then there were the defense lawyers who could easily have been for the other side."

Anne Cocroft stood by Adams's side as he graciously greeted well-wishers. "It was kind of a grotesque huge party," she remembered, "and there were ice sculptures saying CBS and people were walking around saying 'Congratulations' and 'Good job' and this sort of thing; where actually it was dreadful because if you were to ask them 'Who won?' they would have said 'CBS, or was it Westmoreland?' It was such an unclear ending, and I think for Sam it must have been tremendously disappointing."

*

By March, Anne was two months' pregnant. She and Adams were planning a trip to Machu Picchu but Adams, having assessed the Shining Path guerrilla threat, decided that Costa Rica would be safer. During their two weeks in Costa Rica the couple traveled to the cool heights of the cloud forest, to the sultry Caribbean coastline, and to the arid Pacific shore. Adams talked little of the trial, yet the stress of that ordeal had left its mark. Now fifty-two, Adams for the first time in his life looked his age: His neatly trimmed hair (he always cut his own hair) had turned entirely gray, and he was also fast gaining weight. He was still a handsome man, though, and while walking through a Costa Rican neighborhood he caused quite a stir among a giggling group of uniformed schoolgirls. In trepidation one of them finally came up and asked in halting English, "Are you Paul Newman?"

*

The couple returned from Central America and to the little house in Purcellville. Space would somehow have to be found for baby when he or she arrived. "My files are 50 linear feet of paper," Adams explained to an inquiring graduate student. "And yes, in answer to your question, they are pretty well indexed. The files include 5 feet of transcripts of the trial, 10 feet of trial exhibits, 3 file drawers (4 drawers each), 2½ feet thick, of my folders on People — everyone from Acheson to Zorthian — right, Barry. Westmoreland is about 3 linear feet thick. There are 300–400 folders, 5 feet of documents from the trial, 2½ feet, mostly legal stuff and 2½ feet of Who's-in-What. Then, about 200–300 books on intelligence."[2]

Ostensibly working on his book, among his files Adams was again at loose ends. He wrote to the capitals of all fifty states requesting an official state map, and soon his mailbox was crammed with hefty envelopes stuffed with highway guides, tourist brochures, and amusement park coupons. Seeing that Adams had time to spare, his friend Joan Gardiner asked him for a favor. "We took him to the Montessori school to read *Just So Stories* to the preschoolers," she said, "and he came with bags of Clayton's toys and he had all the characters, stuffed animals, and some of them weren't elephants or whatever they were supposed to be, but he made do with what he had and kids were just bursting, they couldn't believe how great it was. He was the greatest narrator ever."

Life for Adams had returned to normal, although the lawsuit was still topmost on his mind. Patricia Roth had kept a diary throughout her four months of jury duty and was now — having gotten a book contract — rewriting it for publication. In going over her daily entries, however, Roth realized that she had not quite mastered the meaning of all the acronyms. "If anybody is going to complicate anything," she explained, "it is the government." Roth telephoned Adams, and the former defendant talked about the acronyms, the details of the intelligence dispute, and many other things. "Sam loved to talk," Roth said. "I thought he was a special person." Adams would call every day. "Talked an hour," Roth remembered, "hour and a half on the phone."

In helping Roth with her book Adams was constructively reliving the trial, but Adams's friend Peter Hiam believed that the legal episode and the way it ended were eating away at Adams. "He was terribly upset about the outcome," Hiam recalled. "He had what I think was an unrealistic view that the light of history would be shining on this whole thing — with people under oath, and that all would be revealed — and he went through a period of great excitement going around the country interviewing these people and coaching the lawyers who were doing the depositions. And then the way it all worked out was very disappointing to him. The settlement wasn't what he wanted. He wanted the judgment of history. And I think he was very depressed for months after that, truly depressed."

Adams never did sign the settlement, the only defendant not to do so, and he felt horribly cheated. The ambiguous ending to the trial was yet one more example of his cause being rent asunder by forces unrelated to the intelligence dispute. The trial ended, Adams knew, not because right had triumphed over wrong but because Dan Burt, who had mishandled Westmoreland's lawsuit from start to finish, was terrified of losing in a jury verdict and because, frankly, CBS was happy to rid itself of the whole affair.

On the second floor of his little house in the country Adams worked, once again, in solitude, searching for the smoking gun that intuition told him must have been in the White House. Adams slowly went through his pile of chronologies, his unearthed documents, and his well-indexed fifty linear feet of paper. He already knew all of this material by heart, but Adams the intelligence analyst was still searching for time lines, for patterns of relationships, for anything that could shed light on where the conspiracy had originated. "In terms of the facts," Robert Baron explained of what happened after the trial, "everybody else's appetite for the facts of this controversy was amply sated; their thirst was slaked. Except for Sam."

*

Adams had always favored small vehicles, and his newest was a tiny Honda Civic. Dressed in a seersucker suit, Adams pulled the Honda into the convenience store parking lot. His best man, Clayton, asked, "Are you nervous, Daddy?" "No," he answered, but all the same a beer wouldn't hurt. Adams went into the store and brought out a six-pack.

It was a June wedding on a beautiful day. The ceremony — the military historian and justice of the peace Bryon Farwell officiating — was held on the front porch of the little house with an American flag hanging in the background. Sam and Anne Adams were beaming. The reception was on the front lawn, the groom performing the honors of shucking oysters by the dozen.

That September, Abraham, named for the sixteenth president, was born. To help pay the bills for his new family Adams had earlier signed on with a lecture bureau. Armed with a copy of the CBS film, he did the college circuit, appearing before audiences whose members had in 1967 been either in or just out of diapers. At the Ivy League schools, where Adams could feel a natural affinity, he made it a point to remind the students that it was not those like themselves who had fought in the war and it was not the sons of privilege like him who had died in Vietnam; it was rather the young men of working-class or impoverished backgrounds who had done the fighting and the dying there.

"The Uncounted Enemy," especially when projected onto the big screen, was powerful and compelling, and Adams was a natural speaker. But still for the undergraduates the war was a long, long time ago, and the intelligence episode itself was confusing. At Tufts University when the film concluded it was question-and-answer time. Some in the audience wondered about what McArthur had done after the war, and why McChristian had decided to testify at the trial. Adams responded to these queries. Then a young woman stood up and wanted to know, "Whatever happened to MacVee?"

*

In 1986, at the time of Anne's and Sam's first anniversary, a two-part article written by Renata Adler appeared in the June 16 and June 28 issues of *The New Yorker* magazine. Adler, who was a journalist, essayist, novelist, and graduate of Yale Law School, wrote of two recent trials, *Sharon v. Time* and *Westmoreland v. CBS et al.* The Sharon trial had been heard in Room 110 at the same time the Westmoreland trial was taking place upstairs in Room 318, and besides their physical and temporal proximities the two trials bore a remarkable degree of semblance to each other. Both were libel suits brought against a large media company by a former general intent upon restoring— what the generals each claimed to be — his lost honor, and in both the defendant was represented by Cravath Swaine and Moor (*Time* magazine's attorney was Thomas Barr, in whose conference room Adams had once made his homestead).

Adler had plenty to say about the Sharon trial, but in regard to the Westmoreland suit she used the words *absurd* and *preposterous* a dozen times to describe the thesis of the CBS documentary, a documentary that she called "factually false and intellectually trivial." Adler was amazed that the CBS program "was not just enthusiastically endorsed; it was perhaps more implausibly, *believed*, without reservation, by almost the entire American press." That anyone, let alone professional journalists, would take the CBS documentary seriously was all the more incredible to Adler because "As an intellectual and historical matter, the thesis that underlay 'The Uncounted Enemy: A Vietnam Deception' was, of course, preposterous."

Adler's reason for denying that the dispute amounted to anything of consequence was that General Westmoreland would never have deliberately underestimated enemy strength because, as a military man, it would not have been in his best interests to do so. "What motive would a general have," she asked rhetorically, "to *underestimate* to his commanders the size and strength of the enemy when his every interest and inclination would fall more naturally on the other side: to overestimate."

Adler was not enamored of Westmoreland (she found it "odd" that when asked his age he answered, "I am seventy and one-half"), although she did admire the general's witnesses (especially, of all people, Carver and Davidson). In terms of the defendants' witnesses, however, Adler's feelings were of utter disdain; she believed these individuals to be, without exception, ineffectual or worse. In particular, Adler berated her fellow journalists for perpetuating the "lore" and the "myth" that McChristian and Hawkins had broken the back of the plaintiff's case. Actually, Adler stated, General McChristian's "rambling" testimony was "devastating" to the defense, being little more than "increasingly unintelligible gabble," "sullen muttering and waffling," and "maundering disquisition." And Hawkins's testimony was, if possible, even more pathetic. The former colonel, an "amiable cornball" "babbling happily" on the stand, Adler wrote, was a "boozy" and "convivial anecdotalist and a well-rehearsed, clownishly beguiling witness" who "showed an irrepressible need, almost aimlessly, and without limitation, to prattle." Hawkins, according to Adler, was given to using "the odd Yidishism" like "the whole shmear," and although not "some monster of coarseness" or even "some utter fool" Hawkins was still, Adler believed, "the lawyers', and also the presses', pawn, trying to oblige, but failing again and again even at that."

More darkly, however, Adler (who disliked Adams but not as intensely) suggested that Hawkins was not just a well-meaning clown but at times displayed "a preposterous evasion" when answering questions put to him. "The possibility became distinct," she warned, "that *both* Adams and Hawkins were prepared to be less than honest, on the broadcast and in court."

In her article Adler explained that the MACV–CIA fight over SNIE 14.3-67 was meaningless because President Johnson had been — all along according to Adler — getting his intelligence from "Source X" (the cover name given to the NSA for the trial). Adler said that George Crile had been forced to invent the story about suppressed NVA infiltration figures because the "honest" dispute over the Viet Cong order of battle could not by itself have carried the documentary. "Adams, the hero as 'intelligence' analyst," Adler explained, "totally alone, was not, even for television, a credible story."

*

Sam Adams was furious, George Crile was furious, Gregory Rushford (whom Adler in the article had called "a devout believer in Adams" and a "kook" and "far out") was furious, and CBS News President Van Gordon Sauter was furious. Adams got right to work. He spent hours on the phone each day with Rushford to go over the article for mistakes, and he cross-referenced Adler's piece with trial transcripts and depositions in search of more factual errors, as well as misrepresentations and derisive comments. He found plenty — hundreds in fact. Meanwhile Crile went right back to Cravath. Robert Baron recalled that "George Crile calls me up, and for the next week or two in the middle of working my senior associate's hours we put together a point-by-point refutation of Renata Adler on the facts."

In July, Sauter sent the editor of *The New Yorker*, William Shawn, Crile's and Baron's forty-nine-page CBS critique of Adler's piece accompanied by a cover letter that accused Adler not just of being "merely unfair, mean spirited, or misguided" but also of having committed "plainly false, gross misrepresentations and distortions of the record." The president of CBS News strongly suggested to Shawn that he "undertake a thorough review of that article," and he also asked for the opportunity to reply in *The New Yorker* to Adler's assertions. Shawn ignored the CBS complaint, and Renata Adler announced that Alfred A. Knopf was going to publish her article in book form.

Sauter and Crile at CBS had done what they could, and Baron went back to working his senior associate's hours at Cravath. Adams and Gregory Rushford, however, did not let go. In late October, Adams and Adler met, quite by accident, at Yale University, and Adler later told the *New York Times* that Adams had told her, "You'll be hearing from me." Adams's friend John Gardiner could see that Adler and her article were drawing Adams away from completing his own book. "I thought, *He will never finish this*," Gardiner recalled. "He was so upset and so distraught."

That summer and into the fall Adams had been laboring over the complaint that he was writing to *The New Yorker*, and over the demands that he intended to make on William Shawn. The nineteen-page letter was finally sent November 7. In it Adams asked that the magazine retract the untrue parts of Adler's article, that he be provided fifteen pages in *The New Yorker* to rebut her untrue statements, and that he be given fair compensation (Adams suggested $150 per hour) for the time he had been forced to spend in responding to Adler's untrue statements.

Shawn afforded Adams the same courtesy that he had displayed toward Sauter: He ignored him. In January, however, Renata Adler herself called Adams and offered to meet with him to discuss the matter. Adams declined, explaining afterward that "My last and only encounter with her was a less-than-a-minute one in New Haven on 25 October, 1986. She apparently gave an account of what was said to the *New York Times* because two days later I found myself misquoted in that paper."[3]

*

After the Westmoreland trial Gains B. Hawkins returned to his home on twenty-two acres just outside West Point, Mississippi. His brief stint as a national news item was over, but he was still a local celebrity. "I'm a free man at last," Hawkins explained to columnist Mary McGrory. "The monkey is off my back." Hawkins told McGrory that the outcome in New York had been "an utter defeat for Westmoreland," although he took no pleasure in Westmoreland's debacle. "I left my integrity in the same damn place he left his honor, over there in Vietnam. I helped perpetrate a gigantic fraud," Hawkins said. "We were in a damn swamp over there. We were up to our asses in alligators. That's something the country was entitled to know. Putting a ceiling on those figures meant we didn't know what we were up against — meant almost six more years of war, almost 20,000 more lives. The statute of limitations never runs on a fraud like that."[4]

In downtown West Point friends and well-wishers came up to Hawkins whenever his small pickup truck was stopped at the light and the retired colonel was in a jovial mood. Before the trial, though, Hawkins's mood had been anything but jovial. His son, Gains Jr., said of the weeks before Hawkins was due to testify, "I think it was clearly a black period for him. As the trial approached he was depressed and would drink heavily and go to bed inebriated a lot of times. He felt he was betraying his government by going up against his commander. He knew it was the right thing to do, but he thought people were going to find him traitorous for doing it. He got letters which were very unkind."[5]

Hawkins, though, would not have long to enjoy his new celebrity. A smoker since age thirteen, he was diagnosed with cancer and had a lung removed. In remission for a while, the cancer came back. George Crile hosted a dinner party at his home in New York for Gains and Bettye Hawkins in the colonel's honor. It was January 1987 and Sam Adams was of course there, as were George Allen, David Boies and his four associates (some of whom had already gone their own way), Mike Wallace, Gains Hawkins Jr., David Halberstam, and many others including — and perhaps best of all — Joseph McChristian, who had flown in for the occasion from Hobe Sound, Florida. Hawkins had always stood up for both Crile and his documentary when others had abandoned them both, and that evening in his home Crile repaid the loyalty by speaking movingly of Hawkins's courage and integrity. The day after the dinner Crile, Hawkins, and McChristian went off together to see *Platoon*.

Only a few weeks later the old colonel's health deteriorated rapidly. "He was not happy," Gains Jr. said. "His food stopped tasting good, even his martini stopped tasting good." In late February, Hawkins went out to the field behind his house and shot himself.

In West Point, Mississippi, the American flags and red, white, and blue bunting were brought out, and after the service in the First Presbyterian Church, Colonel Hawkins was buried with full military honors at Greenwood Cemetery. "Gains B. Hawkins was a great American and a fine man," General McChristian had said on the day Hawkins died. "I personally had the honor to pin the Legion of Merit on him." McChristian also noted that Hawkins volunteered for service in Vietnam. "Not many men did that," McChristian stated. "He was one of the best soldiers I ever knew."[6]

Baron and Crile had flown down together and joined Adams in West Point. After the burial, Adams and Baron went out into the pasture where Hawkins had committed suicide. "Sam and I walked around," Baron remembered. "That's the last time I saw Sam."

*

Unquestionably, Adams admired Gains B. Hawkins more than he admired anyone else in the world, and old Hawkins's death was a devastating blow. Afterward, and with grim determination, Adams turned his attentions to the Adler affair. His patience was at an end. Just before flying down to the funeral, in fact, Adams had written to Robert Gottlieb, Shawn's successor, and complained that "Surely the magazine has had enough time — over 15 weeks or more than 5 days a page — to look things over." Adams then explained exactly why he had taken this matter so seriously.

"When Ms. Adler indicates that I am a sloppy researcher who makes things up and lies under oath," Adams wrote, "she questions not only my integrity and motives, but those of the many people who testified on my, and CBS's, behalf. I feel personally responsible for these people. Of the 40-odd intelligence officials who signed affidavits or gave trial or deposition testimony for CBS during the Westmoreland litigation, I had known or contacted all but three of them. Many are my friends. Some, including US Army and CIA officers on active duty, came forward at considerable risk to their own careers. All felt they were doing right, and that what went wrong with American Intelligence during 1967 and 1968 needed public airing."[7]

"We've now had a chance to review your letter," Gottlieb responded. "But I don't feel that *The New Yorker* should be a forum for such a disagreement, anymore than I think it would be appropriate for your publisher to give Adler a forum to respond to your book. Critics, historians, Vietnam experts, government people, serious readers who are concerned with issues are bound to take up your account of what happened when [your book] appears, that you, in essence, will be having the last word between you and Adler; and the verdict of history will be given by disinterested parties. Isn't this the way it should work when sincere people disagree about important matters?"[8]

There was evidently going to be no recourse for Adams within the pages of Gottlieb's magazine — and then there was Adler's book, *Reckless Disregard*, to contend with. The book was a hardbound version of her article but with an acid-tongued addendum — a coda, as Adler called it — directed against those CBS witnesses whom she had neglected to savage in her magazine article.

Adler got going early, explaining at the outset of her coda why in the original *New Yorker* piece "I had ignored the testimony of the minor, low-level 'military intelligence officers and C.I.A. officials' whom CBS put on the stand to bolster its own case. Specifically, the [CBS complaint] named: Ronald L. Smith, Richard D. Kovar, Douglas Parry, John Barrie Williams, Donald W. Blascak, George Hamscher, Michael Hankins, Bernard Gattozzi, Russell Cooley and (as it turned out, the trial's last witness) one Colonel (at the time Major) Norman House. I will turn to them in a moment. I was almost seriously tempted to use them. I left them out, however, not only because none of them had or could testify from any personal knowledge of the events at issue at the trial but because I wanted to avoid what Cravath would presumably pride itself on: overkill. More precisely, I did not want to make these altogether minor characters appear, by their own testimony, ridiculous."

Warmed up, Adler had only just begun. In the pages that followed she bluntly accused Adams and Allen of lying; she said that Gattozzi had perjured himself; she called Parry "a young, minor and inexperienced analyst"; she called Blascak "another minor official" and "a particularly ineffective witness"; she stated that Smith, Kovar, and House were "thoroughly and almost comically discredited on the stand"; she said that Williams was, if not an outright liar, then at the very least given to "self-deception"; she said that these "minor witnesses" were driven to testify only because they wanted to play the role of "underdogs and heroes" (this being "a sincerely desirable part" she explained); she reiterated the "absurdity of the defendants' case"; and she derided the "C.I.A. folk" for believing "in what they had been told, over a period of years, by Sam Adams."[9]

*

Adams, not for the first time in his life, had had enough and was propelled to action. The course he decided to follow next would, after all he had just been through, though, seem almost unimaginable: litigation.

The seventy-five-million-dollar libel action was brought by Adams on June 9, 1987, at the U.S. District Court in Alexandria, Virginia. It named Renata Adler, The New Yorker Magazine, Inc., Alfred A. Knopf, Inc., and the magazine's and book publisher's parent company, the Condé Nast Corporation, as defendants. Adams accused Adler of writing that he had lied under oath at the Westmoreland trial and had encouraged other CBS witnesses to do likewise. Unlike other cases that Adams had been involved in, however, this one was an anonymous event that earned only brief mention in the press. Adams managed to keep news of the lawsuit from his family and friends, and even from Gregory Rushford who, having been called "a kook" and "far out," was himself suing *The New Yorker*.

Rushford's lawsuit, however, did not get far, a federal appeals court ruling that Adler's "kook" and "far out" quotes were based on the Westmoreland trial transcript and were thus "libel-free." Undoubtedly this played a role in Adams's wish to drop his own lawsuit. On July 16, 1987, barely two months after filing it, Adams terminated his legal action, explaining to his lawyer James Clark that "I have made this decision not because I believe my complaint is unmeritorious" but because "I have come to believe that such distortions and falsifications are better remedied by an accurate presentation of the facts in my forthcoming book."[10]

The "forthcoming book," however, was only a half-completed manuscript that had sat in a box untouched for a decade. Meanwhile, Adler's book had been a literary sensation, earning rave reviews. *Reckless Disregard* was lovingly called by the *New York Times* "acutely reasoned to the point of wittiness" and admiringly described by the *Washington Post* as "brilliant in its analysis, relentlessly argued, and unsparing in its moral and journalistic judgments." Adler was also being thanked for showing CBS's so-called documentary to be nothing more than "pernicious and contrived," "wholly fictitious," and, in the words of respected Vietnam War journalist Peter Braestrup, "vivid, antihistorical entertainment."[11]

Renata Adler had triumphed and could now count herself among the ranks of people who had, like Daniel Graham, run down all those who stood in their way and prospered by the intelligence deception. George Crile, the person most responsible for publicizing the deception, was only now regaining his professional stature. Not one lieutenant, captain, major, or colonel who had opposed the Graham side in the intelligence fight ever made general officer. Not one analyst at Langley who had supported the Adams side ever made it out of middle management; many military and civilian intelligence officers in cynicism and disgust had abandoned their careers altogether. Adams knew all this, and it gnawed at him.

*

Summers in Virginia were always unbearably hot and sticky, and Adams was convinced that they were becoming ever hotter and stickier. "He was very worried about climate change," John Gardiner recalled. In early 1988 Sam, Anne, and Abraham drove north to Vermont for a visit and thought that Vermont might indeed be a good place to make a home. They stayed with the author Tom Powers, who accompanied them while looking at some property. At one point the car got stuck in the snow and all had to get out and push. Adams did his part and, with the car freed and on its way up a little hill, walked the remaining distance himself. Afterward Powers noted that his friend "was huffing and panting as if he had run ten miles. It was forty yards. I was thinking at the time, *Wow, he's really out of condition*."[12]

Adams's health was, in fact, not ideal. When undergoing a physical needed for life insurance Adams was told he had high blood pressure and should avoid salt. Adams did little, though, to alter his diet. "He didn't stop himself," explained John Gardiner. "If there was a plate of cheese or stuff at a party, he would vacuum them up. It probably wasn't good for him. He was gaining weight, his circulation wasn't good." Suffering from gout, Adams was not one to complain. "He had an incredible pain threshold," Joan Gardiner recalled. "He couldn't climb the stairs, his foot hurt so badly." Peter Hiam added, "Sam had a lot of denial. He had arthritis in his fingers and they were swollen badly and I said, 'That must hurt' and he said, 'Oh no, no, it doesn't hurt at all.' Later I learned that he actually stuck a knife into his joints to get rid of the swelling." Because of his blood pressure, Adams was denied the life insurance; it was only through a brother-in-law that he was finally able to get a policy.

Adams was also drinking too much. Powers noticed that his friend would have straight Scotch nightcap after nightcap; Clayton recalled the time his father polished off an entire bottle of whiskey in a single evening.

That summer back in Virginia, Adams continued with his research, making one of his many trips out to Carlisle, Pennsylvania, trips that would become more difficult with the planned move to New England. He was warmly welcomed by the staff that day and then disappeared into the inner recesses of the military archives. Adams was still looking, still searching — but for what exactly he was not exactly saying. After hours in the archives, he bid good-bye to the staff and climbed into the little Honda. On the drive home as the flat farmland of southern Pennsylvania sped by, Adams was lost in thoughts of a war long ago.

*

A house was found in Vermont, a small and newly built one in the village of Strafford, and with a down payment and a mortgage secured the move was imminent. First, though, Alex Alben was getting married out in Los Angeles, and Adams was to be an usher. "He was so happy to be in the wedding," Alben remembered. "He was animated." Alben found Adams housing. "Stayed with a friend of mine. Sam had no airs about creature comforts. I think he slept on my friend's floor." It was a Beverly Hills wedding and, Alben explained, "for Sam this must have been this totally strange bizarre environment but he really enjoyed being there and hanging around with my friends. Everyone he met with he would tell the story of the Vietnam documentary, and he was recruiting more disciples and making a strong impression on a lot of people."

Back east the Strafford house was nearing completion and, importantly, more shelves were needed to handle all of Adams's books. To get a jump start on the movers, Adams began to ship parts of his library himself. The little Honda would be packed full and he would embark northward upon the almost six-hundred-mile drive, not including detours made to visit his sister Alix in New Jersey and his sister Cally in Connecticut. "He was moving books," Cally recalled, "book by book, and he would stop on the way, which was way out of his way. And I said, 'Sam, let's trade cars for God's sake.' I had a station wagon. He refused, didn't want to bother me."

The extensive traveling worried the Gardiners. "He had the house," John reasoned, "and he could have coordinated having to deal with some aspects of the move all at once instead of this frantic dashing." Adams told Joan that while driving he would place a book on the steering wheel, hold the covers with his two thumbs, and read. To assuage her fears, however, Adams explained that he had made the trip so many times, "The car knows the way." Joan remained concerned. "That summer when he was driving back and forth," she said, "it couldn't have been healthy."

By October the books were all moved. They were soon followed by the rest of the belongings from Purcellville. Inside the new house was a mass of opened and unopened boxes, and outside the fall foliage was at its height. There were new neighbors to meet, some of them being quite far to the left. One was the Reverend William Sloane Coffin, prominent Vietnam War opponent. "The story I heard," Abraham Adams said, "is that when he moved to Strafford, Bill Coffin was living there and when they met the first thing my father said was, 'I want you to know that I liked the CIA.'" Too young to remember that incident, Abraham does recall his father's ability to make animal noises of all types and also of his father's "reading to me a lot in the chair in the living room. He used to read me books about Vietnam and Vietnamese history. I was about three."

*

Because of Adams, George Allen had gone through quite a lot — having been dragged along over the years into his various congressional inquiries and documentaries and trials — and Allen remembered the last time he saw Adams. "Sam was still — I think he was still seeking absolution from me in some respect when we were all together at the Gains B. Hawkins dinner in New York," Allen said. "Sam took me aside, he said, 'George I did do the right thing, didn't I?'

"And I said, 'Well I can't say it was wrong.'"

Blowing whistles and burying secret documents did not constitute the type of behavior Allen believed in, but he had seen the intelligence corruption for himself and he could understand. "You know," Allen explained, "Sam took it very, very seriously. Bless his heart."

*

Sue Johnson Yager got a phone call from a friend in Vermont: Vermont Public Radio was reporting that Sam Adams had died behind his barn and that it looked suspicious. "The next day," Yager explained, "they said it wasn't suspicious. He was only fifty-five and had high blood pressure."

Adams, in fact, had died not behind a barn but in the new house sometime during the night, not yet a week after having moved in. Anne discovered her husband sitting back on the living room couch. A first-aid book with its pages opened was next to him. Perhaps there had been chest pains, difficulty breathing . . . Adams was apparently going to do his research and analyze and solve the problem for himself.

The service was held October 13, 1988, a week later. The flag-draped casket seemed incredibly heavy as the bearers struggled with the few short steps leading up into the Congregational church. Family and friends were there. Patricia Roth had driven up from New York with George Crile. They had been listening to the radio when, close to Strafford, it had eerily gone silent. This, it seemed, was appropriate. Roth would miss Adams and his telephone calls. "It was like," she said, "the music had died."

Inside the church family, friends, and former CIA colleagues were assembled. George Crile, John Gardiner, Peter Hiam, and Alex Alben each rose to give eloquent witness to a remarkable life. They talked not only of what Adams had done but who Adams was. Alben, taking the pulpit when his turn came, said, "I was blessed to know Sam Adams for eight short years and to have his friendship. He had tremendous charm. He loved nature. He loved history. He loved literature. At last count he told me he had read *Anna Karenina* six times. He loved to read aloud. He had a passion for words and he imparted that passion to others.

"I have never met a less pretentious person. I have never met a more giving man. Sam loved daffodils. He planted more and more every year in Virginia until they burst out each spring all over the farm. One time — this must have been in the spring of 1981 — I was working with Sam at the farm and we had to go back to New York for a meeting. Before we went out on one of those mad dashes in his Datsun down bumpy Virginia roads, he paused, looked at the daffodils in bloom, and began to cut bundles and bundles of the fresh flowers. We scooped them up in gigantic plastic bags and headed for the airport. Along the way, Sam gave bouquets of daffodils to old ladies waiting in the airport lounge, to every stewardess on our flight, to passengers on the plane. Finally he stormed through the halls of CBS dropping bunches of daffodils on every secretary's desk. All of a sudden our office was transformed into a field of blooming flowers."

Samuel Alexander Adams was buried high in the cemetery that overlooked the village. To fill the new emptiness Anne devoted herself to the mail. There was the letter that had just come for Sam from W. W. Norton. "I'm sorry," an editor at the publisher wrote, but too much time had elapsed and Norton was no longer interested in his book; would he please start repaying the twenty-thousand-dollar advance? The life insurance company had also recently written. Sam had stopped paying his premiums months before, and the policy was canceled.

Letters of condolence began arriving by the bundle. One was from William C. Westmoreland. The general wrote awkwardly at first, obviously struggling for words, before giving up entirely and ending the note quickly. "I always thought," Westmoreland's last line said, "that Sam was a nice person." Flowers were also arriving. One bunch came from Langley. The note was unsigned, although Anne knew it was from compatriots still at the agency. It read:

> *Oh hey Sam,*
> *A truer friend of his country,*
> *a better analyst and warrior*
> *is yet to come.*

Acknowledgments

I would like to thank Clayton Adams for approving and supporting my plans to write a biography of his father. I also thank Eleanor McGowin Adams and Anne Cocroft Adams for their help and encouragement over my four years of research and writing. I thank as well Abraham Adams and the other members of the Adams and Clark families who were so quick to assist me in my endeavors.

Through the kind cooperation of so many people, this project has become much more of an oral history than I ever hoped it would or could be. I am truly appreciative to all who answered my call and took time away from their busy schedules to share their thoughts and memories of Adams. They are: Alex Alben, George W. Allen, Ned Ames, Robert Appel, Kirk Balcom, Dana Ball, Janet Ball, Robert Baron, Howard Beaubien, Don Blascak, Joseph M. Carrier, Lael Chester, Nathaniel Ching, Catherine "Cally" Adams Christy, H. Nichols B. Clark, Chester Cooper, Caroline Davidson, Alix Clark Diana, David M. Dorsen, Bill Duker, David Elliott, Harold P. Ford, Joan Gardiner, John Gardiner, Bernard A. Gattozzi, Carlson Gerdau, David C. Gordon Jr., Leon Goure, David Halberstam, Andrew Hamilton, John Hardegree, Gains Hawkins Jr., Richard Helms, Helen Hiam, Peter Hiam, Joseph Hovey, Hunter Ingalls, Jerry Jacobson, Charles H. Kivett, Robert Klein, Richard Kovar, Jean Kraemer, Waldron Kraemer, Mary S. Kreimer, William LaBarge, Bobby Layton, David Lederman, Mary Adams Loomba, John Lorenz, Randy M. Mastro, Clark A. McCartney, Ray McGovern, Douglas Parry, Tom Powers, Edward Proctor, Patricia Roth, Gregory Rushford, Anthony J. Russo, Robert Sinclair, Judith Smith, Nicola Smith, R. Jack Smith, Byam K. Stevens, Roger Stone, William Stratton, Joseph C. Stumpf III, Dale Thorn, Mike Wallace, J. Barrie Williams, Jim Witker, Gertrude "Sue" Johnson Yager, David Zucchino, and those few who asked to remain anonymous. Whenever possible I arranged for an actual visit because to personally meet those who knew Adams at different epochs of his life was an honor for me, but for those whom I was not able to meet and to thank in person, I thank them again now.

Sean Noël and his staff hosted my two visits to the Samuel A. Adams Collection in the Howard Gotlieb Archival Research Center, Boston University, once for one week in 2001 and again for two weeks in 2003, and I am thankful for their attentive hospitality. I thank my editor Tom Powers for his advice and direction. I also thank Chip Fleischer, Laura Jorstad, Kristin Sperber, and everyone else at Steerforth Press for their help.

I guess one could always ask more of one's agent but when it comes to mine, Albert LaFarge, I can't think of anything. To him I extend my heartfelt gratitude. To my parents I give thanks for many things, naturally, but specific to this book I give thanks to them for surrendering their library to me while I wrote the manuscript. And finally to Marina, Hannah, and Eliana — I thank them for everything.

Abbreviations and Acronyms

ACSI	Assistant Chief of Staff for Intelligence
ARVN	Army of the Republic of Vietnam
BNE	Board of National Estimates
CDEC	Combined Documents Exploitation Center
Chieu Hoi	"Open Arms" program
CICV	Combined Intelligence Center, Vietnam
CIIED	Current Intelligence, Indications, and Estimates Division
CINCPAC	Commander in Chief, Pacific
Cong Bo An	Ministry of Public Security
COMUSMACV	commander, U.S. Military Assistance Command, Vietnam
CORDS	Civil Operations and Revolutionary Development Support
COSVN	Central Office for South Vietnam
DDI	Deputy Directorate for Intelligence
DDP	Deputy Directorate for Plans
DIA	Defense Intelligence Agency
FBIS	Foreign Broadcast Information Service
G-2	staff intelligence officer at division or corps level
IG	inspector general
J-2	staff intelligence officer at joint-command level
JCS	Joint Chiefs of Staff
JEC	Joint Evaluation Center
JOT	Junior Officer Training
KIA	killed in action
MACV	U.S. Military Assistance Command, Vietnam
MACV J-2	head of military intelligence for MACV
NSA	National Security Agency
noi tuyen	penetration agents
NSC	National Security Council
NVA	North Vietnamese Army (same as PAVN)

OB	order of battle
OCI	Office of Current Intelligence
OER	Office of Economic Research
ONE	Office of National Estimates
ORR	Office of Research and Reports
OSS	Office of Strategic Services
PFIAB	President's Foreign Intelligence Advisory Board
POW	prisoner of war
PRB	Publication Review Board
RAND	The RAND Corporation
S-2	staff intelligence officer at battalion or brigade level
SAVA	Special Assistant for Vietnamese Affairs
SD/SSD	self-defense and secret self-defense forces
SEA	Southeast Asia Branch
SITREP	situation report
SNIE	Special National Intelligence Estimate
SNIE 14.3-67	Special National Intelligence Estimate for Indochina, 1967
Tet	Tet Mau Than (the major annual Vietnamese holiday, which in 1968 was marked by large-scale Viet Cong attacks across the country)
USARPAC	U.S. Army, Pacific
USIB	United States Intelligence Board
VASRAC	Vietnamese Affairs Staff Related Activities Center
VC	Viet Cong
VCI	Viet Cong Infrastructure
VC/NVA	Viet Cong and North Vietnamese Army
Viet Cong	Viet Nam Cong San (Vietnamese Communist)
Viet Minh	Viet Nam Doc Lap Dong Minh Hoi (League for the Independence of Vietnam)

Notes

Abbreviations

Adams Collection, From the Samuel A. Adams Collection in the Howard
  Gotlieb Archival Research Center, Boston University.
Westmoreland v. CBS, *Westmoreland v. CBS, Inc., et al.*, 752 F.2d 16 (2d Cir.
1984).

Prologue: Tet, 1968

1. Adams, *War of Numbers*, 130–44.
2. Nolan, *The Battle for Saigon: Tet 1968*, 118.
3. Oberdorfer, *Tet!* 168–69.
4. The Hué CIA station staff was hidden by a South Vietnamese family in their attic
   during the three-week Communist occupation. The head of the station realized that he
   and his men were safe when the foulest swearing in English could be heard from the
   floor below: The U.S. Marines had arrived. (Source requests to remain anonymous.)
5. *New York Times*, February 1, 1968; *New York Times*, February 4, 1968.
6. Oberdorfer, *Tet!* dedication page.

Chapter One: A Downwardly Mobile WASP

1. Quotes from Malcolm Gordon School letters, school records, and Adams's work are
   courtesy of Malcolm Gordon's grandson, David Gordon Jr. This material is now in the
   Adams Collection.
2. In researching his ancestry two centuries later, Adams learned that his ancestor John
   Adams lost both shoes during the war and later petitioned the Continental Congress for
   compensation. (Clayton P. Adams interview.)
3. Peter Hiam is my father, and he made Adams my godfather.
4. Saint Mark's, Sam Adams report cards, Adams Collection.
5. *Boston Globe*, June 16, 1951.
6. Navy records, Adams Collection.
7. Philadelphian and American patriot George Clymer (1739–1813) signed the Declaration
   of Independence.
8. Chapter interviews: (Adams's family) Anne Cocroft Adams, Clayton P. Adams, Eleanor
   McGowin Adams, Catherine "Cally" Adams Christy, H. Nichols B. Clark, Caroline
   Davidson, Alix Clark Diana, Mary Adams Loomba, Judy Smith, and Nicola Smith;
   (Adams's friends and classmates) Ned Ames, Edward Ballantyne, Nathaniel Ching,
   Joan Gardiner, Carlson Gerdau, Andrew Hamilton, Peter Hiam, Hunter Ingalls,

Charles Kivett, Jean Kraemer, Waldron Kraemer, John Lorenz, Clark McCartney, Byam Stevens, Roger Stone, William Stratton, Dale Thorn, Jim Witker, and Gertrude "Sue" Johnson Yager; and (Adams's shipmates) John Hardegree and William LaBarge.

Chapter Two: Crisis in the Congo

1. Kirk Balcom interview. Other interview sources for this chapter were Eleanor McGowin Adams, Dana Ball, Janet Ball, Howard Beaubien, Jerry Jacobson, Ray McGovern, and Robert Sinclair. To avoid excessive notation I will alert the reader early in each chapter regarding all interviews (listed in the acknowledgments) I used as source material and will refrain, except where clarity is needed, from further citations for the remainder of that chapter.
2. The "undisclosed location" was a well-kept secret at the time, although in subsequent years the training site and its location in southern Virginia became widely publicized. For another description of the training experience, Adams's JOT classmate Patrick J. McGarvey provided one in his book *C.I.A.: The Myth and the Madness* (New York: Saturday Review Press, 1972).
3. Adams, *War of Numbers*, 14.

Chapter Three: Vietnam

1. Berman, *Lyndon Johnson's War*, 9.
2. Sam Adams, "What Ed Hauck Knew," unpublished paper, Adams Collection.
3. Adams, *War of Numbers*, 26–27, 29–30. Sadly, this would be the Clymer's third and last war: The Greasy George was scrapped in 1967.
4. Mary Kreimer interview. Other interview sources for this chapter were Eleanor McGowin Adams, George Allen, Kirk Balcom, Howard Beaubien, Joseph Carrier, Leon Goure, David Elliott, Robert Layton, and Anthony Russo.
5. Elliott, *The Vietnamese War*, vol. 1, 227–28, 195.
6. Adams, "Vietnam Cover-Up"; Adams, *War of Numbers*, 34–35.
7. Adams, *War of Numbers*, 41–49.
8. Sam Adams, draft manuscript, Adams Collection.
9. Adams, "Vietnam Cover-Up."
10. Adams, *War of Numbers*, 60.
11. Adams, "Vietnam Cover-Up."
12. Sam Adams, draft manuscript, Adams Collection.
13. Adams Collection.

Chapter Four: George Allen's War

1. George Allen interview. Other interview sources for this chapter were Don Blascak and David Elliott.
2. Allen, *None So Blind*, 8–10.
3. Karnow, *Vietnam*, 193.
4. George Allen interview; Allen, *None So Blind*, 15–17, 24, 38–42.

5. Ibid., 50–59.
6. Lanning and Cragg, *Inside the VC and the NVA*, 21.
7. Allen, *None So Blind*, 70–71, 92–93.
8. Elliott, *The Vietnamese War*, 221; Pike, *Viet Cong*, 194–204. Viet Cong is a contraction of Viet Nam Cong San (Vietnam Communist) — a pejorative term coined by U.S. and allied propagandists early in the war to paint all opponents of the Saigon regime as Communistic. For a discussion of the pitfalls inherent in using the language of either side of the "anti-American Resistance war"/"Vietnam War," see Elliott's *The Vietnamese War*, xviii–xix.
9. Allen, *None So Blind*, 121–25.
10. Newman, *JFK and Vietnam*, 158–60, 174–77, 190–93, 185–86; Don Blascak interview. The six areas at the joint command level are: J-1, Personnel; J-2, Intelligence; J-3 Operations; J-4, Logistics; J-5, Civil Affairs; and J-6, Communications.
11. Allen, *None So Blind*, 134.
12. Newman, *JFK and Vietnam*, 242–44, 251, 254.
13. Ibid., 163–69.
14. Westmoreland, *A Soldier Reports*, 175–76.
15. Allen, *None So Blind*, 199–200.

Chapter Five: The Crossover Point

1. Adams, "Vietnam Cover-Up."
2. Sam Adams, draft manuscript, Adams Collection.
3. Eleanor McGowin Adams interview. Other interview sources for this chapter were Don Blascak and Helen Hiam.
4. Sam Adams, draft manuscript, Adams Collection.
5. *CBS Reports*, "The Uncounted Enemy," 2.
6. Steven S. Biss, "Being Ordered to Lie: A History of the Vietnam Order of Battle Controversy and Johnson Administration Foreign Policy 1966–68," unpublished thesis, Princeton University, Adams Collection.
7. Adams, *War of Numbers*, 64–66.
8. Brewin and Shaw, *Vietnam on Trial*, 6.
9. Sam Adams, George A. Carver Jr. chronology, Adams Collection; Adams, "Vietnam Cover-Up."
10. Adams, *War of Numbers*, 68–73.
11. Adams, "Vietnam Cover-Up."
12. H. Ford, *CIA and the Vietnam Policymakers*, 88.
13. Berman, *Lyndon Johnson's War*, 13–15.
14. Karnow, *Vietnam*, 459.
15. Berman, *Lyndon Johnson's War*, 9–10, 15–20.
16. In describing the Vietnamese Communist order of battle, I was informed by the following sources: George Allen, Don Blascak, and J. Barrie Williams interviews; Allen, *None So Blind*; Adams, *War of Numbers*; *Army Digest*, "The Hidden Enemy"; "Draft Working Paper," author and date unknown, Adams Collection; Elliott, *The Vietnamese*

Wars; Giap, "General Vo Nguyen Giap on the Strategic Role of the Self-Defense Militia"; Hawkins, "The Unconventional Enemy"; and Tanham, *Communist Revolutionary Warfare*.

17. Adams, "Vietnam Cover-Up."
18. Adams, *War of Numbers*, 76–80.
19. Sam Adams, memorandum, November 7, 1966, Adams Collection.
20. Defendant's motion to dismiss, *Westmoreland v. CBS*.
21. Adams, "Vietnam Cover-Up."

Chapter Six: Told to Lie

1. Adams, *War of Numbers*, 89; H. Ford, *CIA and the Vietnam Policymakers*, 87. Interview sources for this chapter were George Allen, Don Blascak, Gains Hawkins Jr., and Richard Kovar.
2. Adams, *War of Numbers*, 88–89.
3. H. Ford, *CIA and Vietnam Policymakers*, 91; Adams, *War of Numbers*, 85–87; Berman, *Lyndon Johnson's War*, 30.
4. Adams, *War of Numbers*, 89; Adams, "Vietnam Cover-Up"; Adams, *War of Numbers*, 90.
5. Sam Adams, draft manuscript, Adams Collection; Adams, *War of Numbers*, 90; Adams, "Vietnam Cover-Up."
6. Hawkins, "A Mississippian's Vietnam Anguish."
7. Gains B. Hawkins, unpublished memoir, Adams Collection.
8. Hawkins, *Mississippian, Roman, Soldier, Writer, Yoda, Dad*, 243–50.
9. Hawkins, "A Mississippian's Vietnam Anguish."
10. Hawkins, *Mississippian, Roman, Soldier, Writer, Yoda, Dad*, 246–50, 257–58.
11. Adams, *War of Numbers*, 90.
12. Robert Sinclair, memorandum, October 20, 1988, Adams Collection.
13. Sam Adams, order of battle chronology, Adams Collection.
14. Adams, "Signing 100,000 Death Warrants."
15. Defendant's motion to dismiss, *Westmoreland v. CBS*.
16. Berman, *Lyndon Johnson's War*, 34.
17. Brewin and Shaw, *Vietnam on Trial*, 233; Berman, *Lyndon Johnson's War*, 35.
18. Ibid., 36–38, 43.
19. Defendant's motion to dismiss, *Westmoreland v. CBS*.
20. Hawkins, *Mississippian, Roman, Soldier, Writer, Yoda, Dad*, 263; Berman, *Lyndon Johnson's War*, 38; Defendant's motion to dismiss, *Westmoreland v. CBS*.
21. Hawkins, *Mississippian, Roman, Soldier, Writer, Yoda, Dad*, 263.
22. Defendant's motion to dismiss, *Westmoreland v. CBS*.
23. Graham, *Confessions of a Cold Warrior*, 48.
24. Graham, *Confessions of a Cold Warrior*, 52; Richard Kovar interview (emphasis added).
25. Hawkins, "A Mississippian's Vietnam Anguish."

Chapter Seven: SNIE 14.3-67

1. H. Ford, *CIA and the Vietnam Policymakers*, 88–91; Richard Kovar interview. Other interview sources for this chapter were George Allen, Andrew Hamilton, Robert Layton, Tom Powers, and J. Barrie Williams.
2. Defendant's motion to dismiss, *Westmoreland v. CBS*.
3. Adams, *War of Numbers*, 93, 96.
4. H. Ford, *CIA and the Vietnam Policymakers*, 93; Adams, *War of Numbers*, 96–97.
5. *CBS Reports*, 9.
6. Table adapted from Adams, *War of Numbers*, 101.
7. *CBS Reports*, 9; Adams, *War of Numbers*, 101, 105.
8. Allen, *None So Blind*, 248.
9. Adams, *War of Numbers*, 105–6; H. Ford, *CIA and the Vietnam Policymakers*, 85.
10. Adams, *War of Numbers*, 106.
11. Sam Adams, George A. Carver Jr. chronology, Adams Collection.
12. Berman, *Lyndon Johnson's War*, 75.
13. Adams, *War of Numbers*, 107–8.
14. Berman, *Lyndon Johnson's War*, 75.
15. Adams, *War of Numbers*, 110–11.
16. Defendant's motion to dismiss, *Westmoreland v. CBS*; J. Barrie Williams interview.
17. J. Barrie Williams deposition, *Westmoreland v. CBS*; Jones, *War Without Windows*, 101.
18. Defendant's motion to dismiss, *Westmoreland v. CBS*.
19. J. Barrie Williams deposition, *Westmoreland v. CBS*; Jones, *War Without Windows*, 101–2.
20. Defendant's motion to dismiss, *Westmoreland v. CBS*; J. Barrie Williams deposition.
21. Davidson, *Secrets of the Vietnam War*, 45.
22. Adams, *War of Numbers*, 112–14; Sam Adams, order of battle chronology, Adams Collection.
23. Davidson, *Secrets of the Vietnam War*, 46–51; Graham, *Confessions of a Cold Warrior*, 55.
24. H. Ford, *CIA and the Vietnam Policymakers*, 93.
25. Sam Adams, George A. Carver Jr. chronology, Adams Collection.
26. Adams, *War of Numbers*, 113–14.
27. Adams, "Vietnam Cover-Up"; J. Barrie Williams deposition, *Westmoreland v. CBS*.
28. Adams, *War of Numbers*, 117.
29. George Carver, cable of August 29, 1967, Adams Collection.
30. Defendant's motion to dismiss, *Westmoreland v. CBS*.
31. H. Ford, *CIA and the Vietnam Policymakers*, 94; George Allen interview.
32. H. Ford, *CIA and the Vietnam Policymakers*, 99.
33. Davidson, *Secrets of the Vietnam War*, 47–50.
34. Adams, *War of Numbers*, 118; Allen, *None So Blind*, 251.
35. Defendant's motion to dismiss, *Westmoreland v. CBS*.
36. Robert Layton interview; Adams, "Vietnam Cover-Up"; Adams, *War of Numbers*, 119.
37. George Allen interview.
38. H. Ford, *CIA and the Vietnam Policymakers*, 100; George Allen interview.

39. Adams, *War of Numbers*, 122.
40. Brewin and Shaw, *Vietnam on Trial*, 306; Berman, *Lyndon Johnson's War*, 68; Adams, *War of Numbers*, 124.
41. Berman, *Lyndon Johnson's War*, 82.
42. H. Ford, *CIA and the Vietnam Policymakers*, 103; Powers, *The Man Who Kept the Secrets*, 239–40.
43. H. Ford, *CIA and the Vietnam Policymakers*, 102–3.
44. Berman, *Lyndon Johnson's War*, 109–10.
45. Defendant's motion to dismiss, *Westmoreland v. CBS*.
46. Adams, *War of Numbers*, 134.
47. Berman, "The Tet Offensive."
48. Berman, *Lyndon Johnson's War*, 121.

Chapter Eight: A Lugubrious Irony

1. Joseph Hovey interview. Other interview sources for this chapter were George Allen, Don Blascak, Robert Layton, and J. Barrie Williams.
2. R. Ford, *Tet 1968*, 211–12, 193; Robert Layton interview.
3. In addition to their prescient alerts in late November and early December 1967, just three days before the Tet Offensive Layton, Ogle, and Hovey attempted to send a cable to Washington pinpointing the date of the attacks. The cable was held up because it had not been properly assigned a CDEC number (*New York Times*, September 22, 1975).
4. Oberdorfer, *Tet!* 17.
5. Subsequent accounts place Ambassador Bunker at a secure location several blocks from the embassy.
6. Prados, "The Warning That Left Something to Chance: Intelligence at Tet."
7. *New York Times*, February 9, 1968.
8. H. Ford, *CIA and the Vietnam Policymakers*, 130.
9. Berman, "The Tet Offensive."
10. Ronald L. Smith affidavit, *Westmoreland v. CBS*.
11. Berman, *Lyndon Johnson's War*, 158–70, 179–80.
12. *New York Times*, March 19, 1968.
13. Defendant's motion to dismiss, *Westmoreland v. CBS*.
14. Berman, *Lyndon Johnson's War*, 184, 195.
15. Powers, *The Man Who Kept the Secrets*, 244–45; H. Ford, *CIA and the Vietnam Policymakers*, 136.
16. Jones, *War Without Windows*, 205.
17. Davidson, *The Secret History of the Vietnam War*, 81.
18. Jones, *War Without Windows*, 192.
19. J. Barrie Williams deposition, *Westmoreland v. CBS*; J. Barrie Williams interview.
20. Davidson, *Secrets of the Vietnam War*, 81; Allen, *None So Blind*, 258–60, 263–65.
21. Sam Adams, order of battle chronology, Adams Collection; Adams, *War of Numbers*, 151.
22. Hawkins, "A Mississippian's Vietnam Anguish."

Chapter Nine: The Adams Phenomenon

1. Ranelagh, *The Agency*, 464.
2. Don Blascak interview. Other interview sources for this chapter were Robert Appel, Richard Helms, Peter Hiam, Robert Klein, Douglas Parry, Edward Proctor, Richard J. Smith, Joseph Stumpf, and J. Barrie Williams.
3. Adams, *War of Numbers*, 150–53.
4. May 27, 1968, Adams Collection.
5. Adams, *War of Numbers*, 158–59, 162, 164.
6. Adams, "Vietnam Cover-Up"; Adams, *War of Numbers*, 165.
7. Ibid., 165–67; Peter Hiam interview.
8. Adams, *War of Numbers*, 166.
9. H. Ford, *CIA and the Vietnam Policymakers*, 90 n.14; Adams, *War of Numbers*, 168.
10. Powers, *The Man Who Kept the Secrets*, 247.
11. Richard Helms interview.
12. Adams, *War of Numbers*, 169.
13. Powers, *The Man Who Kept the Secrets*, 247.
14. Adams, *War of Numbers*, 169.
15. Richard Helms interview.
16. Edward Proctor interview.
17. Adams, "Vietnam Cover-Up."
18. Powers, *The Man Who Kept the Secrets*, 248.
19. Adams, *War of Numbers*, 170, xxxiii.
20. In the 1970s Lydia Weber was party to the first gender discrimination lawsuit brought against the CIA. The class action alleged that women at Langley were denied equal pay and advancement. The plaintiffs won. As part of the settlement Weber was given a sabbatical to attend Harvard University and the assignment of her choice upon returning to Langley — she chose the IG's office.
21. Adams, *War of Numbers*, 171–72.
22. That Adams had independent means was also impressed upon colleagues who noted that his paychecks tended to collect in his desk drawer uncashed, and that on lunch breaks he would go into town and come back to work with a dozen new dress shirts and a pile of just-bought LPs. (Robert Appel and Don Blascak interviews.)
23. Adams, *War of Numbers*, 172–77. Adams was the first person in U.S. intelligence to create a composite table for this structure, and his template served as an invaluable tool for understanding the enemy: The Army Special Warfare School at Fort Bragg agreed by ordering five thousand copies of the Adams chart.
24. Ibid., 180; Adams, "Vietnam Cover-Up."
25. Adams, *War of Numbers*, 178–79.
26. Ray McGovern interview; Powers, *The Man Who Kept the Secrets*, 246.
27. Adams, *War of Numbers*, 173, 184.

Chapter Ten: A Thoreau Type

1. Adams, "Vietnam Cover-Up"; Ronald Smith, fitness report, December 22, 1970, Adams Collection.

2. Adams, "Vietnam Cover-Up."

3. Sam Adams, memorandum, September 16, 1970, Adams Collection.

4. Robert Klein interview. Other interview sources for this chapter were Eleanor McGowin Adams, Robert Appel, Jean Kraemer, and Waldron Kraemer.

5. Adams, *War of Numbers*, 192.

6. Karnow, *Vietnam*, 622.

7. Adams, *War of Numbers*, 193–94; Adams, "The Cambodian Post Mortem."

8. Adams, *War of Numbers*, 196–201; Harold Ford interview.

9. Adams, *War of Numbers*, 201–3.

10. Sam Adams, untitled notes, no date, Adams Collection.

11. Adams, *War of Numbers*, 203.

12. Sam Adams, untitled notes, no date, Adams Collection.

13. Adams, "Vietnam Cover-Up."

14. Adams, *War of Numbers*, 205.

15. Hawkins, "A Mississippian's Vietnam Anguish."

16. Adams, *War of Numbers*, 212–13, 205–6; Sam Adams, memorandum, December 8, 1972, Adams Collection; Adams, "Vietnam Cover-Up."

17. Defendant's motion to dismiss, *Westmoreland v. CBS*.

18. U.S. Army, letter to Sam Adams, January 23, 1973, Adams Collection.

19. Schrag, *Test of Loyalty*, 35–37, 154, 176; *New York Times*, January 19, 1973.

20. Defendant's motion to dismiss, *Westmoreland v. CBS*.

21. Sam Adams, memorandum, January 29, 1973, Adams Collection.

22. Sam Adams, memorandum, January 31, 1973, Adams Collection.

23. Walter P. Southard, untitled note, no date, Adams Collection.

24. Schrag, *Test of Loyalty*, 274–78.

25. *New York Times*, March 9, 1973.

26. *Washington Post*, February 21, 1973.

27. *New York Times*, February 26, 1973.

28. Shrag, *Test of Loyalty*, 291; Hawkins, "A Mississippian's Vietnam Anguish."

29. Adams, *War of Numbers*, 209–10; Sam Adams, letter (to Alex Alben?), undated, Adams Collection.

30. Accounts of Adams's testimony are from the *Los Angeles Times*, *New York Times*, and *Washington Post*, March 7–9, 1973.

31. CIA, notice to employees, March 26, 1973, Adams Collection; Sam Adams, untitled notes, April 1973, ibid.

32. *New York Times*, April 8, 1973; Adams Collection.

33. *New York Times*, April 8, 1973.

34. Source wishes to remain anonymous; Graham, *Confessions of a Cold Warrior*, 57.

35. Sam Adams, memorandum, April 23, 1973, Adams Collection.

36. Robert Sinclair interview. An impossibly high rank, there was no such thing as a "GS-19."

37. Sam Adams, untitled notes, November 17, 1972, Adams Collection.

38. Adams, "The Cambodian Post Mortem."

39. Sam Adams, memorandum, April 24, 1973, Adams Collection; Sam Adams, memorandum, May 2, 1973, ibid.; Sam Adams, memorandum, May 3, 1973, ibid.

40. Ibid.

41. Sam Adams, memorandum (drafts one and two), May 4, 1973, ibid.

42. Sam Adams, memorandum, May 7, 1973, ibid.; Schrag, *Test of Loyalty*, 347.

43. Sam Adams, memorandum, May 17, 1973, Adams Collection.

44. Sam Adams, untitled notes, no date, ibid.

Chapter Eleven: Investigations

1. *New York Times*, June 29, 1973; *Wall Street Journal*, July 5, 1973.

2. Samuel A. Adams testimony, *Westmoreland v. CBS*.

3. Edward Proctor interview. Other interview sources for this chapter were Clayton P.
Adams, Eleanor McGowin Adams, George Allen, Joan Gardiner, Bernard Gattozzi,
Andrew Hamilton, Richard Kovar, and Gregory Rushford.

4. Adams, "Signing 100,000 Death Warrants." When later confronted with the claim that
large numbers of South Vietnamese had not been executed after the war, Adams
responded by pointing out that the Vietnamese Communists were adept at concealing
their massacres. As Adams feared, the victorious Khmer Rouge would carry out a
genocidal vendetta against the Cambodian people.

5. Richard Kovar and Edward Proctor interviews.

6. Adams, untitled notes, May 21, 1975, Adams Collection.

7. House Select Committee on Intelligence, Adams Collection. Upon leaving the conference room a gentleman approached the witness and suggested in a heavy Russian accent
that they meet sometime in private. Smiling with delight, Adams burst out: "Oh I
know — you're KGB!" (Dale Thorn interview.)

8. *New York Times*, September 22, 1975.

9. Prados, "The Warning That Left Something to Chance"; Benjamin, *Fair Play*, 37.

10. Brewin and Shaw, *Vietnam on Trial*, 304–5.

11. Sam Adams, "What Ed Hauck Knew," unpublished paper, Adams Collection.

12. Brewin and Shaw, *Vietnam on Trial*, 16.

13. Sam Adams, untitled notes, no date, Adams Collection.

14. Kowet, *A Matter of Honor*, 22, 25.

15. Adams, *War of Numbers*, 214–15.

16. Kowet, *A Matter of Honor*, 25; Brewin and Shaw, *Vietnam on Trial*, 29.

17. Kowet, *A Matter of Honor*, 21, 70.

18. Bernard Gattozzi interview.

19. Brewin and Shaw, *Vietnam on Trial*, 65.

20. Kowet, *A Matter of Honor*, 20.

21. Brewin and Shaw, *Vietnam on Trial*, 19.

22. James Meacham, collected letters, Adams Collection.

23. Brewin and Shaw, *Vietnam on Trial*, 19.

Chapter Twelve: *CBS Reports*

1. Besides *Fourteen Three*, Adams had also considered *To Square a Circle*. W. W. Norton rejected both as being more suitable for a mathematics text.
2. Kowet, *A Matter of Honor*, 15–16, 21.
3. Benjamin, *Fair Play*, 46, 69.
4. Alex Alben interview. Other interview sources for this chapter were David Dorsen and Mike Wallace.
5. Benjamin, *Fair Play*, 63.
6. No actively serving U.S. government employee, military or civilian, agreed to be on the CBS program.
7. Brewin and Shaw, *Vietnam on Trial*, 35.
8. Kowet, *A Matter of Honor*, 56; Benjamin, *Fair Play*, 67.
9. Benjamin, *Fair Play*, 95, 22–23; Brewin and Shaw, *Vietnam on Trial*, 52.
10. Benjamin, *Fair Play*, 17.
11. Brewin and Shaw, *Vietnam on Trial*, 51.
12. Wallace and Gates, *Close Encounters*, 443.
13. Brewin and Shaw, *Vietnam on Trial*, 58–60.
14. Benjamin, *Fair Play*, 137–47.
15. Brewin and Shaw, *Vietnam on Trial*, 74–78; David Dorsen interview.

Chapter Thirteen: Cravath

1. Brewin and Shaw, *Vietnam on Trial*, 80; Robert Baron interview. Other interview sources for this chapter were Anne Cocroft Adams, William Duker, Bernard Gattozzi, Peter Hiam, and Randy Mastro.
2. In addition to Cravath, CBS involved its own lawyers; George Crile, because of his tenuous relationship with his employer, also retained separate counsel. The CBS et al. defense, however, was firmly controlled by David Boies. One estimate placed the CBS defense at $5 million; Capital Legal said its expenditures on behalf of Westmoreland (the retired general contributed $20,000 to his own case) were $3.3 million.
3. Brewin and Shaw, *Vietnam on Trial*, 82–85, 89.
4. Robert S. McNamara deposition, *Westmoreland v. CBS*.
5. Brewin and Shaw, *Vietnam on Trial*, 188, 191.
6. In federal court it was difficult in civil matters to compel witnesses living outside the jurisdiction where the case was located to appear at trial. Thus many witnesses provided deposition testimony that at trial could be read or, if videotaped, shown to the jury as if the witness was present.
7. Hawkins, "A Mississippian's Vietnam Anguish."
8. Adams wrote Hawkins around the time the program aired to say that the film was "reasonably good" but "as I mentioned before, there's a major problem: The documentary seems to pin the rap on General Westmoreland, when it probably belongs a little higher than that." (Kowet, *A Matter of Honor*, 158.)
9. Brewin and Shaw, *Vietnam on Trial*, 208–9.

10. George Crile did not make himself available to be interviewed for this book. An accomplished journalist, biographer, and writer, Crile may perhaps write his memoirs one day and include in them his own perspective of Adams.

Chapter Fourteen: The Libel Trial of the Century.

1. The Westmorelands had met decades earlier in storybook fashion, she the eleven-year-old horseback-riding daughter of the executive officer of Fort Sill, Oklahoma, and he a young lieutenant in the artillery. When one day Westmoreland was sitting in the officers' club nursing his pride after his girlfriend had gone off and married another officer, Kitsy perched herself on the arm of his chair and said, "Cheer up, Westy. Don't worry. I'll be a big girl soon. I'll wait for you." (Westmoreland, *A Soldier Reports*, 17.)
2. Brewin and Shaw, *Vietnam on Trial*, 211. Up until this chapter I have noted all material arising from the lawsuit with the abbreviation *Westmoreland v. CBS*, but for the remainder of the book I will end this practice when it is obvious I am referring to trial testimony. For those interested in consulting the twenty-thousand-page trial transcript itself, a microfiche copy has been published as *Vietnam, A Documentary Collection — Westmoreland v. CBS* (New York: Clearwater Publishing, 1987).
3. October 21, 1984.
4. David Dorsen interview. Other interview sources for this chapter were Anne Cocroft Adams, Robert Baron, William Duker, Robert Klein, David Lederman (a juror), Randy Mastro, Patricia Roth, and David Zucchino.
5. Adler, *Reckless Disregard*, 200.
6. Roth, *The Juror and the General*, 135.
7. Parkins's testimony dealt with his belief that he had been fired by his boss at MACV, Colonel Charlie Morris, not because he was reporting overlarge NVA infiltration estimates, as Parkins had earlier told Adams, but because of a "personality conflict" that he had with Morris. I have not related Parkins's testimony here, just as I do not relate testimony of other important though more minor witnesses, in an effort to present a brief account of a very long trial.
8. Graham, *Confessions of a Cold Warrior*.
9. H. Ford, *CIA and the Vietnam Policymakers*, 94.
10. Adler, *Reckless Disregard*, 76–77.

Chapter Fifteen: The Colonels' Revolt

1. *Philadelphia Inquirer*, January 8, 1985.
2. Roth, *The Juror and the General*, 189, 198.
3. *Philadelphia Inquirer*, January 11, 14, and 15, 1985.
4. David Dorsen interview. Other interview sources for this chapter were Anne Cocroft Adams, Robert Baron, Don Blascak, David Duker, Robert Klein, Douglas Parry, Patricia Roth, Richard Kovar, and J. Barrie Williams.
5. *Washington Post*, January 10, 1985.
6. *Philadelphia Inquirer*, January 14, 1985.

7. Brewin and Shaw, *Vietnam on Trial*, 302.

8. As a "confessing accomplice," George Allen could directly accuse William C. Westmoreland of wrongdoing.

9. Brewin and Shaw, *Vietnam on Trial*, 315.

10. Roth, *The Juror and the General*, 247.

11. *Philadelphia Inquirer*, February 5, 1986.

12. In the U.S. Army there are two types of colonel: lieutenant colonel, and above that (designated by an eagle insignia) full colonel.

13. Roth, *The Juror and the General*, 293.

14. J. Barrie Williams deposition, *Westmoreland v. CBS*.

15. George Crile, J. Barrie Williams interview, Adams Collection.

Chapter Sixteen: Reckless Disregard

1. Bernard Gattozzi interview. Other interview sources for this chapter were Anne Cocroft Adams, Eleanor McGowin Adams, Alex Alben, George Allen, Robert Baron, Joan Gardiner, John Gardiner, David Halberstam, Gains Hawkins Jr., Peter Hiam, Tom Powers, Gregory Rushford, Patricia Roth, Nicola Smith, and Sue Yager.

2. Josephine Stenson Grund, Sam Adams interview, Adams Collection.

3. Sam Adams, letter to William Shawn, ibid.

4. *Washington Post*, February 21, 1985.

5. *Commercial Appeal*, July 29, 1985; Gains Hawkins Jr. interview.

6. *Daily Times Leader*, February 27, 1987.

7. Sam Adams, letter to Robert Gottlieb, February 24, 1987, Adams Collection.

8. Robert Gottlieb, letter to Sam Adams, March 31, 1987, ibid.

9. Adler, *Reckless Disregard*, coda. I requested an interview from Adler twice, once in a letter that I sent to her in care of her publisher and again in a telephone message I left while she was a visiting professor at Boston University: I was never favored with a reply.

10. Adams Collection.

11. *New York Times*, November, 6, 1986; *Washington Post*, November, 9, 1986; *New York Times*, November, 9, 1986; *Washington Post*, November, 14, 29, 1986.

12. One requirement of Adams's was that any house they bought had to be within half an hour's drive from the Dartmouth Bookstore in Hanover, New Hampshire.

Bibliography

Adams, Samuel A. "Signing 100,000 Death Warrants." *Wall Street Journal*, March 26, 1975.

———. "Truth in the Balance." *New York Times*, June 29, 1973.

———. "Vietnam Cover-Up: Playing War with Numbers." *Harper's*, May 1975.

———. *War of Numbers: An Intelligence Memoir*. South Royalton, VT: Steerforth Press, 1994.

Adams Collection, The Samuel A., in the Howard Gotlieb Archival Research Center, Boston University.

Adler, Renata. *Reckless Disregard: Westmoreland v. CBS et al., Sharon v. Time*. New York: Alfred A. Knopf, 1986.

Allen, George W. *None So Blind: A Personal Account of Intelligence Failure in Vietnam*. Chicago: Ivan R. Dee, 2001.

Army Digest. "The Hidden Enemy." March 1967.

Benjamin, Burton. *Fair Play: CBS, General Westmoreland, and How a Television Documentary Went Wrong*. New York: Harper and Row, 1988.

Berman, Larry. *Lyndon Johnsons's War: The Road to Stalemate in Vietnam*. New York: W. W. Norton, 1989.

———. "The Tet Offensive." In Marc Jason Gilbert and William Head, eds. *The Tet Offensive, 1968*. Westport, CT: Greenwood Publishing, 1996.

Brewin, Bob, and Sydney Shaw. *Vietnam on Trial: Westmoreland vs. CBS*. New York: Atheneum, 1987.

CBS Reports, "The Uncounted Enemy." 1982.

Davidson, Philip B. *Secrets of the Vietnam War*. Novato, CA: Presidio Press, 1990.

Elliott, David W. P. *The Vietnamese War: Revolution and Social Change in the Mekong Delta, 1930–1975*, 2 vols. Armonk, NY: M. E. Sharpe, 2003.

Ford, Harold P. *CIA and the Vietnam Policymakers: Three Episodes, 1962–1968*. Center for the Study of Intelligence: Central Intelligence Agency, 1998.

Ford, Ronnie E. *Tet 1968: Understanding the Surprise*. Portland, OR: Frank Cass, 1995.

Giap, Vo Nguyen. "General Vo Nguyen Giap on the Strategic Role of the Self-Defense Militia." In Patrick J. McGarvey, ed. *Visions of Victory: Selected Vietnamese Communist Military Writings, 1964–1968*. Stanford, CA: Hoover Institution, 1969.

Graham, Daniel O. *Confessions of a Cold Warrior*. Fairfax, VA: Preview Press, 1995.

Hawkins, Gains B. "A Mississippian's Vietnam Anguish: Being Told to Lie." *Jackson Clarion-Ledger*, November 21, 1982.

———. *Mississippian, Roman, Soldier, Writer, Yoda, Dad*. Salisbury, MD: Evans-Coates Printing, 1989.

Jones, Bruce E. *War Without Windows*. New York: Vanguard Press, 1987.

Karnow, Stanley. *Vietnam: A History*. New York: Penguin Books, 1997.

Kowet, Don. *A Matter of Honor: General William C. Westmoreland Versus CBS*. New York: Macmillan, 1984.

Kowet, Don, and Sally Bedell. "Anatomy of a Smear: How CBS News Broke the Rules and 'Got' Gen. Westmoreland." *TV Guide*, May 24, 1982.

Lanning, Michael Lee, and Dan Cragg. *Inside the VC and the NVA*. New York: Fawcett Columbine, 1992.

Newman, John M. *J.F.K. and Vietnam: Deception, Intrigue, and the Struggle for Power*. New York: Warner Books, 1992.

Nolan, Keith W. *The Battle for Saigon: Tet 1968*. Novato, CA: Presidio Press, 2002.

Oberdorfer, Don. *Tet!* New York: Da Capo Press, 1984.

Pike, Douglas. *Viet Cong: The Organization and Techniques of the National Liberation Front of South Vietnam*. Cambridge, MA: MIT Press, 1966.

Powers, Thomas. *The Man Who Kept the Secrets*. New York: Pocket Books, 1983.

Prados, John. "The Warning That Left Something to Chance: Intelligence at Tet." In Marc Jason Gilbert and William Head, eds. *The Tet Offensive, 1968*. Westport, CT: Greenwood Publishing, 1996.

Ranelagh, John. *The Agency: The Rise and Decline of the C.I.A.* New York: Simon and Schuster, 1986.

Roth, M. Patricia. *The Juror and the General*. New York: William Morrow, 1986.

Schrag, Peter. *Test of Loyalty: Daniel Ellsberg and the Rituals of Secret Government*. New York: Touchstone, 1974.

Tanham, George K. *Communist Revolutionary Warfare: From the Vietminh to the Viet Cong*. New York: Frederick A. Praeger, 1967.

Wallace, Mike, and Gary Paul Gates. *Close Encounters*. New York: William Morrow, 1984.

Westmoreland v. CBS, Inc., et al., 752 F.2d 16 (2d Cir. 1984).

Westmoreland, William C. *A Soldier Reports*. Garden City, NY: Doubleday, 1976.

Photo Credits

Index

NOTE: *Photo section pages are in italics.*